Elisabeth Forster
1919 – The Year That Changed China

Transformations of Modern China

—

Edited by
Daniel Leese, Eugenia Lean, Alexander C. Cook,
Nicola Spakowski, and Dong Guoqiang

Volume 2

Elisabeth Forster

1919 – The Year That Changed China

—

A New History of the New Culture Movement

DE GRUYTER
OLDENBOURG

ISBN 978-3-11-068273-1
e-ISBN (PDF) 978-3-11-056071-8
e-ISBN (EPUB) 978-3-11-055829-6
ISSN 2511-6029

Library of Congress Cataloging-in-Publication Data
A CIP catalog record for this book has been applied for at the Library of Congress.

Bibliografische Information der Deutschen Nationalbibliothek
The Deutsche Nationalbibliothek lists this publication in the Deutsche Nationalbibliografie; detailed bibliographic data is available on the internet at http://dnb.dnb.de.

© 2019 Walter de Gruyter GmbH, Berlin/Boston
This volume is text- and page-identical with the hardback published in 2018.
Cover Image: Monument to the People's Heroes on Tian'anmen Square in Beijing (China) designed by Zheng Zhenduo, Wu Zuoren, Liang Sicheng and Liu Kaiqu. Photo © Puck Engman
Typesetting: Konvertus, Haarlem
Printing and binding: CPI books GmbH, Leck
♾ Printed on acid-free paper
Printed in Germany

www.degruyter.com

For Peter Ditmanson

Contents

Acknowledgements —— VIII

Introduction —— 1

1 Early 1919 – Reforms to save the nation —— 27

2 May 4, 1919 – Rumors and conspiracy theories —— 59

3 Late 1919 – Marketing with the "New Culture Movement" —— 91

4 The 1920s and 1930s – The limits of the New Culture Movement —— 130

5 1919 to 2016 – Canonizing a buzzword —— 156

Conclusion —— 195

Glossary of Terms —— 203

Bibliography —— 205

Index —— 248

Acknowledgements

This book would have never been written without the help of the many people who have supported me over the past years. First and foremost, my thanks go to my PhD supervisor Peter Ditmanson for his invaluable help at all stages of the project. I would also like to thank my thesis examiners Margaret Hillenbrand and Leigh Jenco, my academic mentor Rana Mitter, my teachers Henrietta Harrison, Laura Newby and Barend ter Haar, as well as my colleagues Isaac Taylor, Liu Qian, Elisabeth Schleep, Samuelson Yin, Yegor Grebnev, Chen Yunju and Puck Engman. Furthermore, I am very grateful for the input given to me by Isabella Jackson, Toby Lincoln, Taotao Liu, Dirk Meyer, Yang Song, Justin Winslett, David Bowles, Annie Nie and the two reviewers of this book, among them Timothy Cheek.

My thanks also go to the KB Chen Library of the University of Oxford China Centre and its librarians Joshua Seufert, Trevor Langrish, Hannie Riley, Geneviève Wardley, Minh Chung and Caroline Schade. This project was funded by the British Arts and Humanities Research Council (AHRC), the Keller Stiftung of the Maximilianeum in Munich, Germany, the Edwin Arnold Scholarship of University College, Oxford, and the John Fell Oxford University Press Research Fund. I would also like to thank the John W. Kluge Center of the Library of Congress and the Academia Historica in Taibei for hosting me.

Adapted versions of chapters 2 and 3 have been published in *Frontiers of History in China* (vol. 9 no. 4, 2014) and in *Modern Asian Studies* (vol. 51 no. 5, 2017) respectively.

Introduction

1919 was a year of radical cultural transformation in China. Just how radical it was, was illustrated by the U-turn taken in the career of Hu Shi (1891–1962). He had been a professor at Beijing University since 1917. Today he is famous as one of the authors of the magazine *New Youth* (*Xin qingnian*) and as an early advocate of *baihua* (the "Plain Language"), a vernacular based on the Beijing dialect and infused with Western loanwords.[1] But in the spring of 1919, he was in danger of losing his job, a fate which had already befallen his colleague Chen Duxiu (1879–1942).[2] A century later, both of them are known as two of the most important intellectuals of the early 20th century, as both are considered to have been among the stars of the New Culture Movement (*xin wenhua yundong*). But at the time, nobody talked about the "New Culture Movement." The expression had not yet been invented.

Observing Hu Shi's professional difficulties, Huang Yanpei (1878–1965) and Jiang Menglin (1886–1964), two influential educators in Jiangsu, came up with a plan to evacuate him and his network of like-minded colleagues from Beijing University to Nanjing. In a supportive letter to Hu, they stated that Beijing University should be "ceded to the Old Faction."[3] That is, it should be left to those who endorsed a different set of academic ideals, involving, for example, the maintenance of *wenyan* (Literary Chinese)[4] as a written academic language. Hu Shi and his circle had been embroiled in scholarly debates about language with this group over the preceding few months. These debates had been very abstract and nuanced. But for oblique reasons, newspapers had developed a marginal interest in them and had classified these fuzzy discussions into the squabbles between clear-cut "factions of learning" (*xuepai*), namely, the "New Faction" (*xinpai*, the supporters of *baihua* around Hu and Chen) and the "Old Faction" (*jiupai*). It was felt, Huang's and Jiang's letter suggested, that the "New Faction" had lost the

---

[1] Edward M. Gunn, *Rewriting Chinese: Style and Innovation in Twentieth-Century Chinese Prose* (Stanford, California: Stanford University Press, 1991), 217–96; Shu-mei Shih, *The Lure of the Modern: Writing Modernism in Semicolonial China, 1917–1937* (Berkeley: University of California Press, 2001), 71.
[2] Wang Guangyuan, *Chen Duxiu nianpu 1879–1942* (A Chronology of the Life of Chen Duxiu, 1879–1942) (Chongqing: Chongqing chubanshe, 1987), 64.
[3] Huang Yanpei and Jiang Menglin, "Huang Yanpei, Jiang Menglin zhi Hu Shi" (Letter from Huang Yanpei and Jiang Menglin to Hu Shi), in *Hu Shi laiwang shuxinxuan* (Hu Shi's Selected Correspondence), ed. Zhongguo shehui xueyuan jindaishi yanjiusuo Zhonghua minguoshi yanjiushi Fuhui, vol. shang (Beijing: Zhongguo shehui kexue chubanshe, 2013), 35.
[4] I follow Timothy Cheek and Geremie Barmé in translating *wenyan* as "Literary Chinese."

debate. China's culture, their evacuation proposal implied, appeared en route to being shaped by the ideals endorsed by the competing group, the "Old Faction."

Hu Shi did not evacuate, and only a few months later, this turned out to be a good idea, since cultural preferences had radically shifted within a very short amount of time. A set of ideals had become influential that was not only much more favorable to Hu, but within which he and his network were even seen as stars. This had happened under the auspices of a new expression, namely, the "New Culture Movement," a phrase that had only been coined in the summer of 1919. Those who negotiated it – namely, well and less well-known intellectuals across China – treated Hu Shi, as well as some other members of his network (Chen Duxiu, Fu Sinian [1896–1950] and Luo Jialun [1897–1969] among them), as the "masters" or the "center" of the New Culture Movement.[5] Among the other elements of this matrix of associations around the New Culture Movement were a vocabulary (such as *baihua*) and a political event (the demonstrations of May Fourth. These were nation-wide protests beginning on May 4, 1919, against a deal made in the Treaty of Versailles that the formerly German concessions in Shandong Province would be transferred to Japan at the end of the First World War, rather than being returned to China.)

But while Hu Shi and his circle enjoyed their newly found stardom, they, once more, found themselves complaining about the state of affairs: They felt that, although the vocabulary they had favored was now in vogue among broad circles of intellectuals, it was used to express things they disagreed with. "*Baihua*," for example, was deployed in a "blasphemous" way, Lin Yutang (1895–1976) lamented in a letter to Hu. This "blasphemy" consisted in "considering the popularization of education as the only goal of *baihua* literature," rather than seeing *baihua* as a new literary language suited to present times, as Hu and his network saw it.[6]

Creating a language of the common people designed to spread education was not a new idea, but had long been promoted by a variety of reformers under the headline of "National Language" (*guoyu*, a vernacular designed to unify China's dialects). The ideal had stayed the same, just the label had changed. While the

---

[5] "Masters": Miao Jinyuan, "Suowei 'xin wenhua yundong' de chachao yu pochan" (Confiscation and Bankruptcy of the So-Called "New Culture Movement"), *Piping* (Criticism), October 20, 1920, 3–4, 2, Shanghai. "Center": Ye Yun, "Ji Beijing daxue shiye shi (xu)" (Remembering Beijing University's Opening Ceremony for the New Academic Year [Continued]), *Shenbao* (Shanghai News), September 15, 1920.

[6] "Blasphemy": Geng Yunzhi, *Hu Shi nianpu* (A Chronology of Hu Shi's Life) (Chengdu: Sichuan renmin chubanshe, 1989), 85. An example for *baihua* as the language of present times is Fu Sinian, "Wen yan heyi caoyi" (The Integration of Written and Spoken Language), in *Fu Sinian quanji* (Collected Works of Fu Sinian), vol. 4 (Taibei: Lianjing chuban shiye gongsi, 1980), 1065–66.

dismay about the new usage of the expression "*baihua*" could be put down to the academic tendency to take theoretical minutiae overly seriously, there was also relabelling that is more astonishing to us today – with "us today" obviously being shaped by a century worth of history writing on the New Culture Movement: In late 1919 and the early 1920s, some presented Christianity as the New Culture Movement. In Taiwan, intellectuals deployed it to call for Taiwanese independence from Japanese colonial rule. One scholar (on the mainland), Liu Boming (1887–1923), even claimed that writing in Literary Chinese was the "true meaning of the New Culture Movement."[7]

In this book, I seek to make sense of these various facets of paradoxicality in order to arrive at an explanation of how the cultural change of 1919 occurred. I argue that the New Culture Movement was not so much a descriptive term for a set of new ideas. Instead, it was a buzzword used by a variety of people to market an even larger variety of competing agendas, all of which had existed before the invention of the term in the summer of 1919. Among such agendas were differing programs for cultural reform that included topics like *baihua*, Literary Chinese, Christianity, women's rights, popular education, anarchism, the National Language and so forth. However, through mechanisms to be discussed at length in this book, the New Culture Movement came with a matrix of associations (Hu Shi, Chen Duxiu, *baihua*, May Fourth and so forth) that needed to be referenced, at least implicitly, when marketing with it. Therefore this marketing tactic worked better for those agendas that arguably had something in common with these reference points (for example, the National Language, women's rights or popular education) than for others (Christianity or Literary Chinese). In this way, the New Culture Movement, as a buzzword, reweighted the persuasiveness of programs. To put it differently, it made some agendas – such as the National Language, women's rights or popular education – appear more convincing to contemporaries than others, so that some agendas ended up being more influential. It was in this way that Chinese culture started transforming one century ago.

The New Culture Movement as a buzzword

Numerous conceptual frameworks have been developed in a variety of disciplines, which have been applied to individual sub-aspects of the New Culture

---

[7] Xi Ping, "Duiyu 'Liu Boming jun yanjiang xin wenhua yundong zhi yiyi ji biyao' de piping" (A Criticism of "Liu Boming's Talk on the Meaning and Necessity of the New Culture Movement"), *Juewu* (Enlightenment), July 1, 1920, 4, Shanghai.

Movement. However, the vaunted political and social stature of the New Culture Movement has resisted a complete reinterpretation in light of these frameworks.

Reinhart Koselleck and Raymond Williams, for example, have introduced the ideas of "concept[s]" (*Begriff[e]*)[8] or "keywords,"[9] respectively, to analyze the nexus of intellectual and social change. "Concepts" or "keywords" are vague,[10] and can therefore be filled with differing meaning by contemporaries. In this way, we can "track" social change through their study. But more than that, "concepts" can also produce social change, as Koselleck argues.[11] This framework makes it possible to see the ability of the "New Culture Movement" as an expression to create change. However, I call it a buzzword to tap into another helpful theoretical conceptualization, which aids in explaining the precise mechanisms through which it enacted the transformation: namely, marketing – selling ideas, convincing peers, superiors and subordinates of their merit. This marketing can be understood if we conceive of China's culture in 1919 as what Pierre Bourdieu calls a "market" or "field." By this he means a "site of struggles" and of competition, in which individuals or groups seek to gain a better "position" over their fellow competitors.[12] What they compete for is what Bourdieu calls "capital," by which he does not just mean the "economic" variety (money), but also aspects like prestige ("symbolic capital") and skills or degrees ("cultural capital").[13]

This conceptualization has long been successfully applied to the Republican Chinese field of ideas and literature,[14] but it has wider implications for the New Culture Movement as a whole. In 1919, intellectuals were competing for capital

---

8 Reinhart Koselleck, "Begriffsgeschichte and Social History," trans. Keith Tribe, *Economy and Society* 11, no. 4 (November 1982): 410.
9 Reinhart Koselleck, *Keywords: A Vocabulary of Culture and Society* (London: Croom Helm, 1976), 13.
10 Reinhart Koselleck, *Futures Past: On the Semantics of Historical Time* (Cambridge, Massachusetts: MIT Press, 1985), 419.
11 Melvin Richter, "Begriffsgeschichte and the History of Ideas," *Journal of the History of Ideas* 48, no. 2 (June 1987): 252. See also Daniel Leese, "'Revolution': Conceptualizing Political and Social Change in the Late Qing Dynasty," *Oriens Extremus*, no. 51 (2012): 26–28.
12 John B. Thompson, "Editor's Introduction," in *Language and Symbolic Power*, by Pierre Boudieu, ed. John B. Thompson, trans. Gino Raymond and Matthew Adamson (Cambridge: Polity, 1991), 14. See also Pierre Bourdieu, *Language and Symbolic Power*, ed. John B. Thompson, trans. Gino Raymond and Matthew Adamson (Cambridge: Polity, 1991), 61.
13 Thompson, "Editor's Introduction," 14.
14 Examples are Milena Doleželová-Velingerová and Oldřich Král, eds., *The Appropriation of Cultural Capital: China's May Fourth Project* (Cambridge, Massachusetts: Harvard University Asia Center, 2001); Michael Gibbs Hill, *Lin Shu, Inc.: Translation and the Making of Modern Chinese Culture* (Oxford: Oxford University Press, 2013); Michel Hockx, ed., *The Literary Field of Twentieth-Century China* (Richmond: Curzon, 1999).

for their agendas too. By the summer of 1919, these proponents of such programs sought to achieve, in Thomas Bender's words, "hegemony"[15] for these agendas by claiming that they instantiated the most influential buzzword of the time – the New Culture Movement.

Jeffrey N. Wasserstrom suggests a very helpful model to explain this mechanism, which has been elaborated on by Timothy Cheek:[16] Talking about "rhetorical strategies" in a specific community ("mudslinging strategies in the press of the 1920s" in Wasserstrom's case and debates about "the concept of revolution" in the Yan'an Rectification movement of 1942–1944 in Cheek), they distinguish between "three zones of value": "the legitimating core," to which everybody wants to belong, "the neutral buffer zone," and finally "the delegitimizing periphery," from which everybody wants to stay away. Intellectuals now seek to associate themselves (or in my case, their agendas) with the "legitimate terms" that are the hallmarks of the "core," and, vice versa, their opponents with the "delegitimizing terms," which would move them to the periphery.[17]

To explain the maneuverings of 1919, it is expedient to slightly modify this model, and to talk about "positions" within the cultural field, rather than values within rhetoric.[18] Intellectuals sought to move their agendas towards the "legitimate core" and steer clear of the "non-legitimate periphery" (as they could be called in minor adjustment). For example, at the beginning of the year, various groups of intellectuals sought to identify their agendas with the big topic of that time: the end of World War I and the things this allegedly made necessary. In January 1919, for instance, the Jiangsu Educational Association (*Jiangsu sheng jiaoyuhui*) claimed that it needed funding for the foundation of a New Education Society, because this Society was supposedly particularly suited to the demands China was facing at the "end of World War I."[19] Once the New Culture Movement

---

[15] Thomas Bender, "The Cultures of Intellectual Life: The City and the Professions," in *Intellect and Public Life: Essays on the Social History of Academic Intellectuals in the United States* (Baltimore: John Hopkins University Press, 1993), 14.
[16] The paper in which Wasserstrom puts forward this model has, to my knowledge, never been published. I therefore cite the framework from a paper by Timothy Cheek, in which Cheek elaborates on Wasserstrom. Timothy Cheek, "The Names of Rectification: Notes on the Conceptual Domains of CCP Ideology in the Yan'an Rectification Movement," *Indiana East Asian Working Paper Series on Language and Politics in Modern China*, no. 7 (January 1996): 26–27.
[17] "Rhetorical strategies": Ibid., 26. Wasserstrom on "mudslinging strategies": Ibid. Cheek on "the concept of revolution": Ibid., 1. The discussion on the "three zones of value": Ibid., 26–27.
[18] "Positions": Thompson, "Editor's Introduction," 14.
[19] Jiangsu sheng jiaoyuhui, "Cheng jiaoyu zongzhang zuzhi Zhonghua xin jiaoyushe wen" (Petition to the Minister of Education Regarding the Foundation of the Chinese New-Education Society), *Jiangsu sheng jiaoyuhui yuebao* (Jiangsu Educational Association Monthly Report), January 1919, 2.

had become the "hegemonic" "legitimating term,"²⁰ that is, the hegemonic buzzword, in the summer of 1919, intellectuals of various stripes tried to identify their agendas with it: from Liu Boming, who identified Literary Chinese as the New Culture Movement, to Christians, to the advocates of the National Language, anarchism, communism, Taiwanese independence and women's rights.

Of course, where political trends ran counter to agendas, influence could not be marketed into the world. In a time of rising Japanese imperialism, for example, calls for Taiwanese independence did not stand a chance. Nevertheless, this approach shows why ideas become important: It is not so much because they have more merit and answer the big questions of the time better than their competition. They sometimes become more important because they meet the marketing criteria of the day better. Such criteria, however, can be created in a way that is not always primarily motivated by what contemporaries consider "best" for the nation, but in a rather messy way, as I discuss in the following paragraphs.

This model of cultural change through marketing not only provides a new way of looking at the mechanisms behind cultural change. More importantly, it says something about the direction of cultural change and why it is non-teleological, non-linear and why it therefore tends to leave contemporaries confused, as it did in 1919. It also explains why this nevertheless does not mean that the change of 1919 was completely random.

The cultural change of 1919 hinged upon the matrix of reference points that came with the New Culture Movement (to whom belonged, as mentioned before, Hu Shi, Chen Duxiu, *baihua* and May Fourth). A hundred years of history writing suggest to "us" that these associations were very obvious. However, as I will show in this book, they were not. That they were combined and associated with the New Culture Movement can only be explained through the combination, not of the events of 1919, but through what Clifford Geertz calls the "patterning" of events.²¹ By this Geertz means that reality is reshaped by being interpreted. For example, ideologies, Geertz says, can be read as "a ... symbolic framework in terms of which to formulate, think about, and react to political problems."²²

This framework about the importance of the patterning of reality helps to break through the myths that have been layered upon the New Culture Movement. For example, it is often assumed that the debates about *baihua* versus

---

20 'Hegemonic': Cheek, "The Names of Rectification," 6. "Legitimating term": Ibid., 27.
21 Lit. "pattern," Clifford Geertz, *The Interpretation of Cultures: Selected Essays by Clifford Geertz* (New York: Basic Books, 1973), 216.
22 Ibid., 221.

Literary Chinese of the early months of 1919 and the May Fourth protests were interlinked.[23] However, as I will argue in this book, technically they had nothing much to do with each other. What happened was that the reality of ivory tower academic debates of its early months was patterned by newspapers into clear-cut "factions." While the purpose of this was to simplify a complex reality, this then had wide-reaching implications: It was possible to ascribe to these "factions" warlord political allegiances, that is, rumors soon emerged that the "New Faction" was being suppressed by the warlord government, while the "Old Faction" was supposedly in league with it. This eventually associated the "New Faction" with the May Fourth demonstrators (who, incidentally, had displayed very violent behavior, but a spin – another form of patterning – was soon put upon it in newspapers that depicted the demonstrators as heroes).

The matrix of reference points around the New Culture Movement emerged through a complex combination of these patternings of reality. The surprise that contemporaries experienced at the change this produced – indicating the non-linearity of this change – lay in this combination too. Non-linearity has been studied in detail by scholars exploring contingency in history, and contemporaries' confusion and incorrect predictions are often the markers through which such scholars identify instances of contingency. The reason for such contingency is frequently pinpointed to the introduction of an unexpected and unpredictable event, which disrupts long-term "structures." The assassination of Archduke Franz Ferdinand (1863–1914) set off World War I.[24] England remained Anglican in the 16th century, because Elizabeth I (1533–1603) was on the throne, and she was on the throne because her predecessor, the Catholic Mary Tudor (1516–1558), did not conceive a child.[25] HIV was spread to humans because one person was bitten by a monkey.[26]

But while wrong predictions and retrospective confusion were present in 1919, no really unexpected event, nor in fact any unexpected patterning of reality, had occurred. Academics had debated for centuries, and they had been classified into "factions" for a very long time too. Western imperialism had long been disdained. That Shandong would not be returned to China had also been clear

---

23 For details, see Chapter 2.
24 Richard Ned Lebow, "Learning from Contingency: The Case of World War I," *International Journal* 63, no. 2 (2008): 456.
25 Robert Livingston Schuyler, "Contingency in History," *Political Science Quarterly* 74, no. 3 (September 1959): 331–33.
26 Ian Shapiro and Sonu Bedi, "Introduction," in *Political Contingency: Studying the Unexpected, the Accidental, and the Unforeseen*, ed. Ian Shapiro and Sonu Bedi (New York: New York University Press, 2007), 2.

for a few months.²⁷ In other words, non-linearity was created through a different route, one that lay in the combination of these long-term structures: the academic debates that were interpreted as "factions," then politically polarized, which suddenly made them fit with the May Fourth demonstrators, who had been judged to be the heroes of the protests. There was no linearity, and also no predictability, in the way in which the various structures interacted with each other; how they were applied to other trends and developments; how one interpretation piled upon the next, and how they thus suddenly fit with a previously unrelated trend. Marshall Sahlins calls this the "structure of the conjuncture,"²⁸ by which he means that, when various structures coincide, this can produce "contingency" and "change."²⁹

Incidentally, this also says something about agency in the making of the cultural change of 1919, which was highly complex on two levels: In a way, many people were involved in making the New Culture Movement, since many groups participated in the patterning of reality that led to the network of reference points later inscribed into the buzzword. The academics debated. The newspapers invented conspiracy theories. The politicians made their deals with foreign powers about Shandong. But in a way, no one really made the New Culture Movement, since no one group was responsible for combining all these patterns into the New Culture Movement's matrix of reference points. After the buzzword "New Culture Movement" had been coined, agency became complex on a different level. Lesser-known intellectuals claimed that their ideas originated with the star personnel of the New Culture Movement, while, in reality, it was the lesser-known people who had produced the ideas. In other words, agency lay somewhere other than where it was claimed to be.

If the cultural transformation of 1919 was not linear and therefore not inevitable, it was not, however, random. Instead, it was what Douglass C. North calls "path-dependent."³⁰ For example, Chinese culture could not have come to be dominated by Islam or Hinduism. The reason is that the "paths" it was able to

---

27 "Shandong wenti Zhong-Ri huanwen zhi pilu" (Disclosure of Sino-Japanese Diplomatic Correspondence on the Shandong Question), *Shenbao* (Shanghai News), February 22, 1919, 6, Shanghai; [] An, "Shandong wenti zhi Beijing xiaoxi" (News from Beijing on the Shandong Question), *Shenbao* (Shanghai News), April 25, 1919, 6, 6.
28 Marshall Sahlins, "Introduction [Islands of History] [1985]," in *Readings for a History of Anthropological Theory*, ed. Paul A Erickson and Liam D. Murphy (Toronto: University of Toronto Press, 2010), 192.
29 Paul A Erickson and Liam D. Murphy, eds., *Readings for a History of Anthropological Theory* (Toronto: University of Toronto Press, 2010), 626.
30 Douglass C. North, *Institutions, Institutional Change and Economic Performance* (Cambridge: Cambridge University Press, 1996), 99.

take were limited by the pool of competing agendas that existed at the beginning of the year – and which were, of course, shaped by various historically Chinese cultural ideals and Western ideas that had been introduced in the context of 19th-century imperialism. (I will outline in some more detail which roads Chinese culture ended up not taking in the conclusion to this book.)

The point I am making is that intellectual change through marketing means that Chinese culture could have easily taken a different route. The reason that its culture changed in the way it did was rooted in intellectuals' habits of marketing agendas with whichever buzzword seemed opportune; and in the uncoordinated concatenation of a variety of patternings of the reality of 1919, which shaped the parameters of this buzzword.

The new interpretive framework

If we view the cultural transformation of 1919 in terms of cultural fields, patternings of reality and shifting marketing reference points, a new interpretive framework of the New Culture Movement emerges. It reads like this:

Before the introduction of the buzzword "New Culture Movement" in the summer of 1919, a plethora of intellectual, social and educational reform agendas competed in China's cultural field. These agendas included, for example, the program of the warlord of Shanxi Province Yan Xishan (1883–1960), who endorsed Literary Chinese, a version of Confucianism, women's education, popular education, science and the vernacular to communicate with the common people. They comprised similar ideas proposed by a political-educational group called the Jiangsu Educational Association, who additionally supported vocational education. Others were endorsing Christianity, anarchism and women's rights. All of these groups sought to make their agendas more influential in the cultural field by identifying them with the hot topics of the day (see the funding bid for the Jiangsu Educational Association's New Education Society in January 1919)[31]. Many groups also claimed that their programs would further China's "national salvation," another important theme of the time. To put it differently, these groups and individuals tried to co-opt a variety of buzzwords for their programs, in order to convince their peers, superiors and subordinates of their necessity.

One group among these many was a loose network of academics and students at Beijing University, among them Hu Shi, Chen Duxiu, Fu Sinian, Luo Jialun, Qian Xuantong (1887–1939), Li Dazhao (1888–1927) and many more. They

---

[31] Jiangsu sheng jiaoyuhui, "Cheng jiaoyu zongzhang zuzhi Zhonghua xin jiaoyushe wen."

propagated a range of ideas in their student journals *New Tide* (*Xinchao*) and *Weekly Critic* (*Meizhou pinglun*) and in their teachers' journal *New Youth*. Contemporaries did not consider them a force to be reckoned with in the cultural competition of the day. *New Youth*, which Chen Duxiu had founded in 1915, sold very badly and was therefore almost closed down in 1918.[32] Their ideas were not unique either, but intersected with parts of the programs endorsed by others. For example, they shared some ideals with people like Yan Xishan and the Jiangsu Educational Association (such as feminism and popular education) and others with groups proposing *baihua* for written and spoken purposes. This advocacy of *baihua* gave rise to a highly theoretical squabble with a dissenting academic group at Beijing University. These were the people whom the above-cited letter by Huang Yanpei and Jiang Menglin had labelled the "Old Faction," and whose program included maintaining Literary Chinese as the written academic language. Soon these two groups of academics were therefore caught up in a debate, which the public outside of Beijing University did not care much about and which the *baihua* advocates seemed to be losing in the spring of 1919, again, as Huang's and Jiang's letter, but also others like the newspaper *Shanghai News* (*Shenbao*) diagnosed.[33]

That this situation was reversed a mere few months later hinged upon the invention of the expression "New Culture Movement" in the summer of 1919. The "New Culture Movement" was deployed as yet another buzzword, but it turned out to be especially powerful. Its meaning was relatively flexible, but it did come with a matrix of associations, which intellectuals needed to reference when marketing their agendas with the "New Culture Movement." These reference points included star personnel (Hu Shi, Chen Duxiu and so forth), a vocabulary (such as *baihua*) and the association with one of the big political events of the year 1919: the May Fourth protests. These associations, especially the reference to May Fourth, I suspect, were what made it so powerful. But they were also the reason why the New Culture Movement worked better for the marketing of some agendas and less well for others: It was easier to argue that the National Language was essentially "*baihua*" and something that Hu Shi, Chen Duxiu and others supported, than it was to claim the same for Literary Chinese. After all, the National Language was, in practice if not in the minutiae of theory, very close to *baihua*,

---

[32] Letter from Lu Xun from 1 January 1918, cited in Chen Shuping, *Beixin shuju yu Zhongguo xiandai wenxue* (New Northern Press and China's Contemporary Literature) (Shanghai: Shanghai sanlin wenhua chuanbo youxian gongsi, 2008), 20.
[33] Xin Wei, "Riben dui wo xin sixiang shishi zhi tongqing" (Japan's Sympathy for Our New Intellectual Tide Losing Power), *Shenbao* (Shanghai News), April 25, 1919, 6.

whereas Literary Chinese had in the debates of early 1919 been set up as its very opposite.

Looking back over a century of history writing on the New Culture Movement, it seems quite obvious that Hu Shi, Chen Duxiu, *baihua* and May Fourth belonged together and that they should be associated with the "New Culture Movement." But this was not immediately evident to contemporaries. For many of them, Beijing University's academic debates about *baihua* and the May Fourth demonstrations were not a series of events, but separate phenomena. Originally, the vice-president of the Jiangsu Educational Association, Huang Yanpei, was worried that the May Fourth demonstrations would distract from his educational program, rather than give it a boost.[34] While the Jiangsu Educational Association would soon catch on to the potential May Fourth had for its agenda, others remained flummoxed. The missionary and Yanjing University professor Philippe de Vargas (1888–1956, Chinese name: Wang Kesi) observed the connection between *baihua* and May Fourth, but called it a "historical puzzle."[35] The warlord Yan Xishan failed to see it throughout 1919.

The reason for this confusion lay in the way the New Culture Movement's matrix of associations or reference points came together. It hinged upon the conjuncture, not so much of events and phenomena, but of interpretations, constructions and patternings of events, which suddenly combined things that were previously quite independent from each other.

This piling-up of patternings of reality was also the reason why Huang Yanpei and Jiang Menglin did not at the beginning of the year foresee the cultural developments of the next few months, and why, more than that, these cultural transformations could easily have turned out differently. In 1919, reality was interpreted through rumors and conspiracy theories, a longstanding belief in the perennial clustering of academics into squabbling factions, a generally low opinion of warlord politics and a very black-and-white interpretation of the May Fourth protests.

---

34 Huang Yanpei, *Huang Yanpei riji* (Huang Yanpei's Diary), ed. Zhongguo shehui kexueyuan jindaishi yanjiusuo, vol. 2 (Beijing: Huawen chubanshe, 2008), 64. I translate *"hui"* here as synonymous to *shifeng* ("just when"), following "Gudai hanyu cidian" bianxiezu, "Hui" (Can, Meeting, Etc.), *Gudai hanyu cidian: suoyin ben* (A Dictionary of Classical Chinese: Short Version) (Beijing: Shangwu yinshuguan, 2007), Beijing.
These notes were written on the pages of the entries of 8 to 11 June, which the editors feel do not belong to the diary as such. See Huang, *Huang Yanpei riji*, 2:64.
35 Philippe de Vargas, "Some Elements in the Chinese Renaissance (Manuscript)" (Beijing, February 15, 1922), 18, Container 221, Lewis Nathaniel Chase Papers, Manuscript Division, Library of Congress, Washington, D.C., Beijing.

While Chinese academics were debating at Beijing University, the First World War had ended in Europe. China had participated in this war on the side of the Allies, in the hope of gaining a better standing on the international stage and thus regaining the German concessions in Shandong Province. However, since simultaneously Japan was furthering its own imperialist ambitions, the previous German concessions were given to Japan at the Paris Peace Conference in Versailles, rather than being returned to China. This in turn provoked a national political event: the protests of May Fourth against the deal about Shandong. During the protests, the students committed violent acts (the famous burning-down of Finance Minister Cao Rulin's [1877–1966] house and the beating-up of his guest Zhang Zongxiang [1879–1962], both of whom were held responsible for the debacle at Versailles). Simultaneously, the government tried to control the script about Versailles and claimed that it had made an honest attempt at playing Big Power politics, but had honorably failed against greater odds.[36] Nevertheless, public opinion decided that the student protesters were the heroes and the government the villains of the event. This was one way in which reality was patterned.

Meanwhile, newspapers had interpreted and in this way patterned and reshaped the ivory-tower debates at Beijing University about language. They formulated them as clashes between "factions of learning," the "Old Faction" and the "New Faction." In this way they tapped into a centuries-old tradition of classifying debating academics in this very manner. While this initially appeared to merely have the goal of simplifying the highly sophisticated debates to make them more palatable for a newspaper-reading audience, rumors soon started to be spread in newspapers: The "Old Faction" was allegedly in league with the warlord government and the "New Faction" was being suppressed by it. It was this rumored oppression by the government that in early 1919 was considered the central reason for the "New Faction's" impending demise.

In the weeks after May Fourth, however, this combined with the black-and-white interpretation of the protests (students as heroes, government as villains) to turn into the exact opposite of "New Faction" demise: The (constructed) "New Faction" came to be associated with the May Fourth demonstrators, since they both (allegedly, in the case of the "New Faction") were suppressed by the warlord government. Debating ideas traced back to (though not necessarily actually originating from) Hu Shi and Chen Duxiu was quickly equated with

---

36 Duan Qirui, "Beijing Duan Qirui ban jing dian" (Telegram of the 24th [of May 1919] by Duan Qirui in Beijing), in *Yan Xishan dang'an* (Yan Xishan Papers), ed. Lin Qingfen, vol. 5 (Taibei: Guoshiguan, 2003), 48–50.

marching on the streets against the Treaty of Versailles. That is, it became very popular.

A few months later, in the summer of 1919, the expression "New Culture Movement" was invented, associated, as outlined above, with a matrix of reference points and used to sell a variety of the cultural reform agendas that were then competing. As this marketing strategy worked better for some programs (National Language, feminism, popular education) and less well for others (Literary Chinese, Christianity), the New Culture Movement as a buzzword determined which of the agendas would be successful in the competition they were all engaged in, and in this way it shaped China's cultural path.

Initially, the New Culture Movement was only an expression used within quite a small circle of intellectuals in the humanities and education and among certain political groups. But this circle brought forth people who had the power to shape canons and specifically to anchor the New Culture Movement in the canonical narratives about 20th-century China. One of these people was Mao Zedong (1893–1976). Others were Chinese Christians, missionaries to China and individuals like Hu Shi, all of whom were tapped into networks that had global audiences. Over the next decades, they continued using the New Culture Movement as a buzzword by redefining it for their respective purposes: For Mao, the New Culture Movement was the beginning of communist China, with him as a leading figure in both. For Christians, this was a China modernized in the Western style, which, their vain hope went, would soon endorse Christianity. For Hu Shi, this was a China whose culture was heavily shaped by him. Once canonized in this way, the New Culture Movement was later used by others – Chinese dissidents of the 1980s and in 21st-century Taiwanese politics, education and art – to argue for their new agendas.

The story of the New Culture Movement proposed in this book is thus a lively and at times ironic one about cultural change through academic infighting, rumors and conspiracy theories, newspaper stories and intellectuals (hell-) bent on selling agendas through a powerful buzzword.

The need for a new framework

The writing of its history started almost as soon as the expression "New Culture Movement" was invented. Since then, multiple interpretations of the event have been put forward, some of them politically inspired, some academically minded. Academic works have explored at great length New Culture individuals like Hu Shi or Lu Xun (1881–1936), themes like *baihua* and iconoclasm, and related topics like student protests, the "Wilsonian moment" (referring to the US President

Woodrow Wilson's [1856–1924] endorsement of national self-determination) or local manifestations of May Fourth and New Culture.[37] However, in the past couple of decades, rich new research has provided fresh insights into individual themes pertaining to May Fourth and New Culture, and into aspects of Republican society that touch upon May Fourth/ New Culture. This corpus of literature has pointed to the importance of unpredictability, personal fads and down-to-earth pragmatism at the time.

Among such works is that of Chen Pingyuan, who writes about the importance of the mild and sunny weather on May 4, 1919. On a cold and rainy day, the protesters would have been less motivated to spend time outdoors.[38] Feng Xiaocai argues how Shanghai's common people did not much care or know about the Treaty of Versailles, but instead assumed that the Japanese had poisoned the

---

[37] The following list is in no way exhaustive. Among books on Hu Shi are Jerome B. Grieder, *Hu Shih and the Chinese Renaissance: Liberalism in the Chinese Revolution, 1917–1937* (Cambridge, Massachusetts: Harvard University Press, 1970); Cao Boyan and Ji Weilong, *Hu Shi nianpu* (A Chronology of Hu Shi's Life) (Anhui: Anhui jiaoyu chubanshe, 1989); Geng, *Hu Shi nianpu*. On Lu Xun Vladimir Ivanovich Semanov and Charles J. Alber, *Lu Hsün and His Predecessors* (White Plains: M. E. Sharpe, 1980); Leo Ou-fan Lee, ed., *Lu Xun and His Legacy* (Berkeley: University of California Press, 1985); Eva Shan Chou, "Learning to Read Lu Xun, 1918–1923: The Emergence of a Readership," *The China Quarterly* 172 (December 2002): 1042–64. On *baihua*: Gunn, *Rewriting Chinese*; Gang Zhou, *Placing the Modern Chinese Vernacular in Transnational Literature* (New York: Palgrave Macmillan, 2011); Bing Sang, "The Divergence and Convergence of China's Written and Spoken Languages: Reassessing the Vernacular Language during the May Fourth Period," *Twentieth-Century China* 28, no. 1 (January 2013): 71–93. On iconoclasm: Yü-sheng Lin, *The Crisis of Chinese Consciousness: Radical Antitraditionalism in the May Fourth Era* (Madison: University of Wisconsin Press, 1979); Vera Schwarcz, "A Curse on the Great Wall: The Problem of Enlightenment in Modern China," *Theory and Society* 13, no. 3 (May 1984): 455–70. On student protests: Jeffrey N. Wasserstrom, *Student Protests in Twentieth-Century China: The View from Shanghai* (Stanford, California: Stanford University Press, 1991). On the "Wilsonian moment": Erez Manela, *The Wilsonian Moment: Self-Determination and the International Origins of Anticolonial Nationalism* (Oxford: Oxford University Press, 2007). On local manifestations of May Fourth/New Culture: Tianjin lishi bowuguan and Nankai daxue lishixi "Wu si yundong zai Tianjin" bianxiezu, eds., *Wu si yundong zai Tianjin: lishi ziliao xuanji* (The May Fourth Movement in Tianjin: Selected Historical Materials) (Tianjin: Tianjin renmin chubanshe, 1979); Shanghai shehui xueyuan lishi yanjiusuo, ed., *Wu si yundong zai Shanghai shiliao xuanji* (The May Fourth Movement in Shanghai: Selected Historical Materials) (Shanghai: Shanghai renmin chubanshe, 1980); Wen-hsin Yeh, *Provincial Passages: Culture, Space, and the Origins of Chinese Communism* (Berkeley: University of California Press, 1996); James Hugh Carter, *Creating a Chinese Harbin: Nationalism in an International City, 1916–1932* (Ithaca, N.Y.: Cornell University Press, 2002); Shakhar Rahav, *The Rise of Political Intellectuals in Modern China: May Fourth Societies and the Roots of Mass-Party Politics* (New York: Oxford University Press, 2015).

[38] Pingyuan Chen, *Touches of History: An Entry into "May Fourth" China*, trans. Michel Hockx (Leiden: Brill, 2011), 17–20.

wells and that they were protesting against that.³⁹ In recounting her interviews with New Culture activist Zhang Shenfu (1893–1986), Vera Schwarcz shows that Zhang advocated women's emancipation, because he liked to womanize and only a May Fourth "new woman" would have entered the sorts of liberal relationships he was interested in. This personal inclination was set off by another coincidental event: the death of Zhang's first wife, of whom he was very fond, and his subsequent arranged marriage to a woman he did not like.⁴⁰

A growing body of literature depicts Republican intellectuals as pragmatic, marketing-oriented people, rather than as the visionary, idealistic scholars of older narratives, an approach that has often been inspired by Pierre Bourdieu.⁴¹ It has been emphasized that *baihua* was not the language of the common people, as many understandings of it maintained for a long time, in spite of contemporary criticisms. Instead it was full of Western loanwords and sentence structures, and therefore quite incomprehensible to the average Chinese person.⁴² Works on everyday culture have reminded us that May Fourth intellectuals were people of flesh and blood, not abstract agents of a vision.⁴³ Reform programs often associated with May Fourth/New Culture, such as popular education, have been shown to have developed independently of these Movements.⁴⁴

Such works on individual aspects of May Fourth, New Culture and Republican China have broken up the overarching narratives of May Fourth/New Culture, which

---

39 Feng Xiaocai, "Shanghai xiaceng minzhong dui 'wu si yundong' de fanying: yi 'Riren zhidu' fengchao wei zhongxin" (The Reactions towards the May Fourth Movement of the Masses of Shanghai's Lower Classes: The Agitation about "the Poisoning [of Wells] by the Japanese"), *Dongfang lishi pinglun* (Oriental History Review), no. 3 (2013): 84–101.
40 Vera Schwarcz, *Time for Telling the Truth Is Running Out: Conversations with Zhang Shenfu* (New Haven: Yale University Press, 1992), 40–42, 54–56.
41 Doleželová-Velingerová and Král, *The Appropriation of Cultural Capital*; Hill, *Lin Shu, Inc.*; Leo Ou-fan Lee, "Incomplete Modernity: Rethinking the May Fourth Intellectual Project," in *The Appropriation of Cultural Capital: China's May Fourth Project*, ed. Milena Doleželová-Velingerová and Oldřich Král (Cambridge, Massachusetts: Harvard University Asia Center, 2001), 39–45. The same impression is conveyed in studies of May Fourth-era networks, Xu Jilin, *Jindai Zhongguo zhishi fenzi de gonggong jiaowang* (Interactions between Modern Chinese Intellectuals) (Shanghai: Shanghai renmin chubanshe, 2007); Rahav, *The Rise of Political Intellectuals in Modern China*.
42 Gunn, *Rewriting Chinese*, 217–96; Shih, *The Lure of the Modern*, 71. Qu Qiubai had expressed this criticism in the 1930s, Yi-tsi Mei Feuerwerker, *Ideology, Power, Text: Self-Representation and the Peasant "Other" in Modern Chinese Literature* (Stanford: Stanford University Press, 1998), 39.
43 Fabio Lanza, *Behind the Gate: Inventing Students in Beijing* (New York: Columbia University Press, 2010).
44 Paul John Bailey, *Reform the People: Changing Attitudes towards Popular Education in Early Twentieth-Century China* (Edinburgh: Edinburgh University Press, 1990); Timothy B. Weston, *The Power of Position: Beijing University, Intellectuals, and Chinese Political Culture, 1898–1929* (Berkeley, Calif.: University of California Press, 2004).

were put forward in earlier milestone works. Among those was Chow Tse-tsung (1960), according to whom May Fourth/New Culture was an "intellectual revolution" on many political, social and cultural levels, in which intellectuals called for "a complete transformation of traditional Chinese civilization";[45] Vera Schwarcz's earlier book (1986), which interpreted New Culture as the "Chinese enlightenment"; and Rana Mitter (2005), who described May Fourth/New Culture as the making of a largely Western-style modernity and a first manifestation of student violence in China.[46] Diverse as these flagship works offering overall narratives are, they share the assumption that New Culture was a movement led by visionary and idealistic intellectuals, and which had been in the making for a long time, one that was the most important trend of the time and that was unavoidable. To put it differently, they paint a linear picture of the making of cultural change in the early 20th century.

The recent works that have revamped our understanding of Republican China and on the various edges of May Fourth/New Culture have broken these overarching narratives apart. It is the goal of this book to put together a new narrative about the New Culture Movement and the cultural change of 1919. It moves beyond a story rooted in a faith in the idealism and linearity of the New Culture Movement, to take into account this new picture of a messy, cantankerous and flesh-and-blood image of the time period.

The milieu in 1919

Part of the long-term "structures" that contributed to the cultural change of 1919 was the various ways in which reality was "patterned."[47] But among them were also the international situation (outlined briefly above) and the domestic Chinese milieu, in which this "patterning" and marketing occurred. For the sake of simplicity, it is helpful to divide this milieu into three spheres: education and academia, politics and the press. The New Culture Movement was mainly invented and debated in towns and cities.[48] So even though the three spheres extended to the countryside, the following discussion will be limited to China's urban centers.

---

45 Tse-tsung Chow, *The May Fourth Movement: Intellectual Revolution in Modern China* (Cambridge, Massachusetts: Harvard University Press, 1960), 13.
46 Vera Schwarcz, *The Chinese Enlightenment: Intellectuals and the Legacy of the May Fourth Movement of 1919* (Berkeley: University of California Press, 1986); Rana Mitter, *A Bitter Revolution: China's Struggle with the Modern World* (Oxford: Oxford University Press, 2004).
47 Geertz, *The Interpretation of Cultures*, 216.
48 Mitter, *A Bitter Revolution*, 25.

The division into academia/education, politics and the press is in some ways artificial and mostly a conceptual aid, as people were mobile and well-connected across these spheres. Cai Yuanpei (1863–1940), for example, was a teacher at Nanyang Public School, became minister of education in 1912, took up the post of chancellor of Beijing University in 1916 and was then a member of virtually every important educational committee in the country. People were also mobile geographically. Fu Sinian, for example, was born in Shandong, studied in Beijing, got his first job at Zhongshan University in Canton, eventually returned to Beijing and later on moved to Taiwan. Even when people stayed in one locality and job, there was the infrastructure to bring other parts of China to them: Students in Beijing read the Shanghai newspaper *Shanghai News*, made possible by that paper's postal service. Academics in Beijing could correspond with others in Jinan or Suzhou.[49] The New Culture Movement was born out of this milieu of interconnected spheres and regions.

Politics

Chinese intellectuals of the late 1910s loved to loathe governmental politics.[50] The reason was their disappointment with the 1911 Revolution, which had not ushered in the era of democracy which it had promised, but instead given way to rule by military men. The revolution itself had ended the older dynastic system, which had lost its legitimacy after the shock of 19th-century Western imperialism and the subsequent influx of Western ideas. Almost immediately after the Republic

---

49 Teaching in Jinan: Lewis Nathaniel Chase, "Letter to E.A. Chase," June 17, 1923, 3, Container 171, Lewis Nathaniel Chase Papers, Manuscript Division, Library of Congress, Washington, D.C. Socializing in Suzhou: Lewis Nathaniel Chase, "Letter to Shurman," June 2, 1924, Container 222, Lewis Nathaniel Chase Papers, Manuscript Division, Library of Congress, Washington, D.C. Reading the *Shanghai News* in Beijing: Tsing Tuh Zung, "Contemporary Drama of China" (Student essay, July 29, 1924), 3, Container 220, Lewis Nathaniel Chase Papers, Manuscript Division, Library of Congress, Washington, D.C.; Cai Yuanpei, *Cai Yuanpei riji* (Cai Yuanpei's Diary), ed. Wang Shiru, vol. 1 (Beijing: Beijing daxue chubanshe, 2010), 254. On the *Shanghai News*' postal service, see "Chubanjie xiaoxi" (News from the Publishing World), *Shenbao* (Shanghai News), March 31, 1925, 15, Shanghai; Pang Ju, *Kua wenhua guanggao yu shimin wenhua de bianqian: 1910–1930 nian Shenbao kua-wenhua guanggao yanjiu* (Developments in Cross-Cultural Advertisement and Urbanites' Culture: Research on Cross-Cultural Advertisement in the *Shanghai News*, 1910–1930) (Shanghai: Shanghai jiaotong daxue chubanshe, 2010), 53.
50 This sentiment was, for example, expressed in Fu Sinian, "'Xinchao' zhi huigu yu qianzhan" (*New Tide*: Looking Back and Looking Ahead), in *Wu si yundong huiyi lu* (Records of Memories of the May Fourth Movement), ed. Zhongguo shehui kexue yuan jindaishi yanjiusuo (Beijing: Zhongguo shehui kexue chubanshe, 1979), 175.

of China had been officially founded in 1912, its presidency was taken over by General Yuan Shikai (1859–1916). To the dismay of republican enthusiasts, Yuan Shikai tried to restore the monarchy with himself as emperor in 1915, a project foiled by his death in 1916.

But this did not strengthen the republican form of state either. Instead, increasingly powerful local generals, who had been kept in check by Yuan, took over power. This ushered in the period that has become known as the "warlord era," which only ended when Chiang Kai-shek (1887–1975) unified China through a military campaign in 1927. During the warlord era, China was nominally a republic, with a parliament, a premier, a president, political parties and elections. But *de facto* most political offices were occupied by warlords and their allies.

These warlords had the official title of "military governor" (*dujun*) and usually had a regional powerbase. One warlord who will play a role in this book was Yan Xishan, the military governor of Shanxi Province. Warlords were also very diverse, ranging from modernizers like Yan Xishan to those who tried to turn back the clock. Among the latter was Zhang Xun (1854–1923), who was dubbed the "Pigtail General," because he made his troops wear the long outmoded queue of the Qing Dynasty (1644–1911). Warlords of course derived their power from their armies. But they also teamed up in cliques and alliances. Especially the latter changed frequently. But this should not give the impression that China was in fact divided into different countries. Particularly while warlords were in alliance with the central government in Beijing, they maintained a degree of national cohesion. For example, through constant correspondence, they exchanged information, requested instructions and sometimes even followed the central government's orders.[51]

One of the most important warlords of 1919 was Duan Qirui (1865–1936). Duan had been premier of Yuan Shikai and after Yuan's death he became the leader of

---

51 Examples of correspondence between warlords and the central government: Canmou benbu and Lujunbu, "Beijing guowuyuan can, lubu ge dian" (Telegram of the 5th [of September 1919] from the General Staff and the Army Ministry of the State Council in Beijing), in *Yan Xishan dang'an* (Yan Xishan Papers), ed. Qingfen Lin, vol. 5 (Taibei: Guoshiguan, 2003), 84; Chun Li, "Nanjing Li dujun geng dian" (Telegram of the 8th [of June 1919] from Military Governor Li in Nanjing), in *Yan Xishan dang'an* (Yan Xishan Papers), ed. Qingfen Lin, vol. 5 (Taibei: Guoshiguan, 2003), 58–59; Neiwubu, Lujunbu, and Jiaotongbu, "Beijing neiwubu, lujunbu, jiaotongbu dong dian" (Telegram of the 2nd [of December 1919] from the Ministry for Internal Affairs, the Army Ministry and the Ministry of Communications in Beijing), in *Yan Xishan dang'an* (Yan Xishan Papers), ed. Qingfen Lin, vol. 5 (Taibei: Guoshiguan, 2003), 88–89. On warlords implementing the central government's instructions: Zhongping Chen, "The May Fourth Movement and Provincial Warlords: A Reexamination," *Modern China* 37, no. 2 (March 2011): 148.

the warlord faction Anhui Clique – named after Duan's native province Anhui.[52] Duan Qirui quickly made many enemies. In 1917, he fell out with President Li Yuanhong (1864–1928) over the question of whether China should enter World War I. Duan was in favor, Li was not, and neither was Sun Yat-sen (1866–1925), the leader of the GMD (*Guomindang*, at the time mostly called the Revolutionary Party, *Gemingdang*). Giving this and other factors as reasons, Sun Yat-sen split off in 1917 and founded a separate government in South China, with its capital in Canton. Incidentally, in the end Sun's government still declared war on Germany. His original opposition, according to Marie-Claire Bergère, had merely been a ploy in a domestic power game.[53]

Meanwhile in Beijing a warlord group was forming that during May Fourth would come into disrepute with the newspaper-reading public: the Anfu Club. One version of the Anfu Club's foundation reads that, in the late 1910s, members of parliament close to the Anhui Clique came into the habit of spending time at the house of Liang Shitang (1871–1937), which was located on the street Anfu Hutong. This gave Duan Qirui the idea to formally organize these parliamentarians into a club, the Anfu Club. Its declared aim was to gain control over Chinese politics and topple the rival Zhili Clique, which was another warlord grouping. Duan's protégé Xu Shuzheng (1880–1925), who will also play a role in this book, was entrusted with implementing this idea, and the Anfu Club was formally established on March 8, 1918.[54] After 1919, the Anfu Club would fall victim to one of the countless coups and wars between the warlord cliques. In 1920, the Zhili and Fengtian Cliques joined forces to destroy the Anhui Clique, just to fight each other in the two big Zhili-Fengtian Wars in 1922 and 1924.[55]

Another political group at the time was the Research Clique. The Research Clique owned some of the newspapers that are important for the story of the New

---

52 Andrew J. Nathan, "A Constitutional Republic: The Peking Government, 1916–28," in *The Cambridge History of China*, 1st ed., vol. 12 (Cambridge: Cambridge Histories Online, 1983), 272, http://universitypublishingonline.org/cambridge/histories/; Liang Yiqun, "Duan Qirui" (Duan Qirui), ed. Qu Lindong, *Zhongguo zhongxue jiaoxue baike quanshu* (Chinese Middle-School Teaching Encyclopedia) (Shenyang: Shenyang chubanshe, 1991), Shenyang.
53 Marie-Claire Bergère, *Sun Yat-Sen*, trans. Janet Lloyd (Stanford, California: Stanford University Press, 1998), 270–73.
54 Liu Jingquan, *Beijing minguo zhengfu, yihui, zhengzhi yanjiu* (Research on Government, Parliament and the Politics of the Beijing Republic) (Tianjin: Tianjin jiaoyu chubanshe, 2006), 499–500.
55 James E. Sheridan, "The Warlord Era: Politics and Militarism under the Peking Government, 1916–28," in *The Cambridge History of China*, 1st ed., vol. 12 (Cambridge: Cambridge Histories Online, 1983), 297, http://universitypublishingonline.org/cambridge/histories/; Wu Xiang, "Lun Xu Shuzheng yu Wanxi junfa de xingshuai" (The Rise and Fall of Xu Shuzheng and the Anhui Warlord Clique) (Master's, Huazhong shifan daxue, 2009), 63.

Culture Movement. Its most prestigious leader was Liang Qichao (1873–1929), the 19th-century reformer. After fleeing to Japan following the Hundred Days Reform of 1898, Liang assembled a number of "disciples" from among the Chinese intellectuals there.[56] After his return to China in 1911, these disciples formed a political party called the Progressive Party, which backed Yuan Shikai until they realized that Yuan had no intention of maintaining the republic. After Yuan Shikai's death, the Progressive Party changed its name into "Constitution Research Clique" and became known as the "Research Clique."[57]

The Clique supported Duan Qirui on a number of questions, such as the issue of whether China should enter World War I (Duan and the Research Clique were in favor). When Sun Yat-sen built his own government in the south in 1917, the Research Clique stayed with Duan in Beijing and formed an important force in parliament. However, it lost most of its seats in the parliamentary elections of 1918, whereupon many of its leaders traveled abroad. Liang Qichao famously went on a trip to Europe. During May Fourth, the Research Clique backed off from the Duan's Anfu Club. But when the Anfu Club vanished after the warlord wars of the 1920s, the Research Clique ceased its activities as well.[58]

It was this warlord politicking that intellectuals in China disliked, and the image of which would come to be crucial to the matrix of persuasion that was attached to the buzzword "New Culture Movement."

Academia and Education

A story of the New Culture Movement can of course not be told without academia and education. Academia and education were experiencing major upheavals and innovations in the 1910s, trying to define their institutional structure, intellectual ideals and intellectuals' role in society. In using the tricky word "intellectual," Timothy Cheek's very pragmatic approach is helpful. Acknowledging that he uses the term "intellectual" as "our word," rather than as a translation for "*zhishi fenzi*," he deploys it as "a general marker that points to quite different kinds of thinker and writer."[59]

---

[56] Andrew J. Nathan, *Peking Politics, 1918–1923: Factionalism and the Failure of Constitutionalism* (Berkeley, Calif.: University of California Press, 1976), 241.
[57] Ibid., 160.
[58] Ibid., 239–44, 160.
[59] Timothy Cheek, *The Intellectual in Modern Chinese History* (Cambridge: Cambridge University Press, 2015), 5.

The story about academia and education started with an earlier shift in intellectual and educational ideals: in 1905, when the Empress Dowager Cixi (1835–1908) abolished the centuries-old civil service examination system as part of her New Policies. The examination system had previously defined what scholars had to learn – a varying canon of Confucian works. It had also shaped their relationship to society and politics – after a successful examination, most of them hoped to become the administrators of the realm, although for long periods of Chinese history this did not work out in practice, since there was often a higher number of successful candidates than of administrative jobs. The examination system came to an end in 1905 and education began to take place within a new paradigm. Students now attended new-style (read Western- and Japanese-style) schools and universities. There they learnt about the world through new subjects: in science subjects and in the humanities, which read the Confucian classics as part of history or the history of literature, rather than as timeless truths. They could choose from a variety of different types of schools, depending on their ability, inclination and financial resources. There were missionary-run schools (Yanjing University) and state-funded ones (Beijing University), the latter of which were constantly in dire financial straits. Some schools were prestigious (Yanjing and Beijing Universities) some less so (for example Normal Schools, which trained teachers).[60] But again these institutions were permeable. Hu Shi, for instance, simultaneously taught at Beijing University, at Women's Higher Normal School and at Private Chinese University.[61]

Intellectuals' relationship to politics became trickier. Some of them made a point of disliking politics, by which they then referred to the corrupt dealings of the warlord government. Nevertheless, academia remained connected with other aspects of "politics," such as social and cultural ones. This difficult relationship to politics is mirrored in the anecdote about Hu Shi, who announced in 1917 that he would not talk about politics for 20 years. Yet two years later, he participated in the May Fourth Movement of 1919.[62]

Apart from political protest, the most obvious interface between academia/education and politics was educational politics. At the head of educational politics in 1919 was the Minister of Education Fu Zengxiang (1872–1949), a scholar of the prestigious Hanlin Academy, which was an elite club of the time of the

---

[60] Wen-hsin Yeh, *The Alienated Academy: Culture and Politics in Republican China, 1919–1937* (Cambridge, Massachusetts: Council on East Asian Studies, Harvard University, 1990), 3–5.
[61] Jing Guan, "Dumen xuejie xiaoxi" (News from Academia in the Capital), *Shenbao* (Shanghai News), November 5, 1919, 6, Shanghai.
[62] Grieder, *Hu Shih and the Chinese Renaissance*, 175–78.

civil service examinations.⁶³ The Ministry of Education in Beijing drew upon an infrastructure that reached out into the provinces to implement its educational ideals. Part of this infrastructure was the Educational Associations. Huang Yanpei and Jiang Menglin, the authors of the letter from the opening anecdote, were members of the Jiangsu Educational Association, which will play a major role in this book. Huang Yanpei was even its vice-president. Educational Associations existed on province-, county- and town- or village-level all over China. They had some autonomy from the Ministry of Education, but they were also commissioned to make policy suggestions to the Ministry and, vice versa, help implement its policies. Precursors of the Educational Association of Jiangsu Province emerged under varying names in the mid-1900s, when the Qing Dynasty's ban on societies was lifted. It started being called "Jiangsu Educational Association" in 1912 and established its headquarters in Shanghai.⁶⁴

Like Cai Yuanpei, the Jiangsu Educational Association's vice-president Huang Yanpei was someone in whom the spheres of politics and academia/education meshed. Under the civil service examination system, he had received the degrees of Xiucai and Juren. After 1905, he started receiving a new-style education at Nanyang Public School, where Cai Yuanpei was a teacher. Over the next few years, Huang was a member of various committees, associations and government institutions concerned with educational politics. In the first few years of the Republic (when Cai Yuanpei was minister of education), Huang was even minister of education of Jiangsu Province.⁶⁵ Huang Yanpei and the Jiangsu Educational Association were also among those who used the New Culture Movement as a buzzword to market their own agendas in late 1919.

---

63 Nathan, *Peking Politics, 1918–1923*, 145; Guo Fengqi and He Huanzhen, eds., "Fu Zengxiang" (Fu Zengxiang), *Zhiming renwu 100 wei* (100 Famous People) (Tianjin: Tianjin guji chubanshe, 2009), Tianjin.
64 Marianne Bastid and Jian Zhang, *Educational Reform in Early Twentieth-Century China*, trans. Paul John Bailey (Ann Arbor: Center for Chinese Studies, University of Michigan, 1988), 128; Gu Xiuqing, *Qing mo Min chu Jiangsu sheng jiaoyuhui yanjiu* (A Study of the Jiangsu Education Association in the Late Qing and Early Republic) (Guilin: Guangxi shifan daxue chubanshe, 2009), 35–53.
65 Chen Zhuyun, Xu Jilin, and Chen Qicheng, "Huang Yanpei" (Huang Yanpei), ed. Hu Hua, *Zhong-Gong dangshi renwu zhuan* (Biographies of Figures in CCP History) (Xi'an: Shaanxi renmin chubanshe, 1988), Xi'an; Wen-hsin Yeh, *Shanghai Splendor: Economic Sentiments and the Making of Modern China, 1843–1949* (Berkeley, Calif.: University of California Press, 2007), 36–37.

The Press

A third sphere that is important for this story is the press. The press experienced a period of rising significance at the time, reflected in the increasing sales numbers of periodicals. According to the newspaper *Shanghai News*' own indications, its sales increased from 20,000 issues in 1917 to 30,000 in 1920. It also showed in the increasing number of periodicals, from under around 15 different periodicals prior to 1895, to just under 500 in 1913, to somewhere between 840 and 2,000 in the late 1910s and early 1920s.[66]

These numbers are still low when compared to China's overall population. But the press was still highly visible for the part of the population that marketed itself with the New Culture Movement and sought to define it: namely, intellectuals, educational politicians and students in education and the humanities. First of all, more people read newspapers than bought them. This had to do with reading practices. The person who bought a newspaper would go on to lend it to his or her friends or read it out aloud to an audience.[67]

Secondly, those who deployed the New Culture Movement were also the audience of the newspapers. Newspapers are mentioned on student reading lists and in scholars' diaries. They advertised themselves in school journals, suggesting that they identified students as their readership.[68] Sometimes newspaper journalists simultaneously held positions at schools.[69] The weight the press carried in these circles was also reflected in intellectuals' reactions to it. The Beijing University professor Liu Shipei (1884–1919), for example, wrote an angry letter to the newspaper *Public Voice* (*Gongyanbao*), after it had characterized him in an article in a way with which he did not agree.[70] Liu Shipei was already ill at the time and

---

[66] *Shanghai News* sales numbers: "Ben bao de guanggao, faxing ji qita" (This Newspaper's Advertisement, Distribution and so on), *Shenbao* (Shanghai News), September 20, 1947, 22–23, Shanghai. The increase of periodicals: Lee, "Incomplete Modernity," 52.
[67] Li Xiaofeng, "Xinchaoshe de shimo" (Beginning and End of the New Tide Society), in *Wu si yundong huiyilu xu* (Records of Memories of the May Fourth Movement, Part Two), ed. Zhongguo shehui kexueyuan jindaishi yanjiusuo (Beijing: Zhongguo shehui kexue chubanshe, 1979), 209; Henrietta Harrison, "Newspapers and Nationalism in Rural China 1890–1929," *Past & Present*, no. 166 (February 2000): 181.
[68] Zung, "Contemporary Drama of China," 3; Cai, *Cai Yuanpei riji*, 1:254; "The *Shanghai Gazette*," *Moti* (McTyeirean), no. 2 (June 1918); "Read the *Shanghai Gazette*," *Moti* (McTyeirean), no. 3 (June 1919).
[69] Wang Yuanfang, *Huiyi Yadong tushuguan* (Remembering East Asia Library) (Shanghai: Xuelin chubanshe, 1983), 112.
[70] Liu Shipei, "Liu Shipei zhi Gongyanbao han" (Letter by Liu Shipei to the *Public Voice*), *Beijing daxue rikan* (Beijing University Daily), March 24, 1919, 6, Beijing; "Guogu yuekanshe zhi

would die later in the same year. He would probably not have bothered to correct the *Public Voice* if he had not considered the paper influential.

As with the schools, there were a variety of newspapers and periodicals to choose from in the late 1910s. Virtually every school and university had its journal, as did almost every intellectual association. Beijing University had *Beijing University Daily (Beijing daxue rikan)*. The Hu Shi-Chen Duxiu circle had *New Youth, New Tide* and *Weekly Critic*. Their academic opponents had *National Heritage (Guogu)*. Newspapers were sometimes run by political parties. The Research Clique owned the *Morning Post (Chenbao)* in Beijing and the *China Times (Shishi xinbao)* in Shanghai. The Anfu Club ran the *Public Voice* in Beijing. Other newspapers were privately owned or commercial. *Social Welfare Tiensin (Yishibao)* was published by American Catholics in Tianjin. The *Shanghai News* in Shanghai was commercial, and *Impartial (Dagongbao)* in Changsha prided itself on its independence.[71]

But even here and in spite of all this variety, in reality these individual newspapers and periodicals intersected, as they often printed the same articles. The reason was publication practices. Newspapers and periodicals across regions and the political spectrum shared journalists and authors, or they copied articles from each other. The press also overlapped with academia and education. Not only did many intellectuals and schools run journals. Sometimes professional newspaper journalists also simultaneously held jobs in education. For example, one journalist of the *Republic Daily (Minguo ribao)* had a day job as a teacher and wrote the editorials for the newspaper after classes in the evening.[72]

A central issue with which intellectuals and newspapers had to struggle in the 1910s was censorship. In this, ironically, they benefitted from the chaos of

---

Gongyanbao han" (A Letter from the National Heritage Society to the *Public Voice*), *Beijing daxue rikan* (Beijing University Daily), March 24, 1919, 6, Beijing.

[71] On the *Morning Post*, see Peng Peng, *Yanjiuxi yu wu si shiqi xin wenhua yundong: yi 1920 nian qianhou wei zhongxin* (The Research Clique and the New Culture Movement in the May Fourth Period: With a Focus on the Time around the Year 1920) (Guangzhou: Zhongshan daxue chubanshe, 2003), 173, 183. *Public Voice*: Nathan, *Peking Politics, 1918–1923*, 147. *Social Welfare Tiensin*: "Yingyin shuoming" (Explanations to the Photo-Offset), in *Yishibao* (Social Welfare Tiensin), vol. 20 (Tianjin: Nankai daxue chubanshe, 2004), i. *Shanghai News*: Barbara Mittler, *A Newspaper for China?: Power, Identity, and Change in Shanghai's News Media, 1872–1912* (Cambridge, Massachusetts: Harvard University Asia Center, 2004), 3. *Impartial*: Yu Chunmei, *Dadao wei gong: Changsha "Dagong bao" (1915–1927) yu Hunan shehui sichao* (The Grand Course Pursues a Public Spirit: *Impartial* in Changsha (1915–1927) and Intellectual Tides Hunanese Society) (Changsha: Hunan renmin chubanshe, 2011), 23; Liu Jianming, ed., "Dagong bao" (Impartial), *Xuanchuan yulunxue da cidian* (Great Dictionary of the Study of Propaganda and Public Opinion) (Beijing: Jingji ribao chubanshe, 1993), Beijing.

[72] Wang, *Huiyi Yadong tushuguan*, 112.

warlord politics, which they so despised. It was not that warlords did not want to prosecute and censor. But they were unable to do so effectively.[73] China's relative division into warlord territories and, importantly, foreign concessions, made it possible to flee to the land of one ruler to avoid persecution or censorship by another. When Cai Yuanpei quit during May Fourth, for example, he made sure to go to the French concession in Shanghai.[74] When Chen Duxiu was arrested in Beijing a bit later, the *Shanghai News* suspected that the government would also have wanted to arrest Cai. But since Cai was not in Beijing anymore, the government could not get to him.[75]

This was not always a watertight solution. Warlords and foreigners sometimes cooperated in censorship, for example, when they all equally disliked a new idea. For instance, in the summer of 1919, the central government recommended that the provincial leaders should censor all and any publications on anarchism.[76] In the same year, the Shanghai bookshop of the publisher East Asia Library (*Yadong tushuguan*) was victim of a Sino-foreign crackdown on anarchist works. The nephew of East Asia Library's owner, Wang Yuanfang (1897–1980), remembered that someone had asked them to sell books with titles of which they could not make much sense. They contained words like, in Wang's parlance, "something or other Kropotkin," and they sold quite well. But one day, three undercover policemen – Chinese and foreign – tricked the publisher East Asia Library into admitting that they were indeed selling these anarchist books. The owner of East Asia Library was arrested, the business faced a lawsuit and they had to pay a fine.[77]

Another method of censorship was to cut off the routes of distribution. In order to get out of one region and to readers in other places, most periodicals employed a postal service. The *Shanghai News*, for example, had one in place.[78] In 1915, the publisher East Asia Library had to watch how the post refused to send issues of the magazine *Tiger* (*Jiayin*), which criticized Yuan Shikai.[79] Sometimes, local sellers such as bookshops also refused to distribute sensitive

---

73 Yutang Lin, *A History of the Press and Public Opinion in China* (Chicago: University of Chicago Press, 1936), 117; Diana Lary, "Warlord Studies," *Modern China* 6, no. 4 (October 1980): 444; Stephen R. MacKinnon, "Toward a History of the Chinese Press in the Republican Period," *Modern China* 23, no. 1 (January 1997): 16.
74 Cai, *Cai Yuanpei riji*, 1:253.
75 "Chen Duxiu bei bu" (Chen Duxiu Arrested), *Shenbao* (Shanghai News), June 15, 1919, 7–8, Shanghai.
76 Canmou benbu and Lujunbu, "Beijing guowuyuan can, lubu ge dian," 84.
77 Wang, *Huiyi Yadong tushuguan*, 49–50. Kropotkin of course refers to Peter Kropotkin (1842–1921).
78 "Chubanjie xiaoxi," 15; Pang, *Kua-wenhua guanggao yu shimin wenhua de bianqian*, 53.
79 Wang, *Huiyi Yadong tushuguan*, 29.

publications on the same grounds.⁸⁰ In spite of these difficulties, the warlord years gave Chinese intellectuals more freedom to express challenging thoughts than periods with a stronger, more centralized government.

It was out of these structures – though these media, these institutions and these people, as well as through their prejudices, images and practices – that the story of the New Culture Movement and the change of 1919 emerged.

Book structure

This book is divided into what Prasenjit Duara would call a "bifurcated history":⁸¹ It discusses the making of cultural change through the New Culture Movement in 1919 and the early 1920s as one of Duara's "forks." It also traces the way the meaning of the expression "New Culture Movement" changed over the ensuing century as part of the other "fork." Chapters 1 and 2 are about the making of the matrix of reference points. They trace the patterning of academic squabbles into factions and their combination with May Fourth. Chapter 3 describes the usage of the New Culture Movement as a buzzword. Chapters 4 and 5 discuss the new and changing meanings inscribed into the New Culture Movement, which had by then been rewritten into a canonized "event" of Modern Chinese History, to the present.

---

80 Li, "Xinchaoshe de shimo," 209.
81 Prasenjit Duara, *Rescuing History from the Nation: Questioning Narratives of Modern China* (Chicago: University of Chicago Press, 1995), 5.

1 Early 1919 – Reforms to save the nation

The year 1919, according to the newspaper *Shanghai News'* assessment in April of that year, was when Literary Chinese (*wenyan*) reconsolidated its position as the main written language. This happened after some small-scale and abstract, if somewhat fierce, academic debates on language reform had temporarily tried to challenge its "position" within the cultural "field."[1] That is, some of the academics who advocated writing in Literary Chinese had quarreled with an "academic faction" (*xuepai*), in the *Shanghai News'* reading, that endorsed *baihua* as a written language. Both groups were based at Beijing University. But over the course of 1919, these *baihua* advocates had lost the debate. Writing would continue being conducted in Literary Chinese.[2] This was the *Shanghai News'* prediction.

History, of course, turned out differently. Only a few months later, the advocates of *baihua* – the circle around Hu Shi and Chen Duxiu – gained considerable prestige among intellectuals and educational politicians. Ideas traced back to them became influential. For example, the National Language, a form of language close to *baihua*, started being taught in primary schools from 1920 onwards.[3]

The late 1910s would therefore enter history as the time of the "*baihua* movement," and the *baihua* movement would be regarded as an essential part of the "New Culture Movement," which came to be associated with ideas such as women's rights, science, democracy, individualism, popular education and also communism. In addition to *baihua*, these were ideas that the network around Hu Shi and Chen Duxiu had endorsed as well.

Retrospectively, it would look as if this circle at Beijing University was the main, maybe even the only, group in the 1910s that had set out to reform Chinese culture, in order to "save the nation" (*jiuguo*) from the weakness into which Western imperialism had plunged it. In this, the retrospective argument sometimes went, the group followed a "Confucian" mindset, which suggested that cultural reform automatically led to political strengthening.[4] And because their goal was to "save the nation," they would find a backing in the May Fourth protests of 1919, which were also seeking to save China. In their efforts to reform culture, the story would claim, the Hu Shi-Chen Duxiu circle, who were "progressive" "iconoclasts," had to battle a handful of "conservatives" (the advocates of Literary Chinese), who did not recognize the trends of the times and wanted to turn back

---

[1] "Positions": Thompson, "Editor's Introduction," 14. "Field": Bourdieu, *Language and Symbolic Power*, 61.
[2] Xin, "Riben dui wo xin sixiang shishi zhi tongqing," *Shenbao*, 25 April 1919.
[3] Wang, "Chinese Literature from 1841 to 1937," 466.
[4] Lin, *The Crisis of Chinese Consciousness*.

the clock. But these "last-ditch attempt[s]"⁵ by the "conservatives" were easily overcome by the "progressives" at Beijing University.

However, the *Shanghai News*' above-cited assessment of the situation in April 1919 indicates that events were in fact not that "foreordained."⁶ At the time, there was no notion of a "New Culture Movement" – the expression had not yet been invented. A group of academics and students at Beijing University, Hu Shi and Chen Duxiu among them, did propose reformist ideas. But these were only a few among a huge variety of competing ideas and agendas put forward by very many groups at the time, and virtually all these groups claimed to be wanting to "save the nation" through their programs. Most of them called for women's rights, science and popular education. But some wanted to see these demands combined with Literary Chinese, others with English as forms of communication. While it was obvious that China's cultural development was "dependent" on one of the "paths" set out by these reform proposals, to draw upon Douglass C. North's formulation, "at every step along the way there were choices ... that provided real alternatives."⁷ In other words, any of these programs could have, as it were, "won" the competition, and come to dominate Chinese culture. The *baihua* advocates at Beijing University were only one small group among the many, and virtually no contemporary expected them to exert much influence in the cultural field. To put it differently, if, with Cheek and Wasserstrom, intellectuals seek to move from the "non-legitimate periphery" of the field over the "neutral buffer zone" to the "legitimate core," the group of *baihua* advocates that included Hu Shi and Chen Duxiu were in the "buffer zone" en route to the "periphery," and others were much closer to the "core" than they were.⁸

"Academic factions" at Beijing University

Newspaper coverage

In the first few months of 1919, a few academics and students at Beijing University were debating differing ideals for Chinese scholarship and culture, and a central

---

5 Lydia Liu, *Translingual Practice: Literature, National Culture, and Translated Modernity – China, 1900–1937* (Stanford: Stanford University Press, 1995), 247.
6 North, *Institutions, Institutional Change and Economic Performance*, 98.
7 Ibid.
8 In modification of Cheek, "The Names of Rectification," 26. As outlined in the Introduction, the expressions used by Wasserstrom and Cheek are "the legitimating core, the neutral buffer zone, and the delegitimizing periphery."

bone of contention was which style of language should be preferred for writing, Literary Chinese or *baihua*. These academic debates were at the time not of major interest to the Chinese newspaper-reading public, and newspapers from the *Shanghai News* and the *China Times* in Shanghai, the *Public Voice* and *Morning Post* in Beijing, to the *Social Welfare Tiensin* in Tianjin and the *Citizen News* (*Guomin gongbao*) in Chengdu only reported about them very occasionally. When they did, they pressed the reality of the debates into a very specific "pattern":[9] they classified the academics there as the "Old Faction" (*jiupai*) and the "New Faction" (*xinpai*). Sometimes the wording differed and they spoke about "the two sides of new and old," "old and new thought" or the "old [learning] people" and "new [learning] people."[10]

Who was behind these "factions" the newspapers wrote about?

When the papers discussed the "Old Faction," they meant a circle around Liu Shipei and Huang Kan (1886–1935), who were professors at Beijing University's humanities department, and a few of their like-minded students. These students had founded a journal called *National Heritage*, in whose publication, newspapers suspected, Liu Shipei and Huang Kan were more involved than they liked to admit.[11] The idea for the journal had been sparked in early 1919, when the students Yu Shizhen (no dates), Xue Xiangsui (no dates), Yang Shisheng (no dates) and Zhang Xuan (no dates) were worried about the "decline of national learning" and decided to rescue it by means of a journal. They received funding from Beijing University and persuaded a professor to take charge of printing and distribution. They also got a few other professors and members of the National Historiography Institute – an institution tasked with recording China's history and at the time incorporated into Beijing University – to advise them. In March 1919, the *National*

---

9 Lit. "patterned," Geertz, *The Interpretation of Cultures*, 216.
10 For "Old Faction", see Jing, "Beijng daxue xin jiu zhi anchao"; "Qing kan Beijing xuejie sixiang chao bianqian zhi jinzhuang," *Gongyanbao*, 18 March 1919, 6. "New Faction": "Beijing daxue zhi yaoyan," *Guomin gongbao*, 31 March 1919; "Beijing daxue yaoyan zhi wugen," *Chenbao*, 10 March 1919; Jing, "Beijng daxue xin jiu zhi anchao"; Yi, "Zuijin zhi xueshu xinchao." "The two sides of old and new": "Beijing daxue zhi yaoyan," 2; "Beijing daxue yaoyan zhi wugen," 2. "Old and new thought": "Beijing daxue zhi yaoyan," 2. "Old [learning] people" and "new [learning] people": Yun Chao, "Lun Daxue xin jiu zhi zheng" (Discussing the Quarrel between New and Old at the University), *Yishibao* (Social Welfare Tiensin), April 7, 1919, 2, Tianjin; Shou Chang, "Xin jiu sichao zhi jizhan" (The Fierce Battle between New and Old Intellectual Trends), *Chenbao* (Morning Post), March 4, 1919, 7, Beijing; Shou Chang, "Xin jiu sichao zhi jizhan" (The Fierce Battle between New and Old Intellectual Trends), *Shishi xinbao* (China Times), March 10, 1919, 3.3, Shanghai.
11 Chen Qi, *Liu Shipei nianpu changbian* (A Comprehensive Chronology of the Life of Liu Shipei) (Guiyang: Guizhou renmin chubanshe, 2007), 351; "Qing kan Beijing xuejie sixiang chao bianqian zhi jinzhuang," 3, 6; Jing, "Beijng daxue xin jiu zhi anchao," 6.

Heritage could get underway with the declared mission "to promote China's traditional scholarship."[12] The journal's writing style projected a particularly old-style image: It was written in Literary Chinese, some of it even unpunctuated.[13]

By "New Faction," the newspapers meant a similar set of academics and students at Beijing University's humanities department, among them Hu Shi and Chen Duxiu (professors) and Fu Sinian, Mao Zishui (1893–1988) and Luo Jialun (students). These students had also founded a journal, which they called "*New Tide.*" The process of its establishment had happened in similar ways as that of *National Heritage*, only a few months earlier. *New Tide*'s first editor Fu Sinian remembered later that he, his dorm-mate Gu Jiegang (1893–1980, the later famous historian) and another friend called Xu Yanzhi (1897–1940) had first come up with the idea in 1917. Among other motivations, they wanted to "practice a bit" for their envisioned future in academia.[14] Running journals was, then as now, a useful experience to have for this career.

In 1918, they decided to put their plans into practice. Like the authors of *National Heritage*, they received funding from Beijing University, recruited a few more of their classmates to make up the New Tide Society, persuaded the head of the Beijing University Publishing Department to help them with printing and distribution and got Professor Hu Shi to advise them. Beijing University's librarian Li Dazhao – then Mao Zedong's boss – allowed them to use a room in the library as an office. The students settled on a title for the journal. Xu Yanzhi felt "The Renaissance" would be a good English title, and Luo Jialun suggested "*Xinchao*" as its Chinese version. In January 1919, the first issue of *New Tide* saw the light of day. The declared mission of the journal was to promote "a critical spirit," "a scientific mindset" and a "reformed language."[15] Especially with this last item – the "reformed language" – *New Tide* clashed with *National Heritage* as soon as the latter was founded, and the two printed articles that directly criticized each other's views.[16]

Another journal which the newspapers regarded as a mouthpiece of the "New Faction" was *New Youth*. *New Youth* had been founded in Shanghai in 1915,

---

12 "Ben she jishi lu" (Records of This Society), *Guogu* (National Heritage), no. 1 (1919).
13 An example is Ibid.
14 Fu Sinian, "'Xinchao' zhi huigu yu qianzhan" (*New Tide*: Looking Back and Looking Ahead), *Xinchao* (New Tide) 2, no. 1 (October 30, 1919): 199.
15 Ibid., 199–200.
16 Mao Zishui, "Guogu he kexue de jingshen" (The *National Heritage* and the Scientific Spirit), *Xinchao* (New Tide) 5, no. 1 (January 5, 1919); Zhang Xuan, "Bo Xinchao guogu he kexue de jingshen pian" (Against the Article "The *National Heritage* and the Scientific Spirit" in the *New Tide*), *Guogu* (National Heritage), no. 3 (May 20, 1919): 1B–4A; Mao Zishui, "'Bo Xinchao "Guogu he kexue de jingshen" pian' dingwu" (Corrections of "Against the Article 'the *National Heritage* and the Scientific Spirit' in the *New Tide*"), *Xinchao* (New Tide) 2, no. 1 (October 30, 1919): 37–57.

but it was brought to Beijing University by its editor, Chen Duxiu, when he was hired by the university in 1916. *New Youth* is now the most famous journal of the May Fourth period. But in early 1919, this outcome would have surprised contemporaries. It sold so badly that it almost ceased publication at the end of 1918.[17] For much of 1916, it was indeed not published.[18] Even people generally interested in *New Youth*-style ideas were not aware of it. Lan Gongwu (1887–1957), the editor of the Beijing-based newspaper *Citizen News* and a supporter of the *baihua* project, only became aware of it in 1919. In January 1919, he confessed to Fu Sinian that he had only read four of its issues.[19]

This was not for lack of confidence on editor Chen Duxiu's part. One day in 1913 he came rushing into the bookshop of the publisher East Asia Library, whose owner Wang Mengzou (1878–1953) was his friend. Wang's nephew Wang Yuanfang remembered later that at the time Chen Duxiu often hung out in East Asia Library's bookshop, because "he had nothing to do." On that day in 1913, Chen announced his intention to publish a magazine that "would certainly have a great impact after the effort of only ten or eight years." But Wang Mengzou refused to publish *New Youth*. East Asia Library was not doing well at the time, and clearly Wang did not expect *New Youth* to yield much profit. He therefore persuaded his colleagues at Qunyi Book Company (*Qunyi shushe*) to publish *New Youth* instead.[20]

At the time, *New Youth* was still called *Youth Magazine* (*Qingnian zazhi*). But soon Qunyi Book Company received a complaint from the Shanghai YMCA, declaring that the name of Chen Duxiu's *Youth Magazine* sounded too similar to their own *Shanghai Young Men* (*Shanghai qingnian*). The reference to "youth," later so intensely associated with Chen Duxiu, carried different connotations at the time, such as an association with the YMCA. When the journal went into its second volume in 1916, it therefore started being called "*New Youth*."[21]

---

[17] Letter from Lu Xun from 1 January 1918, cited in Chen, *Beixin shuju yu Zhongguo xiandai wenxue*, 20.
[18] Weston, *The Power of Position*, 125.
[19] Peng, *Yanjiuxi yu wu si shiqi xin wenhua yundong*, 135. There was a newspaper called *Citizen News* in Beijing and a different one in Chengdu.
[20] Wang, *Huiyi Yadong tushuguan*, 32.
[21] Ibid., 32–33. Wang Yuanfang only talked about a "Shanghai Youth Association" (*Shanghai qingnianhui*), without mentioning their Christian nature. But he did say that they had a "very strong religious flair." The National Index of Chinese Newspapers and Periodicals, moreover, identifies the YMCA as founders of the *Shanghai Young Men* journal, "*Shanghai qingnianhui*" must be an abbreviation for the Shanghai YMCA. Ibid., 32; *Quanguo baokan suoyin, qikan daohang* (National Index of Chinese Newspapers and Periodicals, Guide), accessed August 1, 2013, http://www.cnbksy.com/shlib_tsdc/originNavSearch.do.

None of these journals – *New Youth*, *New Tide* and *National Heritage* – appeared to have the potential to make history, and lack of significance shone through on every front. First of all, these magazines were not unique. Virtually every school, study society and association had its own journal, so there was nothing special about them. There were, for example, the *Beijing University Daily*, the *Alumnae of the Second Women's Normal School of Jiangsu Province* (*Jiangsu shengli di-er nüzi shifan xuexiao xiaoyouhui huikan*), the *Jiangsu Educational Association Monthly Report* (*Jiangsu sheng jiaoyuhui yuebao*), the *Chinese Christian Advocate* (*Xinghua*) and many more.

Secondly, the journals and their authors were not considered unique by their contemporaries either, and this was reflected by the newspapers' decision to label them "academic factions" (*xuepai*). Chinese academia had seen plenty of academic factions in its history (or at least many academic debates that had been classified into "factions"), and so had Beijing University. Only earlier in the decade, readers were reminded, two factions at the university had competed with each other for academic positions. This was when the students of the famous scholar Zhang Taiyan (1868–1936) had driven the Tongcheng Scholars from their jobs at Beijing University in the early 1910s.[22] These Tongcheng Scholars, the *Shanghai News* explained, had populated the university in the 1900s and early 1910s.[23] This "faction" was considered famous for its writing style of *guwen* ("ancient-style prose," a form of Literary Chinese inspired by authoritative anthologies of classical literary compositions) and for their fondness of the eight-legged essay in the civil service examinations.[24] Many of them came from Tongcheng, a county in Anhui.

Michael Gibbs Hill has identified two ways of recounting the origins of this school. One option traces a lineage starting from Fang Bao (1668–1749), who liked Han Yu's (768–824) Tang/Song style of prose and who argued for the "unity between moral purpose and style."[25] His teachings were transmitted to Zeng Guofan (1811–1872), Wu Rulun (1840–1903) and Yan Fu (1854–1921). Another way (preferred by Hill) is to see Yao Nai (1732–1815) as the school's inventor. He endorsed Tongcheng teaching to counteract the rise of *kaozheng* ("evidential learning")-style scholarship. In order to give his ideas more gravitas, he claimed to stand in the

---

[22] Jing, "Beijng daxue xin jiu zhi anchao," 6; "Qing kan Beijing xuejie sixiang chao bianqian zhi jinzhuang," 3, 6, 3, 6.
[23] Jing, "Beijng daxue xin jiu zhi anchao," 6; "Qing kan Beijing xuejie sixiang chao bianqian zhi jinzhuang," 3, 6, 3.
[24] Hill, *Lin Shu, Inc.*, 43. The translation of "ancient-style prose" follows Ibid., 4. I would like to thank Yegor Grebnev from the University of Oxford for his further input on *guwen*.
[25] Hill, *Lin Shu, Inc.*, 41.

tradition of Fang Bao.²⁶ People regarded as Tongcheng Scholars were hired by Beijing University under chancellor Zhang Baixi (1847–1907, tenure January 1902 to February 1904). Among them was Lin Shu (1852–1924), who was often classified as a Tongcheng Scholar, although he was not from Tongcheng. He taught at Beijing University from 1910 to 1913.²⁷

However, as the *Shanghai News* and the *Public Voice* explained, in the early 1910s under the chancellorship of He Yushi (1878–1961, chancellor from December 1912 to November 1913) and Hu Renyuan (1883–1942, chancellor from January 1914 to December 1916), these Tongcheng Scholars were replaced by the Taiyan Disciples, because Tongcheng scholarship had fallen out of fashion. Among the Taiyan Disciples was Huang Kan, who in 1919 was classified as "Old Faction."²⁸

The designation "Taiyan Disciple" referred very broadly to everyone who had studied with Zhang Taiyan. As a member of the Revolutionary Alliance (*Tongmenghui*), Zhang Taiyan had been arrested in 1903 and fled to Japan after his release in 1906. There he had met many of his future "disciples." As having studied with Zhang Taiyan was the only criterion necessary for applying to oneself the label "Taiyan Disciple," these disciples included people ranging from Huang Kan and Liu Shipei (in 1919 regarded as "Old Faction"), to Qian Xuantong and even Lu Xun ("New Faction").²⁹ In spite of this variety, contemporaries neatly claimed that Taiyan Disciples did evidential research and historical phonology, and wrote in the prose-style of the Six Dynasties.³⁰

The current "factional" strive of 1919 had emerged at Beijing University, according to this newspaper story, after Cai Yuanpei had become its chancellor in December 1916. Like many university chancellors, past and present, Cai had started to change

---

26 Ibid., 41–44.
27 Diana Lin, *Peking University: Chinese Scholarship and Intellectuals, 1898–1937* (Albany: State University of New York, 2005), 20; Li Fan, "Liu Shipei yu Beijing daxue" (Liu Shipei and Beijing University), *Beijing daxue xuebao (Zhexue shehui kexueban)* (Journal of Peking University [Humanities and Social Sciences Edition]) 38, no. 6 (2001): 111.
28 On the replacement of the Tongcheng Scholars by Taiyan Disciples in this newspaper story, see Jing, "Beijng daxue xin jiu zhi anchao," 6; "Qing kan Beijing xuejie sixiang chao bianqian zhi jinzhuang," 3, 6. On Tongcheng scholarship falling out of fashion, see Hill, *Lin Shu, Inc.*, 223. On the appointment of the Taiyan Disciples to Beijing University, see Lanza, *Behind the Gate*, 81. On Huang Kan's appointment during this wave of hiring, see Pei Xiaowei, "Huang Kan" (Huang Kan), ed. Ma Liangchun and Li Futian, *Zhongguo wenxue da cidian* (Great Dictionary of Chinese Literature) (Tianjin: Tianjin renmin chubanshe, 1991), Tianjin. On He's and Hu's chancellorship, see Lin, *Peking University*, 42–43.
29 Yeh, *The Alienated Academy*, 25.
30 Jing, "Beijng daxue xin jiu zhi anchao," 6; "Qing kan Beijing xuejie sixiang chao bianqian zhi jinzhuang," 3, 6, 3.

the university structure immediately after taking office. This included the university's personnel. Among the many new hires that Cai Yuanpei made was Chen Duxiu, whom he made dean of humanities because he admired Chen's (as yet little read) publication *New Youth*.[31]

Cai was apparently very keen on working with Chen Duxiu, and he ambushed him while Chen was on a fund-raising trip to Beijing with his friend Wang Mengzou (the publisher).[32] Chen Duxiu lived in Shanghai at the time and had not yet started his job at Beijing University. Chen Duxiu and Wang Mengzou were having a good time in Beijing, visiting friends, going to parties and to the theater – until Cai Yuanpei turned up and wanted to talk about arrangements at Beijing University. Cai visited Chen and Wang "almost every day," "sometimes he came very early and we had not yet gotten up," Wang Mengzou told his family after his return to Shanghai. While Chen and Wang were getting dressed, Cai Yuanpei waited on a chair "at the door of our room." At some point, this became too embarrassing for Chen Duxiu and Wang Mengzou, and they decided: "We should go to bed early in the evenings and get up early in the mornings."[33] Although Cai Yuanpei had spoilt their Beijing trip, Chen took up the job.

Cai Yuanpei also hired Hu Shi who had freshly returned from his PhD studies in the United States.[34] Among others whom Cai Yuanpei employed were his former colleagues from the Revolutionary Alliance, whose member Cai Yuanpei had been, such as Liang Shuming (1893–1988). Others came from the work-study program in France, which Cai had supported. A third cohort was a new wave of Taiyan Disciples. Among them was Liu Shipei. It was in fact Chen Duxiu who had recommended Liu Shipei to Cai.[35] But soon, according to the newspaper story, Hu Shi and Chen Duxiu teamed up with a few colleagues and students and formed the "New Faction." The Taiyan disciples of the hiring wave of the early 1910s and those hired by Cai Yuanpei also joined up with students to constitute the "Old Faction," in the newspaper narrative.[36]

---

[31] Shen Yinmo, "Wo he Chen Duxiu" (I and Chen Duxiu), in *Chen Duxiu yanjiu cankao ziliao* (Study and Reference Material on Chen Duxiu), ed. Anqing shi lishi xuehui, vol. 1 (Anyang: Anyang shi chubanshe, 1981), 90; Lin, *Peking University*, 56.
[32] Wang, *Huiyi Yadong tushuguan*, 35.
[33] Ibid., 36.
[34] Wang, *Chen Duxiu nianpu*, 35.
[35] Li, "Liu Shipei yu Beijing daxue," 108.
[36] Jing, "Beijng daxue xin jiu zhi anchao," 6; "Qing kan Beijing xuejie sixiang chao bianqian zhi jinzhuang," 3, 6.

Beijing University's opinion on the factions

Talking about factions was not only popular with newspapers in Republican China, but had a long history. However, whether such factions were "real," or whether they were constructs, has been a matter of some debate among China historians. Some have talked about "factions" in a way that presumed the classification's accuracy.[37] Others have argued that there was a wide spectrum of reality behind the categorization, ranging from a group with a "shared ... textual tradition"[38] to a brand name designed to give scholars more prestige, by tracing their origins back to a prestigious person.[39]

Contemporary opinion reflected this tension, with some of Beijing University's academics buying into the idea that there were factions at their institution and others denying it. Chen Duxiu and Li Dazhao thought that they were part of factions. Chen spoke about a "National Heritage party" in March 1919. Li Dazhao published newspaper articles on the "Fierce Battle of Old and New Intellectual Trends" at Beijing University, in which he conveyed the impression that there were fights between easily identifiable opponents going on.[40] Even Chancellor Cai Yuanpei implied a belief in academic factions. Cai is famous for advocating *jianrong bingbao* in the early months of 1919. This is sometimes translated as "broad-minded tolerance"[41] or as "broad-minded and encompassing tolerance of diverse points of view."[42] This tenet expressed that Cai refused to favor either the "Old Faction" or the "New Faction," but felt that Beijing University had to accommodate both.

Jianrong bingbao has been glorified as one of Cai's most visionary policies, facilitating a golden age of academic freedom and diversity. In 1954 the former Beijing University student Yang Zhensheng (1890–1956) remembered that *jianrong bingbao* made scenes possible at Beijing University, in which "[i]n [the light of] his lamp and window, someone was gluing his nose to the *Selections of Literature*,

---

37 Li, "Liu Shipei yu Beijing daxue."
38 Benjamin A. Elman, *Classicism, Politics, and Kinship: The Ch'ang-Chou School of New Text Confucianism in Late Imperial China* (Berkeley: University of California Press, 1990), 4.
39 Ibid.; Hill, *Lin Shu, Inc.*, 156–57.
40 Zhi Yan, "Guanyu Beijing daxue de yaoyan" (The Rumors about Beijing University), in *Wu si yundong zai Shanghai shiliao xuanji* (The May Fourth Movement in Shanghai: Selected Historical Materials), ed. Shanghai shehui xueyuan lishi yanjiusuo (Shanghai: Shanghai renmin chubanshe, 1980), 103; Shou, "Xin jiu sichao zhi jizhan," 3.3, March 10, 1919; Shou Chang, "Xin jiu sichao zhi jizhan" (The Fierce Battle between New and Old Intellectual Trends), *Shishi xinbao* (China Times), March 17, 1919, 3.3, Shanghai.
41 Weston, *The Power of Position*, 123.
42 Schwarcz, *The Chinese Enlightenment*, 52.

reading [Tang Dynasty scholar] Li Shan's small-print commentaries. Outside of the window, someone was blaring out Byron's poems [which were admired by Chinese intellectuals across the 'factional' spectrum[43]]. In one corner of the room, someone was bobbing his head self-complacently, reciting the *guwen* of the Tongcheng Scholars with modulations and rhythm. In another corner were a few people discussing how Nora [from Henrik Ibsen's *A Doll's House*] provided for her livelihood after having left 'the doll's house' [In Ibsen's famous play of 1879, the protagonist Nora leaves her husband Torvald Helmer, the life with whom is metaphorically described as a life in 'a doll's house.']."[44]

This has been interpreted as a depiction of the highly individualistic and multifaceted intellectual community at Beijing University and of the "pure and fresh atmosphere" of Cai Yuanpei's chancellorship.[45] But even in this description, a hint of factional stereotypes shines through, in that the portrayed students engage in activities that were associated with certain factions: The *Selections of Literature* were said to be popular with the Taiyan Disciples.[46] "Reciting *guwen*" was explicitly linked to the Tongcheng Scholars. Discussion *A Doll's House* was associated with the "New Faction."[47]

But beyond this description, which was composed much later, Cai Yuanpei argued for his *jianrong bingbao* in terms of factions even at the time. In a letter to Lin Shu of 1919, Cai Yuanpei wrote: "Where scholarship is concerned, I imitate the rule of every university in the world and I follow the principle of 'freedom of thought.' The tenet of '*jianrong bingbao*' really does not contradict the phrase that you propose: 'accommodating and broad.' No matter which academic factions there are, ... even if they oppose each other, we should with all strength pay attention to their free development."[48] Cai's notion of *jianrong bingbao*, in other

---

43 Qian Liu, "Creative Translation and Creativity via Translation: The Transformation of Emotional Expression in Early Modern Chinese Fiction (1900–1925)" (PhD, University of Oxford, 2013), 172–84.
44 Yang Zhensheng, "Huiyi wu si" (Remembering May Fourth), in *Wu si yundong huiyilu xu* (Records of Memories of the May Fourth Movement, Continued), ed. Zhongguo shehui kexueyuan jindaishi yanjiusuo (Beijing: Zhongguo shehui kexue chubanshe, 1959), 53.
45 Chen Pingyuan, "'Shaonian yiqi' yu 'jiaguo qinghuai' – Beida xuesheng de 'wu si' jiyi" ("Youthful Impulse" and "Patriotic Feelings" – Beida Students Remember May Fourth) lecture, Guangming jiangtan (Guangming Forum), Beijing University, April 20, 2012, 6, Beijing University.
46 Li, "Liu Shipei yu Beijing daxue," 111.
47 Schwarcz, *The Chinese Enlightenment*, 112.
48 Cai Yuanpei, "Da Lin Qinnan shu" (Reply to Lin Qinnan), in *Wu si yundong zai Shanghai shiliao xuanji* (The May Fourth Movement in Shanghai: Selected Historical Materials), ed. Shanghai shehui xueyuan lishi yanjiusuo (Shanghai: Shanghai renmin chubanshe, 1980), 99.

words, saw itself as being accommodating towards different factions. But it conceptually assumed that scholars could be classified according to such factions, and that such factions did indeed exist at Beijing University.

Others expressed their belief in factions through the polemics they threw at their rivals. In the pages of *New Tide*, the authors of *National Heritage* were scolded to be "sticking to the deficient and fragmentary," that is, to be conservatives.[49] The *National Heritage* writers called the *New Tide* contributors murderers of the past and ignorant of it anyway.[50] These kinds of polemics were later reflected in the academic classifications of the Hu Shi-Chen Duxiu circle as "iconoclasts" and the Liu Shipei circle as "conservatives."

Some of Beijing University's academics came up with even more drastic and creative ways to badmouth their opponents. In March 1918, Qian Xuantong (Hu Shi's circle) had created a fictional character named Wang Jingxuan in *New Youth*, who vehemently attacked Qian's group of academics. This, of course, provided Qian's likeminded colleague Liu Bannong (1891–1934) with the opportunity to actively defend his position.[51] Huang Kan, from the "Old Faction," was said to have employed his very specific humor to spoil life for Hu Shi. One day during a lecture, Huang Kan allegedly told his students this joke: It is very easy to decide if *baihua* or Literary Chinese is better, he said. If Hu Shi's wife died and a telegram was sent to inform him, this would read in Literary Chinese: "*Qi sang su gui.*" ("Your wife has passed away, return quickly.") In *baihua*, however, this would read "*Ni de taitai si le, gankuai huilai ya.*" ("Your wife is dead, come home quickly.") The *baihua* telegram would be infinitely more expensive.[52]

Another story read that Huang Kan once said to Hu Shi that he, Hu, did not really endorse *baihua*. When Hu Shi asked why, Huang Kan replied that if Hu was really committed to *baihua*, he would be called "going where?" (*wang nali qu*),

---

49 Fu Sinian, "Mao Zishui 'Guogu he kexue de jingshen' shiyu" (Editor's Note on Mao Zishui's "The *National Heritage* and the Scientific Spirit"), in *Fu Sinian quanji* (Collected Works of Fu Sinian), vol. 4 (Taibei: Lianjing chuban shiye gongsi, 1980), 1259; Mao Zishui, "Guogu he kexue de jingshen" (The *National Heritage* and the Scientific Spirit), in *Xinchao* (New Tide), vol. 2 (Beijing: Quanguo tushuguan wenxian suowei fuzhi zhongxin, 2006), 198.
50 Zhang, "Bo Xinchao guogu he kexue de jingshen pian," 2A; Yu Shizhen, "Gu jin xueshu goutong siyi" (Connecting Old and New Scholarship), *Guogu* (National Heritage), no. 1 (1919): 1B. *National Heritage* did not number its pages consecutively throughout the journal. Instead, it assigned a number to each spread, starting anew with each article. I follow this numbering system and additionally refer to the right page of each spread as "A" and to the left page as "B." Like virtually all journals, *National Heritage* was of course read from right to left.
51 Hill, *Lin Shu, Inc.*, 220–21; Liu, *Translingual Practice*, 233.
52 Li Yuanxiu and Wu Di, eds., *Shijie quanshi* (World History), vol. 41 (Beijing: Junshi yiwen chubanshe, 2006), 11012.

instead of "Hu Shi."⁵³ This joke requires some explanation. In Literary Chinese, the interrogative "*hu*" can mean "where," and "*shi*" can mean "to adjust," but also "to go to" (as in *shicong*). Thus "hu shi" could technically mean "going where?" the *baihua* translation of which would be "*wang nali qu.*" Hu Shi was not Hu's birth name, but an abbreviation of his self-chosen style name (*zi*), Hu Shizhi. Of course, Hu Shi had not created his name to mean "going where." It was instead inspired by T.H.H. Huxley's (1825–1895) *Evolution and Ethics*, and it was meant as an abbreviation for the evolutionary tenet of *shizhe shengcun* ("survival of the fittest").⁵⁴ "Hu," which Huang Kan interpreted as interrogative, was simply Hu Shi's surname, which people did not usually change when creating style names.

The most dramatic way of expressing a belief in factions at Beijing University was recalled by Yang Zhensheng. While conveying a certain sense of *jianrong bingbao* idyll in the paragraph cited above, Yang used his description of the diverse scene at Beijing University as an illustration of how everybody was "fighting" with each other, an emphasis that was possibly owed to the Maoist atmosphere of the 1950s, when he recounted this. The student members of the factions, he claimed, even carried around "little knives," which were intended to be used should they encounter members of the rival factions on Beijing University's corridors.⁵⁵

But these polemics, jokes and allegedly threatened knife attacks must not gloss over the fact that others denied the existence of factions at Beijing University, and even of an academic squabble. Among them was Liu Shipei, who showed himself to be outraged at the newspaper *Public Voice*'s article on the factions. Seconded by the National Heritage Society, he published a letter in the school journal *Beijing University Daily* addressed to the *Public Voice*, and explaining that he was far too ill to team up with anyone to fight anyone else. Liu Shipei was indeed ill and he would die in November 1919. *National Heritage*, Liu Shipei went on, was run only by students and its aim was not to attack *New Tide* or similar magazines.⁵⁶ A similar denier of "factions" was a student called Wu Ti (1897–1968), who years later, in 1951, claimed that he only participated in the debate on the side of *National Heritage* because he admired his teacher Liu Shipei. He "relied on Liu" and did not "preserve the old."⁵⁷ Wu Ti wrote this in an obituary of Fu Sinian, so

---

53 Ibid.
54 Grieder, *Hu Shih and the Chinese Renaissance*, 7, 26–27.
55 Yang, "Huiyi wu si," 53.
56 Liu, "Liu Shipei zhi Gongyanbao han," 6; "Guogu yuekanshe zhi Gongyanbao han," 6.
57 Wu Ti, "Yi Mengzhen" (Remembering Mengzhen), in *E'e zhi shi: mingren bixia de Fu Sinian, Fu Sinian bixia de mingren* (Outspoken Gentlemen: Fu Sinian in the Words of Famous People, Famous People in the Words of Fu Sinian), ed. Wang Furen and Shi Xingze (Shanghai: Dongfang chuban zhongxin, 1999), 83.

this would not have been the time to play up any differences he would have had with Fu in the past. However, an analysis of the debate between *New Tide* and *National Heritage* shows that he was on to something.

The debates at Beijing University

When newspapers claimed in the early months of 1919 that Beijing University was experiencing yet another debate between academic factions, they implied that there was nothing spectacular about this. But the classifications had an additional, "patterning"[58] effect on the reality of the debates: They broke down highly academic and abstract discussions into neat categories, making them more tangible to a newspaper-reading public.

The debates themselves were extremely nuanced. The most obvious difference between *National Heritage* and *New Tide* was that the former was written in Literary Chinese and the latter in *baihua*. While this sounds very clear-cut, a closer look shows that the languages used in the journals belonged in fact to a spectrum of styles, the boundaries between which were blurred. Zhang Xuan's (*National Heritage*) very straightforward Literary Chinese was full of neologisms.[59] As such, it was as different from the archaic Literary Chinese of his friend Yu Shizhen, who hardly used any neologisms, as it was from the *baihua* of his opponent Fu Sinian. Fu Sinian's (*New Tide*) *baihua*, on the other hand, was full of classical allusions, and sometimes he even wrote in Literary Chinese.[60] *Baihua* was, moreover, not the only language ideal held by the circle to which Fu Sinian belonged. Some of his associates advocated a Romanization system to replace Chinese characters. Or they were in favor of Esperanto.[61] When I therefore call these authors "groups," "circles" and "advocates of *baihua* or Literary Chinese," this must be understood as a simplification, made necessary by the requirement to refer to them by some sort of shorthand. After all, it would be very tedious to list all their names every time.

---

58 Lit. "patterned," Geertz, *The Interpretation of Cultures*, 216.
59 Zhang, "Bo Xinchao guogu he kexue de jingshen pian," 2A.
60 Fu Sinian, "Zenyang zuo baihua wen" (How to Write Texts in the Plain Language), in *Fu Sinian quanji* (Collected Works of Fu Sinian), vol. 44 (Taibei: Lianjing chuban shiye gongsi, 1980), 1128; Fu Mengzhen, "Qing Liang Yusheng zhi shiji zhi yi sanshiliu juan" (The Doubtful Points in the *Records of the Historian* by the Qing Historian Liang Yusheng, Volume 36), in *Xinchao* (New Tide), vol. 1 (Beijing, 2006), 145–47.
61 Zhou, *Placing the Modern Chinese Vernacular in Transnational Literature*, 35–36; Sang, "The Divergence and Convergence of China's Written and Spoken Language," 74, 77.

Not only was there a spectrum of ideas within the groups. The allegedly opposing "factions" also had a lot in common and only differed in the nuanced interpretations of the same concepts. They were, in Thomas Bender's words, part of the same "coummunit[y] of discourse" and as such they shared "the collective concepts, the vocabulary of motives, and the key questions that give shape to their work."[62] One such shared concept and a core argumentative strategy for both *baihua* and Literary Chinese was evolution, a theory that the authors of both magazines endorsed. The authors of *New Tide* and *National Heritage* even agreed with respect to some basic patterns in the evolution of the Chinese language. Authors of both journals believed that the Zhou Dynasty had been a golden age for language: in the Zhou Dynasty, language had been right, according to both Fu Sinian from *New Tide* and Zhang Xuan from *National Heritage*.[63] The authors of *New Tide* and *National Heritage* also agreed that the scholar was rooted in both past and present: He (at the time still mostly he) had to study the past, but he also had to prescribe the current and future criteria for the culture.[64] They even shared the same vocabulary to describe their theories: They wanted culture to be "alive" (*sheng, huopo*), rather than "dead" (*si*),[65] and they all referred to the culture they had inherited from old times, the "national heritage," as "material" (*cailiao* or *cai*).[66]

So how did they differ in their analysis of the evolution of the Chinese language? The differences lay in the diagnosis of what had gone wrong in evolution since the golden days of the Zhou Dynasty. According to Fu Sinian, written language had stagnated. According to Zhang Xuan, it had evolved wrongly.

For Fu Sinian, language in the Zhou Dynasty had been perfect because people wrote like they spoke, and because they did both in the language of their times. The downfall had come in the Han Dynasty, when Sima Xiangru (179-127 BC) and Yang Xiong (53 BC-18 AD), who were keen on writing but bad at speaking, had started again to write in the language of the Zhou Dynasty.[67]

---

62 Bender, "The Cultures of Intellectual Life," 3.
63 Fu, "Zenyang zuo baihua wen," 1123; Zhang Xuan, "Wen yan heyi pingyi" (The Integration of Written and Spoken Language), *Guogu* (National Heritage), no. 1 (1919): 1B–2A.
64 Zhang, "Bo Xinchao guogu he kexue de jingshen pian," 2B, 3A; Fu Sinian, "Xiju gailiang gemian guan" (A Comprehensive View of the Reform of Drama), in *Fu Sinian quanji* (Collected Works of Fu Sinian), vol. 4 (Taibei: Lianjing chuban shiye gongsi, 1980), 1075–97.
65 For "*sheng*," see Zhang, "Bo Xinchao guogu he kexue de jingshen pian," 2A. For "*huopo*," see Fu, "Wen yan heyi caoyi," 1066. For "*si*," see Zhang, "Bo Xinchao guogu he kexue de jingshen pian," 2A; Fu, "Wen yan heyi caoyi," 1065.
66 For "*cailiao*," see Fu, "Mao Zishui 'Guogu he kexue de jingshen' shiyu," 1258. For "*cai*," see Zhang, "Bo Xinchao guogu he kexue de jingshen pian," 2B.
67 Fu, "Zenyang zuo baihua wen," 1123.

While spoken language had thus continued evolving in keeping with the trend of times, written language was stuck in the Zhou Dynasty until the present day: Therefore "the living were being given the language of the dead to use."[68] Fu Sinian expressed this problem of stagnation most vividly when talking about Chinese drama, which was "as if an ape had evolved into a hairy man, stopped there, and could never change into a man."[69] It was now the responsibility of a scholar to make sure that Chinese culture would get back in touch with the times.

If Fu Sinian saw the virtue of the Zhou as people who wrote as they spoke, Zhang Xuan saw it in the exact opposite way. In his view, language had been perfect in the Zhou Dynasty because people spoke like they wrote.[70] The downfall came in the Han Dynasty, when Han Gaozu (256-195BC), an uneducated "managing clerk" became emperor, and people started writing like they spoke, that is, in mutually unintelligible dialects, which changed from generation to generation. As a result, a scholar in the north could not understand a scholar in the south, and a scholar in the Ming Dynasty could not understand a scholar from the Han Dynasty. Zhang Xuan therefore concluded that "when the vernacular was introduced into written texts, they became quite difficult to understand."[71] Therefore the *baihua* project, he felt, was a development into the wrong direction – as wrong a direction, incidentally, as were tendencies to use ever more complicated characters in Literary Chinese, a practice that newspapers would have ascribed to Zhang Xuan's very own group, the "Old Faction."[72]

These two differing diagnoses of the ills of the Chinese language were based on different understandings of how evolution worked and how past and present were, and should, therefore be related to each other. For Fu Sinian, evolution meant a succession of individual time periods, in which each new time period was different from its predecessor. They were like a "child [that] is born from its mother, [but] should develop distinct features of its own."[73] Evolution thus showed Fu Sinian how different the old and the new were – an opinion shared

---

68 Fu Sinian, "Hanyu gaiyong pinyin wenzi de chubu tan" (Abandoning Characters in Favour of Pinyin in Chinese: A Preliminary Discussion), in *Fu Sinian quanji* (Collected Works of Fu Sinian), vol. 4 (Taibei: Lianjing chuban shiye gongsi, 1980), 1138.
69 Fu, "Xiju gailiang gemian guan," 1078.
70 Zhang, "Wen yan heyi pingyi," 1B.
71 Ibid., 2B.
72 Zhang Xuan, "Zhongguo wenxue gailiang lun" (The Reform of Chinese Literature), *Guogu* (National Heritage), no. 4 (1919): 4B.
73 Fu Sinian, "Wenxue gexin shenyi" (An Explanation of the Reform of Literature), in *Fu Sinian quanji* (Collected Works of Fu Sinian), vol. 4 (Taibei: Lianjing chuban shiye gongsi, 1980), 1053.

by others in his circle.⁷⁴ In each time period, Fu Sinian held, "the times" made all things social and cultural adjust to the "demands of the times."⁷⁵ For instance, in the Zhou Dynasty, times were ripe for the literature of the Zhou; in the Ming Dynasty, times were ripe for the literature of the Ming; and today, times were ripe for the literature of today.⁷⁶

This meant that, in each new era, it was a scholar's task to grasp the "demands of the times" and to implement them in culture. Consequently, Fu Sinian kept asking about methods of doing so: How should we write *baihua* texts?⁷⁷ How should we periodize history?⁷⁸ This had practical implications for academic study: *New Tide* was full of theoretical discussions about all those new methods and theories, among them logic, science or the language of present times. Articles exclusively dedicated to actual research on China's past were rare. The *New Tide* writers, in other words, were very much concerned with exploring and expounding the theories and paradigms of this new age they lived in.

What happened to culture when a new time had begun, according to these writers? The past culture was "dead," and the new one "alive." In the past, for example, Literary Chinese had felt "spontaneous" or "natural"⁷⁹ – a view with which present China scholars disagree, as they argue that Literary Chinese was always the constructed lingua franca of the nobility.⁸⁰ Still, Fu Sinian went on to say that Literary Chinese in his times was "outdated" and had become "already stale and dead." *Baihua*, however, was "alive and full of *joie de vivre*" because it "suited today's world."⁸¹ In the present, the past should only be the "material" for academic study.⁸²

---

74 Leigh Jenco, "The Problem of the Culturally Unprecedented: Cultural Difference as Historical Discontinuity after May Fourth" n.d., 15–16; Luo Zhitian, "Xin wenhua yundong shiqi guanyu zhengli guogu de sixiang lunzheng" (Intellectual Debates about "Tidying up China's National Heritage" in the Period of the New Culture Movement), in *Guojia yu xueshu: Qingji minchu guanyu "guoxue" de sixiang lunzheng* (Country and Scholarship: Intellectual Debates on "National Learning" at the End of the Qing and in the Early Republic) (Beijing: Shenghui dushu xinzhi sanlian shudian, 2003), 230.
75 Fu Sinian, "Duiyu Zhongguo jinri tan zhexue zhe zhi gannian" (Feelings on People Who Talk about Philosophy in China Today), in *Fu Sinian quanji* (Collected Works of Fu Sinian), vol. 4 (Taibei: Lianjing chuban shiye gongsi, 1980), 1253.
76 Fu, "Wenxue gexin shenyi," 1053.
77 Fu, "Zenyang zuo baihua wen."
78 Fu Sinian, "Zhongguo lishi fenqi zhi yanjiu" (Research on the Periodization of Chinese History), in *Fu Sinian quanji* (Collected Works of Fu Sinian), vol. 4 (Taibei: Lianjing chuban shiye gongsi, 1980), 1224–33.
79 Fu, "Wen yan heyi caoyi," 1070.
80 Ping Chen, *Modern Chinese: History and Sociolinguistics* (Cambridge: Cambridge University Press, 1999), 7–9.
81 Fu, "Wen yan heyi caoyi," 1065–66.
82 Fu, "Mao Zishui 'Guogu he kexue de jingshen' shiyu," 1258.

This implied that Fu Sinian rejected the prescriptive functions of the past. The past should not determine the way of presenting arguments, of writing texts and of behavior in the present. However, calling the past "material" not only meant reducing it. It also meant preserving it as "material" for academic study. In Fu Sinian's words, the study "material" should be "tidied up" (*tiaoli*) with the paradigms that suited the current time period.[83]

Judging from how Fu Sinian combined this "material" with contemporary theories, this appeared to mean that a scholar should examine how these up-to-date theories like logic or science had developed in China, or how Chinese culture had, or had not, responded to the "demands of the times" over the course of its history. In this way, it was possible to determine China's current stage in evolution. The story usually read that evolution had started out well in the beginning, but had then come to a point of stagnation. Language, for instance, had stagnated in the Han Dynasty. Drama had stagnated in the Yuan Dynasty and was now stuck at the "hairy man"-stage – between ape and man.[84] Similar things had happened to the notion of "logic," according to Hu Shi.[85]

This story of evolutionary stagnation sounds quite drastic. But it was, in fact, an alternative to an even more hopeless story, which was told in the West: the story that "in its innate nature, Eastern scholarship is unable to fully develop," as Fu Sinian put it.[86] This narrative had been told and retold by Western thinkers since the 18th century, including Johann Gottfried von Herder (1744–1803), Georg Wilhelm Friedrich Hegel (1770–1831) and John Stuart Mill (1806–1873).[87] Fu Sinian was well aware of it, as the citation above shows. When he said that China had fallen back in evolution, he implicitly challenged the idea that China was unable to develop: the current stagnation was only a temporary setback, which could be remedied through the intervention of scholars who could identify the evolutionary mishap. This was what Fu Sinian called the "first duty" of *New Tide* in his manifesto to the magazine.[88]

---

[83] Fu Sinian, "Gu shu xin ping" (A Re-Evaluation of Old Books), in *Xinchao* (New Tide), vol. 1 (Beijing, 2006), 145.
[84] Fu, "Xiju gailiang gemian guan," 1078.
[85] On "doubting antiquity," see Fu, "Qing Liang Yusheng zhi shiji zhi yi sanshiliu juan," 147. On logic in China, see Shi Hu, "The Development of the Logical Method in Ancient China" (PhD, Columbia University, 1922).
[86] Fu Sinian, "Zhongguo xueshu sixiangjie zhi jiben wumiu" (The Fundamental Faults in Chinese Scholarship and Thought), in *Fu Sinian quanji* (Collected Works of Fu Sinian) (Taibei: Lianjing chuban shiye gongsi, 1980), 1213–14.
[87] Paul A. Cohen, *Discovering History in China: American Historical Writing on the Recent Chinese Past* (New York: Columbia University Press, 1984), 59.
[88] Fu Sinian, "Xinchao fakan zhiqushu" (Aims behind the Publication of *New Tide*), in *Fu Sinian quanji* (Collected Works of Fu Sinian), vol. 4 (Taibei: Lianjing chuban shiye gongsi, 1980), 1398.

Fu Sinian and his circle, in other words, learnt from cultural evolution that history was a succession of individual time periods. In each new time, a scholar had to explore the theories that suited the age and analyze their development in the past culture.

If Fu Sinian was worried about evolutionary stagnation, the worst fear of *National Heritage* author Zhang Xuan was that culture could develop in the wrong direction. Through studying the past, a scholar had to make sure that this did not happen. This idea was based on a notion another *National Heritage* writer, Yu Shizhen, expressed most clearly when he said about general patterns of change that "past and present are of one tally. They do of course not follow separated tracks."[89] Evolution and the patterns of change were thus a continuum of eternal "trails." If these patterns showed Fu Sinian how different past and present were, they showed the *National Heritage* writers the ways in which past and present were connected. It showed them the "joints" or "rhythm" (*jiezu*) that linked the old and the new.[90]

This implied, Yu Shizhen went on, that "if we try to understand [lit. 'strive for'] the present on the basis of the old, we will understand the system of the present." Significantly, this also worked the other way around: "If we want to try and preserve the old, we must comprehend the present."[91] Finally, if the knowledge of past and present was brought together, both past and future could be comprehended.[92] Zhang Xuan, for example, argued that historical phonology could enable a scholar to uncover a "general law of pronunciation change." Since past, present and future all followed the same "tracks," it was possible to determine the pronunciation of the future.[93]

This notion of evolution again had practical implications for academic study. While *New Tide* was full of theory discussions, most articles in *National Heritage* contained actual, often *kaozheng*-style, research on old texts, with the aim to uncover the "tracks" of change. Xue Xiangsui, for example, reconstructed the original pronunciation of historical books.[94] Zhang Xuan also used the "new," Western concepts differently than Fu Sinian and Hu Shi. While Fu and Hu had deployed them to show China's stagnation within evolution, Zhang Xuan used them to illustrate China's past more clearly. After all, according to his colleague,

---

89 Yu, "Gu jin xueshu goutong siyi," 2B.
90 Ibid., 1B.
91 Ibid., 2B.
92 Ibid., 1B.
93 Zhang, "Bo Xinchao guogu he kexue de jingshen pian," 3A.
94 Xue Xiangsui, "Du gushu fa ju yu" (How to Read Old Books), *Guogu* (National Heritage), no. 1 (1919): 2B.

the past, present and future could be better understood if they were brought together.⁹⁵ In one article, for example, Zhang Xuan explained a paragraph from the *Mozi* by saying that it could be understood as an exposition of the "law of causality."⁹⁶ Unlike Fu Sinian, Zhang did not ask how "causality" had not developed in China. He asked how the notion of "causality" helped him to understand the *Mozi* better.

The past, for Zhang Xuan, had another advantage: It could help create a good future, by preventing culture from evolving wrongly. The "general law of pronunciation change," Zhang wrote, was sometimes broken. While this law claimed that pronunciation became easier over time, pronunciation sometimes became more difficult in reality. Apparently oblivious to the many loanwords in his own writing, and mixing the ideas of pronunciation and language, Zhang Xuan complained that this usually happened when foreign words were introduced into a language.⁹⁷ The *baihua* of the Hu Shi-Chen Duxiu circle, however, was full of foreign loanwords. To avoid this, in Zhang Xuan's view, mistake, a scholar had to use the past as a reference to identify good and bad turns in evolution, to abandon the bad ones, and to create a new culture in accordance with the "true" laws of change. The past, together with the new European culture, thus "provides [scholars] with material for transformation."⁹⁸ On the other hand, treating the past as "material for the history of scholarship," "making stale lists of stale and dead people," as *New Tide* proposed to do, meant to be killing off the past.⁹⁹ The terms "material," "alive" and "dead," which both *New Tide* and *National Heritage* authors used to describe evolutionary patterns, therefore did not show something Fu Sinian and Zhang Xuan had in common, but revealed the different ways in which they perceived the relationship between past and present.

Evolution was not the only issue under debate, but there were other ideas too. For example, the authors of the two magazines engaged in similarly sophisticated discussions about how China should position itself to the West and its

---

95 Yu, "Gu jin xueshu goutong siyi," 1B.
96 Zhang Xuan, "Mozi jing shuo xin jie: xu" (New Explanations of the *Mozi*, Continued), *Guogu* (National Heritage), no. 3 (1919): 1B.
97 Zhang, "Bo Xinchao guogu he kexue de jingshen pian," 3A.
98 Ibid., 2B. Zhang Xuan uses the expression "*ouhua*," instead of "*Ouzhou*" here. Literally this means "Europeanization." But with Axel Schneider, I translated it as "European culture," Axel Schneider, *Wahrheit und Geschichte: zwei chinesische Historiker auf der Suche nach einer modernen Identität für China* (Truth and History: Two Chinese Historians in Search of a Modern Identity for China) (Wiesbaden: Harrassowitz, 1997), 151.
99 Zhang, "Bo Xinchao guogu he kexue de jingshen pian," 2A.

culture.¹⁰⁰ Nor was language the only notion the journals cared about. *New Tide*, for example, also wrote on "The Beginnings of the Question of Life" or "The Disposition of the Chinese Nation."¹⁰¹ *National Heritage* featured scholarly discussions about the *Sunzi*, the *Spring and Autumn Annals* or the *Erya*.¹⁰² But the level of abstraction and sophistication, with which this particular discussion about the evolution of language was conducted, suffices to show how academic these debates were. While debates about language and about evolution as such were widespread, it is hard to imagine how this particular version of the discussion could have become connected to a political event like May Fourth without the tweaking undertaken by the newspaper coverage. Neither of the positions derived from the sophisticated reasoning, moreover, could convince commercial newspapers like the *Shanghai News*. In March 1919, this paper explained that, while it could do no harm when "scholars were twisting their brains," both positions taken in the debate were too extreme for actual application. A middle way would be much more desirable, the *Shanghai News* stated.¹⁰³

Lin Shu and the end of the "New Faction"

If they were so indifferent about the debates' content, why then did newspapers write about them at all? The reason was that the Hu Shi-Chen Duxiu circle had attracted an enemy, and a prestigious one at that: the famous translator Lin Shu.

Lin Shu had made a name for himself in the last years of the 19th and the early years of the 20th centuries, when he had produced famous translations of Western works like *The Lady of the Camellias*, *Uncle Tom's Cabin* or *Aesop's Fables*.¹⁰⁴ After his dismissal from Beijing University in 1913 (when the Tongcheng Scholars had to leave), he continued translating and writing, and his earlier translations continued being reprinted on a large scale. In these years, Hill argues, Lin Shu became a brand name for a large-scale translation and book production operation, deployed by the publisher Commercial Press (*Shangwu yinshuguan*).¹⁰⁵

---

100 For a discussion of this, see for example Leigh Jenco, "Culture as History: Envisioning Change across and beyond 'Eastern' and 'Western' Civilizations in the May Fourth Era," *Twentieth-Century China* 38, no. 1 (January 2013): 34–51.
101 Fu Sinian, "Rensheng wenti faduan" (The Beginnings of the Question of Life), in *Xinchao* (New Tide), vol. 1, 1966, 9–23; Kang Baiqing, "Lun Zhongguo zhi minzu qizhi" (On the Disposition of the Chinese Nation), in *Xichao* (New Tide), vol. 1, 1966, 211–58.
102 "Mulu" (Table of Contents), *Guogu* (National Heritage), no. 3 (1919).
103 Jing, "Beijng daxue xin jiu zhi anchao," 6.
104 Hill, *Lin Shu, Inc.*, 4–6.
105 Ibid., 196–98.

In February of 1919 (before the press had taken notice of the debates and shortly before *National Heritage* was launched), Lin Shu started taking sides with the scholars whom the newspapers would soon classify as the "Old Faction." This was somewhat surprising, since some of the members of the "Old Faction" were scholars considered "Taiyan Disciples," and it had been Taiyan Disciples, according to the factional narrative, who had driven Lin Shu and the Tongcheng Scholars from Beijing University in the early 1910s. Lin Shu was not from Tongcheng, but he was still often considered to be an honorary Tongcheng Scholar. When people like Chen Duxiu and Hu Shi were appointed to Beijing University, the Tongcheng Scholars were said to have followed the popular logic of "the enemy of my enemy is my friend" and started sympathizing with the circle around Liu Shipei and Huang Kan.[106] In the words of Yang Zhensheng: "Most teachers at the time stood on the side of the Old [Faction], particularly those at the department for Chinese literature. Before the New Culture Movement, Mr. Huang Kan was teaching parallel prose [*pianwen*, associated with the Taiyan Disciples] and railed against prose [*sanwen*, associated with the Tongcheng Scholars] in his classes. Mr. Yao Yongpu [(1862–1939), a Tongcheng Scholar] was teaching prose and railed against parallel prose in his classes. In the time of the new-literature movement, they did not rail against each other, but all railed against *baihua* literature in their classes."[107] Lin Shu must have undergone the same transformation and he started writing polemics against the circle around Hu Shi and Chen Duxiu in newspapers.

The first round of his attacks was a short story called "scholar Jing." This was published in the newspaper *New Shanghai News* (*Xin Shenbao*) on February 17 and 18, 1919. In this story, Scholar Jing, a mighty warrior and a "giant" (*weizhangfu*), came across three intellectuals: Tian Qimei, Jin Xinyi and Di Mo. He overheard them blaming Confucian morality and Literary Chinese for China's weakness. One of them, Scholar Jin, even admitted that he promoted *baihua* because his Literary Chinese was bad. As his name (*jin*, "gold") indicated, he was only in it for the money. Losing his patience with this heretical talk, Scholar Jing beat the three up.[108]

Soon afterwards (from March 18 to 22), Lin Shu brought out a second short story, "Nightmare," in the same newspaper, which also dreamt of physical violence against "New Faction"-style people. In this story, a fictional student told the narrator about a nightmare, in which he had visited the "netherworld." There "madmen" had established a "Baihua Academy" and were saying things like

---

106 Yang, "Huiyi wu si," 53.
107 Ibid.
108 Lin Shu, "Jing sheng" (Scholar Jing), in *Canchun* (Last Days of Spring), ed. Zhang Ren (Changchun: Jilin shying chubanshe, 1996), 212–13. The translation of "Jing sheng" as "scholar Jing" is taken from Wang, "Chinese Literature from 1841 to 1937," 466.

Literary Chinese "is a dead language." The dreamer also had the displeasure to meet the leaders of the Academy, Tian Heng, Tai Ershi and the principal Yuan Xu. On his way out, the student saw how a demon attacked the academy and ate everybody there. Lin Shu closed with a commentary that unfortunately there was no such demon in real life to eat up the *baihua* advocates.[109]

By mid-April, the public had concluded that the fictional characters were badly veiled allusions to Beijing University's Hu-Chen circle. The three friends from "scholar Jing," it was said, referred to Chen Duxiu ("Tian Qimei, a man from Anhui"), Qian Xuantong ("Jin Xinyi, from Zhejiang") and Hu Shi ("Di Mo, recently returned from the States").[110] Yuan Xu in the "Nightmare" referred to Cai Yuanpei, Tian Heng was Chen Duxiu and Tai Ershi was Hu Shi.[111]

As Michael Gibbs Hill recounts, "Nightmare's" attack on Cai Yuanpei was particularly untimely. Cai Yuanpei had just agreed to introduce a publisher to Lin Shu, with the goal that Lin would write an introduction to a book managed by that publisher. Getting a prestigious person to write an introduction to a book was a popular marketing strategy. But Lin Shu only received Cai Yuanpei's introduction letter after he had sent "Nightmare" off to the *New Shanghai News*. Lin Shu, who was in Beijing at the time, tried to prevent the publication of "Nightmare" in Shanghai, but it was too late.[112]

Consequently, the reactions from Beijing University were sharp. Cai Yuanpei was outraged at a friend and student of Lin Shu's at Beijing University, Zhang Houzai (1895–1955), who had forwarded the manuscript of "Nightmare" to the *New Shanghai News*. According to Hill, Zhang had also told the *Public Voice* that Chen Duxiu and Hu Shi were about to be dismissed from Beijing University, because their ideas had met with too much resistance.[113] Zhang Houzai wrote a very apologetic letter to Cai Yuanpei, defending Lin Shu and appealing to Cai's "magnanimity and tolerance."[114] Cai Yuanpei's tolerance, however, apparently

---

[109] Lin Shu, "Yaomeng" (Nightmare), in *Canchun* (Last Days of Spring), ed. Zhang Ren (Changchun: Jilin shying chubanshe, 1996), 214–16. All translations taken from Shu Lin, "Nightmare," in *Modern Chinese Literary Thought: Writings on Literature, 1893–1945*, ed. Kirk A. Denton, trans. Timothy Wong (Stanford, 1996), 147–48.
[110] Lin, "Jing sheng," 212.
[111] On the associations being made, see Zhang Juncai, *Lin Shu pingzhuan* (A Critical Biography of Lin Shu) (Beijing: Zhonghua shuju, 2007), 226; Hill, *Lin Shu, Inc.*, 217–18. For an early mention of the associations, see the reprint of an article of the *Beijing New Post* in the *Weekly Critic* on 13 April 1919, Yi, "Zuijin zhi xueshu xinchao," 107.
[112] Hill, *Lin Shu, Inc.*, 218.
[113] Ibid., 220.
[114] Zhang Liaozi, "Zhang Liaozi yuan han" (Original Letter from Zhang Liaozi), in *Cai Yuanpei xiansheng quanji* (Collected Works of Mr. Cai Yuanpei), ed. Sun Changwei (Taibei: Taiwan shangwu yinshuguan, 1968), 1093.

drew a line when it came to public slander of Beijing University. His reply to Zhang Houzai sounded very angry, and Zhang was soon expelled from Beijing University.[115]

It was this involvement of Lin Shu that incited the press' interest, giving the debates a broader audience. This showed itself through timing: The articles in the newspapers *Shanghai News*, *Public Voice*, *Morning Post*, *Social Welfare Tiensin* and *Citizen News* (Chengdu) about Beijing University's factions were all published in March or early April 1919, that is, during or after Lin Shu's interventions. The *Public Voice* and the *Shanghai News* also made explicit reference to Lin Shu. The *Public Voice* even printed an article about Beijing University's "academic factions" right after a copy of the third round of Lin's involvement, which was an open letter to Cai Yuanpei.[116] In this letter, after briefly apologizing for the mess-up around the introduction to the publisher, Lin Shu went on to criticize the *baihua* project and attacks on Confucianism at Beijing University.[117] In his reply, Cai denied all charges, explaining that Confucianism was not being "overthrown" at Beijing University, that Literary Chinese was still being taught, and that only a minority of teachers was writing in *baihua*. Besides, it was quite possible to teach the old texts in *baihua*.[118] This was very close to Fu Sinian's suggestion that the "material" of the past should, and could, be explained through the methods and language of the present.

The press' interest in the debates was productive for two reasons. First of all and as mentioned before, it broke down the nuanced debates at Beijing University into neat categories – a struggle between "New Faction" and "Old Faction" – which were easier to grasp. It is reasonable to assume that the average newspaper reader, who would have been a businessman, a politician, a teacher or a member of the families of someone in these professions, and who would have had his or her own life and line of work to worry about, would not have bothered to delve into the nuanced and abstract debates at Beijing University. The shorthands "New Faction" and "Old Faction," however, would have been something this reader could have remembered. This is comparable to the public today (which includes

---

115 Cai Yuanpei, "Fu Zhang Liaozi han" (Reply to Zhang Liaozi), in *Cai Yuanpei xiansheng quanji* (Collected Works of Mr. Cai Yuanpei), ed. Sun Changwei (Taibei: Taiwan shangwu yinshuguan, 1968), 1093; Hill, *Lin Shu, Inc.*, 222.
116 Jing, "Beijng daxue xin jiu zhi anchao," 6; "Qing kan Beijing xuejie sixiang chao bianqian zhi jinzhuang," 3, 6.
117 Lin Shu, "Da daxuetang xiaozhang Cai Heqing taishi shu" (Reply to the Chancellor of the University, Hanlin Scholar Cai Heqing), in *Lin Shu wenxuan* (Selected Works of Lin Shu), ed. Xu Guiting (Tianjin: Baihua wenyi chubanshe, 2006), 106–9.
118 Cai, "Da Lin Qinnan shu," 96–98.

this author) that presumably would not much care about "the observation of an excess of events above the expected background, consistent with the production of a new particle with mass near 125 GeV,"[119] but that surely does care about the discovery of a "God particle."

Secondly, and the importance of this will be the topic of chapter 2, it interpreted the debates in a way that gave them a new meaning: It started depicting these *baihua* advocates at Beijing University as victims. Newspapers started spreading rumors that the "New Faction" was losing the debate. In March 1919, stories were circulating that Chen Duxiu and Hu Shi were about to be dismissed.[120] Chen Duxiu was being accused of having a questionable social life, which involved frequenting brothels and injuring a prostitute in unbridled passion.[121] Hu Shi and Cai Yuanpei denied these rumors vigorously.[122] But on April 10, 1919, Chen Duxiu was indeed dismissed, casting doubt on the earlier refutations. Cai Yuanpei had found the relatively face-saving method of abolishing Chen's post of dean of humanities, while Chen was away.[123] In May, there were the aforementioned plans to evacuate the whole "New Faction" from Beijing.[124] In light of these developments, the *Shanghai News*' assessment of the competition between the advocates of *baihua* and those of Literary Chinese, made in April 1919, seemed plausible: The "New Faction" appeared to have been "elbowed out [of Beijing University] by the Old-Learning Faction," the newspaper wrote. The "conservative faction ha[d] succeeded."[125]

---

119 S. Chatrchyan et al., "Observation of a New Boson at a Mass of 125 GeV with the CMS Experiment at the LHC," *Physics Letters B* 716, no. 1 (September 2012): 31. I would like to thank Julian Scharnagl from the Center for Telematics, Würzburg, Germany, for his input.
120 Wu Wang, "Xin jiu sixiang zhi chongtu" (The Clash between Old and New Thought), *Guomin gongbao* (Citizen News), March 9, 1919, 1, Beijing; Zuo Xuexun, "Wen Beijing daxue jiaoyuan bei zhu xiaoxi jinggao ge fangmian" (Comprehensive Information about the News That Beijing University's Professors Are Being Pursued), *Shishi xinbao* (China Times), March 11, 1919, 3.3, Shanghai.
121 Letter from Hu Shi to Tang Erhe (1878–1940) from 28 December 1925, cited in Gao Pingshu, *Cai Yuanpei nianpu changbian* (A Comprehensive Chronology of the Life of Cai Yuanpei), vol. 2 (1917–1926) (Beijing: Renmin jiaoyu chubanshe, 1996), 181. See also "Xin jiu sichao chongtu zhi di-yi sheng" (First Voice on the Clash between New and Old Intellectual Trends), *Guomin gongbao* (Citizen News), March 30, 1919, 1, Beijing.
122 Wang, *Chen Duxiu nianpu*, 61.
123 Chen Sihe, "Xu Shuzheng yu xin wenhua yundong" (Xu Shuzheng and the New Culture Movement), *Zhongguo xiandai wenxue yanjiu congkan* (Studies on Modern Chinese Literature), no. 3 (1996): 278.
124 Huang and Jiang, "Huang Yanpei, Jiang Menglin zhi Hu Shi," 35.
125 Xin, "Riben dui wo xin sixiang shishi zhi tongqing," 6.

A multitude of competing reform programs

Literary Chinese and English

The debates at Beijing University have often been written about, and therefore they have taken on the halo of an epoch-making event. But not only did the abstractness of these debates not intuitively lend itself to "making an epoch." The reality was much more complex, dynamic and competitive. The *baihua* advocates at Beijing University were also but one small group among huge numbers of people who tried to reform culture and put forward different programs for this purpose. They usually suggested some of a range of elements that were being promoted around the globe (most of them partially, though not exclusively, under the impact of Western imperialism). Among them was women's education, the end of foot binding, popular education and science, to name just a few – but combined them differently, and especially with different ideals for language. Some of them, for example, favored Literary Chinese or English over *baihua*.

Among these competitors was Yan Xishan, for instance, the warlord of Shanxi Province.[126] Yan himself had originally received a classical education. But after his father's bank had gone bankrupt, he had joined a military academy, first in China and later in Japan, where he was educated in the modern style. He participated in the 1911 revolution and, thanks to the alliances he had made in the process, he was appointed military governor of Shanxi. Once in this position, he set out to reform the province. His projects started before 1919 and continued well into the 1920s. He sent students of Shanxi's universities to study abroad, hired foreign-educated professors, established science and engineering courses at Shanxi University and fostered cooperation between Western and Chinese scientists. He also promoted women's rights: He established schools to educate women and was staunchly against bound feet. Popular education was also on Yan Xishan's agenda. He recommended a basic four-year education for all children and built "people's schools." Apart from that, he was against using the lunar calendar and campaigned for hygiene.[127]

Even Yan Xishan's language program was radical. In order to educate, communicate with (and indoctrinate) the common people, he supported using

---

[126] Donald G. Gillin, "Portrait of a Warlord: Yen Hsi-Shan in Shansi Province, 1911–1930," *The Journal of Asian Studies* 19, no. 3 (May 1960): 290; Henrietta Harrison, *The Man Awakened from Dreams: One Man's Life in a North China Village, 1857–1942* (Stanford, California: Stanford University Press, 2005), 97.

[127] Donald G. Gillin, *Warlord: Yen Hsi-Shan in Shansi Province, 1911–1949* (Princeton: Princeton University Press, 1967), 9, 19–22, 34–36; Donald G. Gillin, "Education and Militarism in Modern China: Yen Hsi-Shan in Shansi Province, 1911–30," *The Journal of Modern History* 34, no. 2 (June 1962): 161–65; Yan Xishan, "Shanxi sheng zhengfu zhi Shilou zhishi han" (Letter by the Shanxi

a "phonetic spelling" system in vernacular newspapers and government documents that should be read by the people.[128] He advised a county magistrate in 1919 that, in "implementing politics," it was better to issue documents in *baihua* rather than in Literary Chinese, and better yet to talk to the people directly in simple words.[129]

Nevertheless, Yan Xishan's own writings were in Literary Chinese. Clearly Shanxi's elite should continue writing in this style, Yan Xishan felt. Yan also differed from ideals that would later be associated with the New Culture Movement in that he advocated a version of Confucianism, with the goal, in Donald G. Gillin's interpretation, "of inculcating respect for authority."[130] A speech to the officers of his army of August 1919, for example, sounds very much at odds with a New Culture-style agenda. He told them that all of China's "ills" were caused by the general lack of "rites" and "shame." Japan, on the other hand, was strong because the "rites" were widespread there.[131] Yan Xishan's vision for Chinese culture thus looked quite different from the one that would eventually be produced under the headline "New Culture Movement."

Yan Xishan was just one who threw programs of this style into the field of culture. Other influential individuals and groups advocated agendas quite close to this. Beijing University professor Liu Shipei wrote in a very formalized Literary Chinese. But he was also an anarchist and married to one of China's most famous feminists with anarchist leanings, He-yin Zhen (1884-?).[132] Commercial newspapers like the *Shanghai News*, in themselves products of the new, Western-dominated age, usually still wrote in Literary Chinese in early 1919. The Jiangsu Educational Association wrote its documents in the same style. Its vice-president, Huang Yanpei, composed his diary in Literary Chinese too.[133]

Provincial Government to the County Magistrate of Shilou) (Taiyuan, 1919), 0224, Ge fang minguo 8 nian wanglai dianwen lucun (er), Taibei Guoshiguan Yan Xishan shiliao (Telegram correspondences of 1919 [2], Yan Xishan papers, Academia Historica, Taibei), Taiyuan.
128 Gillin, "Education and Militarism in Modern China," 162.
129 The manuscript does not indicate the month in which this document was written, Yan, "Shanxi sheng zhengfu zhi Shilou zhishi han."
130 Gillin, *Warlord*, 59.
131 Yan Xishan, "Dujun yu zixing shi dui ge ji junguan jiangci" (Speech before the Officers of All Ranks by the Military Governor While Self-Reflecting) August 3, 1919, 1400, Ge fang minguo 8 nian wanglai dianwen lucun (shi yi), Taibei Guoshiguan Yan Xishan shiliao (Telegram correspondences of 1919 [11], Yan Xishan papers, Academia Historica, Taibei).
132 Lydia He Liu, Dorothy Ko, and Rebecca E. Karl, eds., *The Birth of Chinese Feminism: Essential Texts in Transnational Theory* (New York: Columbia University Press, 2013), 51; Peter Zarrow, *Anarchism and Chinese Political Culture* (New York: Columbia University Press, 1990), 83–95, et passim.
133 Jiangsu sheng jiaoyuhui, *Jiangsu sheng jiaoyu hui yuebao* (Jiangsu Educational Association Monthly Report), 1919; Huang, *Huang Yanpei riji*.

Nevertheless, the Jiangsu Educational Association called for popular education and the National Language for the common people. With this it participated in a larger project sponsored by the central government in Beijing for the promotion of these two agendas.[134] Popular education had been endorsed by broad circles since the Qing Dynasty, and in the 1910s the Ministry of Education frequently established official associations or called upon institutions like the Jiangsu Educational Association to promote popular education. As Paul J. Bailey has shown, such popular-education activities comprised the establishment of evening and spare-time schools and of public libraries, the organization of public lectures for common people and the censorship of themes in popular culture deemed (mostly sexually) inappropriate.[135]

The goal to create a National Language for China went back to the 19th century, when scholars like Wu Rulun saw that a National Language had been successfully established in Japan, and started advocating a similar project for China. In 1911, the project got underway when the Qing Dynasty's Board of Education convened a conference to unify the National Language. After the Republic was established one year later in 1912, the project was continued. These efforts were interrupted when General Yuan Shikai lost interest in them, after he had become president of the Republic in 1912. But it was resumed after his death in 1916. In that year, for example, the Ministry of Education convened the Committee for Research on the National Language. In April 1919, it founded the Preparatory Committee for the Unification of the National Language.[136]

Another competing project that was important to the Jiangsu Educational Association was vocational education. Vocational education dated back to 19th-century calls for practical learning. It followed the logic of a businessman who lamented: "On the side of the unemployed, they sigh that ways to make one's living are hard to find. On the side of the realm of enterprises, they are worried that the talent they need is scarce."[137] The Jiangsu Educational Association had long been committed to vocational education. Together with the chancellor of

---

134 Bailey, *Reform the People*, 186–202; Gu, *Qing mo Min chu Jiangsu sheng jiaoyuhui yanjiu*, 172.
135 Bailey, *Reform the People*, 186–202.
136 On the project before Yuan Shikai: Chen, *Modern Chinese*, 14–17. On Yuan Shikai's lack of interest: John DeFrancis, *Nationalism and Language Reform in China* (Princeton, N.J.: Princeton University Press, 1950), 59. On the foundation of the two committees: Li Jinxi, *Guoyu yundong shigang* (A Survey of the National-Language Movement) (Beijing: Shangwu yinshuguan, 2011), 133, 144.
137 Cited from Dong Baoliang and Zhou Hongyu, *Zhongguo jin xiandai jiaoyu sichao yu liupai* (Intellectual Tides and Schools in Education in China's Modern and Contemporary Period) (Beijing: Renmin jiaoyu chubanshe, 1997), 291.

Beijing University Cai Yuanpei, the future chancellor Jiang Menglin and a few others, the Association's vice-president, Huang Yanpei, had founded the Chinese Society for Vocational Education in 1917. Its manifesto argued that universities produced a lot of unemployable graduates, and that consequently "there are high-level vagrants everywhere."[138] These graduates could not find employment, as they lacked the practical skills needed in the industry, in agriculture or in commerce. Unfortunately, however, universities continued "emphasizing theory in their classes, and they do not regard internships as important."[139] If vocational education was promoted, the manifesto claimed, graduates would find jobs. Thereby they would "serve society" and improve the country's economy as a whole.[140]

With its advocacy of vocational education, the Jiangsu Educational Association also overlapped with another important social group in Republican China, namely, businesspeople.[141] Many businesspeople, according to Marie-Claire Bergère, enjoyed modern material culture: They wore Western clothing, had Western furniture and modern comforts such as electricity and running water. They also organized themselves in new-style associations, often sent their children to study abroad and let their daughters study at new-style schools.[142]

But as a language, these business circles preferred Literary Chinese for communication within China and English for interaction with foreign countries. This was exemplified in a student journal of the Peking School of Commerce, the *Commercial Student* (*Shangye xuesheng*), which was mostly written in Literary Chinese, occasionally even unpunctuated, but also had an English-language section.[143] This again reflected the broader education these students

---

[138] Huang Yanpei, "Zhiye jiaoyu shishi zhi xiwang" (Hopes for Implementing Vocational Education), *Jiaoyu zazhi* (Education Magazine) 9, no. 1 (1917): 6. Translation reworked from Bailey, *Reform the People*, 208.
[139] "Zhonghua zhiye jiaoyushe xuanyanshu" (Manifesto of the Chinese Society for Vocational Education), *Dongfang zazhi* (Eastern Miscellany) 14, no. 7 (1917): 165.
[140] Huang Yanpei, "Talks about Vocational Education" (*Zhiye jiaoyu tan*) of 1918, cited in Dong and Zhou, *Zhongguo jin xiandai jiaoyu sichao yu liupai*, 297.
[141] Marie-Claire Bergère, *The Golden Age of the Chinese Bourgeoisie, 1911–1937* (Cambridge: Cambridge University Press, 1989), 4; Xiaoqun Xu, *Chinese Professionals and the Republican State: The Rise of Professional Associations in Shanghai, 1912–1937* (Cambridge: Cambridge University Press, 2001), 2.
[142] Bergère, *The Golden Age of the Chinese Bourgeoisie*, 47, 129, 134.
[143] Yeh, *The Alienated Academy*, 12; Dai Xian, "Shangye xuesheng di-er ji bianyan" (Foreword to the Second Issue of *Commercial Student*), *Shangye xuesheng* (Commercial Student), no. 2 (December 1919): 1–3; Zhong Hengxu, "The Triumph of the Students," *Shangye xuesheng* (Commercial Student), no. 2 (December 1919): 22–29.

received: In the first two years of their courses, the students had to do English-language studies, before moving on to a focus on economics.[144]

"National salvation" rhetoric

In seeking to move to the "legitimizing core" of a field, Timothy Cheek has expounded on Jeffrey N. Wasserstrom's model, one strategy is "to identify oneself with the legitimate terms."[145] One such "legitimate term" or concept in the 1910s was "national salvation," which, consequently, the competing parties all claimed to be pursuing with their projects. The "national salvation" rhetoric was not new in the 1910s. Ever since the imperialist incursions of the 19th century, it had been high up on intellectuals' agendas to restore China to its "wealth and power," to use Benjamin Schwartz's words.[146] The "national salvation" rhetoric could be applied to educational reforms, because reformers were able to tap into a historical Chinese notion, according to which culture and politics were so intricately connected that the reform or downfall of the former could lead to the reform or downfall of the latter. If the ruler and the people had made sure that "[t]heir hearts [were] rectified" and "their persons … cultivated," the country was in order, the Confucian Classic *Great Learning* had claimed.[147]

This logic is central to the well-known story that purported to tell how the later famous New Culture novelist Lu Xun became an author of fiction. Originally Lu Xun was studying medicine in Japan. But, the anecdote goes, on one fateful day in 1905, he saw a lantern slide that showed the execution of a Chinese national by Japanese, with the Chinese onlookers just standing there. In this moment, according to the story, Lu Xun decided that first Chinese culture needed to be reformed so as to awaken the Chinese people, before politics could change, and that this could best be done by writing novels.[148] He therefore abandoned his studies of medicine and became an author.

The reformers of the 1910s deployed the "national salvation" rhetoric on many occasions, mostly when trying to convince their superiors, peers or subordinates

---

144 Zhang Jianming and Qi Dazhi, *Hua shuo Jing shang* (Talking about Business in Beijing) (Beijing: Zhonghua gongshang lianhe chubanshe, 2006), 38.
145 Cheek, "The Names of Rectification," 27.
146 Benjamin Isadore Schwartz, *In Search of Wealth and Power: Yen Fu and the West* (Cambridge: Belknap Press of Harvard University Press, 1964).
147 Translation from James Legge, *The Chinese Classics*, vol. 1 (Hong Kong: Hong Kong University Press, 1960), 359.
148 Jonathan Spence, *The Search for Modern China*, 2nd ed. (New York: Norton, 1999), 238.

of the merit of their agendas. In his speech before the army officers, Yan Xishan invoked China's political crisis and then promoted his Confucian-inspired morality as its remedy.[149] Similarly, when Shanxi hosted a conference of the Union of Educational Associations in October 1919, Yan flattered the educators by saying that China was in "danger," which could only be overcome through education.[150] Business circles claimed that the economic growth, which they nurtured, was aimed at national salvation too.[151] When the Jiangsu Educational Association sought funding for a New Education Society, which it wanted to found, it wrote to the government in January 1919: "The European War has already come to an end. Afterwards, the establishment of the country will be based on scholarship."[152] Therefore, the argument went on, this new Society needed to be financed by the government. In January 1915, the National Language activist Wang Pu (1875–1929) wrote in a petition to the government that popular education was "the fundament of national strengthening." The basis for popular education, however, was the "the unification of written and spoken language," which happened to be the agenda he was trying to sell.[153] References to national salvation, in other words, were used by virtually all reformers to gather support for their agendas.

To what extent this was a mere marketing tool to acquire, in Bourdieu's parlance, "symbolic capital" (i. e. prestige),[154] and to what extent these people genuinely believed that their programs could save the nation, is impossible to say. But there is one instance, in which the reference to national salvation seemed to be rather pragmatically inspired. This was the story about how another New Culture intellectual converted to work in the area of culture: Hu Shi. Like Lu Xun, Hu Shi had originally studied a more application-oriented program at, in his case, Cornell University. Hu Shi was at first enrolled in botany. In his own diary,

---

149 Yan, "Dujun yu zixing shi dui ge ji junguan jiangci," 1400.
150 Yan Xishan, "Shanxi dujun jian shengzhang wei quanguo jiaoyu lianhehui di-wu ci kaihui zhici" (Speech by the Shanxi Military Governor and Provincial Governor on the Fifth Conference of the National Union of Educational Associations) October 10, 1919, 1452, Ge fang minguo 8 nian wanglai dianwen lucun (shi yi), Taibei Guoshiguan Yan Xishan shiliao (Telegram correspondences of 1919 [11], Yan Xishan papers, Academia Historica, Taibei).
151 Bergère, *The Golden Age of the Chinese Bourgeoisie*, 49–50; Xu, *Chinese Professionals and the Republican State*, 6.
152 Jiangsu sheng jiaoyuhui, "Cheng jiaoyu zongzhang zuzhi Zhonghua xin jiaoyushe wen."
153 Li Jinxi, ed., "Duyin tongyihui Zhili daibiao Wang Pu deng cheng jiaoyubu qing banxing zhuyin zimu wen" (Petition to the Ministry of Education from Wang Pu, Etc., Representative of the Commission for the Unification of Pronunciation, Requesting the Promotion of Bopomofo), in *Guoyuxue jiangyi* (Lecture Notes on the Study of the National Language) (Shanghai: Shangwu yinshuguan, 1919), xia 19. For the dating of this petition, see Ibid., xia 21.
154 Thompson, "Editor's Introduction," 14.

Hu Shi claims that over time, he realized that humanities subjects were equally important for national salvation, and this was why he allowed himself to change subjects, from botany to philosophy. His biographer Jerome B. Grieder, however, has looked at Hu Shi's transcripts at Cornell and notes that he had much better results in philosophy than he ever had in botany.[155] Hu Shi was just not very good at botany, and the idea of national salvation through culture appears to have been deployed after the fact.

It is difficult to say whether Hu Shi was the exception or the rule. What is clear, however, is that a huge variety of competing reform agendas was being proposed by very many groups and people in the 1910s and that these people often promoted it by claiming that their agendas were suited to save the nation. This was the sort of rhetoric capable of moving one's agenda towards the "legitimate core."[156] Beijing University's *baihua* advocates were not unique in either respect.

Baihua *without Beijing University*

There was another dimension in which the *baihua* advocates of Beijing University were not unique: They were not the only ones to support the type of program that ended up becoming dominant in China, namely, one that included *baihua*.

Hu Shi was later praised as the originator of the *baihua* movement, and Hu himself claimed that he was the first to give *baihua* an evolutionary narrative.[157] But others said things that were very similar to his arguments. For instance, in 1917, Wei Tingsheng (1890–1977), at the time reading for a Master's degree at Harvard University, distinguished between "living" and "dead" languages. Among the dead languages was Literary Chinese, while among the living ones was *baihua*. Wei Tingsheng also claimed that some dead languages used to be alive in the past.[158] This was very close to what Hu Shi's student Fu Sinian would argue later on, as shown earlier in this chapter. Just how easily *baihua* could have been associated with others than the Hu-Chen circle becomes clear from the fact that, when

---

[155] Grieder, *Hu Shih and the Chinese Renaissance*, 41–42. Hu Shi's diary is also cited on these pages.
[156] In modification of Cheek, "The Names of Rectification," 26. Original expression: "legitimating core."
[157] Hu Shi, *Hu Shi riji quanji* (Hu Shi's Collected Diaries), ed. Cao Boyan, vol. 4 (Taibei: Lianjing chuban shiye gongsi, 2004), 346; Hu Shi, "Jieshao wo ziji de sixiang" (Introducing My Own Thought), in *Hu Shi wenxuan* (Selected Works of Hu Shi) (Shanghai: Yadong tushuguan, 1930), 18.
[158] Li Jinxi, ed., *Guoyuxue jiangyi* (Lecture Notes on the Study of the National Language) (Shanghai: Shangwu yinshuguan, 1919), shang 29.

National Language advocate Li Jinxi (1890–1978) lectured on language in 1919, he did discuss *baihua*. But he chose to cite Wei Tingsheng, rather than Hu Shi, on the topic.[159] So even if there had been a linear development towards the importance of *baihua*, it would not have been inevitable that Hu Shi, Chen Duxiu, Fu Sinian, Luo Jialun and the others of the group would rise to stardom too.

Conclusion

An observer in the first few months of 1919 would have seen that there were competing cultural programs being put forward, and that China was set to undergo some sort of cultural transformation. But that this transformation would lead to the dominance of, among other ideas, *baihua* in the cultural field, and that a narrative would be established that traced the transformation to the academics and students at Beijing University might have surprised the observer, as the wrong diagnosis of the state of affairs in the *Shanghai News* of April 1919 shows.[160]

For this shift to happen so soon afterwards, it was crucial that newspapers shaped reality by restructuring it through their interpretation: that is, by claiming that the debating academics belonged to "factions of learning." Whether academic factions were real has been a matter of some debate, both among contemporaries at the time and among academics today. When newspapers started subscribing to the idea that there were factions, they, it is reasonable to assume, did so to simplify what was going on at Beijing University, a practice that newspapers are wont to pursue. But this compartmentalization was crucial, because it turned the murky, abstract and complicated debates into palpable entities. It made them accessible to a public. It also formed the basis, upon which a second layer of patterning would be placed: It made them into the sort of tangible, seemingly clear-cut units that were suitable to allegedly having political allegiances attached to them. Rumors about such allegiances would lead the "New Faction" to be identified with the May Fourth demonstrators over the ensuing months, and the way this happened is the topic of chapter 2.

---

159 Ibid.
160 Xin, "Riben dui wo xin sixiang shishi zhi tongqing," 6.

2 May 4, 1919 – Rumors and conspiracy theories

In June 1919, Huang Yanpei, the vice-chancellor of the Jiangsu Educational Association, complained that the May Fourth protests distracted from his educational reforms: "Now that the student protests have started, and the gaze of the whole country focuses on the actions of the average young people and the changes of current affairs, this matter [his reforms] has been put aside. But once the student protests are over, the educators of the whole country will urgently try to pick up the pieces."[1] Little did he know, apparently, that a few months later much of his educational agenda would gain traction in China, not in spite of the May Fourth Movement, but because of it. Little did he suspect, moreover, that he himself would eventually see this potential of May Fourth and exploit it for his own program.

Yan Xishan, the military governor of Shanxi, who endorsed ideas not unlike those of Huang Yanpei (see chapter 1), did not see these cultural implications either. For him, 1919 was a lot of hassle that came from all sorts of unconnected directions. First, he had to deal with a conspiracy of the Research Clique, his rival political party, who had incited the student protests in the spring of 1919, or so he believed.[2] (We know these protests as May Fourth.) As if this was not enough, he then had to combat "extremism/Bolshevism" (*guoji zhuyi*): Russian agents, the central government told him, had started importing "extremist/Bolshevist" thought into China. Clearly they were intent on "rabble-rousing" (*shanhuo*).[3] "*Guoji zhuyi*" now means "extremism," and it was occasionally used in this sense in 1919.[4] But when the word first started to appear in Chinese newspapers and journals from 1918 onwards,[5] it referred to the Bolshevist brand of communism

---

[1] Huang, *Huang Yanpei riji*, 2:64. These lines can be found on the pages of the diary entries of 8 to 11 June. It is unclear if Huang Yanpei really wrote them on these days, as the editors of the diaries argue that these lines do not belong to the diary as such. Ibid.
[2] Yan Xishan, "Fu Beijing Zhao canmouzhang xian dian" (Telegram of the 15th [of May 1919], in Reply to Chief of Staff Zhao in Beijing), in *Yan Xishan dang'an* (Yan Xishan Papers), ed. Lin Qingfen, vol. 5 (Taibei: Guoshiguan, 2003), 29.
[3] Neiwubu, "Beijing neiwubu hao dian" (Telegram of the 19th [of September 1919] from the Ministry for Internal Affairs in Beijing), in *Yan Xishan dang'an* (Yan Xishan Papers), ed. Qingfen Lin, vol. 5 (Taibei: Guoshiguan, 2003), 86. This letter was dated to September 1919.
[4] Jun Shi, "Guoji zhuyi yu minzhuzhuyi zhi duikang" (The Antagonism of Extremism and Democracy), *Dongfang zazhi* (Eastern Miscellany) 16, no. 8 (1919): 105–10.
[5] One early mention is "Zhan dian" (War Telegrams), *Shenbao* (Shanghai News), November 8, 1918, 2, Shanghai.

most of the time[6] and was even traded as the translation of "Bolshevism," alongside English translations of the word.[7] How was an honest provincial military governor, one almost hears Yan Xishan sighing, supposed to promote enlightened educational and social agendas like the National Language for the people, women's rights and popular education, when all these obstacles kept getting in the way?

In other words, in mid-1919, neither Yan Xishan nor Huang Yanpei saw any connection between a number of things that, to us, appear very closely related to each other. For us, a century worth of narratives on the matter later, May Fourth is virtually synonymous with these various educational and social agendas. These agendas, like women's rights, popular education, the National Language (all of which Yan Xishan liked) seem to us to be closely connected to Beijing University's debates (about which Yan did not appear to care) and to communism (which Yan disliked). That Yan and Huang did not see any connection was not because they did not have enough information about what was going on in mid-1919. Both men were in constant correspondence with their colleagues across the country, and especially Yan Xishan received all the information about May Fourth brand new in confidential letters from his contacts in Beijing.[8]

---

[6] "Guoji zhuyi qinru Siluofaniya" (Bolshevism Invades Slovenia), *Dongfang zazhi* (Eastern Miscellany) 16, no. 8 (1919): 230; "Guoji zhuyi zhi zhenxiang" (The Truth about Bolshevism), *Yuehan sheng* (The Voice of John) 30, no. 2 (1919): 13–16.

[7] "Guoji zhuyi Bolshevism yu puji jiaoyu" (Bolshevism and Promulgating Education), *Xin jiaoyu* (New Education) 1, no. 3 (1919): 10; "Guchui guoji zhuyi zhi jiguan" (Organs of Bolshevist Propaganda), *Yingyu zhoukan* (English Weekly), no. 188 (1919): 1917. Hans van de Ven translates it as "Bolshevism," Hans J. van de Ven, *From Friend to Comrade* (Berkeley: University of California Press, 1991), 46.

[8] For examples of Yan Xishan's correspondence: Canmou benbu and Lujunbu, "Beijing guowuyuan can, lubu ge dian"; Neiwubu, Lujunbu, and Jiaotongbu, "Beijing neiwubu, lujunbu, jiaotongbu dong dian." For examples of the Jiangsu Educational Association's correspondence, whose vice-president Huang Yanpei was: Jiangsu sheng jiaoyuhui, "Zhi da zongtong, guowuyuan, jiaoyubu chenming Shanghai ge xiao xuesheng yin jiaoyu zongzhang yiren deng wenti qun yi bake, qing fuxun yuqing dian" (Telegram to the President, the Cabinet and the Ministry of Education, Explaining That the Students of All Schools in Shanghai Have Gone on Strike, due to Questions such as the Replacement of the Minister of Education, Etc., and Asking to Succumb to Public Sentiment), *Jiangsu sheng jiaoyuhui yuebao* (Jiangsu Educational Association Monthly Report), May 1919, 10; Hunan sheng jiaoyuhui, "Hunan sheng jiaoyuhui, qing zhaoji quanguo jiaoyuhui lianhehui kai linshihui daidian" (Express Mail Letter from the Hunan Educational Association, Asking to Convene a Provisional Meeting of the National Union of the Educational Associations), ed. Jiangsu sheng jiaoyuhui, *Jiangsu sheng jiaoyuhui yuebao* (Jiangsu Educational Association Monthly Report), June 1919, 5–6.

What their confusion shows is that something had to happen first, before the narrative of May Fourth and New Culture that we know could emerge – a narrative in which May Fourth is pretty much synonymous with New Culture and inseparable from Beijing University. Reality had to be reshaped, or, in Clifford Geertz's words, "patterned,"[9] before a set of independent events could become a series of events. Part of this "something" that had to happen were rumors and conspiracy theories, which were spread in newspapers in early and mid-1919. These rumors and conspiracy theories first reinterpreted the obscure academics at Beijing University as neat academic factions, as shown in chapter 1. They then went on to ascribe political allegiances to them, depicting the "New Faction" as government victims. The demonstrators of May Fourth were equally described as government victims with a patriotic agenda. Thus May Fourth came to be associated with the entity called the "New Faction," as well as with ideas attributed to this "New Faction." But that these ideas, too, became appropriated, I will show in chapter 3. For people like Yan Xishan and, initially, Huang Yanpei, who did not subscribe to these conspiracy theories spread in the press – Yan Xishan believed in a different set of conspiracies – this (particular) merger of political protest, academic personnel and ideas therefore came as a surprise.

The success of the *baihua* advocates of Beijing University

Another group that must have been taken aback by the cultural ramifications of May Fourth were the people at Beijing University whom the newspapers had classified as the "New Faction." After the imminent end of their careers had been predicted in April and even still in May 1919, people like Hu Shi and Chen Duxiu became stars only a few months later. As a reminder, in April the *Shanghai News* diagnosed that the "New Faction" had lost the battle against the "Old Faction." In May, Huang Yanpei and Jiang Menglin proposed to Hu Shi to evacuate the "New Faction" from Beijing.[10] Soon after that, however, the circle became what Michel Hocks has called "cult heroes"[11] of the cultural field and of the New Culture Movement. They were referred to as the "masters," the "center" or "central figures" of

---

9 Geertz, *The Interpretation of Cultures*, 216.
10 Xin, "Riben dui wo xin sixiang shishi zhi tongqing," 6; Huang and Jiang, "Huang Yanpei, Jiang Menglin zhi Hu Shi," 35–36.
11 Lit. "cult hero," Michel Hockx, ed., "Playing the Field: Aspects of Chinese Literary Life in the 1920s," in *The Literary Field of Twentieth-Century China* (Richmond: Curzon, 1999), 65.

the "New Culture Movement,"[12] an expression that first appeared in print in the late summer of 1919, as I will discuss in detail in chapter 3.

The second half of 1919 and 1920 also saw what Fabio Lanza has called the "explosion of publications":[13] A huge number of journals were founded, many of which styled themselves after *New Youth* or *New Tide* and many of which claimed to be promoting the ideas of Hu Shi, Chen Duxiu and their circle. Many of these publications were short-lived, which makes precise calculations difficult. But contemporaries who tried to count them often claimed that there were 400 of them.[14] The Shanghai publisher Wang Yuanfang (the nephew of Chen Duxiu's friend Wang Mengzou, whose fundraising trip to Beijing had been spoilt by Cai Yuanpei) remembered that these journals "sprang up like spring bamboo after the rain" (*yuhou-chunsun*), that is, they "sprang up like mushrooms."[15] I therefore dub them "spring-bamboo journals."

These spring-bamboo journals were not the only ones to adopt ideas they associated with Hu Shi and Chen Duxiu. Already established publications too started changing their agendas to become more accepting of such ideas. For example, from 1920 onwards the "politically conservative" *Eastern Miscellany* (*Dongfang zazhi*) started printing articles in *baihua*.[16] So did the *Ladies' Magazine* (*Funü zazhi*), which targeted a similar audience as *Eastern Miscellany*.[17] Another major breakthrough happened in the same year, when the Ministry of Education made the National Language a compulsory subject for the first two years of primary school. This replaced the subject of *guowen* ("national language"), which was then a different name for Literary Chinese.[18]

At this point, people stopped considering the network around Hu Shi and Chen Duxiu an "academic faction." This was more than a rhetorical change. It also had tangible implications for the prestige and careers of these scholars.

---

12 "Masters": Miao, "Suowei 'xin wenhua yundong' de chachao yu pochan," 3–4, 2. "Center": Ye, "Ji Beijing daxue shiye shi (xu)." "Central figures": Jing Guan, "Gao xin wenhua yundong de tongzhi" (To the Comrades of the New Culture Movement), *Xin funü* (New Woman) 1, no. 2 (1920): 31.

13 Fabio Lanza, "Of Chronology, Failure, and Fidelity: When Did the May Fourth Movement End?," *Twentieth-Century China* 38, no. 1 (January 2013): 57.

14 Miao, "Suowei 'xin wenhua yundong' de chachao yu pochan," 3–4, 2; de Vargas, "Some Elements in the Chinese Renaissance (Manuscript)," 18; Li, *Guoyu yundong shigang*, 137.

15 Wang, *Huiyi Yadong tushuguan*, 38.

16 Zhou, *Placing the Modern Chinese Vernacular in Transnational Literature*, 117.

17 "On the *Ladies' Magazine*'s readership, see Schwarcz, *Time for Telling the Truth Is Running Out*, 38.

18 Wang, "Chinese Literature from 1841 to 1937," 466. The translation of *guowen* as "national language" is taken from Hill, *Lin Shu, Inc.*, 7.

It indicated that an entirely new amount of "symbolic capital"[19] had been accrued by them. Being an academic faction meant being one in a long line of predecessors, one group among many rivals. But being the "center" or "masters" of a "movement" meant being a star.[20] Hu Shi's lectures at Beijing University reportedly became completely packed. Additional chairs had to be brought into the classrooms to accommodate the multitude of students who wanted to hear him speak, one newspaper story claimed. But even then there were not enough seats and some students had to stand.[21]

Newspapers also started gossiping about Hu Shi and Chen Duxiu in the way that the press usually only gossips about celebrities: The *Shanghai News* reported about banquets in Hu Shi's honor, the contents of his luggage during a trip to Shanghai – he carried books –, the location of his subsequent holidays – he went to the West Lake – and essays he had written in secondary school.[22] About Chen Duxiu, the newspaper reported in detail what he had said at various speeches he was giving in the early 1920s, when he came to Shanghai, and it covered his various arrests over the course of the years.[23] Cai Yuanpei was not exempted from this either. In 1924, the *Ladies' Magazine* featured a photo of Cai Yuanpei and his wife taken on occasion of their first wedding anniversary.[24]

---

19 Thompson, "Editor's Introduction," 14.
20 "Center": Ye, "Ji Beijing daxue shiye shi (xu)." "Masters": Miao, "Suowei 'xin wenhua yundong' de chachao yu pochan," 3–4, 2.
21 Jing, "Dumen xuejie xiaoxi," 6.
22 "Xijujia huanyan Hu Shizhi: Hu yun hui Jing hou zuo changshi juben" (Actors Give a Banquet in Hu Shizhi's Honor: Hu Consents to Write a Trial Script after His Return to Beijing), *Shenbao* (Shanghai News), November 20, 1923, 13, Shanghai; "Hu Shi zuori di Hu" (Hu Shi Arrived in Shanghai Yesterday), *Shenbao* (Shanghai News), May 21, 1927, 11, Shanghai; "Chengzhong xiao zhi xin xun: xianzai xiaoyou Hu Shi zhi tongnian keyi" (News from Chengzhong School: Discovery and Publication of Childhood Essays by Alumnus Hu Shi), *Shenbao* (Shanghai News), December 22, 1922, 17, Shanghai.
23 On Chen Duxiu's speeches, see "Chen Duxiu guo Hu zhi tanpian" (Chen Duxiu's Speeches in Shanghai), *Shenbao* (Shanghai News), February 23, 1920, 14; "Chen Duxiu zai E yanjiang zhi jingguo" (Chen Duxiu's Speeches in Hubei), *Shenbao* (Shanghai News), February 15, 1920, 14. His visits to Shanghai: "Chen Duxiu xingjiang lai Hu" (Chen Duxiu about to Come to Shanghai), *Shenbao* (Shanghai News), July 16, 1921, 14. His arrests: "Chen Duxiu bei bu," 7–8; "Chen Duxiu bei bu" (Chen Duxiu Arrested), *Shenbao* (Shanghai News), October 6, 1921, 14; "Chen Duxiu zai Jing bei bu xun" (News on Chen Duxiu's Arrest in Beijing), *Shenbao* (Shanghai News), February 22, 1923, 14.
24 "Cai Zimin xiansheng yu qi furen jiehun yi nian jinian sheying" (Photo Shooting on Occasion of the First Anniversary of the Wedding of Mr. Cai Zimin and His Wife), *Funü zazhi* (Ladies' Magazine), no. 10 (October 1, 1924): 13.

By contrast, their former rivals, the "Old Faction," were still talked about as academic members of a "faction." When Liu Shipei died on 20 November 1919, the *Shanghai News* remembered him as a "leader of the *National Heritage* faction."[25] Considering Liu Shipei's aversion to the classification, this doubtlessly caused him to turn in his grave. Lin Shu did not completely disappear from the public gaze either. When plays like *Oliver Twist* were staged, the *Shanghai News* usually mentioned him as their most prominent translator.[26] But neither he nor the "Old Faction" were ever again talked about as stars or people instrumental in shaping China's future culture.

This trend was also reflected in the fate of the groups' journals. *National Heritage* ceased publication after four issues in the summer of 1919, while the sales numbers of *New Tide* soared up at around the same time. In the autumn of 1919, many of the first cohort of *New Tide* editors and writers graduated and went abroad. Fu Sinian, for example, went to Britain. But not even this transition to a new editorial cohort could damage *New Tide*. The first volume of *New Tide* (January to May 1919), originally published by Beijing University Publishing Department, was reprinted and sold out twice. The New Tide Society therefore commissioned the professional Shanghai publisher East Asia Library to run the third edition.[27]

This professionalization of the editorial process opened up new marketing strategies and sales avenues for *New Tide*. Before May Fourth, *New Tide* had mainly been promoted through word-of-mouth recommendations.[28] As soon as

---

[25] Ye Yun, "Jing xuejie yaoren zhi diaoxie" (The Passing-Away of Important Figures in Beijing Academia), *Shenbao* (Shanghai News), November 27, 1919, 7.
[26] "Haishang xiaoshuojia manping (yi)" (Commentary of Foreign Novelists [1]), *Shenbao* (Shanghai News), January 16, 1921, 14, Shanghai; "Jimo Xu sheng" (Lonely Scholar Xu), *Shenbao* (Shanghai News), February 20, 1921, 14, Shanghai; "Xiaoshuo xianping" (Casual Evaluation of Novels), *Shenbao* (Shanghai News), February 20, 1921, 14, Shanghai; "Yi xiaoshuo yi xi tan" (A Talk about the Translation of Novels), *Shenbao* (Shanghai News), April 3, 1921, 14, Shanghai; "Meiguo nü xiaoshuojia Shituhuo furen xiaoying" (A Photo of the Female American Writer Mrs. Stowe), *Shenbao* (Shanghai News), April 10, 1921, 14, Shanghai; "Yingguo zhuming xiaoshuo shecheng yingju" (A Famous English Novel Is Adapted for the Screen), *Shenbao* (Shanghai News), December 16, 1922, 18, Shanghai; "Weiwei gongsi xindao dapi xiaoshuo" (A Great Amount of Novels Newly Arrive at Weiwei Company), *Shenbao* (Shanghai News), February 3, 1923, 17, Shanghai; "'Chahua nü' xiaoshuo zhi xin dianying" (The New Film about the Novel "The Lady of the Camellias"), *Shenbao* (Shanghai News), October 26, 1923, 18, Shanghai; Ting Hao, "'Gu'er ku yu' zhi pinglun" (Evaluation of *Oliver Twist*), *Shenbao* (Shanghai News), September 10, 1924, 15, Shanghai; Qian Jian, "Jiake Gegen zhuyan xinming jiang kaiyan" (Lead Actor Jackie Coogan Will Newly Star in a Movie), *Shenbao* (Shanghai News), September 5, 1924, 19, Shanghai.
[27] Wang, *Huiyi Yadong tushuguan*, 44.
[28] Li, "Xinchaoshe de shimo," 209.

East Asia Library had taken over, *New Tide* started being advertised on *Shanghai News* front pages. East Asia Library drove an aggressive marketing campaign, and paid for four front page advertisements from October 23, the date of the first advertisement in the newspaper, to the end of that month, and nine in November 1919 alone.[29] *New Youth*'s publisher Qunyi Book Company started a similar strategy in August 1919, with twelve front page advertisements in the *Shanghai News* in that month alone.[30] Every two or three days, a *Shanghai News* reader would have thus seen *New Youth* advertised. In all the preceding years, it had only been advertised once in the *Shanghai News*, on April 20, 1919.[31] *National Heritage* was not advertised a single time.

This new strategy of East Asia Library and Qunyi Book Company had the effect that a broader reach of *Shanghai News* readers was aware of these journals. But, vice versa, the publishers must also have felt that there was a sufficiently large potential audience for *New Tide* and *New Youth*, otherwise they would not have afforded the advertisement, which would have cost them good money.[32] A few months after May Fourth, in other words, things looked up for the people who had previously been called the "New Faction." This development was a significant change from the situation in April and May 1919, when the demise of these intellectuals' careers had seemed imminent or, as in the case of Chen Duxiu, had already happened.

The May Fourth protests

The game-changing event that happened at that time was, of course, the May Fourth demonstrations.

The May Fourth demonstrations were student-led protests against a clause in the Treaty of Versailles that conferred formerly German concessions in Shandong to Japan, rather than returning them to China. The German presence in Shandong primarily went back to the "Jiao'ao Concession Treaty" of 1897, which permitted

---

29 This is shown through a search of the database *Shenbao 1872–1949* (Shanghai News 1872–1949 [Database]), accessed January 12, 2016, http://shunpao.egreenapple.com. For the first advertisement, see "Advertisement for *New Tide*," *Shenbao* (Shanghai News), October 23, 1919, 1, Shanghai.
30 "Advertisement for *New Youth*," *Shenbao* (Shanghai News), August 3, 1919, 1, Shanghai. This again appears from a search of the database *Shenbao 1872–1949*.
31 "Advertisement for *New Youth*," *Shenbao* (Shanghai News), April 20, 1919, 1, Shanghai.
32 Pang, *Kua-wenhua guanggao yu shimin wenhua de bianqian*, 52–53; "Ben bao de guanggao, faxing ji qita," 22–23.

Germany to station military personnel in the Jiao'ao (present-day Qingdao) region, and which gave Germany railway rights in all of Shandong. Under the leadership of the warlord Duan Qirui, China had entered World War I on the side of the Allies in 1917. The international background to this was that the United States had started rising to prominence and opposed British Empire-style imperialism. Its president Woodrow Wilson promulgated notions of national self-determination, and the European empires' colonies started seeing new hope for independence. In 1917, China therefore entered World War I on the side of the Allies, by sending laborers to help their armies. The goal was for China to gain a better standing on the international stage and regain the German concessions on its territory. When the Central Powers were defeated in 1918, it was therefore expected that the German concessions would be returned to China. However, at the Paris Peace Conference, Japan asserted its claims to the concessions, and did so with success.

After the outbreak of the May Fourth protests, it was a matter of some debate whose fault this was. It was undeniable that on May 9, 1915, Japan had forced Yuan Shikai to sign a document called the Twenty-One Demands. After entering World War I on the side of the Allies in 1914, Japan occupied the German concessions in Shandong, specifically Jiao'ao/Qingdao and the Qingdao-Jinan Railway. The Twenty-One Demands were designed to make Japan's claims to Germany's former rights in Shandong, which it had thus obtained, legal.[33] There was also a notion that Japan had concluded secret treaties with Britain, France and Italy. As a result, these powers backed Japan's claim in Versailles.[34]

There was, however, a debate about the extent to which the Northern Chinese government had concluded additional secret treaties with Japan, which had corroborated Japan's claim to Shandong. On May 9, an alarmed State Council sent a (confidential) telegram to all provincial leaders, explaining that the Yunnan warlord had told the *Shanghai News* that the Northern Chinese government had concluded such agreements. Yunnan was part of Southern China, which was then independent of the North. The State Council (of the North) unsurprisingly claimed that all its agreements with Japan had been completely aboveboard, and that the provincial leaders, if not the public, had been informed about all treaties that existed.[35]

---

[33] Chen, "The May Fourth Movement and Provincial Warlords," 139.
[34] "Qingdao ying jiaohuan Zhongguo zhi wailun" (External Opinions on [Why] Qingdao Should Be Returned to China), *Shenbao* (Shanghai News), May 8, 1919, 7, Shanghai; G. Zay Wood, *The Shantung Question: A Study in Diplomacy and World Politics* (New York: Fleming H. Revell, 1922), 101.
[35] Guowuyuan, "Beijing guowuyuan qing dian" (Telegram of the 9th [of May 1919] from the State Council in Beijing), in *Yan Xishan dang'an* (Yan Xishan Papers), ed. Lin Qingfen, vol. 5 (Taibei: Guoshiguan, 2003), 16–17.

However, the idea that there had been secret agreements with Japan could not be undone. Only in March 1919, the Foreign Ministry had published the content of a series of treaties which the Chinese government had struck with Japan after the Twenty-One Demands. They were reprinted by the press under the poignant headline "The Foreign Ministry Publishes All Secret Agreements" or announced as "Publication of Sino-Japanese Secret Agreements on [March] 14."[36] In 1922, one of China's own diplomats, Ge-zai Wood (no dates), still wrote about them under the headline "The Secret Agreements of 1918" and stated that in some ways "China was her own architect" of the debacle at Versailles.[37] The label "secret" was applied to all these treaties in spite of the fact that at least parts of them had been known to the press before.[38]

Among the treaties published in the press in the spring of 1919 were the details of a series of loans, which China had received from Japan between 1917 and 1918. Many of them were signed by Cao Rulin and have become known as the Nishihara loans.[39] The negotiations for these loans were particularly incriminating for Duan Qirui's government. The *Shanghai News* reported in April 1919 about diplomatic notes that had been exchanged between the Chinese envoy Zhang Zongxiang (1879–1962) and Japanese representatives during the negotiations. In them, Japan demanded far-reaching rights in Shandong. Zhang Zongxiang replied to this, the *Shanghai News* claimed, that "the Chinese government gladly agrees" to Japan's demands.[40] The Chinese warlord government, all these newspaper articles suggested to the public, could not be trusted to pursue China's best interests.

It had thus been clear for a while that Japan was laying claim to Shandong. But on May 3, the Chinese public realized that the diplomat to Paris Lu Zhengxiang (1871–1949) would not be able to negotiate this out of the Treaty of Versailles. Various associations gathered on Saturday, May 3, to plan protests. The Citizens' Diplomatic Association, for example, intended to demonstrate on the symbolic May 7, the National Disgrace Memorial Day. This day commemorated Japan's

---

36 "Waijiaobu gongbiao ge xiang miyue" (The Foreign Ministry Publishes All Secret Agreements), *Dongfang zazhi* (Eastern Miscellany) 16, no. 5 (May 1919): 178–90; "Waijiaobu gongbiao ge xiang miyue (xu)" (The Foreign Ministry Publishes All Secret Agreements [Continued]), *Dongfang zazhi* (Eastern Miscellany) 16, no. 6 (June 1919): 166–79; "Zhong-Ri miyue hanri fabiao shuo" (Publication of Sino-Japanese Secret Agreements on the 14th), *Shenbao* (Shanghai News), March 13, 1920, 3.
37 Wood, *The Shantung Question*, 96.
38 "Zhong-Ri gongtong tiaoyue zhi jinxun" (Latest News on the Sino-Japanese Mutual Treaty), *Shenbao* (Shanghai News), June 3, 1918, 3.
39 "Waijiaobu gongbiao ge xiang miyue"; "Waijiaobu gongbiao ge xiang miyue (xu)."
40 Sheng Gui, "Beijing tongxin" (Newsletter from Beijing), *Shenbao* (Shanghai News), April 12, 1919, 6, Shanghai.

ultimatum for accepting the Twenty-One Demands.⁴¹ The students, however, were too impatient to wait.⁴² The next day, on May 4, 1919, reportedly 3,000 of them therefore gathered on the symbolic Tiananmen Square, where in 1895 another cohort of students had demonstrated and where students would demonstrate again in 1989.⁴³ From there, they marched through the streets of Beijing, until some of them burnt down the house of Cao Rulin, beat up Zhang Zongixang and were arrested by the local police.

But this did not end the demonstrations. With the help of Cai Yuanpei, the chancellor of Beijing University, and Fu Zengxiang, who was the minister of education, the students were quickly released.⁴⁴ Soon afterwards, both Cai and Fu resigned. A student union formed on May 6, which organized further strikes. It called for a refusal to sign the Treaty of Versailles and for the dismissal of the "country-selling traitors" (*maiguozei*), who were quite early on identified as Cao Rulin, Zhang Zongxiang and Lu Zongyu (1876–1941).⁴⁵ As finance minister, Cao had negotiated the Twenty-One Demands and as finance minister he had signed many of the Nishihara Loans. Zhang Zongxiang was the envoy to Japan and was now known as the person who had "gladly agreed" to the demands Japan had made in the wake of the Nishihara Loans.⁴⁶ Lu Zongyu had been an earlier envoy to Japan, and in this function he had negotiated the Twenty-One Demands.

In spite of government prohibition and censorship, the students gave lectures on the streets and boycotted Japanese goods over the next few weeks. Soon the protests spilled over into other cities, among which Shanghai became particularly important in June. Students received support from the media, from a number of provincial military governors and from other strata of society.⁴⁷ From June 5 onwards, merchants, workers and students in Shanghai joined ranks and entered a general strike. As a result, the "country-selling traitors" Cao Rulin, Zhang Zongxiang and

---

41 Chen, "The May Fourth Movement and Provincial Warlords," 143.
42 Yi Wan, "Yi zhou Beijing de gongmin da huodong" (One Week of Great Activities by the Citizens of Beijing), *Meizhou pinglun* (Weekly Critic), May 11, 1919, 1–3, 1, Beijing.
43 Chen, "The May Fourth Movement and Provincial Warlords," 144.
44 Ibid.
45 "Wu yue qi ri zhi guomin dahui" (The National Assembly of 7 May), *Shenbao* (Shanghai News), May 8, 1919, 10, Shanghai; "Waijiao jinji yu heju polie (si)" (The Urgency of Diplomacy and the Destruction of Peace [Four]), *Yishibao* (Social Welfare Tiensin), May 19, 1919, 2, Tianjin. An example of an early identification of these three as the "country-selling traitors": "Zhuandian" (Special Telegram), *Shenbao* (Shanghai News), May 6, 1919, 3, Shanghai.
46 Gui, "Beijing Tongxin," 6.
47 On support from the warlords, see Chen, "The May Fourth Movement and Provincial Warlords," 158. On the support from the media, see Mittler, *A Newspaper for China?*, 384–89.

Lu Zongyu were dismissed on June 10, and China refused to sign the Treaty of Versailles on June 28.[48]

May Fourth and New Culture

The narratives that later emerged about May Fourth and New Culture have conveyed upon us the impression that May Fourth was the same as New Culture, and that the "New Faction" was the leader of both. The logic reads that the "New Faction" put forward reformist ideas with the goal to save the nation in the face of Western imperialism, and that May Fourth also sought to save the nation in the face of Western imperialism. Therefore it was obvious that the two were intricately connected.[49] May Fourth and New Culture, moreover, are said to have shared a general sense of "newness" or "modernity."[50] According to another narrative, May Fourth made the New Culture agenda more plausible. *Baihua*, for example, came to be regarded as a worthwhile project because student demonstrators started communicating with the "common people," who did not understand Literary Chinese.[51] The May Fourth demonstrators, it has also been said, were the same people as, or they were at least led by, the New Culture intellectuals.[52] For all these reasons, the two events were, the narratives state, naturally connected. Even though some scholars have treated the two as separate, if related, events,[53] it is a widespread habit to use "May Fourth" and "New Culture" synonymously.

That this connection was in fact a construction, as I claim, therefore needs some arguing for. The first hint is, as I have shown in the introduction to this

---

[48] Huang Banghe and Pi Mingxiu, eds., "Zhang Zongxiang" (Zhang Zongxiang), *Zhong-wai lishi renwu cidian* (Dictionary of Historical Figures in China and Abroad) (Changsha: Hunan renmin chubanshe, 1987), Changsha; Chen, "The May Fourth Movement and Provincial Warlords," 153.
[49] Lin, *The Crisis of Chinese Consciousness*; Weston, *The Power of Position*, 147; Yi-tsi Mei Feuerwerker, "Reconsidering Xueheng: Neo-Conservatism in Republican China," in *Literary Societies Of Republican China*, ed. Michel Hockx and Kirk A. Denton (Plymoth: Lexington Books, 2008), 144; Rudolf G. Wagner, "The Canonization of May Fourth," in *The Appropriation of Cultural Capital: China's May Fourth Project*, ed. Milena Doleželová-Velingerová and Oldřich Král (Cambridge, Massachusetts: Harvard University Asia Center, 2001), 79.
[50] According to Lanza, the essays in the edited volume by Milena Doleželová-Velingerová and Oldřich Král fall into this category. See Lanza, "Of Chronology, Failure, and Fidelity," 57; Doleželová-Velingerová and Král, *The Appropriation of Cultural Capital*.
[51] Chow, *The May Fourth Movement*, 178; Wasserstrom, *Student Protests in Twentieth-Century China*, 204–05.
[52] Li Quan, *Fu Sinian xueshu sixiang pingzhuan* (A Critical Biography of the Scholarship and Thought of Fu Sinian) (Beijing: Beijing tushuguan chubanshe, 1999), 23–24.
[53] Lanza points this out, see Lanza, "Of Chronology, Failure, and Fidelity," 54–55.

chapter, that even well-informed contemporaries did not always make the connection. Even when they did make it later on and then felt that May Fourth, New Culture and the "New Faction" were somehow the same, they could not put their finger on why exactly this was the case. The head of the History Department of Yanjing University and Hu Shi's friend Philippe de Vargas called the connection a "historical puzzle."[54]

In fact, the connections pointed to in scholarship on May Fourth, New Culture and the Hu-Chen circle do not withstand a closer scrutiny. People then called the "New Faction" were not simply the leaders of May Fourth. Allegedly 3,000 students protested in Beijing on May 4. 1,000 Beijing University students planned the demonstrations the day before. The *New Tide* and *New Youth* societies only had around forty-five members altogether.[55] This is about 1.5 percent of all the demonstrators. The numbers of the protesters should of course be regarded as an educated guess, rather than as precise calculations. But even when they are taken with a pinch of salt, the overall ratio stands.

It would, of course, make little sense to write Beijing University and its *baihua* advocates completely out of May Fourth. *New Tide* editor Fu Sinian led Beijing University into the demonstrations on Tian'anmen Square.[56] Luo Jialun issued a manifesto that purported to speak for "all students of Beijing" and that was said to have been handed out "[a]long the route of the march."[57] His essay "The Spirit of the 'May Fourth Movement'" of May 26 was later on even regarded as the text that invented the expression "New Culture Movement."[58] Xu Deheng, one of the authors of *Citizen* (*Guomin*) and thus close to those labelled "New Faction," was a co-author of another manifesto against the "country-selling traitors."[59]

However, it would be equally problematic to overstate Beijing University's role in May Fourth. Fu Sinian soon abhorred the violence of his fellow protesters

---

54 de Vargas, "Some Elements in the Chinese Renaissance (Manuscript)," 18.
55 On the number of protesters overall, see Chen, "The May Fourth Movement and Provincial Warlords," 144. The planners of the protests from Beijing University: Li, *Fu Sinian xueshu sixiang pingzhuan*, 23. In December 1919, the New Tide Society stated that they had grown from 20 members to 37 members over the course of 1919. Over the course of 1919, no more than 18 people published articles in New Youth, "Xinchaoshe jishi" (Records of the New Tide Society), in *Xinchao* (New Tide), vol. 3 (Beijing, 2006), 200; *Xin qingnian* (New Youth), vol. 6, 14 vols. (Tokyo: Taian, 1963).
56 Li, *Fu Sinian xueshu sixiang pingzhuan*, 23–24.
57 Schwarcz, *The Chinese Enlightenment*, 15.
58 Shen Weiwei, *"Xueheng pai" biannian wenshi* (Compiling the Literary Matters of the "Critical Review Faction"), vol. 1 (Nanjing: Nanjing daxue chubanshe, 2015), 19.
59 Schwarcz, *The Chinese Enlightenment*, 18. On the two manifestos, see also Lanza, *Behind the Gate*, 130.

and withdrew.[60] Luo Jialun's essay may have become the most prominent early usage of the expression "May Fourth Movement," but Luo had not invented it. An earlier mention of the term, for example, can be found in the *Shanghai News* and in the *Morning Post*.[61] Luo's essay on "The Spirit of the 'May Fourth Movement'" does not seem to have been reprinted by very many other journals, after it had appeared the *Weekly Critic*.[62] Even in later years, when people started reflecting on the "spirit of the May Fourth Movement," they did not mention Luo Jialun by name, nor did they appear to engage with the content of his essay.[63] Xu Deheng's manifesto had merely thirty-two signatories.[64] To the extent that his manifesto was reported on at the time, it was treated as one among very many other, similar manifestos written by other groups.[65]

Original reports in internal letters and newspapers consequently were not about how "Beijing University," let alone the "New Faction," was protesting on May 4. They talked about how "the schools of Beijing" were protesting.[66] When Beijing University was at some point associated with the demonstrations more

---

60 Li, *Fu Sinian xueshu sixiang pingzhuan*, 23–24.
61 *Shanghai News*: "Jing xuejie zhi zuijin xiaoxi" (Most Recent News from Academia in Beijing), *Shenbao* (Shanghai News), May 18, 1919, 7, Shanghai. *Morning Post*: Chen, *Touches of History*, 52–53.
62 This, at least, is suggested by a search of the database *Quanguo baokan suoyin* (National Index of Chinese Newspapers and Periodicals [Database]), accessed January 8, 2013, http://www.cnbksy.com, which does not list any reprints for 1919.
63 Yu Ying, "Wu si yundong de zhen jingshen" (The True Spirit of the May Fourth Movement), *Gong jin* (Advancing Together), no. 61 (1924): 1–2; Zhang Liushi, "Beijing xuesheng you you wu si yundong shi de jingshen" (Beijing's Students Still Have the Spirit from the Time of the May Fourth Movement), *Juewu* (Enlightenment), 1924, 4–6, Shanghai.
64 Schwarcz, *The Chinese Enlightenment*, 18.
65 "Guomin duiyu Shandong wenti zhi banfa" (Ways in Which the Citizens Deal with the Shandong Question), *Shenbao* (Shanghai News), May 6, 1919, 6, Shanghai. Searches of the databases *Quanguo baokan suoyin*; *Shenbao 1872–1949* do not turn up any results for the title of Luo Jialun's manifesto "Manifesto of All of Academia in Beijing" (*Beijing xuejie quanti xuanyan*), which indicates that it was not reprinted very widely.
66 Jiangsu sheng jiaoyuhui, "Zhi da zongtong, guowuyuan, jiaoyubu chenming Shanghai ge xiao xuesheng yin jiaoyu zongzhang yiren deng wenti qun yi bake, qing fuxun yuqing dian"; Jiangsu sheng jiaoyuhui, "Kaihui jilu" (Meeting Minutes), *Jiangsu sheng jiaoyuhui yuebao* (Jiangsu Educational Association Monthly Report), May 1919, 21; Jiangsu sheng jiaoyuhui, "Kaihui jilu" (Meeting Minutes), *Jiangsu sheng jiaoyuhui yuebao* (Jiangsu Educational Association Monthly Report), June 1919, 15–18; "Jiang Zhe zhi jinian guochi yu zheng Qingdao" (Jiangsu's and Zhejiang's Commemoration of the National Disgrace and Fight for Qingdao), *Shenbao* (Shanghai News), May 11, 1919, 7, Shanghai; Guowuyuan, "Beijing guowuyuan zhi dian" (Telegram of the 4th [of May 1919] from the State Council in Beijing), in *Yan Xishan dang'an* (Yan Xishan Papers), ed. Lin Qingfen, vol. 5 (Taibei: Guoshiguan, 2003), 26–27.

than other schools (for details on how this happened, see below in this chapter), its chancellor Cai Yuanpei was rumored to have complained that "thirteen schools" were protesting and only Beijing University was held responsible. He, or at least the persona depicted in the rumor, appeared to find this highly unfair.[67]

People associated with the "Old Faction," moreover, did not have anything more or less positive to say about May Fourth than those classified as "New Faction." Hu Shi and Lin Shu had, at least officially, the same opinion of May Fourth. They approved of the patriotic spirit of the demonstrations, but despised the idea of students being outside the classroom – an opinion repeated by Cai Yuanpei one year later in the newspaper *Morning Post*.[68] Students as a "political category" and "student activism" were only just being defined during the May Fourth protests, as Fabio Lanza shows, so it was unsurprising that these members of the teacher generation should be uncomfortable with the protests.[69]

Secondly, there are problems with the idea that May Fourth evidenced the need to speak with the common people in *baihua*: Baihua was not the language of the common people. It was meant to be the (Westernized) language of globally envisioned present times (see chapter 1). As scholars like Edward Gunn and Shih Shu-mei have shown in recent years, it was therefore full of Western and Japanese loanwords and was as incomprehensible to the common people as Literary Chinese, if not more so.[70] Already in the 1930s, Qu Qiubai (1899–1935) therefore called it a "new Literary Chinese."[71] Consequently it could not have been very useful in communicating with the common people. Thirdly, as shown in chapter 1, the group around Hu Shi and Chen Duxiu were by no means the only

---

[67] "Cai Yuanpei ciqu xiaozhang zhi zhenyin" (The True Reasons for Cai Yuanpei's Resignation as Chancellor), *Chenbao* (Morning Post), May 13, 1919, 2, Beijing; "Cai Zimin jue ci Beijing Daxue xiaozhang zhi zhenyin" (The True Reasons for Cai Zimin's Decision to Resign as Chancellor of Beijing University), *Guomin gongbao* (Citizen News), May 13, 1919, 3, Beijing; "Cai Yuanpei cizhi zhi zhenyin" (The True Reasons for Cai Yuanpei's Resignation), *Shishi xinbao* (China Times), May 15, 1919, 2.1, Shanghai; "Fengyu piaopiao zhi Jing xuejie" (Academia in Beijing Shaking in Wind and Rain), *Shenbao* (Shanghai News), May 15, 1919, 7, Shanghai.

[68] Hu Shi and Jiang Menglin, "Women duiyu xuesheng de xiwang" (Our Hopes for the Students), in *Minguo shiqi mingren tan wu si: lishi jiyi yu lishi jieshi* (Famous People of the Republican Period Talk about May Fourth: Historical Reminiscences and Historical Explanations), ed. Yang Hu (Fuzhou: Fujian jiaoyu chubanshe, 2011), 93–97; Zhang, *Lin Shu pingzhuan*, 241; Cai Yuanpei, "Qunian wu yue si ri yilai de huigu yu jinhou de xiwang" (A Review of [Events] since 4 May of Last Year and Hopes for the Future), in *Minguo shiqi mingren tan wu si: lishi jiyi yu lishi jieshi* (Famous People of the Republican Period Talk about May Fourth: Historical Reminiscences and Historical Explanations), ed. Yang Hu (Fuzhou: Fujian jiaoyu chubanshe, 2011), 90.

[69] Lanza, *Behind the Gate*, 16, 11–12.

[70] Gunn, *Rewriting Chinese*, 217–96; Shih, *The Lure of the Modern*, 71.

[71] Mei Feuerwerker, *Ideology, Power, Text*, 39.

ones to endorse reformist agendas at the time, including calls for *baihua* or the National Language. Nor were they the only ones to promote their agendas with the "national salvation" rhetoric, which forecloses the possibility that they were associated with May Fourth because they shared the agenda of saving the nation. A lot of groups could have been connected to May Fourth on the basis of patriotic intent or rhetoric.

This means that there was no obvious connection between May Fourth, the particular discourse of New Culture that emerged later on and the people who were classified as the "New Faction" in early 1919. The "New Faction" and ideas ascribed to them only came to be associated with May Fourth because particular interpretations, particular patternings,[72] of reality were layered upon them: because of one set of conspiracy theories and rumors, which newspapers across the country were spreading at the time of the protests.

Rumors and conspiracy theories in newspapers

Interpreting May Fourth

A few days after the May Fourth demonstrations had started, it became clear to politicians, the public and the press that this was the big event of the year. Consequently, they all tried to make sense of it and to display their role at Versailles in a favorable light.

The central government in Beijing sought to depict itself as the honest defender of China's national interests and its unsuccessful maneuvering at Versailles as the failed attempt of an emerging country to have a play at Big Power politics. In other words, like virtually everybody else, it also claimed that it was trying to save the nation.

On May 6, 1919, the State Council sent a telegram to its provincial leaders, trying to convince them that the government had tried its very best at Versailles and had admonished its ambassador Lu Zhengxiang repeatedly not to give up the regions in Shandong.[73] A few weeks later, on May 24, Duan Qirui of the Anfu Club wrote to various politicians and provincial leaders that, with much foresight and against great resistance, he, Duan, had let China enter World War I, because "Britain [had] allowed Japan to occupy Qingdao" while China was neutral. If

---

[72] Geertz, *The Interpretation of Cultures*, 216.
[73] Guowuyuan, "Beijing guowuyuan ma dian" (Telegram of the 6th [of May 1919] from the State Council in Beijing), in *Yan Xishan dang'an* (Yan Xishan Papers), ed. Lin Qingfen, vol. 5 (Taibei: Guoshiguan, 2003), 9.

China did not sign the Treaty of Versailles now, China would not join the League of Nations, and would forfeit all its other diplomatic achievements. The patriotism of the students was clearly not enough to save the nation. "There are so many people in our country who love it, but our country is still not strong," he argued.[74] The students should therefore better return to their classrooms, because their "patriotism," or in Chinese "love for the nation" (*aiguo*), was in fact "destroying the nation" (*huoguo*).[75]

But the public did not buy this story of its government as China's valiant and visionary defender. Instead, the notion that the government had concluded harmful and secret treaties with Japan during World War I kept circulating and the view that the government had "sold out the country" to Japan could not be subdued.[76] The May Fourth protests were therefore interpreted and judged in a very specific manner: They came to be seen in black-and-white terms, as a struggle between brave and patriotic students against an untrustworthy government. To make things worse, it was observed, this government even suppressed the students. Mentions of this suppression could soon be found everywhere, from the reports of the Jiangsu Educational Association to articles in the *Shanghai News*, in *Social Welfare Tiensin* and in *Impartial* in Changsha.[77] The students themselves developed a cult around being suppressed. Luo Jialun wrote in his article "The Spirit of the 'May Fourth Movement'": "There were some who were wounded and there were also some who were arrested. There were also some who were angered to death because of the wounds."[78]

---

74 Duan, "Beijing Duan Qirui ban jing dian," 49.
75 Ibid., 50.
76 "Waijiaobu gongbiao ge xiang miyue (xu)"; "Zhong-Ri miyue hanri fabiao shuo," 3; "Guomin dahui zhi yuwen" (Miscellaneous News from the Citizens' Assembly), *Shenbao* (Shanghai News), May 9, 1919, 10, Shanghai.
77 For newspaper discussions of the government crackdowns, see "Xuejie fengchao zhong ge fangmian zhi taidu" (The Attitude of All Parties in the Student Protests), *Shenbao* (Shanghai News), May 8, 1919, 6, Shanghai; "Chajin 'fanghai zhi'an' de jihui, chuban zhi jingguo" (The Process of Prohibiting Meetings and Publications That "harm the Public Order"), *Meizhou pinglun* (Weekly Critic), July 27, 1919, 1–2, Beijing; "Waijiao jinji yu heju polie (liu)" (The Urgency of Diplomacy and the Destruction of Peace [Six]), *Yishibao* (Social Welfare Tiensin), May 21, 1919, 2, Tianjin; "Ge xiao xiaozhang zhi jianjue" (The Determination of the Principals of All Schools), *Dagongbao* (Impartial), May 10, 1919, 3, Changsha. For similar discussions by the Jiangsu Educational Association, see Jiangsu sheng jiaoyuhui, "Kaihui jilu," May 1919, 21; Jiangsu sheng jiaoyuhui, "Kaihui jilu," June 1919.
78 Luo Jialun, "'Wu si yundong' de jingshen" (The Spirit of the "May Fourth Movement"), in *Minguo shiqi mingren tan wu si: lishi jiyi yu lishi jieshi* (Famous People of the Republican Period Talk about May Fourth: Historical Reminiscences and Historical Explanations), ed. Yang Hu (Fuzhou: Fujian jiaoyu chubanshe, 2011), 78.

The protesters' suffering was in reality quite mild. The students in Beijing, who had been arrested in the wake of beating up Zhang Zongxiang and burning down Cao Rulin's house – two very violent acts – were only in prison for a few days. But admittedly for privileged people, this must have been a shock. The sacrifices the students took upon themselves were equally bearable. According to the *Shanghai News*, some decided "to be a vegetarian for a whole day, in order to give expression to their oath never to forget the disgrace."[79] The publisher nephew Wang Yuanfang even made fun of Chen Duxiu, who apparently made a big deal about his having been arrested in the wake of May Fourth. Wang remembered: "When Chen Zhongweng [i. e. Chen Duxiu] was in Shanghai, he would sometimes come to the shop [of East Asia Library]. We were all very respectful towards him. [But] behind his back, we regularly said: 'What [is he going on about] prison and jail? He went straight in and straight out!'"[80]

In spite of this private bickering and in spite of the relative mildness of the suppression, a public image was created in newspapers and organizations that May Fourth was about good, patriotic students being oppressed by a selfish government. The government's alternative interpretation was more or less ignored, and nobody much cared for its story that it had with much honesty tried to strengthen China's place on the international stage, and that the students were destroying what was left of their good efforts by their naïve behavior.

Rumors about Beijing University before May Fourth

This black-and-white interpretation of the May Fourth demonstrations soon merged with a black-and-white reportage about Beijing University's debates. Newspapers had not only classified a nuanced academic debate into neat factions, the "New Faction" and the "Old Faction" (see chapter 1). They also started to spread rumors that these factions had warlord-political allegiances. The "Old Faction," it was said, was in alliance with the government. With the government's help, it was trying to oust the "New Faction" from Beijing University, which was why Chen Duxiu was dismissed in April 1919. This conspiracy theory made the "New Faction" appear as the government victims.

Republican China was a society in which rumors abounded, and as Henrietta Harrison argues, even when they were contrived, they could have real-life impacts, because people acted upon them.[81] The rumors about the "New Faction's" suppression

---

79 "Jiang Zhe zhi jinian guochi yu zheng Qingdao," 7.
80 Wang, *Huiyi Yadong tushuguan*, 51.
81 Harrison, "Newspapers and Nationalism in Rural China 1890–1929," 187–88.

by the government emerged gradually. An early mention of somewhat unspecific threats can be traced to March 1919. At that time, Li Dazhao published two articles, both with the title "The Fierce Battle between the New and Old Intellectual Tides," in which he claimed that the "old [learning] people" were drawing upon "forces outside of academia" to push their points.[82] They refused to "come out in an upright manner, and debate and discuss with the thinkers of this 'New Faction,'" Li complained, and he denounced them for "always hiding behind people's back, wanting to hold on to that tough guy's legs, to that aggressive force to subdue people who oppose you."[83] These articles were printed in the *Morning Post* (Beijing) on March 4 and 5, 1919, in the *Weekly Critic* (Beijing) on March 9 and in the *China Times* (Shanghai) on March 7 and 10.[84] The *Morning Post* and the *China Times* belonged to the Research Clique and the *Weekly Critic* was based at Beijing University. Li Dazhao had been quite vague with his comment on the "forces outside of academia."[85] Other papers were more specific on where the threat was coming from. On March 6, the *Shanghai News* (commercially run) claimed that the "New Faction" was about to be dismissed at the initiative of the "head of state."[86]

It is impossible to say if there was any truth to these rumors, and historians have held conflicting opinions on the question.[87] But it is conspicuous that these stories started just when Lin Shu had published his short story "Scholar Jing," which he had done in late February. In this story, a "tough guy" beat up individuals who were identified as Hu Shi, Chen Duxiu and Qian Xuantong (see chapter 1).[88] Li Dazhao's often-reprinted articles too mentioned a "tough guy," behind whose "legs" the "Old Faction" was hiding. "[I]n the conspiracist world," the political scientist Michael Barkun explains, the "commonsense distinction between fact and fiction melts away."[89]

---

82 Shou, "Xin jiu sichao zhi jizhan," 7, March 4, 1919.
83 Shou Chang, "Xin jiu sichao zhi jizhan" (The Fierce Battle between New and Old Intellectual Trends), *Chenbao* (Morning Post), March 5, 1919, 7, Beijing.
84 Shou, "Xin jiu sichao zhi jizhan," 7, March 4, 1919; Shou, "Xin jiu sichao zhi jizhan," 7, March 5, 1919; Shou Chang, "Xin jiu sichao zhi jizhan" (The Fierce Battle between New and Old Intellectual Trends), *Meizhou pinglun* (Weekly Critic), March 9, 1919, 3, Beijing; Shou, "Xin jiu sichao zhi jizhan," 3.3, March 17, 1919; Shou, "Xin jiu sichao zhi jizhan," 3.3, March 10, 1919.
85 Shou, "Xin jiu sichao zhi jizhan," 7, March 4, 1919.
86 Jing, "Beijng daxue xin jiu zhi anchao," 6.
87 Scholars who tend to believe them: Weston, *The Power of Position*, 171–75; Schwarcz, *The Chinese Enlightenment*, 53. Scholars who consider them to be without a basis in reality: Zhang, *Lin Shu pingzhuan*, 223; Chen, "Xu Shuzheng yu xin wenhua yundong," 274; Hill, *Lin Shu, Inc.*, 221.
88 Lin, "Jing sheng," 212.
89 Michael Barkun, *A Culture of Conspiracy: Apocalyptic Visions in Contemporary America* (Berkeley: University of California Press, 2003), 29.

It is possible that this happened here as well and that the boundaries between Lin Shu's fiction and reality became blurred.

Then something strange happened. It appeared clear to newspapers that the stories about the government's threat to the "New Faction" and the "New Faction's" imminent demise were nothing but rumors. But this did not keep them from spreading them. On the contrary, they soon started repeating them in articles that were seemingly designed to refute them. The rumors were disseminated as rumors. For example, on March 7 the *China Times* wrote that according to the *Shanghai News* Chen Duxiu and Hu Shi were "being expelled." But fortunately, the *China Times* claimed, it (the *China Times*) had found out that this was untrue.[90] On March 10, the *Morning Post* denied that, "because of the clash between new and old thought, professors [at Beijing University] have been dismissed and the *New Tide* magazine closed down." Nevertheless, it informed its readers, these rumors could be read in "all newspapers in Beijing and Shanghai."[91] Soon even the newspaper of the Anfu Club, the *Public Voice*, repeated the story about how Chen and Hu should be dismissed, but it downplayed the involvement of political figures.[92] The rumors also spread outside of these metropoles at the end of March. On March 31, *Citizen News* in Chengdu reprinted the *Morning Post* (Beijing) story that all the rumors were untrue – thus not only denying, but also informing its readers about the rumors.[93]

Towards the end of March and the beginning of April, these rumors also became more explicit. On May 31, 1919, the *Shanghai News* claimed that the censor and member of the senate Zhang Yuanqi (1858–1922) was threatening to "impeach" the Minister of Education Fu Zengixang, if Fu did not do something about the "New Faction." Fu Zengxiang thereupon wrote a letter to Cai Yuanpei "commanding him to tread carefully." Needless to say, the "New Faction" remained relentless.[94] On April 5, the *Shanghai News* added that Zhang Yuanqi had been "lobbied" by Lin Shu.[95]

The fact that similar stories were printed in many different newspapers seems to suggest that there was some truth to the rumors. After all, it is improbable that

---

[90] Kuang Seng, "Daxue jiaoyuan wuyang" (University Professors Safe), *Shishi xinbao* (China Times), March 7, 1919, 3.3, Shanghai.
[91] "Beijing daxue yaoyan zhi wugen," 2.
[92] "Qing kan Beijing xuejie sixiang chao bianqian zhi jinzhuang," 3, 6.
[93] "Beijing daxue zhi yaoyan," 2.
[94] "Jinghua duanjian" (Short Letters from the Capital), *Shenbao* (Shanghai News), March 31, 1919, 7, Shanghai.
[95] "Jinghua duanjian" (Short Letters from the Capital), *Shenbao* (Shanghai News), April 5, 1919, 7, Shanghai.

independent sources would come to the same conclusion without cause. But newspapers were not independent from each other and this spread of the rumors had a lot to do with the newspapers' operational practices.

Newspapers technically belonged to different institutions. The *Morning Post* and the *China Times* belonged to the Research Clique, the *Shanghai News* was commercial, the *Public Voice* belonged to the Anfu Club. They were technically also printed in different locations. The *Morning Post* and the *Public Voice* in Beijing, the *China Times* and the *Shanghai News* in Shanghai, the *Citizen News* in Chengdu, and so forth. But behind the scenes, these geographical and institutional lines were blurred: often these newspapers printed the same articles. One reason was that they used the same journalists. As Natascha Gentz writes, newspapers hired correspondents whom they paid by the article.[96] It therefore made economic sense for a freelance journalist to send his article to several papers and collect payment from them. Sometimes the articles of high profile writers were also reprinted in several publications, as was the case with Li Dazhao's "The Fierce Battle between New and Old Intellectual Trends." Sometimes writers also sent their articles to news agencies, which then forwarded them to newspapers.[97] On yet other occasions, David Strand claims, newspapers simply copied other publications' articles.[98]

The symptom of these practices was that articles appeared in different newspapers across regions and institutional affiliations with only minor editorial changes. For example, the *Shanghai News* (commercial, Shanghai) and the *Public Voice* (Anfu Club, Beijing) reprinted the same article on March 6 and on March 18 respectively, with only minor differences in some subclauses and individual sentences.[99] Another example is an article, which appeared in the Beijing *Morning Post* under the title "The Untenable Nature of the Rumors about Beijing University" on March 10, 1919, and in the Chengdu *Citizen News* under "The Rumors about Beijing University" on March 31. In addition to the changed title, the only difference was that the *Morning Post* introduced the printed information with the formula "this society [reports]," whereas the Chengdu *Citizen News*

---

[96] Natascha Gentz (nee Vittinghoff), *Die Anfänge des Journalismus in China (1860–1911)* (The Beginnings of Journalism in China [1860–1911]) (Wiesbaden: Harrassowitz, 2002), 146–48.
[97] Shih Hu, "Failure of Law in Nationalist China," in *The Search for Modern China: A Documentary Collection*, ed. Pei-kai Cheng, Michael Elliot Lestz, and Jonathan D. Spence, 1st ed. (New York: Norton, 1999), 273.
[98] David Strand, "'A High Place Is No Better than a Low Place': The City in the Making of Modern China," in *Becoming Chinese: Passages to Modernity and beyond*, ed. Wen-hsin Yeh (University of California Press, 2000), 104.
[99] Jing, "Beijng daxue xin jiu zhi anchao," 6; "Qing kan Beijing xuejie sixiang chao bianqian zhi jinzhuang," 3, 6.

used the formula "this journalist [reports]."[100] This may have been a case in which a *Morning Post* journalist also sent his article to the *Citizen News*. Sometimes, newspapers even seemed to use the same type script, as they reprinted the same spelling mistakes. This happened with an article that reappeared with a missing quotation mark in the *Morning Post*, the *Citizen News* (Beijing), the *China Times* and, as an excerpt, in the *Shanghai News*.[101]

In this way, one body of rumors spread across China's urban centers. It was admitted in these articles that these were probably nothing but rumors. But the idea that the "New Faction" was suffering under its "clash" with the "Old Faction" and under government suppression nevertheless became very visible.

Rumors about Cai Yuanpei's resignation

These rumors about the government's suppression of the academics who were called the "New Faction" were the first step in associating them with the May Fourth demonstrators, who in the public's view were equally suppressed by a selfish government. The association was completed with the reportage about Cai Yuanpei's resignation, which had occurred on May 9, 1919.

After students were arrested during the May Fourth demonstrations, Cai Yuanpei used all his influence to secure their release, and he soon succeeded. This of course made Cai one of the heroes of May Fourth. But in the night of May 9, 1919, newspapers would report afterwards, Cai secretly packed up his belongings in his office at Beijing University and at 5:30am, he sneaked out of Beijing.[102] When Beijing University woke up the next day, it found itself without its chancellor. The story told in newspapers from the *Shanghai News*, *Social Welfare Tiensin* to the *Citizen News* (Beijing) and *Impartial* (Changsha) was that all he had left was a note that stated:

> I am tired. "The gentleman's horse is killed by the child on the side of the road." "The people are also heavily burdened, perhaps a little ease may be got for them." I want to get a little ease. I have already formally resigned from the post of chancellor of Beijing University. Starting from May 9, I end all contact with all other universities and assemblies that I used to be affiliated with. I merely explain this. Only those who know me will forgive me for this.[103]

---

100 "Beijing daxue yaoyan zhi wugen," 2; "Beijing daxue zhi yaoyan," 2.
101 "Cai Yuanpei ciqu xiaozhang zhi zhenyin," 2; "Cai Zimin' jue ci Beijing daxue xiaozhang zhi zhenyin," 3; "Cai Yuanpei cizhi zhi zhenyin," 2.1; "Fengyu piaopiao zhi Jing xuejie," 7.
102 "Beijing daxue you qi jueda bolan: Cai xiaozhang cizhi chu Jing" (Another Big Wave Rises at Beijing University: Chancellor Cai Quits and Leaves Beijing), *Shenbao* (Shanghai News), May 12, 1919, 6, 6, Shanghai; Cai, *Cai Yuanpei riji*, 1:253.
103 "Beijing daxue you qi jueda bolan," 6, 6. Similarly also in "Daxue xiaozhang zhi cizhi" (The Resignation of the Chancellor of the University), *Yishibao* (Social Welfare Tiensin), May 10, 1919,

As Cai Yuanpei was a highly educated scholar, this note was full of classical allusions. The "gentleman's horse" referred to a story in the *Common Meaning in Customs*, a text from the Eastern Han period, in which a horse runs itself to death because it is exhorted by a child who is "on the side of the road."[104] "The people are heavily burdened" is a citation from the poem "The Burden of the People" from the *Book of Odes*.[105] Whether Cai really left this note, is questionable. His diary does not mention it, only that he sent "a letter [explaining] the real reason for my resignation" on the 12th.[106] Still, this was the way in which Cai Yuanpei's resignation entered the press and eventually history.

Cai Yuanpei's resignation was of huge interest to the press, and in the first instance this made the May Fourth demonstrations look as if they were a matter, not of "the universities in Beijing" (which they were), but of Beijing University (which technically they were not). This impression was created through a variety of factors. One was the placement of articles. Newspapers from the *China Times* (Shanghai) to *Social Welfare Tiensin* reported about Cai's resignation and the student protests in the same columns. These columns were now considered front page (or at least early page) material, whereas previous reports on the factional strives at Beijing University had been banned to less prominent sections. On May 13, for example, the *China Times* featured articles on "Chancellor Cai Leaves Beijing and Academia" and "News from the East after the Failure in the Shandong Question" in the same section, which it called "Important Foreign and Domestic News."[107] *Social Welfare Tiensin* too launched a column with the title "Citizens Fight in the Diplomatic [Question]," where it reported about Cai's resignation next to articles on the "Shandong Question."[108]

2, Tianjin; "Jing xuejie you fasheng da wenti: Beijing daxue xiaozhang chuzou" (Big Problem Happens Again in Beijing's Academia: The Chancellor of Beijing University Walks out), *Dagongbao* (Impartial), May 15, 1919, 3, Changsha; "Cai Yuanpei qishi" (Cai Yuanpei's Note), *Guomin gongbao* (Citizen News), May 11, 1919, 1, Beijing. Translation of the *Book of Odes* reworked from James Legge, *The Chinese Classics*, 2nd ed., vol. 4: The She King (Taibei: SMC Publishing Inc, 1991), 496.

104 Ge Wujue, *Shiguang yousheng* (Time Has a Voice) (Beijing: Zhongguo qingnian chubanshe, 2011), 166.

105 Translation from Legge, *The Chinese Classics*, 1991, 4: The She King:496.

106 Cai, *Cai Yuanpei riji*, 1:253.

107 "Cai xiaozhang li Jing yu xuejie" (Chancellor Cai Leaves Beijing and Academia), *Shishi xinbao* (China Times), May 13, 1919, 1.2, Shanghai; "Shandong wenti shibai hou zhi dong xun" (News from the East after the Failure in the Shandong Question), *Shishi xinbao* (China Times), May 13, 1919, 2.1, Shanghai.

108 "Daxue xiaozhang zhi cizhi," 2; "Shandong wenti yi jiejue" (Shandong Question Solved), *Yishibao* (Social Welfare Tiensin), May 10, 1919, 2, Tianjin. The *Shanghai News* and the *Public*

A second factor was the content of the articles. Ever since Lin Shu's short stories and the beginning of the rumors, the idea of physical violence against the "New Faction" had been around.[109] The degree of violence was stepped up in stories about Cai Yuanpei's resignation. Rumors were now circulating that the government was planning to burn down or shell the whole of Beijing University. A widespread story went that Cai Yuanpei had met a friend in Tianjin, and the following conversation had transpired: The friend asked Cai what he was doing here. Cai replied: "I have resigned." The friend said that this was clear, but why was Cai "so determined"? He presumably meant that Cai had gone all the way to Tianjin, rather than staying in Beijing after his resignation. Cai then confessed that the government believed that Beijing University had incited all the schools in Beijing to demonstrate on May Fourth, and that he, Cai, had incited Beijing University. Therefore there were "plans to burn down the university and assassinate the chancellor." Obviously, this motivated Cai Yuanpei to get as far away from Beijing as possible. This was also the aforementioned story, in which Cai complained that "thirteen schools" were protesting and only Beijing University was blamed.[110]

It is probable that this particular story was spread by only one journalist, as the same text appeared in two Beijing newspapers (*Citizen News* and *Morning Post*) on May 13 and in two Shanghai newspapers (*China Times* and *Shanghai News*, only an extract in the latter) two days later. All articles missed the same quotation mark.[111] But a similar story also made its way to other papers and journalists. On May 13, *Impartial* in Changsha claimed as well that a story was "widely circulating," according to which "a certain general" wanted to burn down Beijing University.[112] In this way, the media coverage on Cai Yuanpei's resignation associated Beijing University with May Fourth.

Voice also reported about May Fourth and Cai's resignation together, see "Xuejie fengchao you qi" (Student Protests Flare up Again), *Gongyanbao* (Public Voice), May 10, 1919, 2, Beijing; "Hu Renyuan zhang daxue wenti: jiaoyuan xuesheng yizhi fandui" (Chancellor Hu Renyuan's Problem with the University: Professors and Students Unanimously Oppose Him), *Shenbao* (Shanghai News), June 10, 1919, 7, Shanghai; "Jing xuejie jin xun" (Recent News from Academia in Beijing), *Shenbao* (Shanghai News), August 11, 1919, 6–7, Shanghai.
109 Lin, "Jing sheng"; Lin, "Yaomeng"; Shou, "Xin jiu sichao zhi jizhan," 3.3, March 10, 1919; Shou, "Xin jiu sichao zhi jizhan," 7, March 4, 1919.
110 "Cai Zimin' jue ci Beijing daxue xiaozhang zhi zhenyin," 3; "Cai Yuanpei ciqu xiaozhang zhi zhenyin," 2; "Fengyu piaopiao zhi Jing xuejie," 7; "Cai Yuanpei cizhi zhi zhenyin," 2.1.
111 "Cai Zimin' jue ci Beijing daxue xiaozhang zhi zhenyin," 3; "Cai Yuanpei ciqu xiaozhang zhi zhenyin," 2; "Fengyu piaopiao zhi Jing xuejie," 7; "Cai Yuanpei cizhi zhi zhenyin," 2.1.
112 "Jing xuejie you fasheng da wenti," 3.

But why did this coverage bring the "New Faction" into the limelight of public attention? As chancellor of Beijing University, Cai Yuanpei had long been preaching that he was *jianrong bingbao*, that is, that he was endorsing "broad-minded and encompassing tolerance of diverse points of view,"[113] and that he did not favor either the people called the "New Faction" or those labelled the "Old Faction." From this perspective, the hype around Cai's resignation provided no reason to associate the "New Faction" specifically with May Fourth.

Here again, it was the newspapers' treatment of Cai's *jianrong bingbao* that changed this. Ever since the rumors about Chen Duxiu's and Hu Shi's imminent dismissal had started in March 1919, *jianrong bingbao* had been cited as a formula to defend Cai's decision to retain the "New Faction" at Beijing University. When the *Morning Post* reported about rumors that Hu and Chen should be dismissed, it expressed its shock at this. Echoing Cai Yuanpei, it explained that it was entirely natural for the "highest academic institution" to be "*jianrong bingbao*" of old and new thought. "How could this be restrained by force?"[114] The *Shanghai News* wrote a similar article on May 13. When a general of the Anfu Club tried to have the "New Faction" dismissed, the article read, Cai Yuanpei refused on the grounds that "the highest institution of learning had to be *jianrong bingbao* and could not hold sectarian views." Vice-President Qian Nengxun thereupon considered, according to the *Shanghai News*: "If Mr. Cai is dead, would the university [then] be manageable?"[115]

Cai, in other words, was said to have risked life and limb to retain Chen Duxiu and Hu Shi at Beijing University. He was, in these stories, a defender of the "New Faction." When he resigned and fled Beijing during the May Fourth demonstrations, this then must have appeared not only like a story about threats to Beijing University, but also one about threats to the "New Faction."

Simultaneously, the "Old Faction" was drawn ever more closely into the orbit of the ever less popular warlord government. When the rumors about the government intervention at Beijing University had first started, it was already claimed that the "Old Faction" was allying itself with politicians such as the censor Zhang Yuanqi to oust the "New Faction."[116] In the reportage during May Fourth, the assertions that the "Old Faction" was in league with politicians turned into claims that it was in league with the Anfu Club. On May 9,

---

113 Schwarcz, *The Chinese Enlightenment*, 52.
114 "Beijing daxue yaoyan zhi wugen," 2.
115 Shuang Yu, "Daxue xiaozhang wenti zhi guoqu, xianzai, weilai" (Past, Present and Future of the Problems with the University's Chancellor), *Shenbao* (Shanghai News), May 13, 1919, 6, Shanghai.
116 "Jinghua duanjian," 7, March 31, 1919.

the paper changed the story to purport that Lin Shu had lobbied, not censor Zhang Yuanqi, but Xu Shuzheng.[117] This was a big difference. Xu Shuzheng was a general and friend of Duan Qirui. He was also labelled "country-selling traitor" during May Fourth.[118] The "Old Faction" thus came to be equated with the "traitors" of the Anfu Club, whereas the "New Faction" looked increasingly more like the victims of those "traitors," and Cai Yuanpei like their brave defender.

As a result, May Fourth came to be associated with Beijing University's "New Faction" and ideas that people attributed to them. In 1920, a young teacher who wrote under the name "Jing Guan" (no dates) therefore wrote mysteriously that he did not demonstrate during May Fourth. But he did support the cause of the demonstrations, in his view, because he discussed the "question of the new woman." In his interest in this matter he was, he said, just "like the professors at Beida [that is, Beijing University], Mr. Chen Duxiu and Mr. Hu Shizhi."[119] Discussing and promoting their ideas was apparently considered to be the same as demonstrating during May Fourth by the year 1920.

How could these newspapers exert such an influence? After all, newspapers, while increasingly important, were only read by an elite – those who were literate and who had the time and money to spare to buy and read the papers. The reason is that the New Culture Movement would be negotiated by exactly this newspaper-reading elite, as chapter 4 will show. So the few who read the newspapers were also the few who ended up caring about the idea of a New Culture Movement.

As a result, the stories spread in these newspaper rumors kept being recounted in early chronicles of the New Culture Movement. In these accounts, the stories about the government's violence against the "New Faction" were not depicted as rumors nor as newspaper stories, but as the truth. One example is Philippe de Vargas' "Some Elements in the Chinese Renaissance," a lecture which he gave in Hu Shi's presence at the Society of Friends of Literature in 1922, and which he republished later as a book.[120] Up until May Fourth, *baihua* – the focus of his story – was only proposed by few academics at Beijing University, de Vargas said.[121] Then the "conservatives" found an ally in Lin Shu, who published his short

---

117 Shuang, "Daxue xiaozhang wenti zhi guoqu, xianzai, weilai," 6.
118 "Guomin dahui zhi yuwen," 10.
119 Jing, "Gao xin wenhua yundong de tongzhi," 31–32. "
120 De Vargas' later book: Philippe de Vargas, *Some Elements in the Chinese Renaissance* (Shanghai, 1922). Hu Shi's presence during de Vargas' speech, see Hu Shi, *Hu Shi de riji* (Hu Shi's Diary), ed. Zhongguo shehui kexueyuan jindaishi yanjiusuo Zhonghua minguoshi yanjiu, vol. shang (Beijing: Zhonghua shuju, 1985), 267.
121 de Vargas, "Some Elements in the Chinese Renaissance (Manuscript)," 16.

stories.¹²² The "giant" (that is, the "tough guy") of Lin's story "Scholar Jing" was soon identified with the warlord and Duan Qirui-ally Xu Shuzheng. Shortly afterwards, the "reactionary politicians" of the "Anfu conservative party" threatened impeachment to Minister of Education Fu Zengxiang and caused Chen Duxiu to be dismissed in April.¹²³ But the situation was reversed through May Fourth. De Vargas concluded his account of these events, stating: "And there we have an historical puzzle: how on earth could these students' and merchants' strikes affect the academic debate on the language of literature? Yet so they did."¹²⁴

De Vargas was by no means the only one to tell the story of New Culture and May Fourth in this way. Another example was an author writing the *Chronicles of the Student Protests* under the pseudonym Cha An from Xiaoshan (no dates). The *Chronicles* were published with Zhonghua Book Company (*Zhonghua shuju*) in Shanghai in September 1919. Cha An not only repeated the narrative told in the newspapers, he even copied their wording, especially the one used by the *Shanghai News*.

For example, he literally reprinted the note that Cai Yuanpei had, according to many newspapers, left when resigning. ("I am tired. 'The gentleman's horse ...'")¹²⁵ He also copied much of the phrasing of a *Shanghai News* article of May 13, 1919, the resignation of Cai Yuanpei. Cha An, like the *Shanghai News*, talked about various instances preceding May Fourth in which Cai Yuanpei's position had been "shaken" in early 1919.¹²⁶ One of them was the quarrel between "Old Faction" and "New Faction," in the wake of which the "Old Faction" had teamed up with the government to oust their opponents. Cha An also copied how, during May Fourth, "a meeting was held in [Prime Minister] Qian [Nengxun's] house, [discussing] the dissolution of the university and the dismissal of the chancellor." The reason was that "the average old officials in Beijing all thought that [the protests] were the result of the university having initiated the New-Learning Faction."¹²⁷ All this was literally taken from the *Shanghai News* article of May 13, 1919.

It is impossible to know what the relationship was between Cha An and Shuang Yu (no dates), the author of the relevant article in the *Shanghai News*,

---

122 Ibid., 15.
123 Ibid., 16.
124 Ibid., 18.
125 Cha An: Cha An, *Xuejie fengchao ji* (Chronicle of the Student Protests) (Shanghai: Zhonghua shuju, 1919), shang 8. The newspapers: "Beijing daxue you qi jueda bolan," 6, 6; "Daxue xiaozhang zhi cizhi," 2; "Jing xuejie you fasheng da wenti," 3; "Cai Yuanpei qishi," 1.
126 Cha, *Xuejie fengchao ji*, shang 9; Shuang, "Daxue xiaozhang wenti zhi guoqu, xianzai, weilai," 6.
127 Cha, *Xuejie fengchao ji*, shang 9; Shuang, "Daxue xiaozhang wenti zhi guoqu, xianzai, weilai," 6.

because they both wrote under pseudonyms. For all we know, they could have been the same person. But even if they were, the fact that Cha An repeated Shuang Yu's story, and that the story was in this way further disseminated in yet another publication, shows how influential the rumors spread in the newspapers were, not only in merging May Fourth with the "New Faction," but also in reconsolidating the notion of this merger in later narratives.

Control points

Yan Xishan and the conspiracy of the Research Clique

Just how necessary these particular patternings of reality, that is, these particular conspiracy theories, rumors and factional classifications were in associating the *baihua* advocates at Beijing University with May Fourth becomes evident from looking at people who subscribed to a different set of conspiracy theories or to none at all. These people were utterly astonished by the change of ideas in the wake of the demonstrations.

Yan Xishan was among those people. As shown in the introductory section to this chapter, Yan Xishan was caught entirely unawares by the rise of communism in the summer of 1919, even though his active correspondence with the Beijing government, with other provincial warlords and with his subordinates had furnished him with all the information there was.[128] The reason was that Yan Xishan had patterned the events of 1919 differently.

Yan Xishan was an ardent believer in political factions and he mistrusted his rival factions thoroughly. This may not be unrelated to the fact that, in the future, he himself would betray his allies frequently.[129] While being convinced that factions were omnipresent, Yan Xishan did not believe in the existence of the political consciousness or resourcefulness of China's protesters. When discussing May Fourth, Yan Xishan did not usually talk about the "public" or even the "countrymen" as agents of the protests, which was the vocabulary institutions like the State Council in Beijing and the Jiangsu Educational Association were using when describing the demonstrators.[130]

---

[128] For examples for such correspondence, see the following paragraphs.
[129] Gillin, *Warlord*, 115–257.
[130] "Public": The Jiangsu Educational Association spoke of "public sentiment" (*yuqing*) in the context of May Fourth, Jiangsu sheng jiaoyuhui, "Zhi da zongtong, guowuyuan, jiaoyubu chenming Shanghai ge xiao xuesheng yin jiaoyu zongzhang yiren deng wenti qun yi bake, qing fuxun yuqing dian." "Countrymen": Guowuyuan, "Beijing guowuyuan ma dian."

Consequently, the first reaction of Yan Xishan's circle to the May Fourth protests was that they had to be directed by a force that had to be taken more seriously politically. The protests were, the circle concluded, a conspiracy by a rival political faction, the Research Clique. On May 11, Yan received a letter from a contact in Beijing writing that "these protests are, [it appears] on the surface, [instigated] by student groups. But behind the scenes, the Research Clique is inciting them."[131] This story continued in Yan Xishan's circle for a while. On May 14, 1919, another Beijing contact claimed in a telegram to Yan Xishan that the Research Clique was using May Fourth to topple the Anfu Club.[132] Yan Xishan appeared to buy into this, because on May 15 he wrote the same story back to the contact. The Research Clique was "using" the students and "borrowing [the Shandong Question] as an excuse to further their own cause," he claimed.[133] In this interpretation, May Fourth was not a matter of "good," patriotic students versus a selfish government. It was the matter of one political intrigue versus another. Beijing University's "New Faction" did not figure into this at all.

For Yan Xishan, this did not change either when Cai Yuanpei resigned. Yan did know about the resignation, and he did know about the rumors that General Xu Shuzheng was "scheming to burn down the university." But the reaction of his network was the still focused on factions: his network argued that these rumors were spread, again, by "newspapers of the Research Clique."[134] The implication of this story then was not that the government conspired against Cai Yuanpei, Beijing University and the "New Faction." It was that the Research Clique was plotting against the Anfu Club. Again there was no reason to associate May Fourth with the "New Faction" or with any change in ideas.

When the growing power of communism became apparent in September 1919, Yan Xishan and his correspondents did not trace this back to May Fourth, but instead blamed it on Russian agents, as well as on other foreign influences coming from Korea and Japan.[135] Yan's colleague in Shaanxi seemed similarly

---

131 Ge Jingyou, "Beijing Ge canshi zhen dian" (Telegram of the 11th [of May 1919] from Councilor Ge in Beijing), in *Yan Xishan dang'an* (Yan Xishan Papers), ed. Lin Qingfen, vol. 5 (Taibei: Guoshiguan, 2003), 24–25.
132 Daiwen Zhao, "Beijing Zhao canmouzhang han dian" (Telegram of the 14th [of May 1919] from Chief of Staff Zhao in Beijing), in *Yan Xishan dang'an* (Yan Xishan Papers), ed. Qingfen Lin, vol. 5 (Taibei: Guoshiguan, 2003), 32.
133 Yan, "Fu Beijing Zhao canmouzhang xian dian," 29.
134 Li Qingfang, "Beijing Li Fenpu qing dian" (Telegram of the 9th [of May 1919] from Li Fenpu in Beijing), in *Yan Xishan dang'an* (Yan Xishan Papers), ed. Lin Qingfen, vol. 5 (Taibei: Guoshiguan, 2003), 12.
135 Neiwubu, "Beijing neiwubu hao dian"; Waijiaobu, Neiwubu, and Jiaotongbu, "Beijing guowuyuan waijiao deng bu jing dian" (Telegram of the 24th [of April 1920] from the Foreign

flabbergasted at a growing influence of anarchism at the time. While he was unsuspectingly censoring the mail, the warlord of Shaanxi was utterly astonished to find "anarchist" (*wuzhengfu zhuyi*) journals with titles like *Modern Science and Anarchism* (*Jinshi kexue yu wuzhengfu zhuyi*) or *Clothing, Food and the New Life of the Nation* (*Yi-shi yu guojia xin shengming*). These publications, he judged, were "intent on trying to rabble-rouse." Yan Xishan learnt about this matter from a letter which alarmed departments of the central government forwarded to all the provincial leaders.[136] But May Fourth was left unmentioned here too.

In October 1919, Yan Xishan could therefore happily welcome the Union of the Educational Associations to their annual conference in his province. He could tell them that they, as educators, were the people to save the country from its current crisis.[137] Little did he know that this Union conference would successfully petition the government with an agenda which would enter the history books as one of the successes of May Fourth and New Culture, right along with the foundation of the Chinese Communist Party (CCP) in 1921. After year-long efforts, this Union meeting finally convinced the Ministry of Education to introduce National Language classes into primary-school curricula, and this has been interpreted as a success of the *baihua* movement.[138] For Yan Xishan, all these things were separate events, all of which happened to occur in 1919. They did not belong to the purposeful narrative of "May Fourth and the New Culture Movement." A different set of conspiracy theories created an entirely different interpretation of that year.

The Public Voice *and Cai Yuanpei's "neurosis"*

The reportage of the *Public Voice* about the events of the year did not suggest any connections between May Fourth and the "New Faction" either. This was again unsurprising, as the *Public Voice* belonged to the Anfu Club and the Anfu Club was in other newspapers depicted as the villain of the story.

Prior to May Fourth, the *Public Voice* had also constructed the debating academics at Beijing University into the "New Faction" and the "Old Faction," and

---

Ministry, Etc., of the State Council in Beijing), in *Yan Xishan dang'an* (Yan Xishan Papers), ed. Qingfen Lin, vol. 5 (Taibei: Guoshiguan, 2003), 102–4.
136 Canmou benbu and Lujunbu, "Beijing guowuyuan can, lubu ge dian," 84.
137 Yan, "Shanxi dujun jian shengzhang wei quanguo jiaoyu lianhehui di-wu ci kaihui zhici," 1452.
138 Chow, *The May Fourth Movement*, 279.

reported about the "New Faction's" weak position.[139] But it differed in its coverage of Cai Yuanpei's resignation. According to the paper, Cai Yuanpei resigned because he succumbed to illness. He was, it reported on June 26, 1919, "suffering from neurosis." Although feigning illness to avoid official office was a very time-honored strategy that administrators in China had deployed for centuries, Cai's illness was more than just a "pretext," the paper claimed.[140] Instead, Cai Yuanpei and Minister of Education Fu Zengxiang had quit because they "shouldered the blame" for the protests of May Fourth.[141] Cai Yuanpei had said that he had lost his influence over the students and that "the students' actions increasingly transgress the usual boundaries."[142] In this story, Cai was not a brave man who stood up to an untrustworthy government to defend academic freedom. Instead, he was a mentally ill person who had lost control over the situation. The government, certainly, had nothing to do with the resignation, the *Public Voice* implied. Quite on the contrary, it had repeatedly asked Cai Yuanpei to resume his office as chancellor of Beijing University.[143] It was, if anything, on Cai's side, rather than against him.

The *Public Voice* was strechting and manipulating facts, but it was not completely fabricating them out of thin air. Cai Yuanpei did appear to be ill. In his diary, he wrote about a "stomach ailment," from which he was suffering, although he did not write about a neurosis.[144] His resignation could indeed be interpreted as "shouldering the blame" for the students' actions. But in this reading, it would have made very little sense to see May Fourth as yet another attack on the "New Faction" and to regard debating "New Faction"-style ideas as a way to express political discontent, as the teacher Jing Guan had done. Again, through the lens of this interpretation of the events of 1919, the "New Faction" and May Fourth did not appear to be connected.

---

139 "Qing kan Beijing xuejie sixiang chao bianqian zhi jinzhuang," 3, 6.
140 "Cai Zimin zhen huan shenjingbing ye" (Does Cai Zimin Really Suffer from Neurosis?), *Gongyanbao* (Public Voice), June 26, 1919, 3, Beijing.
141 "Beijing xuejie da fengchao xuzhi" (Record of the Great Student Protests in Beijing, Continued), *Gongyanbao* (Public Voice), May 6, 1919, 907 edition, 2, Beijing.
142 On Cai losing his influence over the students: "Cai Zimin zai Hang zhi tanhua" (Talks with Cai Zimin in Hangzhou), *Gongyanbao* (Public Voice), June 17, 1919, 6, Beijing. On the students "transgressing the usual boundaries": "Cai Yuanpei zhi lai dian yu xuejie fengchao" (Telegram from Cai Yuanpei and the Student Protests), *Gongyanbao* (Public Voice), May 21, 1919, 6, Beijing.
143 "Cai Zimin zhen huan shenjingbing ye," 3.
144 Cai, *Cai Yuanpei riji*, 1:257.

Conclusion

Between the beginning of 1919 and the first few weeks after May Fourth, thick layers of interpretation were piled upon events, which structured, patterned and, most importantly, connected them. This layering was crucial to the making of the matrix of reference points that would soon be attached to the buzzword New Culture Movement, because it produced an association of May Fourth with Beijing University's *baihua* advocates. This presaged the shift in marketing ideals, which eventually effected the reweighting of agendas in the second half of 1919 (this is the topic of chapter 3).

The combination of these layers of interpretation was something that took contemporaries by surprise, as Huang Yanpei's initial annoyance and Yan Xishan's continued confusion show. The reason was not that anything out of the ordinary happened. On the contrary, 1919 was full of predictable events and instantiations of longstanding habits and structures. Resentment against imperialism had a long history, the Shandong deal at Versailles had been foreseeable for several months[145] and similar student protests had happened only a year before.[146] There was the long-held Chinese belief that there were factions, political and academic ones. There was the equally longstanding view that politics and academia were somehow related, a notion that went back to the days of the civil service examinations. Warlords had also been loathed for several years. What was new, following Fabio Lanza, was the idea of students as a "political category."[147] But the conceptualization of scholars in the broadest sense as people involved in political protest, also in the broadest sense, had a long history.[148]

The reason for contemporaries' astonishment lay in the unexpected way in which these long-term habits were combined. Sahlins has called this the "structure of the conjuncture,"[149] by which he meant that, when various structures coincide, this can produce "contingency" and "change."[150] This boils down to more than mere unpredictability. This "structure of the conjuncture" of May Fourth shows that the history of Chinese culture could easily have turned out differently.

---

145 "Shandong wenti Zhong-Ri huanwen zhi pilu," 6; [], "Shandong wenti zhi Beijing xiaoxi," 6, 6.
146 Chen, "The May Fourth Movement and Provincial Warlords," 140.
147 Lanza, *Behind the Gate*, 16.
148 Peter Ditmanson, "The Early Ming National University and Xu Cunren," in *Long Live the Emperor! Uses of the Ming Founder across Six Centuries of East Asian History*, ed. Sarah Schneewind (Minneapolis: Society of Ming Studies, 2008), 42.
149 Sahlins, "Introduction," 192.
150 Erickson and Murphy, *Readings for a History of Anthropological Theory*, 626.

Interpretations of reality could have been pressed into a different network of associations, and the buzzword New Culture Movement (or maybe even a different buzzword) would have had different reference points attached to it, with the result that different sets of the existing, competing agendas would have become "hegemonic."[151] (For the mechanisms of the marketing, see chapter 3.)

This "structure of the conjuncture" also says something about agency (in the sense of the "who did what") in the making of the cultural transformation of 1919.[152] On the one hand, a lot of people were involved in it: the academics who debated, the intellectuals who competed with their agendas, the politicians with the bad reputation, the students who protested, the newspapers who restructured reality and so forth. On the other hand, nobody really "made" the change, because the way in which these patternings of reality were combined was not orchestrated by any one group or individual. It was, in other words, made by both many and no one.

How all this then transformed Chinese culture, will be the topic of chapter 3.

---

[151] Cheek, "The Names of Rectification," 6.
[152] "Structure of the conjuncture": Sahlins, "Introduction," 192.

3 Late 1919 – Marketing with the "New Culture Movement"

The New Culture Movement calls upon us to write in Literary Chinese, said the scholar Liu Boming in the summer of 1920. If students started to get used to *baihua*, he expounded, there was no way they would ever return to learning the far more difficult Literary Chinese. He then went on to explain that, contrary to what some had claimed, there was no real "workers' question," because China had not even developed capitalism. Communism, the implication read, was therefore not necessary in China. In the name of the New Culture Movement, China should also refrain from blindly copying the ideas of the West, such as – this time he said it explicitly – communism, of the Marxist variety and otherwise. This would lead to disaster. Finally, he concluded, engaging in the New Culture Movement meant preserving the "old culture," because "the new culture emerges from the old culture. If there is no old culture, then there cannot be a new culture." It was therefore impossible to create a new culture by "overturning" the old culture. This sounded strikingly similar to the sort of evolutionary narrative put forward by the people who had been classified as the "Old Faction" in the months before May Fourth (see chapter 1). "Oh dear! Is this not the view of the hypocrites' faction?" exclaimed the journalist who reported on this speech in the *Republic Daily* supplement *Enlightenment* (*Juewu*).[1]

Liu Boming had indeed managed to call "New Culture Movement" the exact opposite of what we a hundred years later (and clearly the journalist in 1920 too) would call the "New Culture Movement." But Liu was not the only one to put forward ideas that are counterintuitive to our notion of the New Culture Movement today. The reason, as I argue, was that the expression "New Culture Movement" functioned as a buzzword, which intellectuals deployed to market the competing agendas that had already existed previously: the National Language, popular education, women's rights, Literary Chinese, anarchism, communism and even Christianity and Taiwanese independence from Japanese colonial rule.

The New Culture Movement was, as shown in chapter 1, by no means the first buzzword that had ever been used. But judging from the obsessiveness with which intellectuals deployed it after mid-1919, it became the most influential or "hegemonic"[2] buzzword within a circle of intellectuals involved in the humanities and education. (For details on this circle, see chapter 4.) In order to gain prestige and acceptance for their agendas, intellectuals now sought to "identify" their

---
1 Xi, "Duiyu 'Liu Boming jun yanjiang xin wenhua yundong zhi yiyi ji biyao' de piping," 4.
2 Cheek, "The Names of Rectification," 6.

agendas with this buzzword. This was designed to move their agendas towards the "legitimate core" of the community, to speak in terms of Wasserstrom's and Cheek's model.³

This changed Chinese culture, because the introduction of this new buzzword New Culture Movement entailed a shift in marketing ideals, as right from the beginning the term came with a new network of associations, a new matrix of marketing reference points: the notion that New Culture was connected to May Fourth and, thanks to the rumors spread in newspapers (chapter 2), that May Fourth was connected to people like Hu Shi and Chen Duxiu, as well as to a vocabulary traced back to them (*baihua* and so forth). Considering the low prestige the *baihua* advocates had suffered only a few months earlier, this constituted a shift in ideals of persuasiveness. Some agendas fared better under the new paradigm (e. g. those advocating a National Language, communism or women's rights) than others (e. g. Liu Boming and his Literary Chinese, and also Christianity).

The invention of the New Culture Movement

The expression "New Culture Movement" appears to have been coined in the summer of 1919. Who invented it and when is somewhat unclear.⁴ What is known is that it was used in print from the late summer of 1919 onwards in a variety of journals and newspapers. One of its earliest mentions was on August 31 in the GMD-funded Shanghai magazine *Weekly Review* (*Xingqi pinglun*).⁵ (This magazine is not to be confused with the Beijing University journal *Weekly Critic*, whose Chinese name was *Meizhou pinglun*.) The New Culture Movement was debated by the Jiangsu Educational Association in October of 1919, in a provincial school journal and in the *Shanghai News* in November and by the missionary journal *Chinese Christian Advocate* in December 1919.⁶ Most of these publications have since then

---

3 In modification of Cheek, "The Names of Rectification," 26. As outlined in the Introduction, the expression used by Wasserstrom and Cheek is "the legitimating core."
4 Ouyang Junxi claims that it was invented by the Guomindang. Ouyang Junxi, "Guomindang yu xin wenhua yundong: yi 'Xingqi pinglun,' 'Jianshe' wei zhongxin" (The Nationalist Party and the New Culture Movement: With a Focus on *Weekly Review* and *Construction*), *Nanjing daxue xuebao* (Journal of Nanjing University), no. 1 (2009): 73. But if this was the case, it would be quite surprising that the Guomindang never claimed it for itself.
5 Ibid.; Xian Jin, "Xin wenhua yundong de wuqi" (The Weapons of the New Culture Movement), *Xingqi pinglun* (Weekly Review), August 31, 1919, 13 edition, 4, Shanghai.
6 Jiangsu sheng jiaoyuhui, "Kaihui jilu" (Meeting Minutes), *Jiangsu sheng jiaoyuhui yuebao* (Jiangsu Educational Association Monthly Report), October 1919, 45; Jiangsu sheng jiaoyuhui, "Zhi zhongdeng yishang ge xuexiao tongzhi dingqi juxing yanshuo jingjinhui shu" (Letter to All

not been considered the core of the New Culture Movement. However, *New Youth* – the journal now regarded as the New Culture magazine par excellence – only dedicated an article to the expression in April 1920. This was almost eight months after the expression's first known appearance.[7]

Surprisingly, there is no text that introduces the expression and claims authorship of it. In this, it resembles the term "May Fourth Movement," which began appearing in the same sudden and unexplained way a couple of weeks after the May Fourth demonstrations had started.[8] The "New Culture Movement" was immediately used as if it was already well-known to the intended reader, and authors only tried to define it. I therefore speculate that it was originally invented orally in one of the many study and discussion groups that existed at the time, and that it was already circulating in those groups, before making it into print.

As soon as it appeared in print, a specific matrix of rhetoric developed around it. This matrix included associations with people, practices, formats and a vocabulary. The New Culture Movement, it was said, was connected to May Fourth. In the words of the Jiangsu Educational Association, it "continued the May Fourth Movement."[9] The precise debates that would hint at why contemporaries suddenly felt the need to coin the new expression have been lost. I can only speculate that it might have been because they wanted to put a label on the nexus between May Fourth and the culture traced back to Beijing University's *baihua* advocates. This nexus, as outlined in chapter 2, existed because newspaper reports had made May Fourth something cultural. The example (also from chapter 2) of the teacher Jing Guan, who considered marching on the streets and discussing ideas in the purported tradition of Hu Shi and Chen Duxiu to be equivalent, has shown this.[10] Incidentally the *baihua* advocates had by then already left Beijing University

---

[Educational Institutions] from Middle-School Level and Above, Informing Them That a Date Has Been Chosen to Conduct the Lecture Competition), *Jiangsu sheng jiaoyuhui yuebao* (Jiangsu Educational Association Monthly Report), October 1919, 18–21; Zhu Daihen, "Ni yu tongxiang mou jun taolun xin wenhua yundong shixing fangfa shu" (Pretending to Discuss Ways to Implement the New Culture Movement with Someone from My Native Village), *Jiangsu shengli di-er nüzi shifan xuexiao xiaoyouhui huikan* (Alumnae of the Second Women's Normal School of Jiangsu Province), no. 9 (November 1919): 36–38; "Yanshuo jingjinhui yanti zhi jieshi" (Explanation of the Topic of the Lecture Competition), *Shenbao* (Shanghai News), November 2, 1919, 10; "Xin wenhua yundong zhi jieshi" (Explanation of the New Culture Movement), *Xinghua* (Chinese Christian Advocate) 16, no. 44 (November 12, 1919): 28–29.
7 Ouyang, "Guomindang yu xin wenhua yundong," 73; Chen Duxiu, "Xin wenhua yundong shi shenme?" (What Is the New Culture Movement?), *Xin qingnian* (New Youth) 7, no. 5 (April 1920): 1–6.
8 "Jing xuejie zhi zuijin xiaoxi," 7.
9 Jiangsu sheng jiaoyuhui, "Zhi zhongdeng yishang ge xuexiao tongzhi dingqi juxing yanshuo jingjinhui shu," 25.
10 Jing, "Gao xin wenhua yundong de tongzhi," 31–32.

(Chen Duxiu), were just leaving (as in the case of students like Fu Sinian, who were graduating) and had ceased to see themselves as a group (which has been read as the post-May Fourth split between those with communist and those with more academic leanings).[11]

Nevertheless, the New Culture Movement was claimed to have been inspired by this group of "masters," of a "center" or of "central figures,"[12] who were frequently referenced, either with praise or criticism, when talking about the New Culture Movement.[13] To borrow Michel Hockx's words, the discourse around the New Culture Movement was "structure[d]" by being given "cult heroes."[14] As shown in chapter 2, Hu Shi and Chen Duxiu became stars, with students crowding their ways into their classrooms and newspapers gossiping about them.[15] They had, in other words, not only made their way into the "legitimate core."[16] They had become this "core."

In addition to the political event May Fourth and the star personnel, practices also figured into associations with the New Culture Movement. There was a widespread notion that engaging in the New Culture Movement meant producing books or journals, which was the reason why new journals "sprang up like spring bamboo after the rain" after May Fourth.[17] Founding journals and producing books had been a longstanding practice before that, of course. But now, more people engaged in it (what Fabio Lanza calls the "explosion of publications"),[18]

---

11 Li, *Fu Sinian xueshu sixiang pingzhuan*, 18.
12 "Masters": Miao, "Suowei 'xin wenhua yundong' de chachao yu pochan," 3–4, 2. "Center": Ye, "Ji Beijing daxue shiye shi (xu)." "Central figures": Jing, "Gao xin wenhua yundong de tongzhi," 31.
13 Zung, "Contemporary Drama of China," 3; Nai Yi Chen, "China Now and England in the 19th Century" (Student essay, Beijing, June 12, 1922), 3, Container 216, Lewis Nathaniel Chase Papers, Manuscript Division, Library of Congress, Washington, D.C., Beijing; Miao, "Suowei 'xin wenhua yundong' de chachao yu pochan," 3–4, 3; de Vargas, "Some Elements in the Chinese Renaissance (Manuscript)," 14; Tang Xiu, "Du Chen Duxiu de 'Xin wenhua yundong shi shenme?'" (Reading Chen Duxiu's "What Is the New Culture Movement?"), *Meishu* (Art [Shanghai]) 2, no. 2 (1920): 105–8; Chen Qitian, "Shenme shi xin wenhua de jingshen" (What Is the Spirit of New Culture), *Shaonian zhongguo* (Young China) 2, no. 2 (August 15, 1920): 2.
14 Lit. "cult hero," Hockx, "Playing the Field," 64–65.
15 Jing, "Dumen xuejie xiaoxi," 6; "Xijujia huanyan Hu Shizhi," 13; "Hu Shi zuori di Hu," 11; "Chengzhong xiao zhi xin xun," 17; "Chen Duxiu guo Hu zhi tanpian," 14; "Chen Duxiu zai E yanjiang zhi jingguo," 14.
16 In modification of Cheek, "The Names of Rectification," 26. Originally "legitimating core."
17 Zhou Lingsun, "Xin wenhua yundong he meiyu" (The New Culture Movement and Aesthetic Education), *Meiyu* (Arts Education), no. 3 (June 1920): 1; Ye, "Ji Beijing daxue shiye shi (xu)." For the expression, "springing up like spring bamboo after the rain," see Wang, *Huiyi Yadong tushuguan*, 38.
18 Lanza, "Of Chronology, Failure, and Fidelity," 57.

and it was also redefined by the founders of the spring-bamboo journals as being part of the "New Culture Movement."

One manifestation of this was that they tried hard to make their magazines resemble *New Youth* and *New Tide*. This became evident in the titles they chose. Beijing University student Miao Jinyuan (?-1943) mocked that, as soon as "there was a 'New Tide Society' in Beijing, Shanghai also launches one in imitation."[19] He could have said the same about Zhejiang, where a *Zhejiang New Tide* (*Zhejiang xinchao*) had been founded, or about Sichuan (*Sichuan Educational New Tide, Sichuan jiaoyu xinchao*, launched in 1920), Jiangsu (*Novels New Tide, Xiaoshuo xinchao*, launched in 1921) or Fujian (*Xiehe University New Tide, Xieda xinchao*, launched in 1927).[20] Journals with "youth" or "new youth" in the title were created too. In Taiwan, there was the *Taiwan Youth* (*Taiwan qingnian*, launched in 1920), and in Hankou a *Buddhicise the New Youth* (*Fohua xin qingnian*) was founded in 1923.[21]

Many of the spring-bamboo journals journals not only looked like *New Youth* and *New Tide* on the cover, but also on their pages inside. For example, they usually used new-style punctuation. Punctuation as such was not a hallmark of New Culture. Forms of punctuation had been used for private purposes for centuries, and even *National Heritage* punctuated many of its articles, using the symbol "。" to mark the end of sentences and reading pauses.[22] *New Youth* had used this type of punctuation in its early years too.[23] But soon, it had switched to new-style punctuation marks that were close to a Western punctuation system. In 1916, Hu Shi, for example, had promoted the now familiar "。", "、", "；", "：", "？", "！", "（）", """", "《》", "……" and "——."[24]

---

19 Miao, "Suowei 'xin wenhua yundong' de chachao yu pochan," 3–4, 2.
20 On the *Zhejiang New Tide*, see Yeh, *Provincial Passages*, 135. For the other journals, see *Sichuan jiaoyu xinchao* (Sichuan Educational New Tide) (Sichuan, 1920); Chen Tiesheng and Chen Gongzhe, *Xiaoshuo xinchao* (Novel New Tide) (Nanjing, 1921); Sili Fujian Xiehe daxue xueshenghui xuanchuanbu, *Xieda xinchao* (Xiehe University New Tide) (Fuzhou, 1927).
21 Taiwan qingnian zazhishe, *Taiwan qingnian* (Taiwan Youth) (Tokyo, 1920); Erik J. Hammerstrom, "Buddhists Discuss Science in Modern China (1895–1949)" (PhD, Indiana University, 2010), 220.
22 On the history of punctuation marks, see Yuan Hui, *Hanyu biaodian fuhao liubianshi* (A History of the Development of Chinese Punctuation Marks) (Wuhan: Hubei jiaoyu chubanshe, 2002), 5.
23 Chen Duxiu, "Jinri zhi jiaoyu fangzhen" (Contemporary Guiding Principles in Education), *Qingnian zazhi* (Youth Magazine) 1, no. 2 (October 15, 1915): 113–18.
24 Yuan, *Hanyu biaodian fuhao liubianshi*, 11; Yuan Hui, "Jiushi biaodian fuhao" (Old-Style Punctuation Marks), *Biaodian fuhao cidian* (A Dictionary of Punctuation Marks) (Shanghai: Shanghai chubanshe, 2000), Shanghai.

This sort of punctuation projected trendiness, and the *New Youth* circle started claiming it as its signature layout. When Qian Xuantong invented the fictional icon of conservatism Wang Jingxuan in 1919 (see chapter 1), he let him complain about the peculiar symbols that had replaced the "circle dot" ("。"). By 1919, *New Youth* deployed this system, in addition to a variety of options to underline names, book titles and so on. *New Tide* followed suit, and so did some of the newly founded spring-bamboo journals after mid-1919.[25]

A certain vocabulary, too, was associated with the New Culture Movement, but this vocabulary was not clearly defined. It included words like "*baihua*," "superstition," "free love," "enlightenment," "science" and "new." Beijing University's "New Faction" had been among those who had used this vocabulary previously. But they had by no means been the only ones to do so. Phrasing ideas in this vocabulary nevertheless became an important hallmark of the New Culture discourse. The prevalence of this practice was shown not least by criticism of it, expressed by people who wondered if "merely using a few words like 'universal love,' 'self-determination,' 'workers,' 'holy' and so forth, and expounding on them everywhere, [really] already counts as the New Culture Movement."[26]

"Movement"

May Fourth, new publications, the Hu-Chen circle and a certain vocabulary were not the only features associated with the New Culture Movement. From the time of its invention, there were at least two more. These were the elements that made up its name: the words "movement" (*yundong*) and "New Culture" (*xin wenhua*).

When exploring the meaning of expressions, it is possible to trace their definitions or a "range of meanings."[27] But it is also possible to ask what they projected and communicated at a given time. According to Rudolf Wagner and Tani Barlow, this is the more fruitful approach when discussing "movement" and "culture" in China's Republic.[28] Both "movement" and "New Culture" were, I argue, suitable

---

25 *New Youth*: Chen Daqi, "Gonghe xinxi" (Happy New Year), *Xin qingnian* (New Youth) 6, no. 1 (January 15, 1919): 1–5. *New Tide*: Tan Mingqian, "Laodong wenti zhi jiejue" (The Solution of the Workers' Question), *Xinchao* (New Tide) 1, no. 4 (April 1, 1919): 603–10. Spring-bamboo journals: "Xin Funü xuanyan" (Manifesto of *New Woman*), *Xin funü* (New Woman) 1, no. 1 (reprint) (October 10, 1920): 1; Wang Jingfang, "Fakanci" (Manifesto), *Xin qun* (Social Reconstruction), no. 1 (November 1919): 1–7.
26 Ye, "Ji Beijing daxue shiye shi (xu)."
27 Koselleck, *Keywords*, 15.
28 Wagner, "The Canonization of May Fourth," 70; Tani E Barlow, "Zhishifenzi [Chinese Intellectuals] and Power," *Dialectical Anthropology* 16, no. 3–4 (1991): 211.

for adding to the glamour, power and prestige of the New Culture Movement as a buzzword.

"*Yundong*" as such could mean many different things in 1919. Chen Duxiu defined it in 1916 as something signifying a radical break with the past, anti-imperialism, independence and global importance.[29] In practice, its meaning was much broader. In newspapers and journals, it could denote anything from physical movement to any kinds of "activities" and mostly it simply meant "sports."[30] This range of meanings was quite constant over the decades, but at certain points in time usages of "*yundong*" temporarily zoomed in on specific connotation, and broadened out again afterwards. The word did not appear to have been very popular in the 19th century, when it mostly denoted physical movement, for example that of the planet Earth[31] or that of an armada.[32] In the 1900s, its fashionability increased, as did the range of things it meant, including "lobbying/persuading,"[33] "sports,"[34] "activities"[35] and also activities that were close to

---

29 Wagner, "The Canonization of May Fourth," 75–79.
30 "Physical movement": Koo Z. C. and Chang S. L., "This 'Chest Protector' Newly Invented in America ...," *Yingyu zhoubao* (English Language Weekly), no. 154 (1918): 1172. "Activities": "Shijie tang shi yu Riben canxun" (The Global Sugar Market and the Destruction of Japanese Silkworms), *Shenbao* (Shanghai News), April 29, 1919, 6, Shanghai. "sports": "Yuandong yundonghui ji Beibu yundonghui gaiqi" (Changes in the Dates of the Far Eastern Sports Festival and the Northern Sports Festival), *Beijing gaodeng shifan xuexiao zhoubao* (Beijing Higher Normal School Weekly), no. 49 (1918): 11; Malong Maiyuke, "Nüzi fayu shidai zhi yundong" (Exercises for Women during Puberty), trans. Diao Jun, *Funü zazhi* (Ladies' Magazine), no. 1 (January 5, 1915): 16.
31 "Tianwen yi zhi er ke: lun diqiu yundong" (Easy Knowledge about the Heavenly Bodies, Lesson Two: Discussing the Movement of the Earth), *Xiaohai yuebao* (Child Monthly), no. 14 (1876): 3.
32 Hashimoto Kaikan, "Deguo jiandui yundong" (The Movements of the German Armada), *Dong ye bao* (Eastern Business), no. 5 (1898): 7.
33 "Shuo yundong" (Talking about "Movement"), *Shaoxing baihuabao* (Shaoxing Plain-Language News), no. 82 (190?): 1; "Meiren you lai yundong zhengfu" (The Americans Again Lobby the Government), *Di-yi Jin huabao* (The First Shanxi Dialect Newspaper), no. 3 (1905): 39.
34 A sports festival: "Sunduan kai yundonghui" (Sunduan Starts a Sports Festival), *Shaoxing baihuabao* (Shaoxing Plain-Language News), no. 92 (1900): 2; "Juxing yundonghui" (Conducting a Sports Festival), *Dalubao* (Mainland News), no. 5 (1904): 72–73; "Lianhe yundong" (Joint Sports), *Sichuan guanbao* (Sichuan Official News), no. 29 (1905): 36. A song for a sports festival: "Hangzhou jiaoyuhui tiyu jiangxisuo yundonghui ge" (The Sports Festival Song of the Sports Institute of the Hangzhou Educational Association), *Hangzhou baihua bao* (Hangzhou Plain-Language News) 3, no. 16 (1900): 2. Sports: Malong, "Nüzi fayu shidai zhi yundong."
35 "Shanxi Gelaohui zhi yundong" (The Movements of the Elder Brother Society in Shaanxi), *Lu jiang bao* (Lu River News), no. 87 (1904); "Shanxi geming dang zhi yundong" (The Movements of the Shaanxi Revolutionary Party), *Lu jiang bao* (Lu River News), no. 70 (1904).

"political movements."[36] This continued throughout the 1910s, with the meaning of "political/social movement" becoming consolidated.[37]

In 1919, it focused on very specific meanings several times, as an analysis of its usages in the *Shanghai News* indicates. In March and April it often described the Korean Independence Movement, also known as the March First Movement.[38] This was a series of political protests in Korea against Japanese colonial rule and for Korean self-determination. Even though Japan suppressed the protests, the ensuing years saw a liberalization of colonial administration in Korea, which was in part caused by the March First Movement and in part by general trends towards liberalization in Japan as part of the Taishô Democracy.[39] "*Yundong*" thus took on associations of what Erez Manela has called the "Wilsonian moment":[40] it pointed to independence, anti-imperialism and global significance, just like Chen Duxiu had claimed in his theoretical discussion a few years before.

---

36 "Mimi zhi yundong" (Secret Movements), *Dalu (Shanghai 1902)* (Mainland [Shanghai 1902]) 2, no. 8 (1904): 11–12.
37 Lobby: "Yingguo yundong xila jiaru zhanzheng" (Britain Lobbies Greece to Join the War), *Dongfang zazhi* (Eastern Miscellany) 12, no. 12 (1915): 9; "Ao'guo yundong jiaru Zhongguo zhaizhu" (Austria Lobbies to Join China's Creditors), *Xiehebao* (Mutual Understanding) 2, no. 30 (1912): 25. Political movement: "Sailuonijia shimin zhi shiwei yundong" (The Demonstration Movement of Thessaloniki's Citizens), *Dongfang zazhi* (Eastern Miscellany) 12, no. 4 (1915): 11; "Annan duli yundong (xu di-san hao)" (Vietnam's Independence Movement (Continued from the Third Issue)), *Shishi huibao* (Current Affairs), no. 6 (1914): 5–8; "Dizhi yundong yu tiyu yundong" (The Monarchy Movement and the Exercise Movement), *Jiaoyu zhoubao (Hangzhou)* (Education Weekly [Hangzhou]), no. 130 (1916): 28–29; "Mingri huanghua zhi dizhi yundong ji" (A Record of the Obsolete Monarchy Movement), *Xuesheng* (Student) 3, no. 9 (1916): 1–4; "Eguo xuesheng zhi shiwei yundong" (The Protest Movement of Russian Students), *Dongfang zazhi* (Eastern Miscellany) 8, no. 12 (1912): 13. Sports: "Nanfang zhi guoqingri (Guangdong nan-nü xuesheng da yundonghui)" (The National Holiday in the South [Great Sports Festival of Male and Female Students from Guangdong]), *Zhenxiang huabao* (Truth Pictorial) 1, no. 10 (1912): 14; "Yundonghui jishi" (Record of the Sports Festival), *Jiangsu shengli di-er shifan xuexiao xiaoyouhui zazhi* (Alumni of the Second Jiangsu Provincial Normal School), no. 5 (1912): 39–42; "Yuandong yundonghui ji Beibu yundonghui gaiqi."
38 "Chaoxian duli yundong" (The Korean Independence Movement), *Shenbao* (Shanghai News), March 12, 1919, 6–7, Shanghai; "Mei bao zhi Hanren yundong duli shuo" (American Newspapers on Koreans' Lobbying for Independence), *Shenbao* (Shanghai News), March 13, 1919, 6, Shanghai; "Hancheng duli yundong zhi fengqi" (The Rise of the Independence Movement in Seoul), *Shenbao* (Shanghai News), April 6, 1919, 6, Shanghai; "Hanmin duli yundong zhi waixun" (External News on the Korean Independence Movement), *Shenbao* (Shanghai News), April 10, 1919, 6, Shanghai.
39 Michael J. Seth, *A History of Korea: From Antiquity to the Present* (Lanham, Md.: Rowman & Littlefield, 2010), 226–29.
40 Manela, *The Wilsonian Moment*.

During May 1919, it started being used in the combination "May Fourth Movement."[41] But most of the times, it still meant "sports."[42] At around the time when the expression "New Culture Movement" must have been invented, however, there was a change. In July, *Shanghai News* headlines used *"yundong"* almost exclusively to refer to May Fourth.[43] In other words, *"yundong"* had moved on from the Korean March First to denote the Chinese version of the "Wilsonian moment." By attaching the label "movement" to "New Culture," its inventors thus firmly inscribed the connection with May Fourth and the glamour of its global contexts into the expression. This also indicates why the marketing intellectuals had to insist that it was a "movement" and could not say that it was being used as a buzzword: it needed the glamour of the "movement" in order to function as a buzzword. The focus in the meaning of *"yundong,"* incidentally, was not a permanent shift. In October, "sports" and "May Fourth" held each other the balance again,[44]

---

41 "Xuesheng shiwei yundong zhi waiping" (External Comments on the Students' Protest Movement), *Shenbao* (Shanghai News), May 10, 1919, 7; "Jing xuejie zhi zuijin xiaoxi," 7.
42 "Yuandong yundong yusai yuan jinri chufa" (The Participants in the Far Eastern Sports [Festival] Depart Today), *Shenbao* (Shanghai News), May 4, 1919, 10; "Huansong Yuandong yundonghui yusaiyuan" (Seeing off the Participants in the Far Eastern Sports Festival), *Shenbao* (Shanghai News), May 4, 1919, 10; "Gaoxing zhen jiang kai xiaoxue lianhe yundonghui" (Gaoxing Will Hold a Joint Primary-School Sports Festival), *Shenbao* (Shanghai News), May 12, 1919, 11; "Qingnianhui zhongxue yudonghui yuji" (Announcement of a Sports Festival of the Youth Association Middle School), *Shenbao* (Shanghai News), May 14, 1919, 11; "Pudong ge xiao zhi lianhe yundonghui" (The Joint Sports Festival of All Pudong Schools), *Shenbao* (Shanghai News), May 25, 1919, 12.
43 "Xuesheng aiguo yundong chengji zhi wailun" (External Discussions of the Achievements of the Students' Patriotic Movement), *Shenbao* (Shanghai News), July 1, 1919, 6, Shanghai; "Huaqiao aiguo yundong zhi jinxun" (Recent News on the Patriotic Movement of Chinese Abroad), *Shenbao* (Shanghai News), July 7, 1919, 10, Shanghai; "Qian Dian zhi aiguo yundong" (Guizhou's and Yunnan's Patriotic Movements), *Shenbao* (Shanghai News), July 14, 1919, 6–7, Shanghai; "Gaodeng xiaoxue lianhe yundong zhi jijiang" (Prizes Awarded at the Joint Sports [Festival] of the Upper Primary Schools), *Shenbao* (Shanghai News), July 16, 1919, 10.
44 May Fourth: "Yue xuesheng shifang hou zhi da yundong" (The Great Movement after the Release of the Cantonese Students), *Shenbao* (Shanghai News), October 3, 1919, 7; "Duwei boshi lun Zhongguo xuesheng zhi aiguo yundong" (Doctor Dewey Discusses the Patriotic Movement of the Chinese Students), *Shenbao* (Shanghai News), October 18, 1919, 6. Sports: "Guomin xuexiao lianhe yundonghui xiansheng" (First Signs of the Joint Sports Festival of the Citizens' School), *Shenbao* (Shanghai News), October 14, 1919, 10; "Shengli di-yi shangxiao yundonghui ji" (Record of the Sports Festival of the First Provincial Business School), *Shenbao* (Shanghai News), October 10, 1919, 10; "Xian'gao xiaoxuexiao jiang kai yundonghui" (Xian'gao Primary School Will Hold a Sports Festival), *Shenbao* (Shanghai News), October 17, 1919, 10. A non-May Fourth political movement: "Laodongjie zhi jiaxin yundong" (The Pay-Rise Movement of the Workers' World), *Shenbao* (Shanghai News), October 17, 1919, 11.

and in December 1919, *"yundong"* referred to all sorts of non-May Fourth social and political movements.[45]

"New Culture"

"New Culture" projected something similarly powerful. A search for definitions of "New Culture" would lead us to the 19th century, when the word *"bunka"* was coined in Japanese to find an equivalent to the Western word "culture" ("culture" in English, "culture" in French, "Kultur" in German and so on). In the Chinese pronunciation *"wenhua,"* it made its way to China in the 1860 and 1870s.[46]

As *"wenhua"* or *"bunka"* was designed to render the Western word "culture," its definition was in many ways very similar to the Western one at the time. Although the various European-language forms of "culture" had a rich history, in the 19th and early 20th centuries their definitions, according to Raymond Williams, settled to mean "a particular way of life, whether of a people, a period, a group, or humanity in general." By "particular way of life," Williams means notions of, for example, Chinese culture versus Western culture, French culture versus British culture. "Culture" could also mean "the works and practices of intellectual and especially artistic activity ... culture is music, literature, painting and sculpture, theatre and film."[47] Lydia Liu and Tani Barlow identify similar connotations in the Chinese *"wenhua"* at the time.[48] The combination "New Culture" had appeared very occasionally before 1919. In 1918, for example, the *Guangzhou English-Language Times* (*Guangzhou Yingwen shibao*) expressed its hope that China would gradually move towards a "new culture," as soon as it stopped being held back by the "militarism" of the warlords.[49]

---

[45] Political movements: "Mangtong xuexiao dingqi youyi yundong" (The Blind Children's School Has Scheduled a Recreation Movement), *Shenbao* (Shanghai News), December 11, 1919, 10; "Xi bao ji feichu zaohun zhi yundong" (Western Newspapers Chronicle the Movement to Abolish Early Marriages), *Shenbao* (Shanghai News), December 5, 1919, 6. Sports: "Gao xiaoxuexiao fendeng yundonghui zhi yubei" (Preparations for the Graded Sports Festival of Higher Primary Schools), *Shenbao* (Shanghai News), December 6, 1919, 11.
[46] Liu, *Translingual Practice*, 33–34.
[47] Raymond Williams, *Keywords: A Vocabulary of Culture and Society*, Revised edition (New York: Oxford University Press, 1976), 90.
[48] Barlow, "Zhishifenzi [Chinese Intellectuals] and Power," 211; Liu, *Translingual Practice*, 240.
[49] The *Shanghai News* cited the *Guangzhou English-Language Times* in "Waibao lun nan-bei jianghe yaodian" (Foreign Newspapers Discuss Crucial Points about the Peace Talks between South and North), *Shenbao* (Shanghai News), December 17, 1918, 6, Shanghai.

But as with "movement," "culture" projected something even more powerful. "*Wenhua*" in fact was, according to Tani Barlow, a way to refer to the purview of intellectuals. "*Wenhua*" was the sphere of reality that they dealt with, "*wenhua*" was what they did. They were the "knowers of *wenhua*," the "possessors of knowledge about literature and civilization." Consequently, Barlow says, intellectuals were in constant competition about who could dominate this sphere.[50] This then shows why the expression "New Culture" was so powerful. When intellectuals called their agendas the "New Culture," they put themselves in charge of the whole new version of the purview of intellectuals. Combined with the label "movement," the expression "New Culture Movement" had, already through the words it was made up of, the potential to be an extremely convincing, "authoritative"[51] buzzword.

Case studies

Literary Chinese as the New Culture Movement

Contemporaries recognized this potential, and a huge variety of people and groups tried to identify their agendas as the New Culture Movement to move it to the "legitimate core" of the field.[52] That is, they used it to sell many and mutually contradictory competing agendas in late 1919 and the early 1920s. That it was used as a buzzword designed to do something, rather than as the description of something that was already happening, becomes most evident from the example of the people who deployed it to promote programs that did not make it into the permanent New Culture discourse. These cases break with our notions of what New Culture should be. One of these less successful people was Liu Boming, whom I have cited in the opening passage of this chapter and who promoted ideas as the New Culture Movement that would later on be regarded as the very antithesis of New Culture. Among these ideas was, as mentioned above, advocacy of Literary Chinese.

For Liu Boming, calling his ideas New Culture Movement must have appeared as the only way to convince the particular audience he was addressing. These were people who had come to listen to a lecture by John Dewey (1859–1952), Hu Shi's former PhD supervisor. Dewey was visiting China from 1919 to 1921. Dewey's speeches all followed similar patterns: He did not appear at these lectures alone,

---

50 Barlow, "Zhishifenzi [Chinese Intellectuals] and Power," 211.
51 Geertz, *The Interpretation of Cultures*, 218.
52 In modification of Cheek, "The Names of Rectification," 26. Originally "legitimating core."

but was accompanied by several Chinese colleagues. On occasion, Liu Boming was among them. As Dewey did not speak Chinese, these colleagues translated his speeches for him. But Dewey's Chinese colleagues were also established scholars in their own right. Liu Boming, for example, had been educated in the United States and was at the time professor for philosophy and vice principal of Nanjing Higher Normal School.[53] Dewey's Chinese colleagues were therefore not resigned to pure translator roles, but they often gave their own co-lectures as part of the event.[54] One such co-lecture was Liu Boming's comments, given in Xuzhou, on the New Culture Movement as a project embracing Literary Chinese and criticizing the introduction of communism.[55] Dewey's speeches were also well-attended by journalists, which is how Liu's co-lecture has been transmitted.

Liu's speech in Xuzhou was not an exception. In a similar setting one month before in Yangzhou he had used a similar strategy to promote his ideals. A *Shanghai News* report shows how Dewey's lectures were filled with an atmosphere of admiration for the New Culture Movement. The co-lecturer who preceded Liu Boming in Yangzhou praised Dewey as a "star of New Culture."[56] When Liu followed with his own speech, it must have been clear to him that the only way he could get through to this audience was to tap into the vocabulary that was often used to discuss the New Culture Movement. Liu consequently took it upon himself to criticize the audience for their belief in New Culture, using the "delegitimizing terms" New Culture rhetoric provided.[57] He suggested that the *Analects* provided the better recipe for a "new intellectual tide" (*xin sichao*), and that anyone who questioned this had clearly misunderstood them.[58] He also called New Culture debaters' blind belief in anything that was written in "new journals" a "superstition."[59] These "new journals," which I have dubbed "spring-bamboo journals," were considered hallmarks of New Culture, and "superstition" was something deemed anti-scientific and therefore to be avoided.

---

[53] Liu's education in the US: Wang Shanzhi, "Liu Boming boshi shishi" (Dr. Liu Boming Dead), *Xinghua* (Chinese Christian Advocate) 20, no. 47 (December 5, 1923): 23. Liu's position at Nanjing Higher Normal School: Xi, "Duiyu 'Liu Boming jun yanjiang xin wenhua yundong zhi yiyi ji biyao' de piping," 4; "Xuzhou" (Xuzhou), *Shenbao* (Shanghai News), June 1, 1920, 7, Shanghai.
[54] "Yangzhou" (Yangzhou), *Shenbao* (Shanghai News), May 22, 1920, 8, Shanghai; Xi, "Duiyu 'Liu Boming jun yanjiang xin wenhua yundong zhi yiyi ji biyao' de piping," 4.
[55] Xi, "Duiyu 'Liu Boming jun yanjiang xin wenhua yundong zhi yiyi ji biyao' de piping," 4.
[56] "Yangzhou," 8.
[57] Cheek, "The Names of Rectification," 27.
[58] Liu Boming, "Xuesheng yingyou de taidu ji jingshen" (The Attitude and Spirit Students Should Have), *Xuesheng* (Students' Magazine) 7, no. 9 (September 5, 1920): 1.
[59] Ibid., 2–3.

Liu Boming's speeches did not always meet with the favor of his audience.[60] But his ideas for the "New Culture Movement" were not as isolated as they seem from our perspective today. Literary Chinese and New Culture, for example, did not appear to be mutually exclusive, and commercial advertising sometimes combined the two. In 1921 the publisher Commercial Press deployed the slogan "the dawn of New Culture" (*xin wenhua zhi shuguang*) to advertise some of its publications. These were books by Hu Shi and Zhou Zuoren (1885–1967), but also by lesser-known individuals at Nanjing Higher Normal School or at Beijing University. The words "dawn of New Culture" appeared in a cone of light emanating from a lighthouse in the midst of a dark world. They were, however, written in Literary Chinese.[61] Liu Boming's definition of the "New Culture Movement" apparently had some viability at the time.

Christianity as the better New Culture Movement

Christianity was another agenda that seems alien to the New Culture Movement from today's perspective, but which was nevertheless promoted as the "better" New Culture Movement in the early 1920s. In later times, New Culture became associated with the rise of Marxism in mainland China, and Marxism is of course skeptical of all religion. New Culture also came to stand for science, and the dichotomies of the 19th and early 20th centuries often suggested a contradiction between science and religion, the latter of which could then be labelled a "superstition." In the early 1920s, the New Culture franchise was somewhat more flexible in its views on religion. Chen Duxiu, for example, wrote in 1920 that there was space for "new religion" in the New Culture Movement. This "new religion" "eliminates the unscientific superstition of strained interpretations [carried forward in] the traditions of the old religions."[62] But even in this tolerant comment, religion could not get rid of the suspicion that it could easily fall into the trap of being or becoming a "superstition."

Both foreign and Chinese Christians in China were therefore worried about this trend. "Many people" (wrongly, in this view) assumed that "Christianity is a superstition," wrote a Christian in 1920.[63] But Christians also admitted freely that

---

60 Xi, "Duiyu 'Liu Boming jun yanjiang xin wenhua yundong zhi yiyi ji biyao' de piping," 4.
61 "Xin wenhua zhi shuguang" (The Dawn of New Culture), *Beida shenghuo* (Life at Beida), December 1921.
62 Chen, "Xin wenhua yundong shi shenme?," April 1920, 3.
63 "Fakan 'Shengming yuekan' xuanyan" (Manifesto for the Publication of *Life*), *Shengming* (Life) 1, no. 1 (June 1, 1920): 1.

they were jealous of the New Culture Movement. Christianity had been around in China for centuries and the New Culture Movement only for a short time. Nevertheless New Culture had already achieved so much more influence than Christianity, another Christian lamented.[64] Some Christian groups therefore decided to employ the escape-forward approach and to piggyback on its success by selling Christianity as the New Culture Movement. Among them was the Apologetic Group (*Zhengdaotuan*) in Beijing, many of whose members were recruited from the staff of Yanjing University and the YMCA.[65] They also founded a journal in June 1920, called *Life* (*Shengming*).[66]

In promoting Christianity as the New Culture Movement, the Apologetic Group pursued a variety of strategies, all of which sought to identify Christianity with aspects of the New Culture Movement's matrix of reference points. Like Liu Boming, they couched their agenda in New Culture vocabulary: For example, they declared their intention of turning Christianity into a "movement." The journal's manifesto announced a "reform movement of Christianity."[67] Xu Baoqian (1892–1944), one of *Life*'s authors, wrote about the launch of a "Beijing student's conversion movement."[68] Christianity also now experienced a "new intellectual tide," he announced.[69] "Theological questions" would be tackled with the "scientific method."[70]

Christianity was also depicted as having the capacity to deal with the crucial questions that were being addressed under the headline of the New Culture Movement. Like the New Culture Movement, Christianity had long been concerned with social reform, and it "really has a 'standard' for social reform," the manifesto of *Life* claimed.[71] Qinghua University theologian Liu Tingfang (1891–1947) went further and argued that Christianity even had the better methods of social reform. The reason was that Christians derived their answers from God himself, and naturally God knew better what to do than humans ever could. In

---

[64] Xu Baoqian, "Jidujiao xin sichao" (The New Intellectual Tide of Christianity), *Shengming* (Life) 1, no. 1 (June 1, 1920): 1.
[65] Arthur Lewis Rosenbaum, *New Perspectives on Yenching University, 1916–1952* (Leiden: Brill, 2012), 237. "Apologetic Group" was the group's own chosen translation.
[66] "Copyright page," *Shengming* (Life) 1, no. 1 (June 1, 1920).
[67] "Fakan 'Shengming yuekan' xuanyan," 2.
[68] Xu Baoqian, "Beijing jidujiao xuexiao shiye lianhehui gaizu shimo" (The Full Story of the Reorganization of the Beijing Christian Union for School Affairs), *Shengming* (Life) 1, no. 1 (June 1, 1920): 1.
[69] Xu, "Jidujiao xin sichao."
[70] "Fakan 'Shengming yuekan' xuanyan," 1.
[71] Ibid.

Liu Tingfang's hands, Christianity thus became the more effective New Culture Movement.[72]

The *Life* manifesto also expressed the Apologetic Group's intention to imitate New Culture and May Fourth organizational forms and thus to turn Christianity into a replica of the New Culture/May Fourth franchise. This in itself was a rebranding of old structures, because founding organizations and launching journals was not at all an invention of the New Culture Movement. By their own admission, Christians had long had organizations in China.[73] The most famous ones were the YMCA and the YWCA, which had branches all across the country. These organizations also had their own journals. In its early days in 1915, *New Youth* (then called *Youth Magazine*) even had to change its name, because the Shanghai YMCA was already running a journal called *Shanghai Young Men* (*Shanghai qingnian*).[74] At that time, the vocabulary around "youth" was still primarily associated with these Christians, and Chen Duxiu's magazine looked like a derivative.

By 1920, the tables had turned. The authors of *Life* now deemed it necessary to position their organizations within the May Fourth/New Culture tradition. During May Fourth and in the New Culture Movement, associations had turned out to be very successful, Xu Baoqian explained. Therefore the pre-existing Christian organizations had to be restructured, so as to avoid "falling behind."[75] The *Life* manifesto echoed this by saying that "recently" it had become evident that students were strongly involved in the "reform of the world." Therefore the Christian students in China should "connect up," in order to "become a movement."[76]

The Apologetic Group also tried to link itself to the declared New Culture "cult heroes."[77] Just like the authors of spring-bamboo journals, *Life* author Xu Baoqian cited Hu Shi.[78] The group also organized a seminar with Cai Yuanpei, Hu Shi and Jiang Menglin to discuss the relationship of Christianity and New Culture. The talks were, Xu Baoqian wrote, "completely frank."[79]

This strategy of identifying Christianity as the New Culture Movement was important, ironically not in promoting Christianity in China, but in spreading

---

72 Liu Tingfang, "Xin wenhua yundong zhong jidujiao xuanjiaoshi de zeren (xu)" (The Duty of Christian Missionaries in the New Culture Movement [Continued]), *Xinghua* (Chinese Christian Advocate) 18, no. 24 (June 22, 1921): 12.
73 Xu, "Beijing jidujiao xuexiao shiye lianhehui gaizu shimo," 1.
74 Wang, *Huiyi Yadong tushuguan*, 32–33.
75 Xu, "Beijing jidujiao xuexiao shiye lianhehui gaizu shimo," 1.
76 "Fakan 'Shengming yuekan' xuanyan," 2.
77 Hockx, "Playing the Field," 65. Originally "hero."
78 Xu, "Jidujiao xin sichao," 1.
79 Ibid., 2.

knowledge of the New Culture Movement to the West. As I show in chapter 5, Christians in the early 20th century used the New Culture Movement as a tool to show off the success of the Christian mission in China to Western audiences; that is, to legitimize their enterprise to a different audience. On these occasions they claimed that New Culture stood for China's Westernization, and that Christians had laid the groundwork for its rise.

Popular education as the New Culture Movement

Liu Boming and the Chinese Christians, whose agendas did not make it into the New Culture discourse on a long-term basis, are useful to show how the expression was used as a buzzword, because their claims seem so paradoxical from today's retrospective point of view. But there were also those who were successful in moving their agendas towards the "legitimate core"[80] of the cultural field through this buzzword. It was these groups and their success that would determine the cultural shift of the time and, to some extent, the associations we inscribe into the New Culture Movement today.

One of these groups was the Jiangsu Educational Association, which found a particularly cunning way to harness May Fourth and New Culture, namely by playing them as both "legitimating" and as a "delegitimizing terms":[81] It promoted its agenda as a "remedy" against May Fourth to the provincial government, which feared that student protests would flare up again in the autumn of 1919; and it sold the same cluster of agendas to students as being in service of May Fourth and as "the New Culture Movement [that] continues the May Fourth Movement."[82]

The Jiangsu Educational Association had long supported agendas that endorsed popular education, the National Language and vocational education

---

[80] In modification of Cheek, "The Names of Rectification," 26. Originally "legitimating core."
[81] Ibid., 27.
[82] "Remedy": Jiangsu sheng jiaoyuhui, "Cheng Qi shengzhang chenshu taolun xuechao hou jiuji fangfa wen" (Petition to Provincial Governor Qi, Reporting about the Discussions on Rescue Methods after the Student Protests), *Jiangsu sheng jiaoyuhui yuebao* (Jiangsu Educational Association Monthly Report), September 1919, 6. Promotion as service to May Fourth: Jiangsu sheng jiaoyuhui, "Zhi ge zhongdeng xuexiao qing tongzhi xuesheng yu shujiaqi nei zuzhi jiangyantuan shu" (Letter to All Middle Schools, Asking to Inform the Students to Form Lecture Corps during the Summer Holidays), *Jiangsu sheng jiaoyuhui yuebao* (Jiangsu Educational Association Monthly Report), May 1919, 13. "The New Culture Movement that continues the May Fourth Movement": Jiangsu sheng jiaoyuhui, "Zhi zhongdeng yishang ge xuexiao tongzhi dingqi juxing yanshuo jingjinhui shu," 25.

(see chapter 1). It was also in the habit of promoting its ideals under popular buzzwords, such as the "national salvation" rhetoric.[83]

Before newspaper stories connected May Fourth with Hu Shi, Chen Duxiu and the people identified as part of their circle, the Association had not seen any potential in the May Fourth demonstrations to aid their agendas. On the contrary, it and its vice-president were worried that the protests would distract from their educational plans.[84] Nevertheless, the Jiangsu Educational Association soon ended up being involved in May Fourth, and this must have eventually motivated it to tap into May Fourth for its own purposes. Like so many at the time, the Association's members seemed to be genuinely concerned about Japan's claims to Shandong and they repeatedly petitioned the Chinese government not to sign the Treaty of Versailles.[85] Another reason for its involvement was that May Fourth was as much an educational matter as it was a political one, because its most prominent protesters were students.

Since students were involved, the Ministry of Education ordered the Jiangsu Educational Association to calm down the protests in its catchment area.[86] Soon the Association found itself in an unfavorable position, in which it simultaneously tried to dissuade the students from protesting and the government from cracking down on the students.[87] The Association was forced to multitask and deal with Cai Yuanpei's resignation and the student protests all at the same time. Its meeting minutes show that often the Association had to deal with the resignation of Minister of Education Fu Zengxiang, the disappearance of Cai Yuanpei,

---

83 Jiangsu sheng jiaoyuhui, "Cheng jiaoyu zongzhang zuzhi Zhonghua xin jiaoyushe wen."
84 Huang Yanpei, "Huang Yanpei riji zhengli fanli" (Guide to the Structure of Huang Yanpei's Diary), in *Huang Yanpei riji* (Huang Yanpei's Diary), ed. Zhongguo shehui kexueyuan jindaishi yanjiusuo, vol. 2 (Beijing: Huawen chubanshe, 2008), 64; Jiangsu sheng jiaoyuhui, "Zhi da zongtong, guowuyuan, jiaoyubu chenming Shanghai ge xiao xuesheng yin jiaoyu zongzhang yiren deng wenti qun yi bake, qing fuxun yuqing dian."
85 Jiangsu sheng jiaoyuhui, "Zhi Mei zongtong, Mei guohui, Ying, Fa shouxiang, ji Ying, Fa guohui qing zhuchi gongdao dian" (Telegram to the US President, the US Congress, the Prime Ministers of Britain and France, the Parliaments of Britain and France, Asking to Uphold Justice), *Jiangsu sheng jiaoyuhui yuebao* (Jiangsu Educational Association Monthly Report), June 1919, 1; Jiangsu sheng jiaoyuhui, "Zhi da zongtong, guowuyuan qing duiyu Qingdao jiaoshe reng dian zhuanshi kangyi dian" (Telegram to the President and the Cabinet, Asking to Intervene in the Qingdao [Question], and Send a Telegram to the Special Envoy [in Paris] Letting Him Resist), *Jiangsu sheng jiaoyuhui yuebao* (Jiangsu Educational Association Monthly Report), June 1919, 10–11.
86 Gu, *Qing mo Min chu Jiangsu sheng jiaoyuhui yanjiu*, 215.
87 Jiangsu sheng jiaoyuhui, "Zhi Mei zongtong, Mei guohui, Ying, Fa shouxiang, ji Ying, Fa guohui qing zhuchi gongdao dian"; Jiangsu sheng jiaoyuhui, "Zhi da zongtong, guowuyuan qing duiyu Qingdao jiaoshe reng dian zhuanshi kangyi dian."

the student protests and the government's crackdowns on the protests all in one meeting.[88] This mixture of issues must have sparked the idea in Association members to harness the power of May Fourth for one of its own agendas: public lecturing.

May 1919: Promoting public lecturing as May Fourth

Organizations like the Jiangsu Educational Association were extremely successful in selling public lecturing as a May Fourth activity. Successful enough, in fact, for the impression to emerge that public lecturing was invented during May Fourth, with Beijing University's Commoners' Education Lecture Society as part of its vanguard.[89]

However, public lecturing predated May Fourth by a considerable amount of time. David Strand argues that giving speeches in public had long been part of the "political practices" of China's republicanism.[90] For example, Song Jiaoren's (1882–1913) election campaign of 1912–1913 centrally included giving public speeches. Moreover, a variety of intellectuals and activists, such as women's rights activists, drew upon this form of expression, and newspapers wrote about its importance.[91]

Public lecturing had also existed long before May Fourth as a state-sponsored and state-regulated endeavor in the service of popular education, according to Paul J. Bailey. Going back all the way to the Qing Dynasty, it was in the 1910s part of wider trends to promote popular education (see chapter 1).[92] In 1915, the Jiangsu Educational Association had already founded a Popular Education Research Association that should promote lecturing in public.[93] The Ministry of Education too had founded Popular Lecture Institutes, which had the same purpose.[94] Lecture topics should be themes like "encouraging patriotism," "improving morality" and "advocating hygiene." To control these

---

88 Jiangsu sheng jiaoyuhui, "Kaihui jilu," May 1919, 23.
89 Schwarcz, *The Chinese Enlightenment*, 86–93; Nelson K. Lee, "How Is a Political Public Space Made? – The Birth of Tiananmen Square and the May Fourth Movement," *Political Geography* 28, no. 1 (January 2009): 36; Dong and Zhou, *Zhongguo jin xiandai jiaoyu sichao yu liupai*, 374.
90 David Strand, *An Unfinished Republic: Leading by Word and Deed in Modern China* (Berkeley: University of California Press, 2011), 2.
91 On Song Jiaoren: Ibid., 54. On women's rights activists: Ibid., 94–96. Newspapers: Ibid., 78.
92 Bailey, *Reform the People*, 194.
93 Ibid., 187.
94 Ibid., 194.

topics, they needed to be approved by various state or state-sponsored organizations.[95]

Beijing University's Commoners' Education Lecture Society originally operated within these parameters laid out by the state. This applied to the declared goal of the Lecture Society, which was, according to the *Beijing University Daily* on March 7, 1919, the "popularization of education."[96] This was also the case with respect to state control. Far from planning to engage in subversive actions, the Commoners' Education Lecture Society originally cleared its activities with the local police bureau.[97] During the May Fourth protests, the government did censor the Lecture Society's actions. But this must have been motivated by their new choice of topics (boycotting of Japanese goods and so forth),[98] rather than by the chosen form of public engagement.

But public lecturing and speech giving were reinterpreted from being general "political performances"[99] and state-sponsored popular-education activities[100] to something to do with May Fourth, because organizations like the Jiangsu Educational Association started marketing it to students as a May Fourth activity in late May 1919. "After the failure in negotiating the Qingdao [Question]," the Association wrote to middle schools, a lot of actions have been undertaken to get Qingdao back. Among them were petitions and anti-Japanese boycotts. However, people in "remote cities and villages" were not aware of political issues, and therefore the strikes were doomed to fail. Therefore, the Jiangsu Educational Association recommended that students should "use lectures to enlighten [these uneducated people]" when they were in their native villages during the holidays.[101]

---

95 Jiaoyubu, "Tongsu jiaoyu jiangyan guize" (Regulations on Lectures for Popular Education), in *Zhonghua minguo jiaoyu fagui xuanbian* (Anthology of Education Laws and Regulations of the Republic of China), ed. Song Enrong and Zhang Xian (Nanjing: Jiangsu jiaoyu chubanshe, 2005), 533; Bailey, *Reform the People*, 188–200.
96 *Beijing University Daily* from 7 March 1919, cited in Zhongguo shehui kexueyuan jindaishi yanjiusuo "jindaishi ziliao" bianyishi, ed., *Wu si aiguo yundong* (The Patriotic Movement of May Fourth), vol. 1 (Beijing: Zhishi chanquan chubanshe, 2013), 519; Chang-tai Hung, *Going to the People: Chinese Intellectuals and Folk Literature, 1918–1937* (Cambridge, Massachusetts: Council on East Asian Studies, Harvard University, 1985), 10–11.
97 Zhongguo shehui kexueyuan jindaishi yanjiusuo "jindaishi ziliao" bianyishi, *Wu si aiguo yundong*, 1:521.
98 "Jing xuejie zhi zuijin xingdong" (Latest Events in Beijing's Academia), *Shenbao* (Shanghai News), May 27, 1919, 7, Shanghai.
99 Strand, *An Unfinished Republic*, 3.
100 Bailey, *Reform the People*, 194.
101 Jiangsu sheng jiaoyuhui, "Zhi ge zhongdeng xuexiao qing tongzhi xuesheng yu shujiaqi nei zuzhi jiangyantuan shu," 13.

September 1919: A "remedy" against May Fourth

Pro-May Fourth students were not the only ones to whom the Jiangsu Educational Association marketed its agenda. When the academic year ended in the summer of 1919, the students returned home and the protests cooled down. However, in September the students were returning for the new academic year. With some prescience, the government therefore feared that the protests might start again, which they did, especially around October 10, the national holiday. In this situation, the Jiangsu Educational Association saw another opportunity to harness the potential of May Fourth, this time not to convince the students of its agendas, but the government. In September 1919, the Association sent a letter to Provincial Governor Qi Yaolin (1863-?), promising a "remedy," or literally a "rescue method" (*jiuji fangfa*), against the May Fourth demonstrations.[102] Part of this "rescue method" or "remedy" was the suggestion that students should do internships in the local industry and, again, engage in public lecturing.[103]

The Jiangsu Educational Association argued that it had convened a "research conference" of educators, to "discuss a remedy after the student demonstrations."[104] This again was a communicative choice. The conference invitation sent to the educators had read that, "after the student protests had happened," everybody agreed that teaching methods had to change, "in the hope of adjusting to the trends of the times."[105] Still, in September, the Jiangsu Educational Association wrote to Governor Qi that the conference had concluded that the student protests had on the one hand been caused by "patriotic enthusiasm." On the other hand, they had been incited because schools emphasized "book knowledge" too heavily over other skills. To prevent further protests, such other skills had to be trained. For example, schools should promote the "extracurricular service to society," part of which was public lecturing. They should also promote "internships at [places] like farms, factories and shops." As it turned out, this letter was a bid for funding: new money was needed to implement these educational suggestions.[106]

---

[102] Jiangsu sheng jiaoyuhui, "Cheng Qi shengzhang chenshu taolun xuechao hou jiuji fangfa wen," 6.

[103] Ibid., 6–7.

[104] Ibid., 6.

[105] Jiangsu sheng jiaoyuhui, "Zhi zhongdeng yishang xuexiao paiyuan daohui shu" (Letter to Schools of a Higher Level than Middle [Schools, Instructing Them] to Send People to the Conference), *Jiangsu sheng jiaoyuhui yuebao* (Jiangsu Educational Association Monthly Report), June 1919, 6–7.

[106] Jiangsu sheng jiaoyuhui, "Cheng Qi shengzhang chenshu taolun xuechao hou jiuji fangfa wen," 6–7. The "extracurricular service to society" was defined as including popular lectures in a *Shanghai News* article on the Jiangsu Educational Association's conference, "Jiangsu zhongdeng

This "remedy" was certainly surprising, and the Jiangsu Educational Association did not explain how it was to prevent future student protests. But it was suspiciously in line with the Association's longstanding agendas. Among them was public lecturing, as shown above. But among them were also internships, which were an important part of the Jiangsu Educational Association's commitment to vocational education. Already in 1917, the Association's vice-president Huang Yanpei had, together with Cai Yuanpei, Jiang Menglin and a few others, founded the Chinese Society for Vocational Education and this society established a school a year later. The students of that school had to complete internships in the local industry.[107] When the Jiangsu Educational Association now referenced May Fourth in order to promote internships, this was yet another attempt to use the protests as a means to market its own, long-held agendas. The Association was again successful and Governor Qi granted the money.[108]

October 1919: Continuing the May Fourth Movement

While the Jiangsu Educational Association held this conference and sent the resulting letter of September 1919, the expression "New Culture Movement" was coined. The Association appeared to know about this and decided to sell its agenda again to students – this time as the "New Culture Movement [that] continues the May Fourth Movement."[109] On October 24, 1919, it sent out a letter to middle schools and schools of higher levels, announcing a lecture competition on the topic of "the various questions of the New Culture Movement and ways to promote it."[110] A similar lecture competition had been held the year before. The goal of these events was to hone students' skills in the National Language and public lecturing.[111] The announcement of the 1919 competition had a considerable reach within the region. Twenty-eight schools held internal

---

yishang xuexiao jiaoyu yanjiuhui zhi yijue'an" (Resolution of the Educational Research Conference for Schools in Jiangsu of a Middle Level and above), *Shenbao* (Shanghai News), August 20, 1919, 10, Shanghai.
107 Yeh, *Shanghai Splendor*, 38–39; Bailey, *Reform the People*, 208.
108 Qi Yaolin, "Qi shengzhang pi" (Approval by Provincial Governor Qi), ed. Jiangsu sheng jiaoyuhui, *Jiangsu sheng jiaoyuhui yuebao* (Jiangsu Educational Association Monthly Report), September 1919, 9.
109 Jiangsu sheng jiaoyuhui, "Zhi zhongdeng yishang ge xuexiao tongzhi dingqi juxing yanshuo jingjinhui shu," 25.
110 Jiangsu sheng jiaoyuhui, "Zhi zhongdeng yishang ge xuexiao tongzhi dingqi juxing yanshuo jingjinhui shu."
111 Jiangsu sheng jiaoyuhui, "Fu yanshuo jingjinhui jianze" (Attachment: Regulations for the Speech Competition), *Jiangsu sheng jiaoyuhui yuebao* (Jiangsu Educational Association Monthly

competitions to select altogether forty-five candidates, whom they sent to the provincial competition.[112] The competition's announcement was reprinted in journals and newspapers in the area, such as the *Shanghai News* and the *Chinese Christian Advocate*.[113]

The "New Culture Movement [that] continues the May Fourth Movement" again turned out to promote the Association's longstanding agenda. The Association defined the "New Culture Movement" as the "spread of culture to the great majority of our countrymen," which included "promulgating *baihua* literature and establishing free schools and lecture groups."[114] Vocational education was not included in this definition. But popular education and lecture groups were, and the Jiangsu Educational Association had by that time sold them under three different and mutually contradictory labels: twice to students as being in service of May Fourth (and the New Culture Movement that "continued" it) and once to the local government as preventing a repetition of May Fourth.

Communism and the New Culture Movement

Associations that would bring forth later-famous communists, too, marketed themselves with the New Culture Movement. Among such groups was the *Young China (Shaonian Zhongguo)* journal, some of whose authors would later become members of the Chinese Communist Party. The Young China Study Association had first convened informally in 1918, but was "formally inaugurated" in July 1919 in Beijing, that is, at the time when the expression "New Culture Movement" must have been invented.[115] The journal *Young China* was launched in July 1919, and it promoted its ideas, among them a mixture of anarchism and communism, as part of the New Culture franchise.

Report), March 1918, 7–8; Jiangsu sheng jiaoyuhui, "Yanshuo jingjinhui bisai jishi" (Record of the Contest of the Speech Competition), *Jiangsu sheng jiaoyuhui yuebao* (Jiangsu Educational Association Monthly Report), December 1918, 10–12; Jiangsu sheng jiaoyuhui, "Zhi zhongdeng yishang ge xuexiao tongzhi dingqi juxing yanshuo jingjinhui shu," 23.

112 "Yanshuo jingjinhui di-er ci kaihuiji" (Record of the Second Lecture Competition), *Shenbao* (Shanghai News), December 25, 1919, 10, Shanghai; Jiangsu sheng jiaoyuhui, "Zhi zhongdeng yishang ge xuexiao tongzhi dingqi juxing yanshuo jingjinhui shu."

113 "Yanshuo jingjinhui yanti zhi jieshi," 10; "Yanshuo jingjinhui di-er ci kaihuiji," 10.

114 Jiangsu sheng jiaoyuhui, "Zhi zhongdeng yishang ge xuexiao tongzhi dingqi juxing yanshuo jingjinhui shu," 25.

115 On the Young China Study Association's formal inauguration, see Rahav, *The Rise of Political Intellectuals in Modern China*, 109–10.

Knowledge about the various strands of Western thought that endorse social revolution came into China in the late 19th century. It is difficult to distinguish neatly between the different strands of ideas that supported social revolution at the time, since many associations and even individuals subscribed to a potpourri of ideas.

Steven A. Smith describes the approach to such concepts at the time as "eclectic."[116] For example, when elaborating on the concept of "class," workers described their achievement of class consciousness as a form of "enlightenment," which Smith classifies as originating from "New Culture."[117] There was an anarchist element to notions of "class," Smith argues, because the exploitation of one class by another was considered to be caused by "authoritarian power (*qiangquan*) and human selfishness."[118] Finally, even Confucianism shaped notions of "class," in that activists tried their best to depict it as the very opposite of Confucianism. This, Smith says, sometimes led to "overcompensation."[119] For example, pondering the statement in the *Mencius*, which outlines that "[t]hose who work with their minds rule, while those who work with their bodies are ruled," Chen Duxiu was determined to reverse this distribution of roles into its very opposite.[120] Individuals, too, could unite ideas that can be traced to different traditions. For example, in 1918 the Wuhan intellectual and later CCP member Yun Daiying (1895–1931) supported elements taken from anarchism and communism, and also from Daoism and Christianity in what Shakhar Rahav describes as a "hodgepodge of cultural reference points."[121]

The same was the case for *Young China*. In its manifesto, the journal did not announce its adherence to any particular ideology. It even mocked people who "welcomed" a new set ideology every day without creating a suitable one themselves: "As for the so-called reformist faction, today they copy the American constitution, tomorrow they imitate British politics. Today they welcome Marxist socialism, tomorrow they welcome Kropotkin's anarchism. Something Kant, something Dewey. We will welcome it all day long. And we will not at all think of creating [something] ourselves."[122] Its own goals *Young China* consequently

---

116 S.A. Smith, *Like Cattle and Horses: Nationalism and Labor in Shanghai, 1895–1927* (Durham: Duke University Press, 2002), 116.
117 Ibid., 118.
118 Ibid., 120.
119 Ibid., 117.
120 Ibid., 123.
121 Rahav, *The Rise of Political Intellectuals in Modern China*, 1.
122 Wang Guangqi, "'Shaonian Zhongguo' zhi chuangzao" (The Creation of *Young China*), *Shaonian zhongguo* (Young China) 1, no. 2 (August 15, 1919): 2.

framed in ideologically much less set terms as wanting to produce a "constructive life; a social life; a scientific life."[123]

The various strands of ideology that fed into such support for social revolution in its different forms had been introduced into China in the late 19th century. The names of Karl Marx (1818–1883) and Friedrich Engels (1820–1895) were first mentioned in 1899, according to Alexander Pantsov.[124] A translation of one chapter of the *Communist Manifesto* appeared in 1908 in *Heavenly Justice* (*Tianyibao*), a journal which Maurice Meisner classifies as "anarchist."[125] Initially and especially before 1917, ideas that can be categorized as anarchist were particularly popular.[126]

One of the anarchist notions that most interested the intellectuals of the 1910s and 1920s was the concept of "mutual aid." This idea goes back to Peter Kropotkin's (1842–1921) book of the same title of 1902, which had been translated into Chinese in 1908.[127] It countered the idea that Darwinism had to stand for competition and pointed to the importance of "cooperation" in the struggle for survival.[128] The popularity of the concept not only appears from the frequency with which intellectuals discussed or referenced it (for examples, see below). It also becomes clear from the names they gave their societies. For example, in late 1917, Yun Daiying established a Mutual Aid Society, which purported to have the wish of "helping ourselves and helping others."[129]

While this set of ideas had been known in China for a few decades, it – especially its Marxist variety – only gained traction during the time after May Fourth, which eventually led to the foundation of the Chinese Communist Party in 1921.[130] Of course, it would be simplistic to claim that this happened only because activists started marketing their ideas through the New Culture Movement. Other factors unquestionably played a role too. Among them was the inspiration given

---

123 Ibid.
124 Alexander Pantsov, *The Bolsheviks and the Chinese Revolution, 1919–1927* (Richmond: Curzon, 2000), 25–26.
125 Maurice J Meisner, *Li Ta-Chao and the Origins of Chinese Marxism* (Cambridge, Massachusetts: Harvard University Press, 1967), 53. See also Zarrow, *Anarchism and Chinese Political Culture*, 102.The translation of *Tianyi bao* is taken from Pantsov, *The Bolsheviks and the Chinese Revolution*, 26.
126 Meisner, *Li Ta-Chao and the Origins of Chinese Marxism*, 53; Arif Dirlik, *The Origins of Chinese Communism* (New York: Oxford University Press, 1989), 3.
127 Rahav, *The Rise of Political Intellectuals in Modern China*, 61.
128 Colin Ward, *Anarchism: A Very Short Introduction* (Oxford: Oxford University Press, 2004), 7.
129 Rahav, *The Rise of Political Intellectuals in Modern China*, 59.
130 Meisner, *Li Ta-Chao and the Origins of Chinese Marxism*, 54; Pantsov, *The Bolsheviks and the Chinese Revolution*, 26–27.

by the October Revolution of 1917,[131] and the activities by the Comintern, which sent agents to China. For example, in 1920 Grigorij Vojtinskij (1893–1953) came to China as part of a Comintern delegation. There he met with Li Dazhao and Chen Duxiu, helped with the establishment of Marxist associations and pushed for the foundation of the CCP in July 1921.[132] Among these factors that led to the establishment of the CCP was also the organizational impetus given by the May Fourth Movement. Shakhar Rahav and Hans van de Ven, for example, show how the intensified spread of study societies and the way they networked across the country contributed to the foundation of the Communist Party.[133]

In spite of all this infrastructure and these reference points, however, journals like *Young China* apparently saw an advantage in marketing themselves as part of the buzzword New Culture Movement. On the one hand, this concerned the ideas. In *Young China*'s September 1919 edition, Li Dazhao, for example, called for a "youth movement." This "youth movement" needed a "culture movement," which consisted of a "spiritual reform movement" and a "material reform movement." Li argued with anarchist vocabulary for the "spiritual reform movement." For example, he wrote that it was necessary to "propagate the truths [*daoli*] of 'mutual aid' and 'universal love,' based on the spirit of humanism."[134] On the question of why this "spiritual reform movement" was necessary to effect the "material reform movement," he cited Karl Marx, who had, in Li's reading, said that that "material reform" was not sustainable without the "spiritual reform."[135]

In a discussion of "What Is the Best Method for Revolution" in July 1920, Yu Jiayu (1898–1976) called the creation of a "social consciousness" the "culture movement." This "social consciousness" was in his view the basis for revolution and it involved ideals like "free criticism," "the freedom to choose one's ways" or "the freedom to choose one's leaders."[136] A month later, Chen Qitian (1893–1984) asked "What Is the New Culture Spirit?" After criticizing an answer suggested by Hu Shi,[137] Chen Qitian explained that the "New Culture spirit" was, among other

---

131 On the role of the October Revolution, see Meisner, *Li Ta-Chao and the Origins of Chinese Marxism*, 60–70; Pantsov, *The Bolsheviks and the Chinese Revolution*, 27.
132 S.A. Smith, *A Road Is Made: Communism in Shanghai, 1920–1927* (Richmond: Curzon, 2000), 12–14.
133 Rahav, *The Rise of Political Intellectuals in Modern China*; van de Ven, *From Friend to Comrade*.
134 Li Dazhao, "'Shaonian zhongguo' de 'shaonian yundong'" (*Young China*'s "Movement of the Young"), *Shaonian zhongguo* (Young China) 1, no. 3 (September 15, 1919): 1.
135 Ibid.
136 Yu Jiaju, "Shenme shi geming de zuihao fangfa?" (What Is the Best Method for Revolution?), *Shaonian zhongguo* (Young China) 2, no. 1 (July 15, 1920): 40.
137 Chen, "Shenme shi xin wenhua de jingshen," 2.

things, to move "from a life of [Darwinist, as he pointed out later] competition to a life of mutual aid [in the sense of Kropotkin, again as he wrote later]."[138]

The same strategy was deployed in other journals too. Research Clique member Jiang Qi (1886–1951) challenged the role of intellectuals in a similar spirit. He explained that, as long as "civilization" was created by the elite, the New Culture Movement "followed the old tracks of an overturned cart." The new "civilization" of the New Culture Movement should not be created "from top to bottom, [by people] such as rulers, politicians, scholars, educators and so on." Instead, everybody should help create it, "within the scope of his own ability" and through "mutual aid."[139]

Beyond the ideas itself, *Young China* also advertised itself, as a journal, through the New Culture franchise. In a short, five-line manifesto which it printed repeatedly in its issues, *Young China* declared as its goal to "conduct a culture movement based on the scientific spirit."[140] When the Shanghai publisher East Asia Library took over the journal in November 1919, newly printed or reprinted issues sported a similar advertisement. It read: "*Young China* emphasizes – the culture movement; – the explication of scholarly principles; – pure science."[141] The advertisements for other publications, which East Asia Library placed in *Young China*, must also have immediately associated the journal with the New Culture Movement for its readers. *Young China* promoted *New Tide* (by then an East Asia Library publication), *New Youth*, *Construction* (*Jianshe*, also an East Asia Library publication) and the *Morning Post*. It also advertised Hu Shi's collection of poems called *Experiments* (*Changshiji*), which was forthcoming with East Asia Library.[142]

---

138 Ibid., 3.
139 Jiang Qi, "Xin wenhua yundong he jiaoyu" (The New Culture Movement and Education), *Jiefang yu gaizao* (Emancipation and Reconstruction) 2, no. 5 (March 1, 1920): 89–92. On *Emancipation and Reconstruction* belonging to the Research Clique, see Peng, *Yanjiuxi yu wu si shiqi xin wenhua yundong*, 248.
140 "'Shaonian zhongguo' yuekan de xuanyan" (*Young China's* Manifesto), *Shaonian zhongguo* (Young China) 1, no. 3 (September 15, 1919): i; "'Shaonian zhongguo' yuekan de xuanyan" (*Young China's* Manifesto), *Shaonian zhongguo* (Young China) 1, no. 4 (October 15, 1919): i.
141 "Advertisement for *Young World*," *Shaonian zhongguo* (Young China) 1, no. 1 (November 20, 1919): i; "Advertisement for *Young World*," *Shaonian zhongguo* (Young China) 1, no. 6 (December 15, 1919): i; "Advertisement for *Young World*," *Shaonian zhongguo* (Young China) 1, no. 7 (January 15, 1920): i. On East Asia Library taking over publication, see "Ben yuekan jinyao qishi" (Important Notices from This Journal), *Shaonian zhongguo* (Young China) 1, no. 1 (November 20, 1919): 52.
142 "Advertisement for *New Tide*," *Shaonian zhongguo* (Young China) 1, no. 1 (November 20, 1919): 45; "Advertisement for *New Youth*," *Shaonian zhongguo* (Young China) 1, no. 1 (November 20, 1919): 47; "Advertisement for *Construction*," *Shaonian zhongguo* (Young China) 1, no. 1 (November 20, 1919): 46; "Advertisement for *Morning Post*," *Shaonian zhongguo* (Young China) 1, no. 1

For the publishing house, this had the dual effect of promoting these journals in *Young China* and connecting *Young China* to the New Culture franchise. When the journal started being published by Zhonghua Book Company later on, the new publisher continued this method. In 1923, it advertised a Zhonghua Book Company series, which was called "New Culture Collections." Most of these books, among them translations of Charles Darwin's (1809–1882) *Origins of Species*, had been written before and completely independently of the New Culture Movement and had even been popular in China before its invention.[143] Nevertheless they, as well as the journal *Young China*, were now being identified with the New Culture Movement, so as to move them towards the "legitimate core"[144] of the cultural field.

Women's rights as the New Culture Movement

Feminism was another agenda promoted as the New Culture Movement after 1919. Chinese feminism went back to the 1900s, when intellectuals like Liang Qichao and Kang Youwei (1858–1927) advocated women's rights and women's education to ensure the often-invoked salvation of the nation.[145] By the 1910s, the advocacy of feminism was widespread among reformers of different persuasions. Liu Shipei from the *National Heritage* supported his wife, the famous anarcho-feminist He-yin Zhen, in her endeavors.[146] The Minster of Education Fu Zengxiang supported women's rights and even the Shanxi warlord Yan Xishan advocated women's education and the end of foot binding.[147]

But after late 1919, feminism too was marketed as part of the New Culture franchise. One example is the authors of the *Ladies' Magazine*. The *Ladies' Magazine* had been founded in 1915 and was run by Commercial Press in Shanghai. Its agenda had long included notions like women's education. But like so many others, as I have shown in chapter 1, it had combined this with writing in Literary Chinese.[148]

(November 20, 1919): 49; "Advertisement for *Experiments*," *Shaonian zhongguo* (Young China) 1, no. 1 (November 20, 1919): 51.
143 "Xin wenhua congshu" (New Culture Collections), *Shaonian zhongguo* (Young China) 4, no. 6 (August 1923).
144 In modification of Cheek, "The Names of Rectification," 26. Originally "legitimating core."
145 Liu, Ko, and Karl, *The Birth of Chinese Feminism*, 33.
146 Ibid., 5; Zarrow, *Anarchism and Chinese Political Culture*, 130.
147 Guo and He, "Fu Zengxiang"; Yan, "Shanxi sheng zhengfu zhi Shilou zhishi han," 0224.
148 Wang Xiaodan, "'Funü zazhi' dui jindai dushi nüxing shenghuo de suzao he yingxiang" (The Formation Of, and Influence On, the Life of Modern Urban Women by the *Ladies' Magazine*), *Xueshu tansuo* (Academic Exploration), no. 8 (August 2011): 99–100.

After May Fourth, the style of the journal changed. It was increasingly written in *baihua*. It also depicted the New Culture Movement as a watershed moment in the rise of feminism. New Culture had, its author Se Lu (no dates) claimed, caused "average women" to start questioning the old order of society.[149] Other authors started calling the pursuit of women's rights a "movement."[150] The *Ladies' Magazine* had previously also talked about *"yundong,"* but then it had mostly not meant a social movement but "sports."[151] Like other New Culture marketers, the *Ladies' Magazine* sought a connection to the "cult heroes"[152] of New Culture. It printed a speech by Hu Shi on the women's question, cited him, and it gossiped about Cai Yuanpei – it reproduced a photo of his wedding anniversary.[153] Especially when discussing the wider feminist discourse of the time by reviewing other publications, the *Ladies' Magazine* described feminism as part of the New Culture Movement. For instance, it called the magazine *New Woman* (*Xin funü*) a "sharp weapon of New Culture" and claimed that its authors were "catering towards this age of the New Culture Movement."[154]

Others concerned with feminism tied themselves even more tightly into the buzzword "New Culture Movement." An example is *New Woman*. One of its authors, the aforementioned teacher Jing Guan, claimed in 1920 that he had been involved in women's education for five years – he worked at a girls' school. But he nevertheless chose to depict his advocacy of feminism and his decision to found the journal *New Woman*, taken during the May Fourth protests, as part of the New Culture Movement, not as the culmination of a longer-standing interest.[155] Others refranchised feminism in a similar way. *Young China* advocated women's rights on its pages, which were, as argued above, swamped with New Culture

---

149 Se Lu, "Zuijin shi nian nei funü jie de huigu" (Review of the World of Women of the Last Ten Years), *Funü zazhi* (Ladies' Magazine), no. 1 (January 1, 1924): 21.
150 "Beijing nüxuesheng zhi waijiao yundong" (The Diplomatic Movement of Beijing's Female Students), *Funü zazhi* (Ladies' Magazine), no. 7 (January 1, 1921): 11; "Riben furen tongqinghui de zixha fangzhi yundong" (Suicide Prevention Movement of the Japanese Women's Sympathy Organization), *Funü zazhi* (Ladies' Magazine) 7, no. 2 (February 5, 1921): 18; "Funü jiefang yundong de pubianhua" (Generalization of the Women's Emancipation Movement), *Funü zazhi* (Ladies' Magazine) 7, no. 5 (May 5, 1921): 122.
151 Malong, "Nüzi fayu shidai zhi yundong."
152 Lit. "cult hero," Hockx, "Playing the Field," 65.
153 Hu Shi on the women's question: Hu Shi, "Nüzi wenti (yi) Hu Shizhi xiansheng jiangyan" (The Women's Question (1) a Speech by Mr Hu Shizhi), *Funü zazhi* (Ladies' Magazine), no. 5 (May 1, 1921): 6–9. Citing Hu Shi: Wang Su, "Du 'Xin funü' de ganxiang" (Feelings on Reading *New Woman*), *Funü zazhi* (Ladies' Magazine) 6, no. 5 (April 30, 1920): 33. Cai Yuanpei's wedding anniversary: "Cai Zimin xiansheng yu qi furen jiehun yi nian jinian sheying."
154 Wang, "Du 'Xin funü' de ganxiang," 33.
155 Jing, "Gao xin wenhua yundong de tongzhi," 32.

references.[156] As did a journal in Taiwan by the name of *Taiwan Youth* and its successor publication *Taiwan People's News (Taiwan minbao)*.[157]

Taiwanese Independence as the New Culture Movement

Taiwan Youth and *Taiwan People's News* were part of what has come to be known as the Taiwanese New Culture Movement. The Taiwanese New Culture Movement is usually dated to the 1920s and 1930s. Its most famous actors were members of the Taiwanese elite and intellectuals, who were often studying in Tokyo. In 1920, intellectuals around Lin Xiantang (1881–1956) founded the New People Society, which established the *Taiwan Youth*.[158] *Taiwan Youth* was later renamed into *Taiwan People's News*. Another group within the Taiwanese New Culture Movement was the Taiwan Cultural Association. It was founded in 1921 by Jiang Weishui (1890–1931) and its members also published in *Taiwan People's News*.[159] Jiang Weishui and the Taiwanese New Culture Movement are currently used in Taiwan to negotiate the island's national identity, and they will play a major role in chapter 5.

In the 1920s, the *Taiwan Youth* and the *Taiwan People's News* sought to identify themselves as part of the buzzword New Culture Movement and its associated matrix of reference points. The title of *Taiwan Youth* itself imitated the *New Youth* magazine. The publications also sought to establish a connection to the professed stars of the New Culture Movement. The *Taiwan People's News*, for example,

---

156 Xiang Jingyu, "Nüzi jiefang yu gaizao de shangque" (A Discussion of the Liberation and Reform of Women), *Shaonian zhongguo* (Young China) 2, no. 2 (August 15, 1920): 29–37; Hu Shi, "Daxue kai nü de wenti" (The Question of Opening Universities for Women), *Shaonian zhongguo* (Young China) 1, no. 4 (October 15, 1919): 1–3; Li Dazhao, "Funü jiefang yu Democracy" (The Liberation of Women and Democracy), *Shaonian zhongguo* (Young China) 1, no. 4 (October 15, 1919): 27–32.
157 Wang Minchuan, "Nüzi jiaoyu" (Women's Education), *Taiwan qingnian* (Taiwan Youth) 1, no. 3 (September 12, 1920): 41–43; Jian Ru, "Furen zanzheng yunong" (The Movement for Women's Political Participation), *Taiwan minbao* (Taiwan People's News), April 15, 1923, 11, Tokyo; "Chedi de furen jiefang yundong" (A Thorough Movement for the Liberation of Women), *Taiwan minbao* (Taiwan People's News), April 15, 1923, 3–4, Tokyo.
158 Huang Songxian, "1920 niandai Taiwan wenhua xiehui chengli beiying yinsu zhi fenxi" (An Analysis of the Background and Factors Involved in the Foundation of the Taiwan Culture Association in the 1920s), *Mindao Riben yu jiaoyu* (Mindao Japanese Education), no. 2 (July 2008): 265.
159 Steven Lamley, "Taiwan under Japanese Rule, 1895–1945: The Vicissitudes of Colonialism," in *Taiwan: A New History*, ed. Murray A. Rubinstein (Armonk, N.Y: M.E. Sharpe, 2007), 231–32; Huang, "1920 niandai Taiwan wenhua xiehui chengli beiying yinsu zhi fenxi," 265; Zhu Shuangyi, "'Taiwan minbao' dui wu si xin wenxue zuopin de jieshao ji qi yingxiang he zuoyong" (The Introduction, Influence and Function of May Fourth Works of New Literature by the *Taiwan People's News*), *Taiwan yanjiu jikan* (Taiwan Research Quarterly), no. 4 (2008): 84.

introduced the writings of intellectuals like Hu Shi, Chen Duxiu and Lu Xun. A poem to celebrate the foundation of the *Taiwan People's News* referred to Hu Shi and Chen Duxiu as the newspaper's inspiration. The newspaper discussed the "new-literature movement," printed Chen Duxiu's *Call to Youth* and explained its intention to promote the "culture movement" in Taiwan.[160]

The central theme in *Taiwan Youth* and *Taiwan People's News* was not feminism, but calls for Taiwanese self-determination.[161] Taiwan had been a Japanese colony ever since the Treaty of Shimonoseki of 1895 and would continue being one until the end of World War II. In an article on the "culture movement," one author explained that the "culture movement" in Taiwan was to "create a special culture" for the island.[162] This can be read as a cautious call for self-government under the headline of the New Culture Movement, as claims of cultural uniqueness were an important discourse deployed by advocates of national self-determination in Taiwan and beyond.[163]

Demands for Taiwanese self-government under the auspices of the New Culture Movement were again a rebranding of a longstanding goal. Taiwanese

---

160 Introduction of the writings of Hu Shi, Chen Duxiu and Lu Xun: Zhu, "'Taiwan minbao' dui wu si xin wenxue zuopin de jieshao ji qi yingxiang he zuoyong," 84; "Hu Shi wencun" (Selected Works of Hu Shi), *Taiwan minbao* (Taiwan People's News), April 15, 1923, 27, Tokyo. Hu Shi and Chen Duxiu as the newspaper's inspiration: Fang Yuan, "Zhu Taiwan minbao fakan" (Good Wishes for the Foundation of the *Taiwan People's News*), *Taiwan minbao* (Taiwan People's News), April 15, 1923, 24, Tokyo. Discussion of the new literature movement: Xiu Chao, "Zhongguo xin wenxue yundong de guoqu, xianzai he jianglai" (Past, Present and Future of the Chinese New Literature Movement), *Taiwan minbao* (Taiwan People's News), July 13, 1923, 3, Tokyo. Chen Duxiu's "Call to Youth": Chen Duxiu, "Jinggao qingnian" (Call to Youth), *Taiwan minbao* (Taiwan People's News), August 27, 1923, 3–5, Tokyo. The intention to promote the "culture movement": Jian Ru, "Wenhua yundong" (The Culture Movement), *Taiwan minbao* (Taiwan People's News), August 1, 1923, 2–4, Tokyo.
161 Quan Zhe, "Taiwan zizhizhi ping" (An Assessment of Taiwan's System of Self-Government), *Taiwan qingnian* (Taiwan Youth) 1, no. 3 (February 12, 1920): 34–39; Lin Cizhou, "Gaizheng Taiwan difang zhidu gailun (shang)" (Outline of the Reform of Taiwan's Local System [One]), *Taiwan qingnian* (Taiwan Youth) 1, no. 4 (1920): 1–2; "Xingzheng gexin de hao ji" (A Good Opportunity for Administrative Reform), *Taiwan minbao* (Taiwan People's News), November 11, 1923, 1, Tokyo; Zhu, "'Taiwan minbao' dui wu si xin wenxue zuopin de jieshao ji qi yingxiang he zuoyong," 85–87; Huang, "1920 niandai Taiwan wenhua xiehui chengli beiying yinsu zhi fenxi," 265; Lian Qing, "Taiwan yihui shezhi qingyuan weiyuan shang Jing" (The Representatives of the Taiwan Parliament Petition [Movement] Go to Tokyo), *Taiwan minbao* (Taiwan People's News), June 21, 1924, 2, Tokyo.
162 Jian, "Wenhua yundong," 2–4.
163 Steven E. Phillips, *Between Assimilation and Independence: The Taiwanese Encounter Nationalist China, 1945–1950* (Stanford, California: Stanford University Press, 2003), 26; Manela, *The Wilsonian Moment*, 127.

resistance against Japan started as soon as the Treaty of Shimonoseki was concluded in 1895, and Japanese forces had to take Taiwan by military force against the vehement resistance of the island's inhabitants.[164] Resistance against Japan continued in the 1910s, when, for example, members of the local elite around Lin Xiantang and the Japanese politician Itagaki Taisuke (1837–1919) started a short-lived Assimilation Movement. This Movement sought to achieve equal treatment for the Taiwanese with the Japanese, after the Taiwanese would have adjusted culturally to Japan. An important independence movement of the 1920s and early 1930s was activism against the Law Sixty-Three, which granted the Japanese governor-general in Taiwan far-reaching legislative powers. This movement was called "Taiwan Parliament Petition Movement" or "Home Rule Movement."[165] The quest for Taiwanese independence or self-rule, in other words, had been a longstanding and strong concern. Framing these goals as part of the New Culture franchise was thus another strategy deployed by a group to market older agendas under a new buzzword.

Phenomena of co-optation

Contemporary observers in China were aware that the New Culture Movement was being used as a buzzword to promote longstanding agendas. But they did not regard this as an ingenious marketing strategy. Instead, they criticized is as a ploy to use the New Culture Movement as a "signboard" (*zhaopai*) to "deceive people" (*pianren*). [166] Variations of this "signboard" criticism were widespread among New Culture debaters. Miao Jinyuan, a Beijing University student who wrote for the *Republic Daily* supplement *Criticism* (*Piping*), lamented the "bankruptcy" in the New Culture Movement. Often journal authors wrote about the "old," but nevertheless called it "new," he said.[167] By then famous intellectuals like Chen Duxiu were making the same observation. People were using various "new popular words," such as "enlightenment," "new intellectual tide" or "new culture," Chen Duxiu complained. But in reality they were only deploying them

---

164 Murray A. Rubinstein, ed., *Taiwan: A New History* (Armonk, N.Y.: M.E. Sharpe, 2007), 206.
165 Huang, "1920 niandai Taiwan wenhua xiehui chengli beiying yinsu zhi fenxi," 259–66; Rubinstein, *Taiwan*, 204–19; Phillips, *Between Assimilation and Independence*, 2003, 33.
166 Wang Yinxue, "Shishi xinbao: cong wu si yundong yilai Shanghai gua xin wenhua yundong zhaopai de baozhi ..." (The *China Times*: Newspapers That Hang up the Signboard of the New Culture Movement in Shanghai since the May Fourth Movement ...), *Xin fojiao* (New Buddhism) 1, no. 6 (1920): 9–10.
167 Miao, "Suowei 'xin wenhua yundong' de chachao yu pochan," 3–4, 2.

as marketing ploys to sell cigarettes, medicine, books or lottery tickets.[168] Teacher and *New Woman* author Jing Guan discussed the matter from the opposite direction. He complained that people had accused him of "plagiarism" when he and his colleagues founded the magazine in the tradition of the Hu-Chen circle. Of course, he rejected the accusation.[169]

A changed content

The usage of the New Culture Movement as a buzzword and the deployment as a matrix of marketing reference points of ideas that were associated with it filled new meaning into the vocabulary that formed part of this matrix. This dismayed those who were treated as this vocabulary's originators – Hu Shi, Chen Duxiu and the others who had before May Fourth advocated *baihua* at Beijing University.

Before May Fourth, these intellectuals had, as shown in chapter 1, argued for *baihua* on the grounds that it was the language best suited to present times. In his letter to Lin Shu from March 1919, the chancellor of Beijing University Cai Yuanpei specifically explained that the *baihua* advocated by his professors was not the language of "carriage pullers and jam sellers."[170] But the language of "carriage pullers and jam sellers" was exactly what *baihua* was now turned into as it was appropriated and redefined by others. The Jiangsu Educational Association treated "*baihua*" in its announcement for the lecture competition as part of the popular-education project.[171] They were not the only ones. The teacher trainee Zhu Daihen (no dates), for example, discussed it as a tool for popular education as well.[172]

The goal to create a language of the common people, however, was much closer to the National Language project. One famous National Language activist, Li Jinxi, said that at the time, the goal behind the National Language was the idea that a republican form of state could only be maintained if the common people possessed a certain degree of education. A language that was both national and used for writing and speaking was a useful tool to achieve this goal.[173] This was the way in which the National Language was deployed by reformers from Yan

---

168 Wang, *Chen Duxiu nianpu*, 94.
169 Jing, "Gao xin wenhua yundong de tongzhi," 33.
170 Cai, "Da Lin Qinnan shu," 98–99.
171 "Yanshuo jingjinhui yanti zhi jieshi," 10.
172 Zhu, "Ni yu tongxiang mou jun taolun xin wenhua yundong shixing fangfa shu," 37.
173 Li, *Guoyu yundong shigang*, 133.

Xishan to the Jiangsu Educational Association.¹⁷⁴ The quest for a language of the common people was now inscribed into the expression "*baihua*," and this was attributed to Hu Shi, Chen Duxiu and so forth as the "center of the New Culture Movement."¹⁷⁵

This redefinition had far-reaching results. For a long time, *baihua* made it into academic narratives as the language of the common people. It was translated as "the vernacular," treated as the language that wanted to tear down the boundaries between elite and the common people, and that was designed to communicate with the common people.¹⁷⁶ Even though Qu Qiubai had criticized *baihua* to really be a "new Literary Chinese" in the 1930s,¹⁷⁷ the idea that *baihua* was difficult to understand because of its Western loanwords and sentence structures only really took hold in academia after the 1990s, thanks to the work of scholars like Edward Gunn and Shih Shu-mei.¹⁷⁸

In practice, the boundaries between *baihua*-as-the-language-of-present-times and *baihua*-as-the-language-of-the-common-people were blurred. The actual writing styles the proponents of both sides deployed were undistinguishable. People from one camp also worked in institutions of the other, especially before May Fourth. For example, many *New Tide* authors were members of the Commoners' Education Lecture Society, an organ committed to popular education. Hu Shi was a delegate to the Preparatory Committee for the Unification of the National Language.¹⁷⁹ It had even been Hu Shi who had brought the National Language and *baihua* together in the first place. In his now famous article "A Discussion of a Constructive Literary Revolution" of 1918, he had coined the slogan "a literature in the National Language – a literary National Language."¹⁸⁰ Presumably marketing *baihua* as the National Language had then given him clout, rather than vice versa.

Nevertheless, the appropriation of their pet project *baihua* for the National Language argument upset the professed stars of the New Culture Movement con-

---

174 Yan, "Shanxi sheng zhengfu zhi Shilou zhishi han"; "Yanshuo jingjinhui yanti zhi jieshi," 10.
175 "Center of the New Culture Movement": Ye, "Ji Beijing daxue shiye shi (xu)."
176 "The vernacular": Schwarcz, *The Chinese Enlightenment*, 56; Zhou, *Placing the Modern Chinese Vernacular in Transnational Literature*. Tearing down the boundaries between elite and the common people: Schwarcz, *The Chinese Enlightenment*, 79. Communication with the common people: Chow, *The May Fourth Movement*, 178.
177 Mei Feuerwerker, *Ideology, Power, Text*, 39.
178 Gunn, *Rewriting Chinese*, 217–96; Shih, *The Lure of the Modern*, 71.
179 Li, *Guoyu yundong shigang*, 144.
180 Hu Shi, "Jianshe de wenxue geming lun" (Discussion of a Constructive Literary Revolution), *Xin qingnian* (New Youth) 4, no. 4 (1918): 289.

siderably after the second half of 1919.¹⁸¹ In a letter to Hu Shi, his friend Lin Yutang lamented that people treated *baihua* as the language of the common people. This was, in his view, a "blasphemy" of *baihua*.¹⁸² Chen Duxiu too felt that *baihua* should not be primarily "vulgar and easy to understand," but the medium of a "new literature."¹⁸³ *New Tide* editor Fu Sinian started distancing himself from the whole rhetoric of national salvation and the project of connecting academia with society. In autumn 1919 he expressed the unwillingness of the New Tide Society to "go and manage all matters in society."¹⁸⁴ "Managing all matters in society," however, was exactly what many activists, who talked about the New Culture Movement, were interested in (at least in theory). Fu Sinian's autumn article was also a far cry from the proactive, popular-education-style tone of his *New Tide* manifesto a few months earlier in January 1919, in which he had announced to "awaken the countrymen" and to teach the "countrymen" about evolution.¹⁸⁵

The stars and the followers

The people who had formerly been classified as the "New Faction" were not the only ones to notice that power over the New Culture Movement was not in their hands. Their self-declared followers were aware of it as well and this manifested itself in a number of ways.

First of all, these "followers" did not hesitate to criticize their purported idols when their own opinions differed. Such criticism often emerged from the debate about the question of whether the New Culture Movement should primarily be "enhanced" (*tigao*) or "popularized" (*puji*).¹⁸⁶ "Enhancing" meant to conduct further academic research into it. "Popularization" meant to spread it among the common people. Disagreement over this question was one of the biggest stones of contention among those who claimed to be New Culture activists. This "popular-

---

181 For the expression "center of the New Culture Movement," see Ye, "Ji Beijing daxue shiye shi (xu)."
182 Geng, *Hu Shi nianpu*, 85.
183 Chen, "Xin wenhua yundong shi shenme?," April 1920, 3.
184 Fu, "'Xinchao' zhi huigu yu qianzhan," October 30, 1919, 204.
185 Fu, "Xinchao fakan zhiqushu," 1398.
186 Zheng Shiqu, "Wu si hou guanyu 'xin wenhua yundong' de taolun" (Discussions about the "New Culture Movement" after May Fourth) conference paper, "Wu si de lishi yu lishi de wu si" xueshu taolunhui ("The History of May Fourth and the May Fourth of History." An Academic Symposium), Beijing, June 6, 2009, 25, Beijing, http://www.wanfangdata.com; Ye, "Ji Beijing daxue shiye shi (xu)"; Miao, "Suowei 'xin wenhua yundong' de chachao yu pochan," 3–4, 470.

ization"-versus-"enhancement" debate has often been interpreted as the beginning of the split of New Culture activists into Communists (the popularizer) and those who have been called "liberals," more scientifically or apolitically minded people (the enhancers).[187]

This split also manifested itself among the New Culture stars, which means that, while it was doubtful that they were anything resembling an "academic faction" before May Fourth, they were even less of a coherent group afterwards. The "popularizers" are often associated with Chen Duxiu, the "enhancers" with Hu Shi.[188] The reality, as usual, was more blurred, and Chen Duxiu advocated a combination of "popularization" and "enhancement" on at least one occasion.[189]

Nevertheless, the debate existed and one of its symptoms was the exchange of articles on "problems and isms" (*wenti yu zhuyi*). It was started by Hu Shi, who published a paper called "Research a Few More Questions and Talk a Bit Less about Isms" in the *Weekly Critic* of July 20, 1919. Lan Gongwu and Li Dazhao then published counter-articles in the *Citizen News* and the *Weekly Critic*, to which Hu Shi responded with further defenses.[190] In Leo Lee's interpretation, Hu Shi opposed the idea of "'fundamental solutions' for all the problems of a society" in favor of "attention to concrete situations."[191] By "fundamental solutions," Hu Shi in all likelihood meant communism.[192]

Many lesser-known New Culture debaters criticized the alleged leaders of the New Culture Movement in the context of this debate. Student Miao Jinyuan, for example, self-confidently declared that "what I am saying is just the opposite of [what] Mr. Hu Shi [says]. He says: 'Only enhancement is true popularization.' ... I

---

187 On Marxists, see Zheng, "Wu si hou guanyu 'xin wenhua yundong' de taolun," 21; Li, *Fu Sinian xueshu sixiang pingzhuan*, 18. "Liberals": Grieder, *Hu Shih and the Chinese Renaissance*, xi; Chow, *The May Fourth Movement*, 217. "scientifically" minded: Tani E Barlow, *Formations of Colonial Modernity in East Asia* (Durham: Duke University Press, 1997), 67–69. Apolitically minded: Li, *Fu Sinian xueshu sixiang pingzhuan*, 18.
188 Zheng, "Wu si hou guanyu 'xin wenhua yundong' de taolun," 25; Li, *Fu Sinian xueshu sixiang pingzhuan*, 18; Ying-shih Yü, "Neither Renaissance nor Enlightenment: A Historian's Reflection on the May Fourth Movement," in *The Appropriation of Cultural Capital: China's May Fourth Project*, ed. Milena Doleželová-Velingerová and Oldřich Král (Cambridge, Massachusetts: Harvard University Asia Center, 2001), 308–9.
189 Chen Duxiu, "Tigao yu puji" (Enhancement and Popularization), *Xin qingnian* (New Youth) 8, no. 4 (1920): 5–6.
190 Geng, *Hu Shi nianpu*, 76.
191 Leo Ou-fan Lee and Merle Goldman, *An Intellectual History of Modern China* (Cambridge: Cambridge University Press, 2002), 124.
192 Grieder, *Hu Shih and the Chinese Renaissance*, 125. See also Geng, *Hu Shi nianpu*, 76.

say: 'Only popularization is true enhancement.'"[193] Miao Jinyuan was not a critic of Hu Shi as such. Only a few paragraphs earlier, he had praised and cited him.[194] Rather, Miao was first and foremost following his own agenda, and only using Hu Shi to support it as necessary.

Secondly, the New Culture periphery ascribed to itself a pivotal role in the making of the New Culture Movement. In their narratives of the New Culture Movement and May Fourth, they often claimed that New Culture had emerged only *after* May Fourth – that is, when the lesser-known groups had become involved in it. As mentioned above, the Jiangsu Educational Association wrote that "the New Culture Movement continues the May Fourth Movement."[195] When the student Yu Tiandong (no dates) gave his presentation at the Association's lecture competition, he repeated that the New Culture Movement was making progress ever *since* – but not since before – the May Fourth protests.[196] Before the lesser-known people became involved, the narrative implied, new thought was not a movement.

As with so many narratives about New Culture, this one was not the only version that was put forward. As Zheng Shiqu points out, some contemporaries dated the New Culture Movement back to the end of World War I in 1918 or to the foundation of *New Youth* in 1915. Especially later on, the foundation of *New Youth* became increasingly popular as a starting point for New Culture.[197] But the claim that New Culture had only begun after May Fourth, when less famous groups and individuals had started using it as a buzzword, denied to the purported "cult heroes"[198] of the Movement the ability to create the "movement" without aid from the fans.[199]

As a result, Hu Shi, Chen Duxiu, Fu Sinian and the others of their former network at Beijing University experienced a sense of decline at their new height of fame. Hu Shi felt unduly criticized, claimed that it was others, primarily the media, who controlled what New Culture meant and complained that the New Culture Movement had developed a dynamic of its own. "After it has [started]

---

193 Miao, "Suowei 'xin wenhua yundong' de chachao yu pochan," 3–4, 4.
194 Ibid., 3.
195 Jiangsu sheng jiaoyuhui, "Zhi zhongdeng yishang ge xuexiao tongzhi dingqi juxing yanshuo jingjinhui shu," 25.
196 Yu Tiandong, "Xin wenhua yundong zhi zhongzhong wenti ji tuixing fa" (The Various Questions of the New Culture Movement and Ways to Promote It), *Xuesheng* (Students' Magazine) 7, no. 3 (1920): 1.
197 Zheng, "Wu si hou guanyu 'xin wenhua yundong' de taolun," 9.
198 Lit. "cult hero," Hockx, "Playing the Field," 65.
199 "Center of the New Culture Movement": Ye, "Ji Beijing daxue shiye shi (xu)."

moving," he said, "one cannot induce it not to move."[200] Hu Shi did not even like using the expression "New Culture Movement." Instead, he mostly spoke of the "new intellectual tide" (*xin sichao*).[201] Chen Duxiu did not share his qualms about the expression itself.[202] But he agreed that the "New Culture Movement" did not belong to him. Rather it was "currently very popular in our society."[203] "Society" or "many people," moreover, misunderstood the Movement, and Chen Duxiu saw himself compelled to correct these, in his view, misconceptions.[204]

Chen Duxiu and Hu Shi, in other words, tried to reappropriate the meaning of the "New Culture Movement" or the "new intellectual tide" by providing explanations of their own. To put it differently, ironically, the purported stars of the New Culture Movement sought to push their own ideals into the "legitimate core"[205] of the New Culture Movement, by trying to define the buzzword, just like everybody else.

However, they did not seem to have any strategic vision for this and their definitions kept changing. In November 1919, Chen Duxiu claimed that the New Culture Movement was about science. It replaced a "literary way of thinking" with a "scientific way of thinking."[206] In April 1920, he defined the New Culture Movement in very broad terms. It then was the renewal of all culture, which he defined as "science, religion, morality, arts, literature and music."[207] He narrowed this down again in May 1921, when he distinguished between a "cultural movement" and a "social movement." The former was about "literature, arts, music, philosophy and science" and the latter about "the women's question, the laborers' question and the population question." The "cultural movement," he now argued, would not automatically solve the social problems.[208] Hu Shi's explanations

---

[200] Ibid. Criticism of Hu: Geng, *Hu Shi nianpu*, 87. The media control: Hu Shi, "Xin sichao de yiyi" (The Meaning of the New Intellectual Tide), in *Xin qingnian* (New Youth), vol. 7A (Tokyo: Taian, 1963), 9.
[201] Hu, "Xin sichao de yiyi." A similar point has been made by Peng, *Yanjiuxi yu wu si shiqi xin wenhua yundong*, 182; Ouyang, "Guomindang yu xin wenhua yundong," 77.
[202] Chen Duxiu, "Gao xin wenhua yundong de zhu tongzhi" (To All the Comrades of the New Culture Movement), in *Cai Yuanpei, Chen Duxiu, Hu Shi* (Cai Yuanpei, Chen Duxiu, Hu Shi), ed. Gong Haiyan, vol. 14 (Shanghai: Shanghai wenyi chubanshe, 2010), 224–29; Chen, "Xin wenhua yundong shi shenme?," April 1920.
[203] Chen, "Xin wenhua yundong shi shenme?," April 1920, 1.
[204] "society": Chen, "Gao xin wenhua yundong de zhu tongzhi," 224, et passim. "Many people": Chen Duxiue, "Wenhua yundong yu shehui yundong" (The Culture Movement and the Social Movement), in *Xin qingnian* (New Youth), vol. 9A (Tokyo: Taian, 1963), 138.
[205] In modification of Cheek, "The Names of Rectification," 26. Originally "legitimating core."
[206] Chen, "Gao xin wenhua yundong de zhu tongzhi," 229.
[207] Chen, "Xin wenhua yundong shi shenme?," April 1920, 1.
[208] Chen, "Wenhua yundong yu shehui yundong," 138.

of the New Culture Movement kept changing as well. In December of 1919, he claimed that the "new intellectual tide" was about the "critical spirit."[209] In future years, and especially when talking to Western audiences, he would depict New Culture as the "Chinese Renaissance" and heavily emphasize the importance of the *baihua* movement.[210]

The people formerly classified as the "New Faction" were professed to be the stars of the New Culture Movement. But they were not in fact in control of the ideas they were claimed to be inspiring.

Conclusion

The New Culture Movement, as a buzzword, transformed Chinese culture. It did so, because it introduced a new matrix of marketing reference points into the cultural field, which reweighted the persuasiveness of the competing agendas. In other words, marketing with the New Culture Movement worked better for some programs than it did for others. Liu Boming's promotion of Literary Chinese therefore did not work. Neither did Christianity, which probably stood too much in the suspicion of being an unscientific "superstition"; that is, it was too easily associated with a "delegitimizing term."[211] Not even a powerful buzzword could, moreover, overcome strong political trends. Taiwanese independence, for example, could not be talked into the world when Japanese imperialism was in the ascendant. Again, Christianity could not stand a chance in a country where Marxism, an ideology skeptical of religion, would come into power.

However, where politics and the matrix of reference points did not explicitly stand in the way, the New Culture Movement as a buzzword could strengthen agendas and in this way give them the edge over their rivals and move them towards the "legitimate core."[212] The National Language, for example, was similar enough to "New Faction" *baihua* for it to be sold as the New Culture Movement. After years of unsuccessful petitioning, the National Union of Educational Associations finally succeeded in October 1919 in persuading the Ministry of Education to make the National Language a subject of primary schools. In January

---

209 Hu, "Xin sichao de yiyi," 10.
210 Shi Hu, *The Chinese Renaissance*, The Haskell Lectures, 1933 (Whitefish, Montana: Kessinger Publishing, 2010).
211 Lit. "delegitimizing terms," Cheek, "The Names of Rectification," 27.
212 In modification of Ibid., 26. Originally "legitimating core."

1920 the Ministry decreed that the National Language should become part of the primary-school curriculum starting in that year.[213]

Similarly communism rose in popularity, aided additionally, of course, by the efforts of the Comintern and the new organizational initiatives following upon May Fourth. In 1921, the Chinese Communist Party was founded. Feminism, too, got a boost, and even though it would (and will) take many more decades for complete gender equality to be achieved, the lives of women became somewhat more independent. Beijing University, for example, hired its first female professor with Chen Hengzhe (Sophia Chen, 1890–1976) in 1920.[214]

This also says something about agency (here in the sense of the "who did what") in the making of cultural change through the New Culture Movement. If agency was already very complicated in the making of the matrix of reference points (chapter 2), the deployment of the buzzword made it even trickier. If everyone and no one was involved in shaping the matrix of New Culture associations, the question of the "whodunit" is further complicated by the fact that those who did (their part of) it said that they were doing what others were doing. To put it differently, when wielding the buzzword New Culture Movement, the lesser-known reformist groups claimed that they were following ideas of the (never quite coherent, but by then certainly dissolved) Hu-Chen circle. Their goal behind this was to add glamour to their own agendas, by attributing them to more prestigious people. This made agency in the New Culture Movement appear very simple, but in fact only glossed over its complex nature. Nobody made the cultural change of the time, in the sense of orchestrating it. It was created through the concatenation of the actions of many.

---

[213] For a petition in 1914, see Quanguo jiaoyuhui lianhehui, "Tongyi guoyu fangfa'an" (Motion for the Unification of the National Language), in *Lijie jiaoyu huiyi yijue'an huibian* (Collection of the Resolutions of All Historical Meetings of the Educational Associations), ed. Tai Shuangqiu (Beijing: Quanguo tushuguan wenxian suowei zhongxin, 2010), 2–3. For one in 1916, see Quanguo jiaoyuhui lianhehui, "Qing ding guoyu biaozhun bing tuixing zhuyin zimu yiqi yuyan tongyi" (Request for Determination of a Standard for the National Language and the Promotion of Bopomofo, so as to Unify the Language), in *Lijie jiaoyu huiyi yijue'an huibian* (Collection of the Resolutions of All Historical Meetings of the Educational Associations), ed. Tai Shuangqiu (Beijing: Quanguo tushuguan wenxian suowei zhongxin, 2010), 12–13. The National Language in primary school curricula: Wang, "Chinese Literature from 1841 to 1937," 466.
[214] Katrina Gulliver, *Modern Women in China and Japan: Gender, Feminism and Global Modernity between the Wars* (London: Tauris, 2012), 78.

4 The 1920s and 1930s – The limits of the New Culture Movement

"The mood of society has hugely changed [in our favor]," Fu Sinian wrote in September 1919. All of society was now celebrating his circle and the New Culture Movement, he claimed.[1] Even though he and the others who suddenly found themselves at the "center"[2] of the New Culture Movement were somewhat skeptical about it, they were also excited about its (and their) sudden success. But Fu Sinian appeared to be overly optimistic with this assessment of the New Culture Movement's reach. The New Culture Movement was important, Wang Jingwei (1883–1944) wrote in 1921, but only in the humanities. The sciences hardly cared about it.[3] Wang Jingwei would later become known as a collaborator with the Japanese during World War II. But at the time he was head of the Guangdong Educational Association.

Liu Yin (1914-?), daughter of the mayor of Tianjin of 1935–1936, never read Lu Xun in the 1920s and early 1930s. Instead, she preferred Mandarin Duck and Butterfly fiction, such as the novels by Zhang Henshui (1897–1967). Only later, when she came to the United Kingdom in the 1950s, she started reading Lu Xun – mainly because she was helping British students of Chinese with reading the Chinese texts. Her future husband, Liu Jung-en (Liu Rong'en, 1908/09-?), their daughter Taotao Liu, a professor for Chinese literature at the University of Oxford, suspects, "probably would not have bothered" to read *baihua* literature either. Instead he would have read English books, since English was the language of the Western- and science-educated elite.[4]

The claim that New Culture swept over all of (urban)[5] society, in other words, is another construction put forward from within the discourse. The New Culture Movement was important, but only to a limited circle of people. Most of them

---

[1] Fu, "'Xinchao' zhi huigu yu qianzhan," October 30, 1919, 201. This *New Tide* issue was published on 30 October 1919. But Fu Sinian claimed to have written this article on 5 September 1919, Ibid., 205.
[2] "Center of the New Culture Movement": Ye, "Ji Beijing daxue shiye shi (xu)."
[3] Wang Jingwei, "Wang huizhang jiuzhi ri yanshuoci" (Speech given by President Wang upon Taking Office), *Guangdong sheng jiaoyuhui zazhi* (Journal of the Guangdong Educational Association) 1, no. 1 (July 1921): 2.
[4] Taotao Liu, "E-mail message to the author," June 22, 2014; Taotao Liu, "Conversation with the author," June 25, 2014.
[5] Rana Mitter has argued that May Fourth and New Culture were only an urban phenomenon, Mitter, *A Bitter Revolution*, 25.

https://doi.org/10.1515/9783110560718-005

came from the humanities, as Wang Jingwei suggested, education and a few political interest groups.

Many of these people, who did discuss the New Culture Movement, however, were very enthusiastic and well-informed about debates conducted under the headline "New Culture Movement," and this was fostered by the routes along which information about New Culture was transmitted: personal networks and advertising strategies that usually promoted journals in like-minded publications. However, even little-known individuals in the early 20th century were tapped into global networks. Eventually information about New Culture was therefore gradually transmitted through personal networks to new groups of people, who did not appear to become New Culture enthusiasts, but who took a more general or cursory interest in New Culture.

Finally, a note on terminology is called for. The previous chapters have focused on the expression "New Culture Movement" specifically, and distinguished it from "May Fourth." This and the next chapter are different. They bring us to the margins of the New Culture discourse, and they also are about a time when for contemporaries the expressions "New Culture" and "May Fourth" had merged into one concept. Distinguishing between them therefore makes little sense here, and I will consequently discuss all the various terms that could refer to New Culture/May Fourth together.

Limited interest in the New Culture Movement

The people who cared

In the early 1920s, the New Culture Movement was actively discussed in the articles of the many journals that "sprang up like spring bamboo after the rain" in the months after the May Fourth demonstrations.[6] The writers and readers of these journals formed what Thomas Bender calls "communities of discourse,"[7] whom the New Culture Movement, its vocabulary, personnel and ideas provided with a "cluster of shared meanings and intellectual purposes."[8] These spring-bamboo journals often indicated that they were run by "societies," for example, the New Woman Society or the Social Reconstruction Society. This high-sounding nomenclature supported the impression that these "societies" were somewhat

---

6 Wang, *Huiyi Yadong tushuguan*, 38.
7 Bender, "The Cultures of Intellectual Life," 3.
8 Ibid., 4.

larger than life and considerable forces in, to use Fu Sinian's word, "society."[9] But essentially their members were students, teachers and other intellectuals from secondary schools, universities and political parties, and often they had a background in the humanities or in education. Social and natural sciences were hardly represented.

Among these spring-bamboo journals based at educational institutions was *Criticism*. Miao Jinyuan, who was so self-confident in criticizing Hu Shi (see chapter 3), wrote for this journal. *Criticism* bore many of the hallmarks that would become part of a more permanent New Culture discourse. It claimed in its mission statement that it wanted to "bravely and fearlessly appraise, analyze and test all things in mankind and society with the critical spirit, the scientific method and a questioning attitude."[10] It was consistently written in *baihua* and discussed the New Culture Movement in two articles in its first issue alone.[11] *Criticism* was a supplement to the GMD newspaper *Republic Daily* and founded in October 1920.[12] However, the members of the Criticism Society were students of Beijing University and they merely used the *Republic Daily* as a medium to distribute their paper.[13] Miao Jinyuan, for example, was enrolled at the philosophy faculty of Beijing University, where Hu Shi was teaching too.[14]

There were more publications like *Criticism*. *Social Reconstruction* (*Xinqun*), launched in December 1919, was a journal at Shanghai Chinese Public School. Its declared aim was to discuss the "pressing" issues of foreign politics, the "turmoil" of domestic politics and the suffering of the "people."[15] Similarly, *New Student* (*Xin xuesheng*), launched in December 1919, held up the ideal to take "responsibility" in a constantly changing world,[16] and it featured articles on "The New Great

---

9 Fu, "'Xinchao' zhi huigu yu qianzhan," October 30, 1919, 201.
10 "Fakanci" (Manifesto), *Piping* (Criticism), October 20, 1920, 1, 1, Beijing; Shanghai.
11 Zhou Changxian, "Piping de jingshen he xin wenhua yundong" (The Critical Spirit and the New Culture Movement), *Piping* (Criticism), 1920, 2, Shanghai; Miao, "Suowei 'xin wenhua yundong' de chachao yu pochan," 3–4.
12 David Bowles, "Finding the Way: The Nationalist Party Appropriation of Confucius and the Challenges of Revolutionary Traditionalism in China, 1919–1934" (PhD, University of Oxford, 2013), 34, University of Oxford.
13 Qiu Shihuang, Wu Xinxun, and Xiang Chunwu, eds., "Piping" (Criticism), *Xinwen chuanbo baike quanshu* (Encyclopedia of News and Broadcasting) (Chengdu: Sichuan renmin chubanshe, 1998), Chengdu; "Ben she qishi san" (Third Announcement of This Society), *Piping* (Criticism), October 20, 1920, 4, Beijing; "Banner," *Piping* (Criticism), October 20, 1920, 1 edition, 1, Beijing; Shanghai.
14 Miao Jinyuan, "Miao Jinyuan zhi Hu Shi" (Miao Jinyuan to Hu Shi), in *Hu Shi laiwang shuxinxuan* (Hu Shi's Selected Correspondence) (Beijing: Zhonghua shuju, 1979), 117–19.
15 Wang, "Fakan ci," 1.
16 "Fakanci" (Manifesto), *Xin xuesheng* (New Student) 1, no. 1 (December 1919): 1.

Crest of the Young People's New Culture" and "Love Marriages and No-Love Marriages."[17] *New Student* was run by the New Student Society, which belonged to the newly founded Taicang Student Union. Taicang is a place in modern-day Jiangsu. Individual students from this Union came from Nanjing Higher Normal School, which trained teachers, or from Nanyang Public School, where the Jiangsu Educational Association's vice-president, Huang Yanpei, had been a student and Cai Yuanpei a teacher.[18] These spring-bamboo journals, in other words, were run by students mostly at pedagogical and humanities faculties.

Another type of publication that actively negotiated the New Culture Movement was periodicals managed by political interest groups. Among them were the GMD and the Research Clique. Under Chiang Kai-shek, the GMD would later become skeptical of the New Culture Movement. But in 1919, Sun Yat-sen saw the potential of the phenomenon.[19] The GMD therefore founded two journals in August 1919, *Weekly Review* and *Construction*. *Weekly Review* was among the first to use the expression "New Culture Movement" in August 1919.[20] Publisher Wang Yuanfang recalled that *Construction* was so committed to the New Culture discourse that it refused to exchange advertisements with publications that did not support the New Culture Movement.[21] (On the practice of exchanging advertisements, see below.)

Another political party whose publications discussed the New Culture Movement was the Research Clique (for details, see Introduction). A number of newspapers and magazines that framed themselves as part of the New Culture Movement most actively belonged to this group. Among them were the Beijing newspaper *Morning Post*, as well as the journals *Emancipation and Reconstruction* (*Jiefang yu gaizao*) and *Scholar's Lantern* (*Xuedeng*). The *Morning Post* had provided a platform for the circle around Hu Shi and Chen Duxiu even before May Fourth. In March, for example, it had published Li Dazhao's tirades against the "tough guy" who was allegedly attacking his circle.[22] After the May Fourth demonstrations, the *Morning Post* reshaped itself even more according to the New Culture

---

17 "Muci" (Table of Contents), *Xin xuesheng* (New Student) 1, no. 1 (December 1919).
18 "Fakanci," 1; "Ben she qishi yi" (First Announcement of This Society), *Xin xuesheng* (New Student) 1, no. 1 (December 1919). On Nanjing Higher Normal School's teacher-training program, see Yeh, *The Alienated Academy*, 5. On Huang Yanpei studying at Nanyang Public School, see Cai Zhiguang and Xie Zewei, *Pudong mingren shujian baitong* (Collection of Letters by Famous People of Pudong) (Shanghai: Shanghai yuandong chubanshe, 2010), 158.
19 Ouyang, "Guomindang yu xin wenhua yundong," 74.
20 Xian, "Xin wenhua yundong de wuqi," 4.
21 Wang, *Huiyi Yadong tushuguan*, 41.
22 Shou, "Xin jiu sichao zhi jizhan," 7, March 4, 1919; Shou, "Xin jiu sichao zhi jizhan," 7, March 5, 1919.

Movement. On January 31, 1919, it restructured its section "Free Forum" to discuss ideas classified as the New Culture Movement. Among them were themes like "new knowledge" and "new thought."²³ This, Leo Lee argues, turned the section into "an arena for the New Culture Movement."²⁴ The *Morning Post* belonged to the Research Clique in that it was funded by that party and edited by various of its members.²⁵

Similarly, *Scholar's Lantern* endorsed ideas like *baihua* even before the May Fourth demonstrations, and afterwards its support increased, featuring *baihua* texts by Mao Dun (1896–1981) and Guo Moruo (1892–1978). It also negotiated the New Culture Movement in articles such as "The Three Big Dangers to the New Culture Movement Today" of August 1920. *Scholar's Lantern* was a supplement to *China Times*, which was funded by Liang Qichao and it was edited by Zhang Dongsun (1886–1973), another leader of the Research Clique.²⁶ *Emancipation and Reconstruction*, finally, was the journal in which Jiang Qi discussed "The New Culture Movement and Education" in 1920.²⁷ It too was edited by Research Clique members.²⁸ This circle did indeed actively debate the New Culture Movement, but its reach was quite small.

The people who did not care

Other sub-sections of urban society simply ignored the New Culture Movement. Among them were, as Wang Jingwei said, China's scientists.²⁹ But businesspeople also counted among their numbers.

Like Liu Jung-en (from the introductory paragraph), who "probably would not have bothered" to read *baihua* literature,³⁰ businesspeople were not particularly

---

23 Peng, *Yanjiuxi yu wu si shiqi xin wenhua yundong*, 208–9.
24 Lee, "Incomplete Modernity," 55.
25 Peng, *Yanjiuxi yu wu si shiqi xin wenhua yundong*, 207–8.
26 Qiu Shihuang, Wu Xinxun, and Xiang Chunwu, eds., "Shishi xinbao" (China Times), *Xinwen chuanbo baike quanshu* (Encyclopedia of News and Broadcasting) (Chengdu: Sichuan renmin chubanshe, 1998), Chengdu; Peng, *Yanjiuxi yu wu si shiqi xin wenhua yundong*, 163–66, 186, 208.
27 Jiang, "Xin wenhua yundong he jiaoyu."
28 Peng, *Yanjiuxi yu wu si shiqi xin wenhua yundong*, 248; Qiu Shihuang, Wu Xinxun, and Xiang Chunwu, eds., "Jiefang yu gaizao" (Emancipation and Reconstruction), *Xinwen chuanbo baike quanshu* (Encyclopedia of News and Broadcasting) (Chengdu: Sichuan renmin chubanshe, 1998), Chengdu.
29 Wang, "Wang huizhang jiuzhi ri yanshuoci," 2.
30 Liu, "Taotao Liu, e-mail message to the author"; Liu, "Taotao Liu, conversation with the author."

interested in *baihua*. Instead they favored English, which had, in Yeh Wen-hsin's words, become the "language of global commerce."³¹ The *Commercial Student*, a student journal based at the Peking School of Commerce and Finance, wrote in Literary Chinese and in English.³² When reporting about May Fourth in an article of December 1919, one of its authors told a story about the demonstrations that did not feature Beijing University's "New Faction" or the subsequent "New Culture Movement" at all. Instead, he reported only about the anti-government and anti-Japanese nature of the demonstrations.³³

This lack of interest in the New Culture Movement continued in business circles over the next decade. In the 1920s and 1930s, the missionary Emma Lester (1883–1978) received numerous English-language letters from her former Chinese students. These were mostly affluent ladies from Shanghai – the catchment area of the Jiangsu Educational Association –, who were married to businessmen or politicians. Nevertheless, the expression "New Culture Movement" did not appear in their letters. These ladies may just not have mentioned the New Culture Movement in their letters to Lester, while being interested in it outside of the correspondence. But it is conspicuous that they discussed with her other intellectual and political events, such as the rise of communism and the Sino-Japanese war, but not May Fourth and New Culture.³⁴ Lester's Shanghai friends also never referred to any of the New Culture figureheads. Instead, they talked about the English-language books they had read, such as George Bernard Shaw (1856–1950) and John Erskine (1879–1951).³⁵

While again this may have been a choice about what to share with Lester, rather than reflecting their actual interest, it is conspicuous that the National Language did not appear to have played any part in their lives either. This was in spite of the government's ongoing efforts to popularize it, which extended well into the 1930s.³⁶ Students often learned the National Language at school, but then

---

31 Yeh, *The Alienated Academy*, 12.
32 An article in Literary Chinese: Dai, "Shangye xuesheng di-er ji bianyan." An article in English: Zhong, "The triumph of the students."
33 Zhong, "The triumph of the students."
34 See, for example, Tuh Wei Chang, "Letter to Emma Lester," December 15, 1931, 1–2, Container 214, Lewis Nathaniel Chase Papers, Manuscript Division, Library of Congress, Washington, D.C.; Vung Yuin Ting, "Letter to Emma Lester," January 11, 1937, Container 209, Lewis Nathaniel Chase Papers, Manuscript Division, Library of Congress, Washington, D.C.
35 For a mention of George Bernard Shaw, see Sze Be Tsung, "Letter to Emma Lester," September 18, 1929, 2, Container 218, Lewis Nathaniel Chase Papers, Manuscript Division, Library of Congress, Washington, D.C. For a mention of John Erskine, see Chang, "Chang Tuh Wei to Emma Lester," 3.
36 Chen, *Modern Chinese*, 22–23.

hardly ever used it again. This at least was the experience of Liu Yin, the daughter of the future mayor of Tianjin.[37]

This neglect is surprising since at least one of Lester's acquaintances, Sam Moy (Samuel Orne Moy, no dates), would have much benefitted from a National Language. In 1933 Sam Moy moved to Shanghai with his wife, Niu Minghua (no dates), who had been born there.[38] Moy spoke a Chinese dialect as a native language that was incomprehensible to people in Shanghai and vice versa.[39] During the months after moving to Shanghai, Niu Minghua confided in her friend Emma Lester that Moy had considerable trouble gaining a foothold in Shanghai because he did not understand the dialect.[40] On occasion, when he inspected factories as part of his job, he even asked his wife to translate Shanghai's Wu dialect into English for him. Understandably Niu sighed: "Now what do I know about engineering & its technical terms. I had the worst time in the beginning, but getting to be quite an engineer myself now. Well, I'll be glad when this touring around is over."[41] Had the National Language reached business circles by 1933, Sam Moy would have had an easier time getting settled in Shanghai.

The opposition

Indifference to the New Culture Movement was not the only form of lacking enthusiasm. There was also outright opposition. Even though Liu Boming had tried to market Literary Chinese as the New Culture Movement during John Dewey's lectures in 1920, explicit opposition against the New Culture Movement had not died out within the humanities. Soon Liu Boming would join it. In 1922, the academics in Nanjing around Mei Guangdi (1890–1945), Hu Xiansu (1894-1894) and

---

37 Liu, "Taotao Liu, conversation with the author."
38 Minghua Niu, "Letter to Emma Lester," December 10, 1933, 1, Container 209, Lewis Nathaniel Chase Papers, Manuscript Division, Library of Congress, Washington, D.C.
39 Minghua Niu, "Letter to Emma Lester," July 23, 1937, 2, Container 209, Lewis Nathaniel Chase Papers, Manuscript Division, Library of Congress, Washington, D.C.
40 Minghua Niu, "Letter to Emma Lester," June 2, 1934, 3–4, Container 209, Lewis Nathaniel Chase Papers, Manuscript Division, Library of Congress, Washington, D.C. The situation was aggravated for Sam Moy, because he seemed to have lived in the US with his family for a long time. See Minghua Niu, "Letter to Emma Lester," May 9, 1933, 1, Container 209, Lewis Nathaniel Chase Papers, Manuscript Division, Library of Congress, Washington, D.C. However, Sam and his family were Chinese and Ming reported that she did not understand their dialect either. See Niu, "Niu Minghua to Emma Lester," July 23, 1937, 2.
41 Minghua Niu, "Letter to Emma Lester," February 28, 1934, 2–3, Container 209, Lewis Nathaniel Chase Papers, Manuscript Division, Library of Congress, Washington, D.C.

Tang Yongtong (1893–1964) founded the *Critical Review* (*Xueheng*), in which Liu Boming was involved as well.⁴² The *Critical Review*'s "mission," according to Lydia Liu, was to oppose the New Culture Movement and *baihua* literature.⁴³

Mei Guangdi had never stopped pestering Hu Shi. In November 1919, Mei had just returned from the United States, and Hu Shi's friend Ren Hongjuan (1886–1961) told Hu in a letter from Nanjing that "Old Mei is making a big noise there, giving lectures on new literature. In passing, he is also attacking 'Huism.'" Ren Hongjuan expressed his hope that Hu Shi and "Old Mei" would be able to refrain from quarrelling with each other.⁴⁴ Hu Shi and Mei Guangdi used to be close friends but developed insurmountable differences over the *baihua* project in 1917.⁴⁵ Criticism of the New Culture Movement soon became vocal more widely. In 1921 two Chinese students in the United States, Qiu Changwei (1898–1956) and Wu Mi (1894–1978), exchanged articles on the topic. Wu Mi, a master's student in comparative literature, attacked the New Culture Movement, while Qiu Changwei defended it.⁴⁶

The *Critical Review*, co-founded by Wu Mi upon his return to Nanjing in 1922, resumed many of the themes proposed in *National Heritage* in 1919, and has therefore been regarded as its successor magazine.⁴⁷ The journal rejected *baihua* in favor of Literary Chinese.⁴⁸ It also shared argumentative strategies with *National Heritage*. For example, its author Hu Xiansu wrote that spoken language was too unstable over time, and the vernacular of the present would not be comprehensible in the future. Therefore it was preferable to write in the more stable Literary

---

42 Qiu Shihuang, Wu Xinxun, and Xiang Chunwu, eds., "Xueheng" (Critical Review), *Xinwen chuanbo baike quanshu* (Encyclopedia of News and Broadcasting) (Chengdu: Sichuan renmin chubanshe, 1998), Chengdu; Mei Feuerwerker, "Reconsidering Xueheng," 140.
43 Liu, *Translingual Practice*, 250.
44 Geng, *Hu Shi nianpu*, 78.
45 Mei Feuerwerker, "Reconsidering Xueheng," 143; Yü, "Neither Renaissance nor Enlightenment," 314.
46 Qiu Changwei, "Lun xin wenhua yundong (da Wu Mi jun)" (A Discussion of the New Culture Movement [a Reply to Mr. Wu Mi]), *Liu Mei xuesheng jibao* (Chinese Students' Quarterly) 8, no. 4 (1921): 1–13; Wu Mi, "Lun xin wenhua yundong (jielu Liu Mei xuesheng jibao)" (A Discussion of the New Culture Movement [An Excerpt from the *Chinese Students' Quarterly*]), *Xueheng* (Critical Review), no. 4 (1922): 36–58; Wu Mi, "Zai lun xin wenhua yundong (da Qiu Changwei jun)" (Another Discussion of the New Culture Movement [A Reply to Mr. Qiu Changwei]), *Liu Mei xuesheng jibao* (Chinese Students' Quarterly) 8, no. 4 (1921): 13–38. On Wu Mi being a master's student, see Mei Feuerwerker, "Reconsidering Xueheng," 147.
47 Liu, *Translingual Practice*, 246–56.
48 Wu Lichang, ed., *Wenxue de xiaojie yu fan xiaojie: Zhongguo xiandai wenxue paibie lunzheng shilun* (Dispelling Literature and the Opposition to Dispelling It: A History of the Factions and Debates in Modern Chinese Literature) (Shanghai: Fudan daxue chubanshe, 2004), 97.

Chinese.⁴⁹ Zhang Xuan had written something very similar in *National Heritage* in 1919 (see chapter 1).⁵⁰

This does not mean that the *Critical Review* was simply an imitation of *National Heritage*. Its most central debate with its biggest opponent, *New Youth*, was not about understandings of things like evolution, as had been the case with *National Heritage* and *New Tide*. One important difference between the *Critical Review* and *New Youth* was which Western scholars they regarded as worthy models. While authors of *New Youth* admired figures like Bertrand Russell (1872–1970) and John Dewey, the *Critical Review* followed Irving Babbitt (1865–1933).⁵¹ Yi-tsi Mei Feuerwerker even suggests that the difference between the *Critical Review* and *New Youth* was down to the different universities they attended in the United States, Columbia in Hu Shi's case, and Harvard in Mei Guangdi's and Wu Mi's case.⁵²

Even though the *Critical Review* has since been called a serious force in "[t]he struggle between the two camps for recognition as the sole, legitimate voice of Chinese culture,"⁵³ the magazine never gained the same traction as *New Youth*. Hu Shi appears to have been right when he condescendingly commented on the launch of the magazine that it was "probably the epilogue of opposition to the literary revolution."⁵⁴ The *Critical Review*'s sales numbers were notoriously low, and this made its editors resort to very desperate measures.⁵⁵ Zhang Shizhao (1881–1973), the editor of the *Tiger* magazine, once offered to help out with a cash injection. According to Timothy Weston, *Tiger* had been instrumental in instituting the later New Culture "community" and their discourse in the early 1910s. Later, however, Zhang Shizhao became "conservative" and a "critic" of the New Culture Movement.⁵⁶ But Wu Mi refused Zhang Shizhao's offer to help, because, Liu Kedi argues, he feared for the autonomy of the magazine. Instead, he asked his friends to sell the magazine in their home provinces or to the libraries they worked at.⁵⁷

---

49 Ibid., 98; Zhang, "Wen yan heyi pingyi," 2B.
50 Zhang, "Wen yan heyi pingyi."
51 Mei Feuerwerker, "Reconsidering Xueheng," 145; Liu, *Translingual Practice*, 248; Ye Shixiang and Zhang Dongmei, "Xiandaixing shiye zhong de 'guocui pai' he 'Xueheng pai'" (The "National Essence Group" and the "Critical Review Group" from a Modern Perspective), *Wenzhou daxue xuebao* (Journal of Wenzhou University) 21, no. 4 (2008): 3; Yü, "Neither Renaissance nor Enlightenment," 316–18.
52 Mei Feuerwerker, "Reconsidering Xueheng," 145.
53 Liu, *Translingual Practice*, 255–56.
54 Wu, *Wenxue de xiaojie yu fan xiaojie*, 95.
55 Mei Feuerwerker, "Reconsidering Xueheng," 165.
56 Timothy B Weston, "The Formation and Positioning of the New Culture Community, 1913–1917," *Modern China* 24, no. 3 (July 1998): 125, 261.
57 Liu Kedi, *Hua luo chun reng zai: Wu Mi yu "Xueheng"* (The Flowers Have Wilted but Spring Is Still There: Wu Mi and the *Critical Review*) (Beijing: Zhongguo wenlian chubanshe, 2001), 208–09.

The *Critical Review* never seemed to have much public visibility. The *Shanghai News*, for example, hardly ever reported about it and its editors.[58] Soon the magazine also lost some of its most important supporters. Liu Boming died in 1923, and Hu Xiansu and Mei Guangdi left China for the United States in 1924. Consequently, the *Critical Review* had difficulties getting article submissions.[59] It is therefore surprising that it nevertheless managed to last until 1933 and to produce seventy-nine issues.[60] Even though the opposition against New Culture was only moderately successful within the humanities, it was not abandoned.

The people formerly classified as the "Old Faction" were also still active in academia and education, with the exception of Liu Shipei, who died on November 20, 1919.[61] The others, however, continued their careers, although they did not reach the heights of success that their former opponents from the "New Faction" achieved. Huang Kan left Beijing University in 1919 and served as principal and professor at various universities until his death on October 8, 1935.[62] The *National Heritage* students are somewhat more difficult to trace, since they never became famous. But judging from the sort of magazines in which they published over the next decades, and even though this is only a very approximate method, they seemed to have found employment in smaller academic and government institutions.

Zhang Xuan continued publishing until around 1933. The journals in which his articles appeared suggest that he stayed in Beijing in 1920, moved to the Shanghai region in the mid- and late-1920s and lived in Canton in the 1930s. There he may have had an academic position at National Zhongshan University.[63] It seems as if Yu Shizhen remained in Beijing until 1940, when his trace is lost. Until then, he stayed active in scholarly circles. For example, he published in

---

[58] This is indicated by a search of the database *Shenbao 1872–1949*.
[59] Duan Huaiqing, *Baibide yu Zhongguo wenhua* (Babbitt and Chinese Culture) (Beijing: Shoudu shifan daxue chubanshe, 2006), 146; Liu, *Hua luo chun reng zai: Wu Mi yu "Xueheng,"* 207.
[60] Qiu, Wu, and Xiang, "Xueheng."
[61] Chen, *Liu Shipei nianpu changbian*, 357.
[62] On Huang's departure from Beijing University, see Lin, *Peking University*, 47. According to Pei Xiaowei, he became head of the Qinghua Research Institute, of Dongnan University or Wuchang Higher Normal School. He was also professor at Jinling University. See Pei, "Huang Kan."
[63] Zhang Xuan published in the following magazines until 1933: 1920: *New China* (*Xin Zhongguo*), a monthly journal published in Beijing from 1919 to 1920; 1926: *Sound of the Tide* (*Haichao yin*), a fortnightly from Shanghai, run by the Buddhicisation Education Society; 1932: *Southwest Research* (*Xinan yanjiu*), run in Guangzhou by Southwest Research Group of the National Sun Yat-sen University; 1933: *Great Voice* (*Da sheng*), a monthly journal from Guangzhou. See *Quanguo baokan suoyin*; *Quanguo baokan suoyin, qikan daohang*.

the *Critical Review* in 1931.⁶⁴ In the 1930s, he may have been employed at the Beijing Old Learning Academy and taught at National Beijing Women's Teachers' Academy. Xue Xiangsui may also have stayed in Beijing and he seems to have been involved in various study societies. In the early 1930s, he might have moved to Henan, Nanjing or Shaanxi, where he may have been affiliated with local educational-political departments.⁶⁵

Lin Shu, however, was left a frustrated man, according to his biographers Zhang Juncai and Michael Gibbs Hill.⁶⁶ But even he continued being involved in institutions that were skeptical of ideas promoted under the label "New Culture Movement" until his death on October 9, 1924. For example, he participated in the Confucian Society *Shangxian tang* ("Hall for the Veneration of Worthies"), which was revived by the American missionary Gilbert Reid (1857–1927) in 1922. In 1923, Lin Shu wrote a text called "Continued Discussion on the Debate on Treason," in which he called the New Culture activists "great traitors."⁶⁷ In 1924, he was made head of the *guowen* department at Republican University.⁶⁸ The press had not forgotten Lin Shu either. Every time someone staged *Oliver Twist* or *The Lady of the Camellias*, which Lin Shu had translated, the *Shanghai News* mentioned his name.⁶⁹

---

64 Yu Shizhen published until 1940 in these magazines: 1939 and 1940: *Collections of Ancient Learning* (*Guxue congkan*), a fortnightly journal in Beijing founded in 1939. It was edited by the Editorial Group of the Beijing Old Learning Academy and sold by Beijing Old Learning Academy; 1939: *Literature and Art* (*Wenyi*), an irregular journal from Beiping, founded in 1939, and run and sold by National Beijing Women's Teachers' Academy, Literature and Arts Research Group; 1931: the *Critical Review* (*Xueheng*). See *Quanguo baokan suoyin*; *Quanguo baokan suoyin, qikan daohang*.
65 Xue Xiangsui's publication can be traced until 1940 in the following journals: 1939: *Shiboh Review* (*Xibei lunheng*), a monthly journal from Beiping edited and sold by the Shiboh Review Society; 1932: *Northwest Research* (*Xibei yanjiu*), a monthly journal from Beiping edited and sold by Northwest Research Society; 1934: *Henan Education Monthly* (*Henan jiaoyu yuekan*), a monthly journal from Kaifeng, edited and sold by the Henan Education Department; 1935: *Northwest Questions* (*Xibei wenti*), a weekly journal from Nanjing launched in 1932, and edited and run by Nanjing Northwest Question Newspaper Society; 1940: *Resistance and Construction* (*Kang jian*) from Shaanxi, founded in 1939 and edited and sold by the Shaanxi Provincial Government Education Department. See *Quanguo baokan suoyin*; *Quanguo baokan suoyin, qikan daohang*.
66 Zhang, *Lin Shu pingzhuan*, 237; Hill, *Lin Shu, Inc.*, 230.
67 Zhang, *Lin Shu pingzhuan*, 239.
68 Tian Hao, "Beijing zhi daxue xiaoxi" (News from Beijing's Universities), *Shenbao* (Shanghai News), July 3, 1924, 11, Shanghai.
69 "Yingguo zhuming xiaoshuo shecheng yingju," 18; "'Chahua nü' xiaoshuo zhi xin dianying," 18; Ting, "'Gu'er ku yu' zhi pinglun," 15.

Although none of the people formerly classified as "Old Faction" gained the same fame as their counterparts from the "New Faction," they had not disappeared from academia and educational politics, and they continued to oppose the circle around Chen Duxiu and Hu Shi, as well as the label "New Culture Movement" that now surrounded this group.

Grey area of marginal interest

Between these two extremes, those that dedicated journals to discussing the New Culture Movement and those that directly opposed it, was a large group of people who had heard of the New Culture Movement and the features associated with it, who approved of it, but who displayed only moderate interest in it. One example for such people was the English-literature students of the American professor Lewis Nathaniel Chase (1873–1937) at Yanjing, Beijing and Beijing Normal Universities. Chase was the son of a Californian businessman without much enthusiasm for business himself. He left the United States in the 1910s to travel the world, including India, England and France. In autumn 1921 he arrived in Beijing for the new academic year, where he would stay until 1925.[70]

Chase's students knew about the expression "New Cultural movement," as one of them put it, or its popular English rendition as "the Chinese Renaissance" (for details on the "Chinese Renaissance," see chapter 5). They talked about people like Hu Shi in the context of this "New Cultural movement."[71] They also knew about *baihua* advocacy. For example, a student from Beijing Normal University,

---

[70] Chase's background before arriving in China: Lewis Nathaniel Chase, "Letter to Frank Chase," May 1, 1922, Container 173, Lewis Nathaniel Chase Papers, Manuscript Division, Library of Congress, Washington, D.C.; Manuscript Division, "Biographical and Organizational Note: Lewis Nathaniel Chase," *A Finding Aid to the Collection in the Library of Congress*, 2012, http://findingaids.loc.gov. Chase's stay in China: Lewis Nathaniel Chase, "Letter to Family," December 16, 1921, Container 171, Lewis Nathaniel Chase Papers, Manuscript Division, Library of Congress, Washington, D.C.; Lewis Nathaniel Chase, "Letter to Frank Chase," June 4, 1925, Container 191, Lewis Nathaniel Chase Papers, Manuscript Division, Library of Congress, Washington, D.C.; Lewis Nathaniel Chase, "Letter to Pearl Adell Chase," July 23, 1925, Container 205, Lewis Nathaniel Chase Papers, Manuscript Division, Library of Congress, Washington, D.C.
[71] "New Cultural movement": Chen, "China Now and England in the 19th Century," 3. "Chinese Renaissance": Ibid., 2. A mention of Hu Shi: Ibid., 3; Xu Guoyu, "My Reflections and Queries on the Question of the Creation of the Chinese Imaginative Literature of Interest to Non Chinese" (Examination paper, January 22, 1924), 1, Container 221, Lewis Nathaniel Chase Papers, Manuscript Division, Library of Congress, Washington, D.C.

who failed to write his⁷² name on his essay, elaborated his thoughts on the set question of how literature could "reveal" China to foreigners. He introduced his reflections by recapitulating the *baihua* project, the invention of Romanized alphabets for the Chinese language and the changes to Chinese curricula (probably referring to the introduction of the National Language into primary schools).⁷³ The creation of a Romanized alphabet was part of the popular-education and National Language projects, and it was also supported by people like the *New Tide* editor Fu Sinian.⁷⁴

Some of Chase's students were openly in favor of *baihua*. O.C. Wang (Wang Wenqi, no dates), for example, mixed the *baihua* notions of the Hu Shi-Chen Duxiu circle with those of the National Language advocates. The "spoken language" gave literature a "new and living spirit," and would also make literature "democratic and comprehensible," and conducive to the popularization of education, he wrote.⁷⁵ Another student, Xu Guoyu (no dates), approved of the suggestion to produce literature in the "spoken language," and he praised the *baihua* of Hu Shi as being one of the best.⁷⁶

Most importantly, when introducing recent intellectual developments, Lewis Chase's students talked about the New Culture Movement as if it was the only relevant intellectual trend of their times. By contrast, they never mentioned New Culture opponents or any other group. For example, the aforementioned anonymous student from Beijing Normal University wrote in January 1924: "[S]pelling letters of mandarin were invented, a modern language (Pai Hua) movement was started, the course of Chinese in schools was reformed, and even some people wanted to abandon their own language and adopt a foreign in stead [probably a reference to Esperanto, which people like Zhou Zuoren were very fond of]."⁷⁷

---

72 As this student's classmates had male names, such as "Robert C. Lu," it is reasonable to assume that he was male as well. See Cheng Li, "My Reflections and Querries [Sic] on the Question of the Creation of the Chinese Imaginative Literature of Interest to Non Chinese." (Examination paper, 22.1.24), 3, Container 221, Lewis Nathaniel Chase Papers, Manuscript Division, Library of Congress, Washington, D.C.
73 "My Reflections and Queries on the Subject of Revealing or Interpreting China and the Chinese to Non-China, by Means of Imaginative Literature" (Examination paper, January 22, 1924), 1, Container 221, Lewis Nathaniel Chase Papers, Manuscript Division, Library of Congress, Washington, D.C.
74 Chen, *Modern Chinese*, 22; Fu, "Hanyu gaiyong pinyin wenzi de chubu tan."
75 Wang Wenqi, "My Reflections and Queries on the Question of the Creation of the Chinese Imaginative Literature of Interest to Non Chinese" (Examination paper, January 22, 1924), 1, Container 221, Lewis Nathaniel Chase Papers, Manuscript Division, Library of Congress, Washington, D.C.
76 Xu, "My Reflections and Queries on the Question of the Creation of the Chinese Imaginative Literature of Interest to Non Chinese," 1.
77 "My Reflections and Queries on the Subject of Revealing or Interpreting China and the Chinese to Non-China," 1.

In spite of this general awareness and appreciation of ideas and people associated with the New Culture Movement, Lewis Chase's students were by no means New Culture activists. For example, after reviewing the recent changes in language, the aforementioned anonymous student went on to explain that he did not agree with all this: "But in my opinion so far as we have more than four thousand years tradition it is impossible for us to give up all we have kept for generations."[78] Another student, Liu Te Yuan (Liu Deyuan, no dates), who wrote an essay on Chinese characters, explained that he neither agreed with the die-hard admirers of Chinese characters nor with the "return[ed] students blindly in saying it is no good at all."[79]

Sometimes Chase's students also showed themselves to have been remarkably unaware of the arguments and counterarguments exchanged within the New Culture discourse. For people who criticized Chinese characters as part of the Hu Shi-Chen Duxiu circle's debate, the alternative to characters was to write in a different system, for example, a Romanization system.[80] But when Chase let his students write an essay on "The Educational Value of Chinese Character Writing," some of them appeared uninformed about this option. Instead, they argued from the standpoint that the only alternative to "Chinese character writing" was not to write at all. Unsurprisingly, this led them to strongly advocate Chinese characters. Su K'e-Ju (Su Keru, no dates) explained that "we must hav[e] writings to express our thoughts." Otherwise these thoughts could not be shared with "mankind or the generation after us." "Character writing," he therefore concluded, was "a great contribution to the modern education."[81] Although Chase's students in their English-literature classes were aware of the phenomenon "New Culture Movement," they would not have regarded themselves as New Culture activists.

Chase's students were not the only ones to be merely sporadically interested in the New Culture Movement. The *Shanghai News* had mentioned the expression when reprinting the Jiangsu Educational Association's announcement of the lecture competition on the topic (see chapter 3). It did so on October 31 and November 2, 1919.[82] Nevertheless, the *Shanghai News* had not become a passionate

---

78 Ibid.
79 Te Yuan Liu, "The Educational Value of Chinese Character Writing" (Student essay, n.d.), 5, Container 219, Lewis Nathaniel Chase Papers, Manuscript Division, Library of Congress, Washington, D.C.
80 Fu, "Hanyu gaiyong pinyin wenzi de chubu tan."
81 K'e Ju Su, "The Educational Value of Chinese Character Writing" (Student essay, n.d.), 2, Container 219, Lewis Nathaniel Chase Papers, Manuscript Division, Library of Congress, Washington, D.C.
82 "Yanshuo jingjinhui dingqi zai Ning kaihui" (The Lecture Competition Is Schedule to Be Held in Nanjing), *Shenbao* (Shanghai News), October 31, 1919; "Yanshuo jingjinhui yanti zhi jieshi," 10.

New Culture newspaper. It only mentioned the expression "New Culture Movement" these two times in the whole of 1919, and it still largely wrote its articles in Literary Chinese.

The same was the case for local school and association journals. The magazine *Alumnae of the Second Women's Normal School of Jiangsu Province* was among the first to publish an article on the New Culture Movement by teacher trainee Zhu Daihen in November 1919.[83] But this article was the exception, and most other pieces in the magazine were on different topics and written in Literary Chinese. Zhu Daihen's piece on the New Culture Movement was also banished to the very end of the journal, into the "Miscellanea" section. The New Culture Movement was mentioned on only very few other occasions.[84] The Jiangsu Educational Association was influential in shaping opinions on the New Culture Movement in its catchment area. Nevertheless, the announcement of the lecture competition in October 1919 was, to my knowledge, the only mention of the Movement in the Association's monthly reports.[85] An only mediocre interest in the New Culture Movement was, in other words, quite common.

Routes of transmission

How did information about the New Culture Movement spread to these circles that ended up being more or less enthusiastic about it? There were two main mechanisms, which led people to read and possibly write New Culture journals: advertisements in publications they already read and personal networks.

Personal networks

Many of the people debating the New Culture Movement knew each other personally. One of the authors of *Criticism* was Miao Jinyuan, a student at Beijing University's philosophy faculty, where Hu Shi was teaching. Miao had even written Hu Shi a letter, complaining that Hu did not have the opportunity to teach classes

---

[83] Zhu, "Ni yu tongxiang mou jun taolun xin wenhua yundong shixing fangfa shu."
[84] Cai Dun, "Zhu Jingnong xiansheng yanjiang jilu" (A Record of Mr. Zhu Jingnong's Lecture), *Jiangsu shengli di-er nüzi shifan xuexiao xiaoyouhui huikan* (Alumnae of the Second Women's Normal School of Jiangsu Province), no. 16 (November 1923): 6–13; Geng, *Hu Shi nianpu*, 77.
[85] Jiangsu sheng jiaoyuhui, "Zhi zhongdeng yishang ge xuexiao tongzhi dingqi juxing yanshuo jingjinhui shu," 25.

while Miao was at the university.[86] In future years, Beijing University's Criticism Society would continue to give Hu Shi publicity, for example, by trying to put his books onto students' reading lists. Zhou Changxian (no dates), who had written an article on the New Culture Movement in *Criticism*, listed the *Selected Works of Hu Shi* and *An Outline of the History of Chinese Philosophy* as the "ten books young people must read" in 1925.[87]

The authors of spring-bamboo journals and of the star journals like *New Youth* and *New Tide* were also sometimes the same people. *Social Reconstruction*, for example, was co-edited by a former member of the New Tide Society, Liu Binglin (1891–1956). After his graduation, probably in summer 1919, Liu became a teacher at Chinese Public School in Shanghai. In November 1919, his new school launched *Social Reconstruction*, with Liu Binglin as one of its editors.[88] People also contributed articles to each others' journals. Hu Shi published in the *Chinese Christian Advocate* and Huang Yanpei in *China and the Southern Seas* (*Zhongguo yu Nanyang*) as well as in the newspaper *Impartial*.[89]

Even groups of people that were only sporadically interested in the New Culture Movement, such as the Jiangsu Educational Association, often had connections to Beijing University's circle around Hu Shi. The vice-president of the Jiangsu Educational Association Huang Yanpei used to be Cai Yuanpei's student at Nanyang Public School. Cai Yuanpei introduced Huang to the Revolutionary Alliance in 1904, and in 1916 Huang and Cai together founded the Chinese Society for Vocational Education.[90]

---

86 Miao, "Miao Jinyuan zhi Hu Shi."
87 Zhou Changxian, "Fuyuan xuezhang dajian" (To Principal Fuyuan), in *Qingnian bi dushu* (Young People Must Study), ed. Wang Shijia (Kaifeng: Henan daxue chubanshe, 2006), 88–89.
88 Liu Binglin appeared as former member on a membership list of the New Tide Society in the December 1919 edition of *New Tide* (the second issue of the second volume). As his new postal address, the magazine indicated "Chinese Public School in Shanghai," see *Xinchao* (New Tide), vol. 3, Minguo zhenxi qikan (Valuable Republican Journals) (Beijing: Quanguo tushuguan wenxian suowei fuzhi zhongxin, 2006), 201. In the January 1920 edition of *Social Reconstruction*, Liu Binglin appeared among the editors of this magazine. See "Ben zazhi bianji renyuan" (Editors of This Magazine), *Xinqun* (Social Reconstruction), no. 1 (November 1919).
89 Hu Shi, "Women duiyu Xiyang jindai wenming de taidu" (Our Attitude towards Modern Western Culture), *Xinghua* (Chinese Christian Advocate) 23, no. 30 (1926): 8–19; Huang Yanpei, "Nanyang huaqiao jiaoyu shangque shu" (A Discussion of the Education of Chinese Nationals in the Southern Seas), *Zhongguo yu Nanyang* (China and the Southern Seas) 1, no. 1 (1918); Bao Yi, "Wo duiyu baihua wenti de yijian" (My Opinion on the Plain-Language Style of Writing), *Dagongbao* (Impartial), July 12, 1919, 2, Changsha. Bao Yi was Huang Yanpei's pseudonym, see Xu Weiming, ed., "Bao Yi" (Bao Yi), *Zhongguo jin xiandai renwu bieming cidian* (Dictionary of the Pseudonyms of Chinese Figures in the Modern and Contemporary Period) (Shenyang: Shenyang chubanshe, 1993), Shenyang.
90 Cai and Xie, *Pudong mingren shujian baiting*, 158.

The member list of this Chinese Society for Vocational Education reads like a who's who of Republican intellectual leaders. Other members were Yan Fu, Liang Qichao, Zhang Yuanji (1867–1959) and Shi Liangcai (1880–1934).[91] Zhang Yuanji had been manager of the Commercial Press in Shanghai since 1914, and he had also been a teacher at Nanyang Public School.[92] Shi Liangcai was the manager of the *Shanghai News* since 1912, one of whose shareholders was Zhang Jian (1853–1926), the president of the Jiangsu Educational Association in 1919.[93] People involved in shaping the New Culture discourse also cultivated their acquaintanceships on a personal level. Huang Yanpei, for example, mentioned dinner invitations extended to Hu Shi and received by Shi Liangcai in his diary.[94] Chen Duxiu had been a friend of Wang Mengzou, the owner of East Asia Library, since 1903.[95]

This is not to say that everybody who negotiated the New Culture Movement in the early 1920s had personal connections to people who used to be called Beijing University's "New Faction," or was involved in the humanities or in education. There were some publications that had no apparent link to Beijing University. Among them is a magazine by the name of *New Buddhism* (*Xin fojiao*), which nevertheless negotiated the New Culture Movement actively.[96] Nor is it to say that just because people had such connections, they automatically favored the New Culture Movement. Liu Shipei had long been friends with Chen Duxiu and owed his employment at Beijing University to Chen.[97] When Chen Duxiu was arrested in June 1919, Liu Shipei headed the signatories of a document that requested Chen's release, although Liu was already seriously ill at the time. When Liu Shipei died in November 1919, Chen Duxiu held his memorial service at Beijing University.[98] Nevertheless, Chen Duxiu and Liu Shipei had very different opinions on language and belonged to what newspapers had classified as two different "academic

---

91 Ibid.
92 Liang Shu, "Zhang Yuanji" (Zhang Yuanji), *Zhongguo wenxuejia da cidian* (Great Dictionary of Chinese Writers) (Beijing: Zhonghua shuju, 1997), Beijing. While in Germany, Cai Yuanpei edited textbooks for Commercial Press to earn some money. This means that he had an additional connection to this publishing house. See Weston, *The Power of Position*, 80.
93 Qiu Shihuang, Wu Xinxun, and Xiang Chunwu, eds., "Shenbao" (Shanghai News), *Xinwen chuanbo baike quanshu* (Encyclopedia of News and Broadcasting) (Chengdu: Sichuan renmin chubanshe, 1998), Chengdu.
94 On the invitation to Hu Shi, see Huang, *Huang Yanpei riji*, 2:62. On the one by Shi Liangcai, see Ibid., 2:88.
95 Wang Yuanfang, *Yadong tushuguan yu Chen Duxiu* (East Asia Library and Chen Duxiu) (Shanghai: Xuelin chubanshe, 2006), 40.
96 Wang, "Shishi xinbao."
97 Li, "Liu Shipei yu Beijing daxue," 108.
98 Chen, *Liu Shipei nianpu changbian*, 356–57.

factions." But for many other members of the New Culture-debating groups, personal connections could be very important for the transmission of knowledge about the New Culture Movement.

Advertisements

Personal networks were not the only such route. Another one was advertisements. As in today's online culture, selling advertising space was a popular means for publications to earn money. The *Shanghai News* had perfected this method. According to Wang Runian, selling advertising space was the *Shanghai News*' "most important source of income."[99] The newspaper had always featured advertisements of local and national companies. However, against the background of increasing economic development, they became ever more garish and numerous after the 1870s. The 1920s and 1930s were a heyday of *Shanghai News* advertising. Advertisements were expensive and their price depended on their size and location within the newspaper. An advertisement on the front page, for example, was particularly costly.[100] Other periodicals also used this price scaling. In the spring-bamboo journal *Emancipation and Reconstruction*, a "first-class" advertisement, that is, one on the cover and of the size of a whole page, cost twenty Yuan. A "third-class" advertisement, that is, one "in front or behind the texts or in the middle of the texts" covering one fourth of a page, only cost three Yuan.[101]

Advertisements had the potential to spread information about journals to wider audiences. But in reality the reach of advertisements tended to be confined and they reinforced the visibility of the New Culture Movement within those "communities of discourse"[102] that already negotiated it. First of all, the audience of the advertisement's carrier was limited. For example, although the *Shanghai News* was a large newspaper, it was by no means read by every person in China. By definition, its readers had to be literate, and among the literature people, the *Shanghai News* readers were, according to Wang Runian, mainly businesspeople and intellectuals.[103] Even an advertisement in the *Shanghai News* would have therefore only reached a limited circle of people.

---

99 Wang Runian, *Yuwang de xiangxiang: 1920–1930 niandai Shenbao guanggao de wenhuashi yanjiu* (The Imagination of Desire : A Cultural History of Advertisement in the *Shanghai News* in the 1920s and 1930s) (Shanghai: Shanghai renmin chubanshe, 2007), 70.
100 Ibid., 70–96.
101 "Guanggao jia mubiao" (Price List for Advertisements), *Jiefang yu gaizao* (Emancipation and Reconstruction) 1, no. 1+2 (October 15, 1919).
102 Bender, "The Cultures of Intellectual Life," 3.
103 Wang, *Yuwang de xiangxiang*, 108.

Secondly, the reach of advertisements was confined by a pricing strategy that granted more favorable conditions to advertisements of like-minded publications. According to an "Advertising Price List," printed in both *New Tide* and *National Heritage*, the advertising price for "[publications] that this journal regards as beneficial will be calculated at a fifty-percent discount."[104] In other words, although *New Tide* and *National Heritage* were prepared to advertise publications they did not agree with, it is reasonable to assume that people tried to promote their journals in congenial magazines, since this would save them money. Economic common sense would have also suggested that people who had already bought the magazine of a certain strand of thought were more likely to buy another one of a similar persuasion.

Additionally, magazines followed the practice of "introducing" new publications they found particularly commendable (and agreeable).[105] In these cases, the "Price List" stated, no money would be charged. In January 1919, *Beijing University Monthly* introduced *National Heritage*. Luo Jialun in *New Youth* recommended *Pacific* (*Taipingyang*), *Tiger* and *Science* (*Kexue*) in April 1919. In August, the *Weekly Critic* introduced two new "little brothers," among them the spring-bamboo journal *Xiang River Review* (*Xiang jiang pinglun*), run by Mao Zedong in Changsha.[106]

East Asia Library employee Wang Yuanfang even remembered that journals had a policy to "exchange advertisements." This meant that two journals advertised each other for free. It was in this context that *Construction* announced, as mentioned above, that it would only engage in this "advertisement exchange" with journals that supported the "New Culture Movement."[107] The fact that many New Culture journals were printed or sold by the same publishers reinforced the effect. The spring-bamboo journals *New Woman* and *Social Reconstruction*, for example, were managed by East Asia Library.[108] Consequently, they promoted a

---

104 "Guanggao jiamu" (Price List for Advertisements), *Xinchao* (New Tide) 1, no. 1 (January 1, 1919). See also "Guanggao jiamu" (Price List for Advertisements), *Guogu* (National Heritage), no. 1 (March 20, 1919).
105 Li, "Xinchaoshe de shimo," 209.
106 The "Price List": "Guanggao jiamu," January 1, 1919. *Beijing University Monthly*: Chen, *Liu Shipei nianpu changbian*, 349. *New Youth*: Luo Jialun, "Jinri Zhongguo de zazhijie" (The Chinese World of Magazines Today), in *Xinchao* (New Tide), vol. 2, Minguo zhenxi qikan (Valuable Republican Journals) (Beijing: Quanguo tushuguan wenxian suowei fuzhi zhongxin, 2006), 77–78. *Weekly Critic*: "Xiang jiang pinglun ..." (Xiang River Review ...), *Meizhou pinglun* (Weekly Critic), August 24, 1919, 4, Beijing.
107 Wang, *Huiyi Yadong tushuguan*, 41.
108 "Copyright Page," *Xin funü* (New Woman) 1, no. 2 (1920); "Copyright Page," *Xinqun* (Social Reconstruction) 1, no. 1 (November 1919).

number of other East Asia Library publications. In its first issue, for example, *Social Reconstruction* advertised *New Tide*, which was then printed by East Asia Library.[109]

Advertisements thus had the potential to introduce journals and the ideas they transported to broader circles. However, many of the pricing strategies that the suppliers of advertising space employed caused like-minded journals to advertise each other. As a result, information about journals tended to be limited to an audience that was already inclined to agree with them. It also promoted the formation of a discursive circle, which was very well-informed about ideas and actors in the field, and which cited and negotiated them.

This explains how Fu Sinian could claim that the New Culture Movement was sweeping away "society."[110] When he wrote "society," he probably meant the type of circle in which he was socializing, and this was the circle of people who (almost) all knew each other and who advertised each other's journals. Within this community, enthusiasm for the New Culture Movement seemed indeed very vibrant: they all read the same publications, published in each other's journals and cited each other. For example, the journal *Fine Arts* (*Meishu*) in Shanghai referred to a lecture and an article by Chen Duxiu, both with the title "What is the New Culture Movement."[111] People involved in negotiating the Movement responded to each other's comments, such as when Jing Guan from *New Woman* defended himself against accusations that he was "plagiarizing" other publications (see chapter 3).[112] This criticism had most likely come from other New Culture activists. Transmission of information about the New Culture Movement along personal networks and through advertisements in like-minded publications furthered the promotion of such a well-informed in-group.

Moving beyond the circle: The case study of Lewis Nathaniel Chase

But New Culture would soon spread outside of this circle, and personal networks could play a role here, too. The reason was that some individuals were well placed

---

109 "Advertisement for *New Tide*, vol. 1, no. 3," *Xinqun* (Social Reconstruction), no. 1 (November 1919).
110 Fu, "'Xinchao' zhi huigu yu qianzhan," October 30, 1919, 201.
111 Tang, "Du Chen Duxiu de 'Xin wenhua yundong shi shenme,'" 105; Chen Duxiu, "Xin wenhua yundong shi shenme?" (What Is the New Culture Movement), in *Xin qingnian* (New Youth), vol. 8 (Tokyo: Taian, 1963), 697–702.
112 Jing, "Gao xin wenhua yundong de tongzhi," 31, 33.

to spread ideas to global audiences, even if they themselves were little known. These individuals had access to such global audiences because in an age of imperialism and increasing globalization, many people traveled the world, building audiences in the places they traveled to. Those who stayed at home wanted to know about those far-away places the others had visited. Imperialism, in other words, had not only been one of the causes for why the New Culture Movement emerged. It also facilitated the spread of knowledge about it.

One such traveling individual was Lewis Nathaniel Chase, through whom information about the New Culture Movement transitioned out of the circle of New Culture buffs to wider audiences in China and even in the United States. These wider circles did not appear to become part of the group that participated in shaping the New Culture discourse, but instead they seemed to only take cursory notice of it. Chase himself is little-known. But he was part of a broader group of Western academics visiting China in a context provided by imperialism, and this case study about him gives a close-up on the inner workings of knowledge transmission at the time. It shows how what were essentially the side-effects of the personal circumstances, friendships and goals of one little-known person could play a role in the fate of big narratives like the New Culture Movement.

Shortly after his arrival in Beijing in the autumn of 1921, Chase encountered the New Culture Movement. This happened in the form of the lecture given by the Yanjing University historian and Hu Shi's friend Philippe de Vargas (that is, another academic working in China in a setting created by imperialism) on the topic of "Some Elements in the Chinese Renaissance" (see chapter 2).[113] De Vargas gave the lecture in February 1922 before the Society of Friends of Literature, a Sino-foreign group of intellectuals who organized lectures together.[114]

De Vargas was an accomplished linguist, but his native language was French, not English, which was the language commonly used at the Society of Friends of Literature.[115] It seems that he therefore gave his lecture script to Lewis Chase beforehand, with the request to proofread it for him. This at least is suggested by the handwritten corrections in the otherwise typewritten manuscript of the lecture found in the Chase Collection. At the latest by this point, Chase had come into contact with the New Culture Movement. Over the next few years, Chase would continue interacting with Hu Shi and other members of star personnel of the New Culture Movement. He would attend Hu Shi's lectures at the Society of Friends of Literature, and Hu Shi would invite Chase to take up a teaching post at

---

113 de Vargas, "Some Elements in the Chinese Renaissance (Manuscript)."
114 On the Society of Friends of Literature, see Hu, *Hu Shi de riji*, shang:65.
115 For example, the invitation cards and the titles of lectures announced on them were in English.

Beijing University. Chase was furthermore personally acquainted with Lu Xun's brother Zhou Zuoren.[116]

Another man whom Lewis Chase met at the Society of Friends of Literature was also a Western academic in China – A. E. Zucker (1890–1971), a professor for English at Peking Union Medical College, who was very active in the Society.[117] This acquaintanceship appeared to have drawn Lewis Chase's attention to a book Zucker had authored and for which Hu Shi had written an introduction. This four-volume book called *Western Literature: Specimens of Literature with Introductions Embodying the Chief Traditions of Europeans and Americans* was a textbook for Chinese English-language students. It was one of many literature anthologies for such students designed by China-based foreign teachers of the language, and it was designed to introduce them to classical Western works of literature, such as the Iliad, the Bible or Dante.[118]

In his introduction, Hu Shi praised Zucker's accomplishments, as is the duty of a good introduction. But he also took the opportunity to promote his idea that novels and dramas should be more appreciated and developed in China. His argument was that Zucker's book enabled Chinese students to engage in "comparative study" of Western and Chinese literature. As a result of "comparative study," they would come to an appreciation of Western novels, which would lead them to value Chinese novels more highly. Through comparison with Western drama, they would also find out at which evolutionary stage Chinese drama was at the moment. All of this would "help the student in his appreciation of the literature of both the West and the East."[119] This outline of evolutionary patterns was similar to the arguments *New Tide* authors had made in early 1919 (see chapter 1).

---

[116] Attendance of Hu Shi's lectures: Wenyou hui, "Invitation to Hu Shi's Lecture," February 20, 1924, Container 187, Lewis Nathaniel Chase Papers, Manuscript Division, Library of Congress, Washington, D.C.; Wenyou hui, "Invitation to Hu Shi's Lecture," November 17, 1922, Container 220, Lewis Nathaniel Chase Papers, Manuscript Division, Library of Congress, Washington, D.C. Chase's teaching post: L.Y. Chen, "Letter to Lewis Chase," 1923, Container 216, Lewis Nathaniel Chase Papers, Manuscript Division, Library of Congress, Washington, D.C. Acquaintance with Zhou Zuoren: Zuoren Zhou, "Christmas Card to Lewis Chase," 192?, Container 220, Lewis Nathaniel Chase Papers, Manuscript Division, Library of Congress, Washington, D.C.
[117] Hu, *Hu Shi de riji*, shang:65.
[118] A.E. Zucker, *Western Literature: Specimens of Literature with Introductions Embodying the Chief Traditions of Europeans and Americans*, vol. 1 (Shanghai: Commercial Press, 1927); A.E. Zucker, *Western Literature: Specimens of Literature with Introductions Embodying the Chief Traditions of Europeans and Americans*, vol. 2: The Bible and the Middle Ages (Shanghai: Commercial Press, 1922).
[119] Hu Shi, "Introduction to 'Western Literature, Volume 1: Greece and Rome, by A. E. Zucker,'" in *Hu Shi quanji* (Hu Shi's Collected Works), vol. 35 (Hefei: Anhui jiaoyu chubanshe, 2003), 289–97.

Promoting the role of novels had also been one of Hu Shi's long-term missions. Someone reading Hu Shi's introduction to Zucker's book would have thus become acquainted with ideas associated with the proclaimed "center of the New Culture Movement."[120]

Among the readers of the book were Lewis Chase's students, as *Western Literature* became part of Chase's syllabus at Beijing University. A lecture list of the Faculty for English Literature for the academic year 1923–1924 shows that Chase based his course on "European Literature" for third- and fourth-year students on it.[121] Chase also set an examination question for his students, which treated Zucker's book. It read: "Is a knowledge of ancient Greek and Roman literature such as indicated by Dr Zucker's book of interest to you either personally or as [a] Chinese?" When discussing this question, students should also, the examination paper stated, express if "[i]n your opinion ... a knowledge of ancient Greek and Roman literature [is] desirable in order to increase your just appreciation of Chinese literature."[122]

This was a very close reflection of Hu Shi's expressed hope for the book, namely, that it would "help the student in his appreciation of the literature of both the West and the East."[123] No doubt Hu Shi would have been delighted to know that this seemed to have worked for Chase's student Hsi Chen (Xi Zhen [no dates]). Hsi Chen concluded his essay on the question with the statement that a comparative study of Western and Chinese literature would help to "reform our literature," and that "Dr Hu Shih" was advocating the "literary revolution" exactly because he had done such comparative study.[124] By giving them Zucker's book to read, Chase had made his students engage with Hu Shi's thought.

So far, information about Hu Shi stayed within the circle of Beijing intellectuals. But through Chase's interest in Zucker's book, knowledge about Hu Shi and his ideas eventually reached broader groups, to which Hu Shi did not appear to have a connection. Chase seemed to enjoy *Western Literature* so much that he wrote a very positive review of its first volume. In this review, he also discussed Hu Shi's introduction at great length, and he particularly repeated and affirmed

---

120 Ye, "Ji Beijing daxue shiye shi (xu)."
121 Ye Juan, *Deyu wenxue yanjiu yu xiandai Zhongguo* (Research on German Literature and Contemporary China) (Beijing: Beijing daxue chubanshe, 2008), 117.
122 Zhen Xi, "Is a Knowledge of Ancient Greek and Roman Literature such as Indicated by Dr Zucker's Book of Interest to You Either Personally or as Chinese?" (Student essay, Beijing, 1923), 1, Container 220, Lewis Nathaniel Chase Papers, Manuscript Division, Library of Congress, Washington, D.C., Beijing.
123 Hu, "Introduction to 'Western Literature, Volume 1: Greece and Rome, by A. E. Zucker,'" 297.
124 Xi, "Is a Knowledge of Ancient Greek and Roman Literature such as Indicated by Dr Zucker's Book of Interest to You Either Personally or as Chinese?," 4.

Hu Shi's support for novels. Chase then published this review in the English-language newspapers *Japan Advertiser* and *Peking Leader* (*Beijing daobao*).[125] It also reached a Chinese-speaking audience when it appeared in Chinese translation in the school journal of Yanjing University, the *Yen Ching Students' Weekly* (*Yanda zhoukan*).[126] This meant that Chase's review of Zucker's book was accessible even to students who did not read English and who were not in his class.

Eventually, Chase helped to transport knowledge about the New Culture Movement out of the capital, where Hu Shi lived at the time, to a completely new circle: a circle of foreigners in Suzhou. Chase sometimes traveled into different parts of China, for example, to give summer schools in Suzhou and in Jinan.[127] There he met fellow foreigners at some of the local "luncheon clubs" that were so popular with the foreign community, and of which only some admitted Chinese nationals.[128] One day, Chase attended an "Anglo-American tiffin" in Suzhou, where he met a Dr. Shurman (possibly Dr. Jacob Gould Schurman, 1854–1942, the US envoy to China at that time). Chase and Shurman discussed the differences and similarities of ancient Greece and old China. Back in Beijing, Chase wrote a letter to Shurman in June 1924, enclosing a "type-script copy of my review of Zucker's book which bears on the same question."[129]

This may have been a case of academic self-advertisement – Chase was very much aware of the importance of networking and always in search of opportunities to give lectures and earn some extra money in the wake of it.[130] But it also

---

125 Lewis Nathaniel Chase, "Western Classics for Chinese Students: Appreciation of Ancient Greece by Chinese May Lead to Single World Civilization" (Beijing, 1923), 1–3, Container 220, Lewis Nathaniel Chase Papers, Manuscript Division, Library of Congress, Washington, D.C., Beijing.
126 Chase Lewis Nathaniel, "Xifang wenxue jiezhu: wei Zhongguo xuesheng xuan de" (Classics of Western Literature: Chosen for Chinese Students), trans. Shao Ming, *Yanda zhoukan* (Yen Ching Students' Weekly), October 11, 1923, 1, Container 220, Lewis Nathaniel Chase Papers, Manuscript Division, Library of Congress, Washington, D.C., Beijing.
127 On the summer school in Suzhou, see Lewis Nathaniel Chase, "Letter to E.H. Cressy," March 26, 1925, Container 222, Lewis Nathaniel Chase Papers, Manuscript Division, Library of Congress, Washington, D.C. On the summer school in Jinan, see Chase, "Lewis Chase to E.A. Chase," June 17, 1923, 3.
128 Nicholas Rowland Clifford, *Spoilt Children of Empire: Westerners in Shanghai and the Chinese Revolution of the 1920s* (Hanover: University Press of New England, 1991), 71; Robert A. Bickers, *Britain in China: Community, Culture and Colonialism 1900–1949* (Manchester: Manchester University Press, 1999), 83.
129 Chase, "Lewis Chase to Shurman." That all this happened in Suzhou is suggested by the labelling of the relevant folder in the manuscript collection.
130 Lewis Nathaniel Chase, "Letter to Family," October 16, 1921, 2, Container 171, Lewis Nathaniel Chase Papers, Manuscript Division, Library of Congress, Washington, D.C.

had the effect that information about both Zucker and Hu Shi reached a new network of people in Suzhou. This circle may have been easier to reach for Chase, as a foreigner, than for Hu Shi and his Chinese colleagues. The Chase Papers do not contain any information about what Dr. Shurman did with Chase's review of Zucker. But if he liked it, he may well have informed his own friends about Zucker's book and Hu Shi's introduction. In this way, knowledge of the New Culture Movement may again have hopped over to new circles.

In 1925, Lewis Chase returned to the United States, because his eighty-six-year-old mother asked him to finally come home.[131] Once there, he gave lectures on China. Lecturing or writing books on China was a habit shared by many foreigners who had visited China, to the extent that their contemporaries made fun of them. Sometimes, their more cynical contemporaries mocked, these visitors had only been to China for a few weeks and never left the foreign concessions, but still lectured or wrote on the country.[132] Chase certainly had more China experience. But he, too, started to share his experiences. For example, on January 6, 1926, he gave a lecture on China before the "Ladies['] Aid Society of Calvery Presbyterian Church, Riverside," California, the place where his mother lived.[133]

In this lecture before the Ladies' Aid Society, Chase again briefly mentioned ideas promoted as New Culture Movement, when he explained that there was now a new written language. This "is known as the spoken language whcih [sic] recently has been made literary."[134] To be sure, the New Culture Movement was not the main topic of the lecture. Chase did not delve into the argument behind *baihua* either. It is therefore not possible to determine if Chase was talking about Hu Shi's (*baihua*-as-the-language-of-present-times) or the lesser-known activists' (*baihua*-as-the-language-of-the-people) *baihua*. It also stands to reason that his audience did not become New Culture enthusiasts, but took a rather cursory notice of the *baihua* project. Still, they learnt about *baihua* through Lewis Chase. From acquaintance with the New Culture in-group (at the Society of Friends of Literature), and apparently driven by academic self-promotion, family circumstances and choice of teaching materials, Chase had gradually contributed to

---

131 Chase, "Lewis Chase to Frank Chase," June 4, 1925; Chase, "Lewis Chase to Pearl Adell Chase."
132 John W. Colbert, "Journey on the Yangtze" n.d., Container 2, John W. Colbert Papers, Manuscript Division, Library of Congress, Washington, D.C.
133 Lewis Nathaniel Chase, "My Ignorance of China" (Lecture notes, El Centro, California, May 11, 1925), 1, Container 217, Lewis Nathaniel Chase Papers, Manuscript Division, Library of Congress, Washington, D.C., El Centro, California. On his mother's residence, see Lewis Nathaniel Chase, "Letter to E.A. Chase," January 5, 1923, 1, Container 171, Lewis Nathaniel Chase Papers, Manuscript Division, Library of Congress, Washington, D.C.
134 Chase, "My Ignorance of China," 5.

spreading information about New Culture to students, foreigners in China and to a charitable society in the United States.

Conclusion

Fu Sinian exaggerated when he claimed that "society" was now behind the New Culture Movement.[135] Only parts of "society," even only parts of urban society, cared about it. But among these people, the New Culture Movement was indeed enthusiastically discussed, with people reading each others' articles, commenting on and critiquing each other and publishing in each others' journals. The creation of this limited, but intense, community was favored by two central mechanisms, through which the information about the New Culture Movement spread: personal acquaintance and advertisements in like-minded journals. However, as the example of Lewis Chase has shown, personal networks could be so extended in the early 20th century that information about New Culture and its declared stars could spread into completely new circles and even countries.

This effect was reinforced when people who were tapped into such networks decided that they had a stake in spreading information about New Culture. Chapter 5 will show how figures like Hu Shi, Mao Zedong and Christians – all of whom had access to an infrastructure that could reach large audiences – used the New Culture Movement to advertise their own successes and agendas. In this way, they anchored May Fourth and New Culture into narratives about the making of Modern China in both China and the West.

---

135 Fu, "'Xinchao' zhi huigu yu qianzhan," October 30, 1919, 201.

5 1919 to 2016 – Canonizing a buzzword

A hundred years later, memory of the New Culture Movement is alive and well. More than that, it is a central part of the narrative of 20th-century Chinese history. No course on "Modern China" at a Western university can do without it. No story of the foundation of the Chinese Communist Party can omit it. The dissidents of 1989 invoked the spirit of May Fourth and New Culture. Taiwan too has in the past decade started to extol the Taiwanese New Culture Movement to negotiate its national identity. Beijing sports a Lu Xun museum, Taibei a Hu Shi Memorial Hall. The New Culture Movement, in other words, not only shaped Chinese cultural change. It has also become part and parcel of the narrative of "Modern China." Contrary to the previous chapters, this chapter does not trace the usage of the buzzword New Culture Movement as an "agent" of change, in Reinhart Kosellek's conceptualization, but as its "indicator."[1] Change became visible through the perpetually shifting network of reference points that was inscribed into the "New Culture Movement," from the question of who its "true" stars were to the issue of what it was and is said to be prescribing for the mainland China or Taiwan of each time period.

How could the New Culture Movement become part and parcel of the big narratives about Modern (mainland) China and Taiwan, when only so few cared about it in the 1920s? The circle of New Culture enthusiasts at the time may have been small. But some of its members went on to achieve positions that enabled them to shape historical narratives in the first half of the 20th century. Among them were Mao Zedong (a figure whose political importance does not need to be argued for), Hu Shi (who had excellent ties to the future Taiwanese political establishment in the form of the Guomindang and to Western academia) and Chinese Christians and missionaries in China. This last group was very well and especially globally networked and provided a platform to voice ideas about China to Western audiences.

Mao Zedong, Hu Shi and the Christians all made different claims about what the New Culture Movement was, which of its actors were to be commended and which ones to be criticized. But what they had in common was that they made the New Culture Movement part of the narrative about the birth of the sort of China they envisioned to be ideal. In making these narratives, they claimed leading roles in the New Culture Movement for themselves, that is, they used the New Culture Movement as a buzzword to extol their own personas, agendas or accomplishments.

---

1 Richter, "Begriffsgeschichte and the History of Ideas," 253.

Once the New Culture Movement was thus canonized in the first half of the 20th century, its fame became self-replicating. In the second half of the 20th and in the 21st centuries, important groups again justified or negotiated their ideas through it. Mainland Chinese dissidents in the 1980s used it as part of their repertoire to voice their discontent.[2] In contemporary Taiwan, the *Taiwanese* New Culture Movement is currently popular as a buzzword to debate the legitimacy of the GMD and differing visions for Taiwan's national identity. The Democratic Progressive Party (DPP), the press and intellectuals close to it seek to delink the Taiwanese New Culture Movement from its mainland cousin. On the basis of this detachment, they then use the Taiwanese New Culture Movement to critique everything else that is connected to the mainland, from rapprochement with it to the GMD, which originates from the mainland. Meanwhile, the GMD and a GMD-sympathetic public tries to reconnect the Taiwanese New Culture Movement to the mainland to achieve the opposite. Even a hundred years after its invention, the New Culture Movement is still being used as a buzzword to negotiate crucial questions of current affairs.

Making the canon: The early 20th century

Christians as the makers of the New Culture Movement

"Old China hands" and Chinese intellectuals with ties to the West had a pivotal role in securing the New Culture Movement's place in narratives about China in the West. Among them were academics like Lewis Chase (see chapter 4), but also missionaries and Chinese Christians. The Christians' contributions to making New Culture known in Europe and the United States is ironic, seeing as the Movement has entered history as an event opposed to "superstition," which, in many views at the time, included religion. Still, Christians like the Apologetic Group, who tried to market Christianity as the New Culture Movement to Chinese audiences in the 1920s (see chapter 3), also used it to show off with the proclaimed accomplishments of the China mission to the West. Such people claimed that Christianity had been the precondition for the emergence of the New Culture Movement.

---

2 The notion of "repertoire" has, for example, been deployed on China, specifically its student protests, by Jeffrey N. Wasserstrom in *Student Protests in Twentieth-Century China: The View from Shanghai* (Stanford, California: Stanford University Press, 1991), 75–78. In doing so, Wasserstrom draws upon Charles Tilly, *The Contentious French* (Cambridge, Massachusetts: Harvard University Press, 1986), 4, 116–18.

One such Christian missionary was Paul Hutchinson (no dates). Hutchinson was one of the editors of the Chinese journal *Chinese Christian Advocate*, which had reprinted the lecture by the Qinghua theologian Liu Tingfang.[3] Liu had claimed in these lectures that Christianity was the better New Culture Movement (see chapter 3).[4] For Western audiences, Hutchinson published a book called *China's Real Revolution*. This book was written in English. The "real revolution" to which he referred in the title was the New Culture Movement combined with May Fourth. This becomes clear through the caption "Magazines symbolic of China's real revolution," which accompanied photos of the New Culture journals *New China (Xin Zhongguo)*, *Ladies' Magazine*, *Construction* and *New Tide*.[5] By calling New Culture/May Fourth the "real revolution" in China, Hutchinson made it clear that this was an epoch-making event.

The text surrounding the photos of the New Culture journals described the May Fourth protests and Hutchinson argued that May Fourth could not have happened without Christianity. The "Chinese scholar," Hutchinson wrote, had lost his self-confidence ever since the 19th century and in the wake of the warlord era, which valued military power over intellectual prowess. This was, incidentally, also the reason for China's weakness, in this view. But fortunately, Christian missionaries had established modern-style schools. These schools had brought about the "reassertion" of the "Chinese scholar," leading to the May Fourth protests and the end of Chinese decline.[6] Without Christianity, Hutchinson claimed, May Fourth/New Culture would not have happened.

Hutchinson was not the only missionary to deploy this strategy. Another one was the Reverend A.M. Chirgwin (1885–1966). Chirgwin put forward a similar narrative of the New Culture Movement. He called the New Culture Movement the "Chinese renaissance," a formulation suggested by Hu Shi, as I will outline in more detail later on. This Chinese renaissance, according to Chirgwin, put an end to all the ills China had traditionally had, in the Western perception. Among them were "autocracy," corruption, despotism, patriarchy and "superstition."[7] But the Chinese renaissance had not happened out of the blue. Factors leading to it were Western imperialism, the failure of the Republic, the ideas promoted by Woodrow Wilson, the Russian revolution – and, of course, Christianity.[8] Again,

---

[3] "Contents," *Xinghua* (Chinese Christian Advocate) 17, no. 34 (September 8, 1920).
[4] Liu, "Xin wenhua yundong zhong jidujiao xuanjiaoshi de zeren," 12.
[5] Paul Hutchinson, *China's Real Revolution* (New York: Missionary Education Movement of the United States and Canada, 1924), 38–39.
[6] Ibid., 23–37.
[7] A. M. Chirgwin, "The Chinese Renaissance and Its Significance," *Contemporary Review* 125 (January 1, 1924): 65.
[8] Ibid.

in other words, Christianity was depicted as the beginning of a good, renewed China, by laying the ground for the New Culture Movement. In the hand of these two missionaries, Hutchinson and Chirgwin, the New Culture Movement became the end of what were in their view traditional China's problems and of China's decline, and the Christian China mission was turned into the fundament of the New Culture Movement. To put it differently, in order to show off their own accomplishments in China, these missionaries increased the Movement's glamour by giving it a firm place in the making of China's social and cultural developments of the 20th century, as well as an international cachet.

Contrary to the networks of transmissions described in chapter 4, which were strongly limited to a small audience, these sorts of missionary writings had a global and broad reach. Chirgwin's paper, for example, was published twice, once as an article in 1924 in the *Contemporary Review*, and later, in 1928, as part of the book *What China Wants*. The article was advertised in 1924 in the *Times* and in the *American Journal of Sociology*. The 1928 volume was reviewed in the *North China Herald*, the English-language newspaper of the foreign community in China.[9] In this way, it reached academic and general audiences both in China and in the West, and spread knowledge of the New Culture Movement. Contrary to the New Culture enthusiasts from chapter 4, however, these new audiences would not claim to be actively participating in the New Culture Movement themselves. It is more likely that they would have learned about it as something happening in China and filed it under common or academic observational knowledge.

This was not only a strategy of Western missionaries to China. Chinese Christians took on a similar role in making the New Culture Movement known in the West, but they chose a slightly different angle. They depicted the New Culture Movement, not as evidence of the China mission's achievements, but of China's successful Westernization. This was designed to raise the standing of China in the eyes of their Western audiences. Countering any doubts about China's potential to become Christian (and judging from the many counterarguments missionaries and Chinese Christians put forward, those doubts were tenacious), they also described the New Culture Movement as a new chance for Christianity in China.

These narratives were often told by Christian students and academics, who were involved in global Christian organizations. These associations provided them with good platforms to be heard by Western audiences. One such association

---

9 Chirgwin, "The Chinese Renaissance and Its Significance"; A. M. Chirgwin, *What China Wants* (London: Livingstone Press, 1928); "Multiple Display Advertisements," *Times*, January 1, 1924, 18, The Times Digital Archive, London; T.C.W., "Review of 'The Chinese Renaissance and Its Significance' by Chirgwin," *American Journal of Sociology* 30, no. 1 (July 1924): 111; "Review of *What China Wants* by A. M. Chirgwin," *North China Herald*, July 21, 1928, 130, Shanghai.

was the World's Student Christian Federation. In 1925, its member and "first Oriental secretary," T.Z. Koo (Gu Ziren, 1887–1971), gave a speech at a meeting of the Student Christian Conference in Manchester, in which he discussed the New Culture Movement. This earned him and the New Culture Movement a mention in the *Times*.[10] Another group of people to make use of this cosmopolitan interface of Christianity was Liu Tingfang and a few fellow academics around him, among them Hu Shi. Liu Tingfang was at the time member of the World Student Christian Federation.[11] Liu, Hu and their associates published a book targeted at "the delegates of the World's Student Christian Federation Conference" held in Beijing. A central topic of the book was the New Culture Movement.[12] The book's title was *China To-Day through Chinese Eyes*, first published in 1922.

This book's agenda was again to demonstrate China's, from this perspective, positive developments. The introductory chapter already set out this goal. It stated that, even though there were still many problems in China, such as political disunity, governmental inefficiency and international weakness, there was now some real hope in the form of the "Renaissance Movement." This "Renaissance Movement" furthered the import of "modern science and philosophy," the "re-evaluation of Chinese civilisation," a *baihua* movement with the goal to bring education to "the masses" and a reform of religions by uprooting their "superstitions."[13]

In a chapter specifically on "China's Renaissance," Liu Tingfang again described the Chinese Renaissance as being about "science," "democracy," "social reform," "relentless thoroughness" and language reform.[14] The New Culture Movement was a risk for Christianity, but it was also an opportunity, he wrote. It fought Christianity's greatest obstacle in China, namely "indifference." Indifference, the argument read, was not an option in the New Culture Movement, and apparently, in Liu's logic, this meant that now Christianity would not be treated indifferently anymore either.[15] Liu again outlined his argument that the New Culture Movement and Christianity had a lot in common, just as he had done when addressing Chinese audiences in 1921 (see chapter 3).[16] The "Chinese renaissance"

---

[10] "Anti-Foreign Spirit in China," *Times*, January 5, 1925, 9, The Times Digital Archive, London.
[11] Howard L Boorman, "Liu T'ing-Fang," *Biographical Dictionary of Republican China* (New York: Columbia University Press, 1968), 416, New York.
[12] Shih Hu et al., *China to-Day through Chinese Eyes*, 2nd ed. (London: Student Christian Movement, 1922), 7.
[13] Shih Hu et al., "China to-Day," in *China to-Day through Chinese Eyes*, 2nd ed. (London: Student Christian Movement, 1922), 11–17.
[14] T. T. Lew, "China's Renaissance," in *China to-Day through Chinese Eyes*, 2nd ed. (London: Student Christian Movement, 1922), 25–27.
[15] Ibid., 42.
[16] Liu, "Xin wenhua yundong zhong jidujiao xuanjiaoshi de zeren," 12.

pursued social reform, he wrote, as well as work of the sort that Christianity had been undertaking for decades. This highlighted the importance of such social work to the Chinese public and through this they would learn to appreciate the as yet underappreciated work the Christians had been doing all along.[17]

The New Culture Movement, in his interpretation, was thus evidence and impetus for China to become more Christian and Western-style. This, of course, highlighted the importance of people like the Christian theologian Liu Tingfang himself, who would play an important role in any such development. The reception of this book shows again that through this strategy knowledge of the New Culture Movement reached broader circles. The book was published in London. It was reviewed in Western academic journals, such as the English-language *American Journal of Sociology* in 1924. It left the English-speaking world when, in 1923, parts of the book were translated into German and published in the *Swiss Pedagogical Journal* (*Schweizerische pädagogische Zeitschrift*). It also reached American general audiences when the *New York Times* reviewed it in 1923.[18]

Chinese Christians, as well as Western missionaries to China, were thus very well positioned to spread ideas to multiple audiences, as they were tapped into global networks of knowledge transmission. In the early 1920s, they chose to promulgate knowledge of the New Culture Movement to these audiences, because they saw the New Culture Movement as a means to promote their own achievements (in the case of the missionaries) and the success of their own country (in the case of the Chinese Christians). The New Culture Movement made it into the West because it was used as a buzzword.

Visionary Hu Shi

Hu Shi was another person who spread knowledge of the New Culture Movement to the West in the wake of self-promotion. Hu Shi originally did not like the expression "New Culture Movement" and the idea that he did not control it (see chapter 3). But in a mixture of promoting the New Culture Movement through his

---

17 Lew, "China's Renaissance," 44.
18 T.C.W., "Review of 'China's Renaissance' by Timothy Tingfang Lew," *American Journal of Sociology* 29, no. 5 (3.1924): 636; E. Moser, "Das heutige China" (China Today), *Schweizerische pädagogische Zeitschrift* (Swiss Pedagogical Journal) 33, no. 8 (1923): 229–37; "Brief Reviews," *New York Times*, September 9, 1923, 25, New York Times (1923-Current File), New York. In Moser, the chapter on the Chinese Renaissance was not translated. However, in a footnote introducing the original text, "[t]he Life Journal" is mentioned as "one of the organs of the so-called 'renaissance movement.'" Moser, "Das heutige China," 229.

own person and his own person through the New Culture Movement, he soon started to actively advertise himself as the New Culture star par excellence to foreign audiences. The expression he then used to talk about New Culture was the "Chinese renaissance." This formulation had already appeared as the English title of the *New Tide* magazine, so it had long had a connection to New Culture. Presumably because a Western audience could have more easily built associations with something called the "Chinese renaissance" rather than with something called the "New Culture Movement," Hu Shi chose this expression when addressing academics and the public in Europe and America. The feature of New Culture which Hu Shi emphasized most was the introduction of *baihua*, an unsurprising choice, given Hu Shi's academic preferences and activities.

The peak periods of Western interest in Hu Shi and New Culture were when he undertook trips abroad. Among them were trips to Europe, Britain and the United States in 1926 and 1927, and one to Chicago via Japan and Hawaii in 1933. What incited the public's interest in Hu Shi in the first instance was, especially during his first trip, not so much his role as an intellectual, but as someone involved in politics. This was somewhat ironic in light of Hu Shi's announcement of 1917 not to talk about politics for twenty years – in 1926/27 and 1933, this twenty-year period was technically still ongoing.[19] But Hu had long abandoned this intention. He went on the 1926 trip to the UK as a member of the Boxer Indemnity Committee, and newspapers were sure to mention this.[20] The Boxer Indemnity Committee's task was to determine how best to spend the money of the Boxer Indemnity Fund. The money for this fund came from the reparations China had had to pay to, in this case, Britain after the defeat of the Boxer Uprising of 1900. After China's entry into World War I, Britain had suspended China's payments, and after the Treaty of Versailles, the money that China had already paid was rerouted to be used for projects that would benefit both Britain and China.[21]

Hu Shi used this public interest in him in order to style himself as the "father of the Chinese renaissance," a title given to him, for example, by the *Irish Times*, the *Times* in London and the *Manchester Guardian*.[22] In 1926 an (unnamed and

---

[19] On Hu Shi's announcement of 1917, see Grieder, *Hu Shih and the Chinese Renaissance*, 175–78.
[20] "Boxer Indemnity," *Times*, May 3, 1926, 13, The Times Digital Archive, London; "The Chinese Renaissance: Lecture in Trinity College," *Irish Times*, November 17, 1926, 7, The Irish Times (1921-Current File).
[21] Shiona Airlie, *Scottish Mandarin: The Life and Times of Sir Reginald Johnston* (Hong Kong: Hong Kong University Press, 2012), 205.
[22] "Boxer Indemnity Committee," *Times*, February 12, 1926, 11, The Times Digital Archive, London; "The Chinese Renaissance: Lecture in Trinity College"7; "'The Tragedy of China': Dr. Hu Shih on Failure of the Revolution," *Manchester Guardian*, October 11, 1926, 6, The Manchester Guardian (1901–1959), Manchester.

undated) newspaper, whose article Hu Shi preserved, cited an interview Hu had given to the *Daily Mail*. In this interview, Hu had self-confidently declared that "I started the movement of introducing the spoken language into the school of China."[23] He must also have enjoyed the celebrity he thus achieved, as is testified to by the fact that he mentioned many of his newspaper interviews in his diary and even preserved clippings of newspaper articles about him.[24]

This engagement with the press increased when Hu Shi set out on his next big trip in 1933 to Canada and the United States. En route he seems to have been ambushed by journalists at every port at which his ship stopped along the way, and Hu Shi's diary gives no indication that he tried to avoid these encounters. In this diary, Hu Shi wrote about the editor of the *Japan Chronicle*, who wanted to meet him in Kobe,[25] and he collected a clipping from an unnamed newspaper probably from Hawaii that again called him the "Father of the Chinese Renaimance [sic]" and "the first Chinese poet to write in the vernacular."[26]

Hu Shi's self-promotion as "father of the Chinese renaissance" also reached academic circles. During his 1926–1927 trip, Hu Shi lectured on the New Culture Movement at various academic institutions. He spoke, for example, on the topic at the London School of Economics, in Oxford and at Trinity College Dublin.[27] A lecture he gave in November 1926 at the Royal Institute of International Affairs was reprinted in the Institute's journal in the same month.[28] Hu also socialized with various British sinologists, such as Lionel Giles (1875–1958), Arthur Waley (1889–1966), Reginald F. Johnston (1874–1938, who became professor for Chinese at the School of Oriental Studies in the 1930s) and Herbert Allen Giles (1845–1935). During a brief trip to Frankfurt in October 1926, he met Richard Wilhelm (1873–1930), who was just setting up his China Institute there.[29] To the extent to which their conversations were known, they were not all about the New Culture Movement. But they doubtlessly helped with making Hu Shi known in Western academia.

---

23 Hu, *Hu Shi riji quanji*, 2004, 4:346.
24 Ibid., 4:346, 499.
25 Hu Shi, *Hu Shi riji quanji* (Hu Shi's Collected Diaries), ed. Cao Boyan, vol. 6 (Taibei: Lianjing chuban shiye gongsi, 2004), 681.
26 Ibid., 6:716. This was probably a Hawaiian newspaper, as it reported about a lecture Hu Shi had given in Hawaii.
27 Hu, *Hu Shi riji quanji*, 2004, 4:540, 559; "The Chinese Renaissance: Lecture in Trinity College"7.
28 Hu, *Hu Shi riji quanji*, 2004, 4:542; Shih Hu, "The Renaissance in China," *Journal of the Royal Institute of International Affairs* 5, no. 6 (November 1926): 265–83.
29 Hu, *Hu Shi riji quanji*, 2004, 4:475, 529, 534, 540, 542. On Johnston's professorship, see Airlie, *Scottish Mandarin*, 227.

During the trip to Chicago in 1933, Hu Shi continued promoting himself as "father of the Chinese Renaissance" to Western academic circles. During the voyage, his ship stopped in Hawaii. Originally, it was only scheduled to stay there for a brief while. But the ship's crew had not taken Hu Shi's popularity into account. Once the ship had anchored, a Dr. Sinclair (no dates) of the University of Hawaii contacted Hu Shi. He was so keen on hearing Hu Shi lecture that he "had already negotiated with the ship's company that it would depart a bit later in the afternoon."[30] Hu Shi then gave a one-hour speech on the "Chinese Renaissance" at the University of Hawaii, before he hurried back to his ship and continued the journey.[31]

One of the longest-lasting influences on Western academic narratives about the New Culture Movement and Modern China were the Haskell Lectures, which Hu Shi gave at the University of Chicago in 1933. This platform again existed thanks to Christian missionary efforts. The Haskell Lectures were a series of speeches given by foreign guest lecturers at the Department of Comparative Religion in Chicago. The Haskell Foundation was designed to foster knowledge exchange about religions between the "East [and] the Christian West." It was the counterpart to another foundation that gave "a scholarly presentation of Christianity to the Orient" by inviting Asian academics to talk about their religion in Chicago. In 1933, one of these lecturers was Hu Shi, while other guest lecturers spoke on Islam, Judaism, Christianity and Hinduism.[32]

A session in Hu Shi's lecture series was on the "Chinese renaissance." It is certainly surprising that A. Eustace Haydon (1880–1975), one of the organizers, chose to ascribe to Hu Shi "a self-effacing modesty"[33] in the context of these lectures, because Hu Shi depicted the "Chinese renaissance" as the beginning of an enlightened China, and himself as its originator. New Culture was a "conscious movement to promote a new literature in the living language," Hu wrote. It was a "movement of conscious protests against many of the ideas and institutions in the traditional culture" and a "movement of reason versus tradition, freedom versus authority."[34] Hu Shi himself was, according to his own claim, one

---

30 Hu, *Hu Shi riji quanji*, 2004, 6:710.
31 Ibid., 6:711.
32 Hu, *The Chinese Renaissance*, 2010, ix; A. Eustace Haydon, "Foreword," in *The Chinese Renaissance: The Haskell Lectures 1933* (Whitefish, Montana: Kessinger Publishing, 2010), vii; Laurens Hickok Seelye, "Review of *The Chinese Renaissance* by Hu Shih," *Church History* 4, no. 3 (June 1935): 153.
33 Haydon, "Foreword," viii.
34 Hu, *The Chinese Renaissance*, 2010, 44.

of the movement's "leaders" who enacted New Culture as a "fully conscious and studied movement" and who "[knew] what they want[ed]."³⁵

Hu Shi went on to explain that the Chinese Renaissance had started in 1917. This was the year in which he, as he explained later, published his "Tentative Suggestions for the Reform of Literature." This set off the *baihua* movement, which Hu depicted as a most central feature of New Culture. He again was the most visionary proponent of *baihua* literature, who had envisioned the usage of the "vulgar tongue" for all written purposes long before anybody else could stomach such a revolutionary idea, and while he was still a PhD student in the United States.³⁶

By the time he returned to China in 1917, he went on, the "renaissance" was already in full swing and the only important cultural trend to speak of. Any opposition against it was paltry. "What surprised me most was the weakness and utter poverty of the opposition,"³⁷ Hu Shi said with "self-effacing modesty."³⁸ Omitting that Chen Duxiu was dismissed from his post in April 1919, he claimed that Lin Shu's puny attempts at criticism in fact only gave Beijing University "a great deal of free advertising."³⁹ (For my interpretation of Lin Shu's criticism as quite devastating, see chapter 1.) May Fourth then further boosted the *baihua* movement and in 1920 *baihua* was introduced into primary-school curricula.⁴⁰ It was now called by "the more respectable name of the 'National Language of China,'" Hu Shi said.⁴¹ In other words, in order to communicate his success more convincingly, Hu did not hesitate to adopt the idea that *baihua* was the "vulgar tongue" and the "National Language" – both of which had upset him considerably when in dialogue with Chinese audiences ten years earlier.

Hu Shi's Haskell Lectures were one year later published as a book. This book has been part of undergraduate reading lists down to the present day.⁴² Moreover, it was also widely reviewed in journals at the time. These journals included specialist publications of the fledgling Chinese Studies field, such as the *Monumenta Serica*, as well as of other subjects, such as the *Journal of Religion*, the *American Journal of Sociology*, a variety of philosophy journals, *Pacific Affairs* and the

---

35 Ibid., 46.
36 Ibid., 44–62.
37 Ibid., 55.
38 Haydon, "Foreword," viii.
39 Hu, *The Chinese Renaissance*, 2010, 55.
40 Ibid., 55–57.
41 Ibid., 57.
42 Rana Mitter and Micah S. Muscolino, "Further Subject: China since 1900 (History Faculty of the University of Oxford : Reading List)" (Oxford, 2015), Oxford.

Journal of the Royal Institute of International Affairs.⁴³ Many of them displayed the "Chinese renaissance" as the only relevant trend in Chinese culture and they felt that Hu Shi's fame as leader of this renaissance added value to the book. "As the exposition of an originator and outstanding leader of the intellectual revolution through which China is passing the book merits more than passing attention." wrote one reviewer in the *American Journal of Sociology*.⁴⁴

In the ensuing decades, Hu Shi's Haskell lectures would be cited, commented on or included in the bibliographies of many influential academic books on the New Culture Movement, such as Vera Schwarcz's *The Chinese Enlightenment*, Jerome B. Grieder's *Hu Shih and the Chinese Renaissance* or Yü Ying-shi's chapter in *The Appropriation of Cultural Capital*.⁴⁵ It would also be discussed in works on modern China more generally. Among the latter are famous books such as Elisabeth Kaske's *The Politics of Language in Chinese Education*, Prasenjit Duara's *Rescuing History from the Nation* or Shih Shu-mei's *The Lure of the Modern*, to name just a few.⁴⁶ It would be reprinted in many editions, for example in 1963, in 2009 and in 2010.⁴⁷ Hu Shi, in other words, had very successfully advertised himself through the "New Culture Movement" or, in his case, the "Chinese Renaissance." His narrative has been, if not always adopted, so at least become known to very broad circles of those studying China in the West.

---

43 Henri Bernard, "Review of *The Chinese Renaissance* by Hu Shih," *Monumenta Serica* 1, no. 1 (1935): 214–15; Harley Farnsworth MacNair, "Review of *The Chinese Renaissance* by Hu Shih," *American Journal of Sociology* 41, no. 3 (November 1935): 389; H.W.S., "Review of *The Chinese Renaissance* by Hu Shih," *Journal of Philosophy* 31, no. 13 (June 21, 1934): 193; Clarence H. Hamilton, "Review of *The Chinese Renaissance* by Hu Shih," *International Journal of Ethics* 46, no. 1 (October 1935): 121–23; J.J.L. Duyvendak, "Review of *The Chinese Renaissance* by Hu Shih," *Pacific Affairs* 8, no. 1 (March 1935): 102–3; J. P., "Review of *The Chinese Renaissance* by Hu Shih," *International Affairs* 14, no. 2 (1935): 288; R.H. Tawney, "Review of *The Chinese Renaissance* by Hu Shih," *Philosophy* 11, no. 44 (October 1936): 484–85.
44 MacNair, "Review of *The Chinese Renaissance* by Hu Shih," 389. For reviews that display the New Culture Movement as the only intellectual trend of modern China, see Tawney, "Review of *The Chinese Renaissance* by Hu Shih," 484; Hamilton, "Review of *The Chinese Renaissance* by Hu Shih," 122. For reviews that depict Hu Shi as the leader of the New Culture Movement, see Ibid., 122; Duyvendak, "Review of *The Chinese Renaissance* by Hu Shih," 102; P., "Review of *The Chinese Renaissance* by Hu Shih."
45 Grieder, *Hu Shih and the Chinese Renaissance*, 385; Schwarcz, *The Chinese Enlightenment*, 344; Yü, "Neither Renaissance nor Enlightenment," 300.
46 Elisabeth Kaske, *The Politics of Language in Chinese Education, 1895–1919* (Leiden: Brill, 2008), 464; Shih, *The Lure of the Modern*, 395; Duara, *Rescuing History from the Nation*, 244.
47 Shi Hu, *The Chinese Renaissance*, The Haskell Lectures, 1933 (New York: Paragon Book Reprint Corp., 1963); Shih Hu, *The Chinese Renaissance*, The Haskell Lectures, 1933 (LaVergne, TN: Kessinger, 2009); Hu, *The Chinese Renaissance*, 2010.

The CCP and the New Culture Movement

The canonization of May Fourth and New Culture and their usages as a "brand name" or an "allegory," in Rana Mitter's and Vera Schwarcz's words respectively,[48] in the People's Republic of China (PRC) has been discussed at length by others,[49] and therefore a brief treatment of this issue will suffice here. May Fourth is an integral part of the CCP's founding narrative. This story had been formulated by 1940 and has in its core elements remained the same until the present. In the 1930s and 1940s, the CCP deployed a variety of strategies to legitimize its claim to power, and rewriting history was one of them. It was necessary for CCP leaders, William F. Dorrill argues, to show that they "were carrying out the laws of history."[50] In this context, Mao Zedong declared May Fourth to have been a central stage in Chinese history, which led to the foundation of the CCP. Mao himself was then ascribed a leading role in the Movement, showing that he had led China onto the right path.

The 1930s and 1940s were a time when the CCP was growing as a political force, but had not yet convinced everybody. With the goal to achieve legitimacy for his party and leadership for himself, Mao and historians loyal to him repackaged history, not only making it fit with a Marxist worldview, but also playing up Mao's role in the history of the past few decades. May Fourth was one of the elements that were in this way rewritten. In 1939, Mao depicted May Fourth as an important event ushering in the foundation of the CCP. May Fourth had been "incomplete," he said, because its intellectuals failed to connect with the "masses."[51] In 1939 he wrote, "[b]ut the intellectuals will accomplish nothing if they fail to integrate themselves with the popular masses of the workers and peasants. *This is the cause of failure of the Revolution of 1911 and the May Fourth movement.*"[52] Needless to say, the CCP had then managed to complete that process, according to this narrative.

By 1940, Mao had created his own, unique periodization of history, in which May Fourth took the place of a turning point between what he called the "old

---

[48] "Brand name": Mitter, *A Bitter Revolution*, 22. "Allegory": Schwarcz, *The Chinese Enlightenment*, 240.
[49] Lee, *Lu Xun and His Legacy*; Mitter, *A Bitter Revolution*; Wagner, "The Canonization of May Fourth."
[50] William F. Dorrill, "Transfer of Legitimacy in the Chinese Communist Party: Origins of the Maoist Myth," *China Quarterly*, no. 36 (1968): 47.
[51] Schwarcz, *The Chinese Enlightenment*, 248.
[52] Zedong Mao, "The May Fourth Movement (May 1939)," in *Mao's Road to Power: Revolutionary Writings 1912–1949*, ed. Stuart Schram and Nancy J. Hodes, vol. 7 (Armonk, N.Y.: M.E. Sharpe, 2005), 67. Italics in the original.

democracy" and the "new democracy." The old democratic revolutions were "led *entirely* by the bourgeoisie, with the aim of establishing a capitalist society and a state under bourgeois dictatorship,"[53] Mao wrote in 1940. May Fourth was the watershed moment, after which revolutions would be of the "new democratic" variety: "After the May Fourth movement, the *chief* political leader of China's bourgeois-democratic revolution was no longer the *single class of the* bourgeoisie, and the proletariat also participated in the political leadership."[54] The proletariat was, of course, guided by the CCP. This view of history and of May Fourth was taken up by historians close to Mao.[55] Soon it also found its way into high-school history textbooks. Over the next few decades until the present, these books would teach May Fourth as the beginning of "new democracy" and as the prelude to the foundation of the CCP in 1921.[56]

Another salient feature in these textbooks is the extreme emphasis on Mao Zedong's role in the New Culture Movement. Mao Zedong had participated in the New Culture Movement by founding the journal *Xiang River Review* in 1919. The *Xiang River Review* was a local journal based in Hunan and it was one of the many journals that "sprang up like spring bamboo after the rain" in that year.[57] While it received some positive attention, contemporaries in 1919 would have certainly been surprised to learn that it would later be considered a leading magazine. For

---

[53] Zedong Mao, "On New Democracy (January 15, 1940)," in *Mao's Road to Power: Revolutionary Writings 1912–1949*, ed. Stuart Schram and Nancy J. Hodes, vol. 7 (Armonk, N.Y.: M.E. Sharpe, 2005), 334. Italics in the original.
[54] Ibid., 338. Italics in the original.
[55] Huaiyin Li, "Between Tradition and Revolution: Fan Wenlan and the Origins of Marxist Historiography of Modern China," *Modern China* 36, no. 3 (May 2010): 288–91; Mao Zedong, "Xin minzhu zhuyi lun" (On New Democracy), in *Mao Zedong ji* (Collected Writings of Mao Zedong), ed. Takeuchi Minoru (New York: Tianwai chubanshe, 1998), 151–60.
[56] For mentions of "new democracy," see Jilin sheng jiaoyu xueyuan, ed., *Gaozhong lishi fuxi ziliao* (Revision Material for History at Senior High Schools) (Changchun: Jilin renmin chubanshe, 1979), 106; Li Longgeng, ed., *Zhongguo lishi* (Chinese History), vol. 3 (Beijing: Renmin jiaoyu chubanshe, 1987), 1; Huang Wenlin, ed., *Gaozhong lishi* (History for Senior High Schools) (Beijing: Kexue jishu wenxian chubanshe, 1995), 128; 'Gaozhong lishi yongbiao' bianxiezu, ed., *Gaozhong lishi yongbiao* (Tables for Senior High School History) (Beijing: Zhongguo dui wai fanyi chuban gongsi, 2010), 36. For the foundation of the CCP, see Anhui sheng jiaoyu ting bianshenshi, ed., *1961 nian gaozhong lishi fuxi tigang: Zhongguo shi bufen* (Revising Senior High School History, 1961: Chinese History) (Hefei: Anhui jiaoyu chubanshe, 1961), 118; Jilin sheng jiaoyu xueyuan, *Gaozhong lishi fuxi ziliao*, 106; Li, *Zhongguo lishi*, 3:7; Huang, *Gaozhong lishi*, 129; 'Gaozhong lishi yongbiao' bianxiezu, *Gaozhong lishi yongbiao*, 36.
[57] For the expression, "springing up like spring bamboo after the rain," see Wang, *Huiyi Yadong tushuguan*, 38.

example, in 1919 the *Weekly Critic* introduced it, both benevolently and patronizingly, as one of its "little brothers" (*xiao xiongdi*).⁵⁸

Mao also had a connection to Beijing University, where he had been an assistant librarian from late 1918 to early 1919 under Li Dazhao. But he had reportedly been snubbed by the students around Fu Sinian and Luo Jialun, which led to his resentment for them afterwards.⁵⁹ Still, in the PRC Mao and his fellow CCP leaders were written into central roles in the New Culture Movement. One junior-high-school book from 1987, for example, depicted New Culture as an event centrally run by later CCP dignitaries. Its most important publications, it claimed, were not only *New Youth* and *Weekly Critic*. They were also Mao's *Xiang River Review* and even Zhou Enlai's (1898–1976) *Tianjin Student Union News* (*Tianjin xuesheng lianhehui bao*).⁶⁰ The same narrative that plays up Mao's journal has since also been supported by the *People's Daily* (*Renmin ribao*), by history books and by exhibitions.⁶¹

This usage of May Fourth to legitimize the CCP's and Mao Zedong's role in the making of 20th-century China, had additional effects: It firmly inscribed the New Culture Movement into Chinese history and it made some of its other actors well-known too. In the Mao era, Lu Xun was praised as the New Culture writer par excellence, and until the present, Beijing has a Lu Xun museum. On October

---

58 "Xiang jiang pinglun," 4.
59 Schwarcz, *The Chinese Enlightenment*, 248.
60 Li, *Zhongguo lishi*, 3:7.
61 "Jinian Makesi danchen, zhanlanhui zuori zai shoudu kaimu" (Remembering the Birth of Marx, Opening of the Exhibition Yesterday in the Capital), *Renmin ribao* (People's Daily), May 6, 1958, 4, Beijing; Peng Ming, "Jianping 'Wu si shiqi qikan jieshao'" (A Review of *Periodicals of the May Fourth Era*), *Renmin ribao* (People's Daily), March 7, 1959, 7, Beijing; A Ying, "Aidao Li Kenong tongzhi" (Mourning Comrade Li Kenong), *Renmin ribao* (People's Daily), February 14, 1962, 6, Beijing; Shi Zhong, "Wu si shiqi pi Kong douzheng de lishi jingyan – jinian wu si yundong wushiwu zhounian" (The Historical Experience of the Struggle to Criticize Confucius during the May Fourth Period – Commemorating the 55th Anniversary of the May Fourth Movement), *Renmin ribao* (People's Daily), May 5, 1974, 2, Beijing; "Fayang 'wu si' geming jingshen – yi jiu yi jiu nian wu si yundong zhaopian jianji" (Carrying on the Revolutionary Spirit of "May Fourth" – a Montage of Photos of the May Fourth Movement of 1919), *Renmin ribao* (People's Daily), May 3, 1979, 4, Beijing; Li Ruihuan, "Jianchi zhengmian xuanchuan wei zhu de fangzhen: zai xinwen gongzuo yantaoban shang de jianghua (1989 nian 11 yue 25 ri)" (The Policy of Emphasizing the Continuation of Direct Propaganda: A Talk at the News Work Study and Discussion Class [25 November 1989]), *Renmin ribao* (People's Daily), March 3, 1990, 1, Beijing; Meng Xianli, "Guotu zhanchu zhengui wu si wenxian" (The National Library Exhibits Precious May Fourth Documents), *Renmin ribao* (People's Daily), May 5, 1999, 5, Beijing; Liu Weijian, "Shidai huhuan da bianji" (Great Edition of an Epoch's Call), *Renmin ribao* (People's Daily), January 4, 2009, 8, Beijing.

31, 1966, on the 30th anniversary of his death, 70,000 people commemorated Lu Xun's death in Beijing. Among them were Zhou Enlai, Guo Moruo and Chen Boda (1904–1989). One of the reasons for exalting Lu Xun was, according to Rana Mitter, that Lu Xun could be read as an iconoclast.[62] His famous short story *Diary of a Madman* (*Kuangren riji*) of 1918 had, for example, rejected Confucian morality as being equivalent to cannibalism. This criticism of what Lu Xun had constructed as "Chinese tradition" could be made to fit with ideals in Mao-era China.

Hu Shi, on the other hand, was vehemently attacked in the Mao years. As one of the most famous US-educated scholars, he was scapegoated for all foreign-educated intellectuals, whom the CCP was both skeptical of and dependent on. Hu Shi was criticized by his own son, Hu Sidu (1921–1957), who had remained on the mainland, in 1950 and then in two anti-Hu campaigns (1951–1952 and 1954–1955).[63] The collected criticism of Hu Shi was published in an eight-volume work entitled *Critique of Hu Shi's Thought*.[64]

Other works on Hu Shi of the Mao era had titles such as *A Criticism of Hu Shi's Reactionary Thought* (1955) or *The Research on the Water Margins of the Reactionary Literatus Hu Shi* (1975).[65] Jerome B. Grieder recounts that Hu Shi pointed with pride to the collection of criticism of him and said that, better than anything else, it evidenced his importance.[66] The anti-Hu campaigns, incidentally, were also a vehicle to spread a more sympathetic knowledge of Hu Shi to the West. Grieder recounts that he found Hu Shi "vainglorious" and "self-indulgent" when he heard him lecturing for the first time in 1955. But Grieder then started studying the anti-Hu campaigns in the PRC, and this incited not only his sympathy for Hu but also his interest in him.[67]

After the end of the Mao era, Hu Shi was rehabilitated again on the mainland. A number of *nianpu* (chronologies of lives) and biographies were published in the 1980s alone.[68] Some of them felt obliged to address Hu Shi's uncomfortable

---

[62] Mitter, *A Bitter Revolution*, 202.
[63] Grieder, *Hu Shih and the Chinese Renaissance*, 361–63.
[64] Ibid., 367.
[65] Li Da, *Hu Shi fandong sixiang pipan* (A Criticism of Hu Shi's Reactionary Thought) (Wuhan: Hubei renmin chubanshe, 1955); Hu Shi, *Fandong wenren Hu Shi dui "Shui hu" de kaozheng* (The Research on the *Water Margins* of the Reactionary Literatus Hu Shi), ed. Renmin ribao tushu ziliaoshi (Beijing: Renmin ribao chubanshe, 1975).
[66] Grieder, *Hu Shih and the Chinese Renaissance*, 367.
[67] Ibid., ix–x. The word "vainglorious" appears in the adverbial form in the text.
[68] *Nianpu*: Cao and Ji, *Hu Shi nianpu*; Geng, *Hu Shi nianpu*. Biographies: Bai Ji, *Hu Shi zhuan* (A Biography of Hu Shi) (Changsha: Hunan jiaoyu chubanshe, 1987); Shen Weiwei, *Hu Shi zhuan* (A Biography of Hu Shi) (Kaifeng: Henan daxue chubanshe, 1988); Yi Zuoxian, *Hu Shi zhuan* (A Biography of Hu Shi) (Wuhan: Hubei renmin chubanshe, 1987).

political association with Chiang Kai-shek and to point out that in fact Hu Shi was much more "complicated" than his "reactionary" image would suggest.⁶⁹ Chiang himself, of course, was rehabilitated on the mainland as well. The production of books on Hu Shi or reprints of works by him has been flourishing ever since the 1980s and the discussions of his tricky image have subsided.⁷⁰

The usage of May Fourth and New Culture as a buzzword to boost personal fame and to market agendas is ongoing in the PRC. While Mao Zedong's interpretation of May Fourth as the beginning of "new democracy" and the CCP has remained unchanged, details around this core vary and are adjusted to different ideals. For instance, New Culture has since been used to boost the fame of individual CCP cadres. In 1993, for example, the *People's Daily* tried to improve the credentials of the CCP functionary Yang Hansheng (1902–1993). In an obituary, it called him a "pioneer of China's New Culture Movement." Ironically, even from the newspaper article it becomes clear that Yang had not actually pioneered the New Culture Movement. The *People's Daily* wrote that Yang had joined the CCP in 1925. "Following the party's instructions, he edited [the journals] *Flowing Sand* [*Liusha*], *Sunrise* [*Richu*] and [the book] *Social Science Collections*."⁷¹

It is hard to comprehend how this would have made him a "pioneer of the New Culture Movement," especially since in the CCP narrative the New Culture Movement led to the foundation of the party in 1921. The two journals, for example, were only launched in 1928, long after the "pioneering" period was over. What the article shows instead is that Yang Hansheng was a CCP cadre involved in culture just before and after the foundation of the PRC.⁷² The ascribed role in the New Culture Movement was apparently designed to boost his fame.

---

69 Yi, *Hu Shi zhuan*, 1. Similarly also in Li Xin, "Xu" (Preface), in *Hu Shi zhuan* (A Biography of Hu Shi), by Bai Ji (Changsha: Hunan jiaoyu chubanshe, 1987), 1–2; Ren Fangqiu, "Xu" (Preface), in *Hu Shi zhuan* (A Biography of Hu Shi), by Shen Weiwei (Kaifeng: Henan daxue chubanshe, 1988), 4.
70 The foreword of a 2004 edition of *Hu Shi's Autobiography* had nothing but praise for Hu Shi, Hu Shi, *Hu Shi zishu* (Hu Shi's Autobiography) (Zhengzhou: Henan renmin chubanshe, 2004), 1–3. Apart from an abstract mention of some "criticism" that has always surrounded Hu Shi (p.3), the same goes for the preface of *Selected Classical Works by Hu Shi*, Hu Shi, *Hu Shi jingdian wencun* (Selected Classical Works by Hu Shi), ed. Hong Zhigang (Shanghai: Shanghai daxue chubanshe, 2004), 1–4.
71 "Zhongguo xin wenhua yundong de xianqu, wenyi jie zhuoyue lingdaoren Yang Hansheng tongzhi shishi" (The Pioneer of China's New Culture Movement and Outstanding Leader in the Field of Art and Literature, Comrade Yang Hansheng, Has Passed Away), *Renmin ribao* (People's Daily), June 11, 1993, 4, Beijing.
72 On the foundation of the journals, see *Quanguo baokan suoyin, qikan daohang*.

More recent CCP agendas have also been called "New Culture" and "May Fourth." For example in 1999, Beijing Normal University historian Gong Shuduo (1929–2011) wrote in the *People's Daily* that the New Culture Movement was a direct precursor of the "culture of the socialism with Chinese characteristics."[73] In 2009, on the 90th anniversary of the Movement, another *People's Daily* article called for a continuation of the "May Fourth spirit of patriotism," which was even necessary in an age in which "China can say that it is unhappy, [in which] it can say no!"[74] This was very probably an allusion to the nationalist books with the titles *China Can Say No* and *Unhappy China* from 1997 and 2009 respectively.[75] In 2014, President Xi Jinping inserted calls for "realizing the China dream" in a speech on May Fourth at Beijing University.[76]

To be sure, New Culture and May Fourth are not among the major buzzwords of our time on the mainland, especially when they are compared to slogans like "socialism with Chinese characteristics" or the "China dream." But they are so deeply embedded in mainland culture that they can be resurrected and used at any time and for almost any purpose. When politicians refer to them, there is no need for them to explain the importance of "May Fourth" and "New Culture" to a new generation.

Redeploying a canonical event: The past sixty years

In this way May Fourth and New Culture were made part and parcel of narratives about 20th-century Chinese history. Once this had happened, new voices drew upon its canonicity to boost their own fame and agendas, and in this way they reinterpreted the New Culture Movement again. Among the people to do so were

---

[73] Gong Shuduo, "Zhengque pingjia wu si xin wenhua yundong" (Correctly Assessing the New Culture Movement of May Fourth), *Renmin ribao* (People's Daily), May 6, 1999, 9, Beijing.
[74] Chen Shuyu, "Qingchun feiyang de suiyue" (The Time of the Rise of Youth), *Renmin ribao* (People's Daily), May 4, 2009, 16, Beijing.
[75] Song Qiang, Zhang Zangzang, and Qiao Bian, *Zhongguo keyi shuo bu: lengzhan hou shidai de zhengzhi yu qinggan jueze* (China Can Say No: Political and Emotional Choices in the Post-Cold War Era) (Beijing: Zhonghua gongshang lianhe chubanshe, 1996); Song Xiaojun, *Zhongguo bu gaoxing: da shidai, da mubiao ji women de neiyou-waihuan* (Unhappy China: The Great Time, Grand Vision and Our Challenges) (Nanjing: Jiangsu renmin chubanshe, 2009).
[76] Xi Jinping, "Qingnian yao zijue jianxing shehui zhuyi hexin jiazhiguan – zai Beijing daxue shi-sheng zuojianghui shang de jianghua" (The Young People Must Consciously Fulfill the Core Value System of Socialism – Talk at the Beijing University Teacher and Student Forum), *Zhonghua renmin gongheguo jiaoyubu* (Ministry of Education of the People's Republic of China), May 4, 2014, http://www.moe.gov.cn/publicfiles/business/htmlfiles/moe/moe_176/201405/167911.html.

the mainland Chinese dissidents and government critics of the 1980s. Among them were in recent decades also politicians, the press and art in Taiwan, all of whom negotiated Taiwanese national identity.

Government critics in mainland China

The student protests of Tian'anmen Square in 1989 were very consciously modelled on May Fourth and the protesters tapped into a number of elements of the May Fourth repertoire to make this connection. 1989 was the seventieth anniversary of May Fourth. With Tian'anmen Square, they chose the location where the May Fourth protests had started.[77] Even the identity of its organizers shared in the legacy of May Fourth: among the prominent organizers of June Fourth were students of Beijing University. In 1988, the Beijing University student Wang Dan (b.1969) founded a journal called *New May Fourth* (*Xin wu si*). The famous student protester Wu'er Kaixi (b. 1968) wrote a "May Fourth Manifesto" on May 4, 1989, in which he accused the CCP of having failed to implement the "spirit of democracy" of May Fourth.[78] Liu Xiaobo (1955–2017), then a protester and later the famous winner of the Nobel Peace Prize, was an admirer of Lu Xun and of May Fourth.[79]

This usage of New Culture by the government critics brought the Movement again into the Western press, after it had been neglected there for a long time. During the 1989 protests, the *Guardian* called May Fourth the "real intellectual origin of nationalist China,"[80] and "China's first national and cultural revolution."[81] In the wake of this, scholars working on May Fourth became more visible to the public too. The most famous May Fourth scholar of the time was Vera Schwarcz. In July 1989, the *New York Times* wrote how Schwarcz, an "expert in Chinese student movements," was "counselling" Chinese students in the United States who were traumatized by the reports from their home country.[82]

---

77 Hermann Aubié, "Is Liu Xiaobo a Rooted Cosmopolitan? A Critical Examination of His Dissent from a Historical Perspective," in *Cosmopolitanism and the Legacies of Dissent*, ed. Tamara Caraus (New York: Routledge, 2015), 71.
78 Mitter, *A Bitter Revolution*, 274–75.
79 Aubié, "Is Liu Xiaobo a Rooted Cosmopolitan?," 69–71.
80 "Can China Find Its Gorbachev?," *Guardian*, April 24, 1989, 18, The Guardian (1959–2003), London.
81 John Gittings, "Is China Heading towards Revolution? Recapturing 1919's Glory," *Guardian*, May 5, 1989, 14, The Guardian (1959–2003), London.
82 Peggy McCarthy, "A Support for Students Who Grieve for China," *New York Times*, July 2, 1989, CN1, CN7, CN1, New York Times (1923-Current File), New York.

Soon afterwards, in 1990, Schwarcz wrote a review in the *New York Times* of Jonathan Spence's *Search for Modern China*, in which she drew upon 1989 to argue for the importance of the "history of China from imperial to Communist times."[83] Finally, the *New York Times* reviewed Schwarcz's book on New Culture *Time for Telling the Truth Is Running Out* in 1992 and called it a "moving" story.[84] That this public interest in May Fourth and its scholars was dependent on Tian'anmen Square becomes clear from the fact that afterwards the Western press only paid little attention to May Fourth. Even Rana Mitter's *The Bitter Revolution* was hardly reviewed in the general press.[85] This is in spite of the fact that *The Bitter Revolution* is very well-known in academic circles far exceeding China historians, and that Mitter himself is a public intellectual with frequent appearances in the press and with his own BBC radio program.

New Culture and May Fourth continued to sporadically have some traction among Chinese dissidents, and they occasionally continued using it as a reference point to legitimize their own claims. In 1998, Beijing University professor Qian Liqun (b. 1939) and student Yu Jie (b. 1973) praised Cai Yuanpei and May Fourth for their advocacy of academic freedom. This clashed with an interpretation Jiang Zemin (b. 1926) was then putting forward, which emphasized May Fourth's advocacy of "patriotism, progress, democracy, and science."[86]

Ten years later, New Culture and May Fourth popped up again in the Charter 08, a document written and signed by 303 people, among them the later Nobel Prize winner Liu Xiaobo, which demanded far-reaching political reforms.[87] The charter gave an outline of modern China's history in its introduction, which was meant to show where China had strayed from the path to democracy. The "New Culture Movement of 'May Fourth,'" in this story, was the last occasion on which China had called for the desirable "science and democracy," the charter said.

---

[83] Vera Schwarcz, "China: The Hard Road to Now," *New York Times*, May 13, 1990, BR1, BR32, BR1, New York Times (1923-Current File), New York.

[84] Arnold R. Isaacs, "Silencing the Best and the Brightest," *New York Times*, June 28, 1992, BR27, New York Times (1923-Current File), New York.

[85] One exception is *Foreign Affairs* Lucian W. Pye, "Review of *A Bitter Revolution*," *Foreign Affairs*, November–December 2004. The lack of other reviews appears from a search in the following databases: "Times Digital Archive (1785–1985)," Database, (n.d.), http://www.thetimes.co.uk/tto/archive; "ProQuest Historical Newspapers: The Guardian and The Observer," Database, (n.d.), http://search.proquest.com/hnpguardianobserver.

[86] Geremie Barmé, *In the Red: On Contemporary Chinese Culture* (New York: Columbia University Press, 1999), 350–52.

[87] Eva Pils, Jean-Philippe Béja, and Hualing Fu, "Introduction," in *Liu Xiaobo, Charter 08, and the Challenges of Political Reform in China*, ed. Jean-Philippe Béja and Hualing Fu (Hong Kong: Hong Kong University Press, 2012), 1.

Afterwards these demands were sidelined by the necessities of World War II and by the Communist Party's victory after the Chinese Civil War of 1945 to 1949.[88]

However, New Culture and May Fourth are only one element in this narrative, and they are not at all the central reference point. Instead, the Charter 08 claims to be written on occasion of the "hundredth anniversary of the Chinese constitution," the "sixtieth anniversary of the 'declaration of global human rights'" and the "thirtieth anniversary of the birth of the 'wall of democracy.'"[89] Most importantly, the website of the Charter 08 has its own page on Liu Xiaobo and on "June Fourth," that is, the demonstrations of 1989.[90] In other words, Chinese government critics have found a new point of reference with the 1989 demonstrations.[91] Maybe it is because May Fourth and New Culture are occupied by the official CCP discourse to such an extent that they appear to have lost their lustre for the CCP's critics.

The New Culture Movement in Taiwan: A chequered history

In Taiwan, however, the New Culture Movement is experiencing a heyday of its usage as a buzzword in the form of the Taiwanese New Culture Movement.

The New Culture Movement in martial-law era Taiwan

This rebirth of the New Culture Movement in Taiwan is surprising, as the island's relationship to the event was tricky throughout the martial-law era (1949–1987). In 1919, Sun Yat-sen had quickly grasped the potential of the New Culture Movement and tried to use the franchise for himself. A GMD-run journal, the *Weekly Review*, was among the first to use the expression "New Culture Movement" in writing.[92] But under Chiang Kai-shek and at a time when May Fourth had been appropriated by the CCP, the GMD's attitude towards the Movement became

---

[88] "Xianzhang zhengwen" (Text of the Charter), *Lingba xianzhang* (Charter 08), accessed November 11, 2015, http://www.2008xianzhang.info/chinese.htm.
[89] Ibid.
[90] "Liu Xiaobo" (Liu Xiaobo), *Lingba xianzhang* (Charter 08), accessed November 11, 2015, http://www.2008xianzhang.info/000-xiaobo--liebiao.php; "Wu wang 'liu si'" (Do Not Forget June Fourth), *Lingba xianzhang* (Charter 08), accessed November 11, 2015, http://www.2008xianzhang.info/JuneFourth/000198964.html.
[91] A similar point has been made by Aubié, "Is Liu Xiaobo a Rooted Cosmopolitan?," 74.
[92] Ouyang, "Guomindang yu xin wenhua yundong," 73; Xian, "Xin wenhua yundong de wuqi," 4.

difficult. Chiang Kai-shek's GMD on and off either celebrated it cautiously or wrote it out of history. For example, during the Second United Front in 1939, the CCP and the GMD renamed May 4 into "Youth Day," with the goal to mobilize young people for the Sino-Japanese War. In 1943, Chiang Kai-shek created a narrative about recent Chinese history that moved from the Xinhai Revolution in 1911 directly to the re-organization of the GMD in 1924, completely omitting May Fourth and New Culture as an important stage in history.[93]

Once Chiang Kai-shek and his party had moved into exile to Taiwan in 1949, New Culture and May Fourth were almost entirely written out of history. Under the impact of the then-prevalent Cold War mentality, the GMD could not like an event that the CCP had already made its own. This was reflected in high-school history textbooks. A textbook published in 1968, while the Cultural Revolution was raging on the mainland, did not mention the New Culture Movement at all. It grudgingly dedicated six lines to May Fourth under the headline of "Foreign Relations at the Time of the First World War," and depicted the protests as resistance against Japanese imperialism and the country-selling traitors of the warlord government.[94] This story was repeated in 1972.[95]

A 1967 textbook which taught the "history of Chinese culture" did not mention the New Culture Movement either, but only discussed the thought of Sun Yat-sen as the set of ideas important for that time period.[96] Classroom practice, however, may have differed. The *Teachers' Handbook* to the 1972 book contained an extensive description of May Fourth, mentioning New Culture elements such as *baihua* and a critique of Confucian morality. All of this was cited from Chow Tse-tsung's *The May Fourth Movement.*[97]

Still, only towards the end of the martial-law era in 1987 and of the Cold War in 1989, the New Culture Movement made it back into textbooks more visibly. A 1985 book talked about New Culture in some detail and cautiously explained that the Movement had had its positive sides, such as the advocacy of "democracy and science" and the "popularization of education" through the "new literature." However, the book pointed out, other aspects of it had led to "disasters of country

---

93 Wagner, "The Canonization of May Fourth," 108–9.
94 Zhongxue biaozhun jiaokeshu lishike bianji weyuanhui, ed., *Gaozhong lishi* (Chinese History for Senior High Schools), 6th ed., vol. 2 (Taibei: Taiwan xinsheng yinshuachang, 1968), 5, 140.
95 Guoli bianyiguan, *Gaoji zhongxue lishi* (History for Senior High Schools), 1st ed., vol. 3 (Guoli bianyiguan, 1972).
96 Zhongxue biaozhun jiaokeshu lishike bianji weyuanhui, ed., *Gaozhong Zhongguo wenhuashi* (The History of Chinese Culture for Senior High Schools), vol. xia (Taibei: Taiwan xinsheng yinshuachang, 1967), 2.
97 Guoli bianyiguan, *Gaoji zhongxue lishi jiaoshi shouce* (History for Senior High Schools – Teachers' Handbook), 2nd ed., vol. 3 (Guoli bianyiguan, 1978), 297; Chow, *The May Fourth Movement.*

and nation" (*guojia minzu de zaihuo*), among which was, most notably, the popularization of "Marxism" (*Makesi zhuyi*).⁹⁸ This book was used and reprinted all the way into the 1990s.⁹⁹

This skepticism about May Fourth and New Culture during the Chiang Kai-shek era stood in uneasy tension with the fact that many of the New Culture star personnel held high positions in Taiwan's academia. Hu Shi had not only promoted himself in the West. He had also become a well-established intellectual in China and contributed to this actively. In 1921 Hu Shi published the *Selected Works of Hu Shi*, and right away it was brought out by two publishers (East Asia Library in Shanghai and Central Editing and Translation Publisher in Beijing, *Zhongyang bianyi chubanshe*). Over the next decade, new, multi-volume editions of his *Collected Works* appeared almost every year, until in 1935 East Asia Library ran the sixteenth edition of the book series.¹⁰⁰ His *Selected Works* were one of the success stories of an otherwise constantly struggling East Asia Library. By 1922, the publisher had already sold 12,000 copies of the book, which made it the fourth best-selling book of the company. It, as well as the *Selected Works of Chen Duxiu*, was in fact so popular that they were soon pirated – much to the financial

---

98 Guoli bianyiguan, *Gaoji zhongxue lishi* (History for Senior High Schools), vol. 3 (Guoli bianyiguan, 1985), 99.
99 Guoli bianyiguan, ed., *Gaoji zhongxue lishi* (History for Senior High Schools), 9th ed., vol. 3 (Guoli bianyiguan, 1993), 213.
100 Hu Shi, *Hu Shi wencun* (Selected Works of Hu Shi), vol. 2 (Shanghai: Yadong tushuguan, 1921); Hu Shi, *Hu Shi wencun* (Selected Works of Hu Shi), vol. shang (Beijing: Zhongyang bianyi chubanshe, 1921); Hu Shi, *Hu Shi wencun* (Selected Works of Hu Shi), vol. shang-xia (Beijing: Zhongyang bianyi chubanshe, 1921); Hu Shi, *Hu Shi wencun* (Selected Works of Hu Shi), 4th ed., vol. shang (Shanghai: Yadong tushuguan, 1923); Hu Shi, *Hu Shi wencun* (Selected Works of Hu Shi), 4th ed., vol. xia (Shanghai: Yadong tushuguan, 1923); Hu Shi, *Hu Shi wencun* (Selected Works of Hu Shi), vol. 2 (Shanghai: Yadong tushuguan, 1924); Hu Shi, *Hu Shi wencun* (Selected Works of Hu Shi), vol. 3 (Shanghai: Yadong tushuguan, 1924); Hu Shi, *Hu Shi wencun* (Selected Works of Hu Shi), 4th ed., vol. 2.1 (Shanghai: Yadong tushuguan, 1927); Hu Shi, *Hu Shi wencun* (Selected Works of Hu Shi), 4th ed., vol. 2.2 (Shanghai: Yadong tushuguan, 1927); Hu Shi, *Hu Shi wencun* (Selected Works of Hu Shi), 4th ed., vol. 2.3 (Shanghai: Yadong tushuguan, 1927); Hu Shi, *Hu Shi wencun* (Selected Works of Hu Shi), 4th ed., vol. 2.4 (Shanghai: Yadong tushuguan, 1927); Hu Shi, *Hu Shi wencun* (Selected Works of Hu Shi), 4th ed., vol. 1 (Shanghai: Yadong tushuguan, 1928); Hu Shi, *Hu Shi wencun* (Selected Works of Hu Shi), 4th ed., vol. 2 (Shanghai: Yadong tushuguan, 1928); Hu Shi, *Hu Shi wencun* (Selected Works of Hu Shi), 4th ed., vol. 3 (Shanghai: Yadong tushuguan, 1928); Hu Shi, *Hu Shi wencun* (Selected Works of Hu Shi), 4th ed., vol. 4 (Shanghai: Yadong tushuguan, 1928); Hu Shi, *Hu Shi wencun* (Selected Works of Hu Shi), vol. shang (Beijing: Zhongyang bianyi chubanshe, 1929); Hu Shi, *Hu Shi wencun* (Selected Works of Hu Shi), vol. xia (Beijing: Zhongyang bianyi chubanshe, 1929); Hu Shi, *Hu Shi wencun* (Selected Works of Hu Shi), 16th ed., vol. 2 (Shanghai: Yadong tushuguan, 1933); Hu Shi, *Hu Shi wencun* (Selected Works of Hu Shi), 16th ed., vol. 3 (Shanghai: Yadong tushuguan, 1933); Hu Shi, *Hu Shi wencun* (Selected Works of Hu Shi), 16th ed., vol. 4 (Shanghai: Yadong tushuguan, 1933).

chagrin of East Asia Library.¹⁰¹ From the 1930s onwards, Hu Shi published multiple editions of his study-abroad diaries and of his *Autobiography at Forty*.¹⁰² Once the Guomindang had moved to Taiwan this continued, with more editions of Hu's diaries, *Selected Works, Autobiography* and *Collections of Speeches*.¹⁰³

Hu Shi made sure to advertise his works. When publishing an edition of his collection of *baihua* poems, *Experiments*, in 1920, he asked – and told in his preface that he had asked – famous scholars like Lu Xun, Zhou Zuoren, Yu Pingbo (1900–1990) and Chen Hengzhe (Beijing University's first female professor) to select poems for the new edition. This, Chen Pingyuan argues, was a conscious effort to increase the prestige of the book, as his readers must have associated this with the story about how Confucius selected poems for the *Book of Odes*.¹⁰⁴

Hu was also personal friends with Chiang Kai-shek. Although Hu Shi was never unequivocally in agreement with Chiang Kai-shek's policies and criticized him openly on occasion, he was broadly supportive of him.¹⁰⁵ From 1937 to 1942, he served as the GMD regime's ambassador to the United States, and Chiang Kai-shek even paid for part of his flat when Hu returned to Taiwan in 1958 to become president of the Academia Sinica.¹⁰⁶ Other New Culture star personnel had

---

101 On *Selected Works of Hu Shi* being a success and on them being pirated, see Wang, *Huiyi Yadong tushuguan*, 139–42. On the 12,000 copies sold by 1922, see Ibid., 82.

102 Hu Shi's study-abroad diaries: Hu Shi, *Hu Shi riji* (Hu Shi's Diary) (Wenhua yanjiushe, 1933); Hu Shi, *Hu Shi riji* (Hu Shi's Diary) (Wenhua yanjiushe, 1934); Hu Shi, *Hu Shi liuxue riji* (Hu Shi's Study-Abroad Diary), vol. 1 (Shangwu yinshuguan, 1947); Hu Shi, *Hu Shi liuxue riji* (Hu Shi's Study-Abroad Diary), vol. 2 (Shangwu yinshuguan, 1947); Hu Shi, *Hu Shi liuxue riji* (Hu Shi's Study-Abroad Diary), vol. 3 (Shangwu yinshuguan, 1947); Hu Shi, *Hu Shi liuxue riji* (Hu Shi's Study-Abroad Diary), vol. 4 (Shangwu yinshuguan, 1947). Hu Shi's *Autobiography at Forty*: Hu Shi, *Sishi zishu* (Autobiography at Forty) (Shanghai: Yadong tushuguan, 1933); Hu Shi, *Sishi zishu* (Autobiography at Forty) (Shanghai: Yadong tushuguan, 1935); Hu Shi, *Sishi zishu* (Autobiography at Forty) (Shanghai: Yadong tushuguan, 1939); Hu Shi, *Sishi zishu* (Autobiography at Forty) (Shanghai: Yadong tushuguan, 1947); Hu Shi, *Sishi zishu* (Autobiography at Forty) (Shanghai: Yadong tushuguan, 1954).

103 Hu Shi, *Hu Shi wencun* (Selected Works of Hu Shi) (Taibei: Yuandong tushuguan, 1953); Hu Shi, *Sishi zishu* (Autobiography at Forty) (Taibei: Liu yi chubanshe, 1954); Hu Shi, *Sishi zishu* (Autobiography at Forty) (Taibei: Zhengzhong shuju, 1957), 19; Hu Shi, *Hu Shi yanlun ji* (Collection of Hu Shi's Speeches) (Taibei: Huaguo chubanshe, 1953); Hu Shi, *Hu Shi liuxue riji* (Hu Shi's Study-Abroad Diary) (Taibei: Taiwan shangwu yinshuguan, 1959); Hu Shi, *Hu Shi liuxue riji* (Hu Shi's Study-Abroad Diary) (Taibei: Taiwan shangwu, 1960); Hu Shi, *Hu Shi liuxue riji* (Hu Shi's Study-Abroad Diary) (Taibei: Taiwan shangwu, 1961).

104 Chen, *Touches of History*, 275–78.

105 Grieder, *Hu Shih and the Chinese Renaissance*, 250.

106 Tao Yinghui, *Dianxing zai suxi: zuihuai Zhongyang yanjiuyuan liu wei yigu yuanzhang* (A Model of Past Times: Commemorating the Late Sixth President of the Academia Sinica) (Taibei: Xiuwei zixun keji gufen youxian gongsi, 2007), 246.

similarly good ties to Chiang's government, among them Fu Sinian and Luo Jialun. After the Civil War of 1945 to 1949, they therefore moved with Chiang to Taiwan.

There they made up the top ranks of the academic elite institutions. Fu Sinian, for example, had already become the director of the Institute of History and Philology of the Academia Sinica in 1928, which was established in the wake of the Northern Expedition. He then held official positions for the GMD regime and became president of Taiwan University in 1949, a position he held until his death in 1950.[107] Luo Jialun had joined the GMD in the mid-1920s, held various academic positions and educational-political offices for the Nanjing Regime as well as an ambassadorship to India. After the move to Taiwan, he became chair of the GMD Party History Compilation Committee, vice-president of the Examination Yuan and editor of important works such as the *Chronology of the Life of the Father of the Nation*. The "father of the nation" was, of course, Sun Yat-sen. In 1958, Luo was made president of the national archive Academia Historica.[108]

That these people were also stars to a broader Taiwanese public became apparent in the attention the media paid when two of them died, Fu Sinian in 1950 and Hu Shi in 1962. Both of them died a very public death. Fu Sinian collapsed while answering questions in his capacity as chancellor of Taiwan University at the Taiwan Provincial Legislature. Responding to a question, Fu Sinian took to the rostrum to lament that students from poor backgrounds were unable to obtain higher degrees for financial reasons. An eye witness remembered a year later that, when Fu returned to his seat after giving this answer, he looked unhealthily pale. The eye witness therefore rushed to the nearest hospital, located a doctor and brought him to Fu. But it was too late and Fu Sinian could not be saved.[109]

Hu Shi died at a conference in 1962. According to the Taiwan-based *Independent Evening News* (*Zili wanbao*), he had spent all day chairing a committee at the

---

[107] Howard L Boorman, "Fu Ssu-Nien," *Biographical Dictionary of Republican China* (New York: Columbia University Press, 1968), 44–45, New York.
[108] Howard L Boorman, "Lo Chia-Lun," *Biographical Dictionary of Republican China* (New York: Columbia University Press, 1968), 430–31, New York.
[109] Shangguan furong, "Fu Sinian shishi qianhou jixiang" (Detailed Record of the Time around Fu Sinian's Death), in *Fu guxiaozhang aiwanlu* (Elegies on the Former President Fu), ed. Guoli Taiwan daxue jinian Fu guxiaozhang choubei weiyuanhui aiwanlu bianyin xiaozu (Taibei: Taiwan daxue, 1951), 19; Cheng Weixian, "Zhuiyi Fu guxiaozhang zai sheng canyihui" (Remembering the Late President Fu at the Consultative Meeting), in *Fu guxiaozhang aiwanlu* (Elegies on the Former President Fu), ed. Guoli Taiwan daxue jinian Fu guxiaozhang choubei weiyuanhui aiwanlu bianyin xiaozu (Taibei: Taiwan daxue, 1951), 18.

Academia Sinica. In the evening, he had given a one-and-a-half-hour long lecture at a party. This exhausted him too much and he suffered a heart attack.[110]

Each time, the events were reported on a large scale in the press. Photos of both corpses were circulating in the press. One showed Hu Shi lying on a couch or a stretcher, with a group of men standing around him and one of them feeling his pulse. The caption to the picture reads "The last ten minutes" (*zuihou shi fenzhong*). A further explanatory text states that the photo shows Hu Shi after he had lost consciousness from his heart attack and while a doctor was "feeling his pulse."[111] Hu Shi, in other words, was a celebrity and his death was of human interest to the Taiwanese public.

Photographing Hu Shi's last moments was not the only way of doing this. The Taibei-based newspaper *Shin Sheng Daily News* (*Xinshengbao*) claimed to have gotten hold of Hu's driver. The driver explained that he had always taken good care of Hu Shi, who had long suffered from a weak heart. But during the party, his employer had been surrounded by guests. As soon as the driver had looked the other way, Hu Shi had collapsed. The driver immediately brought Hu's "oxygen cylinder." But it was too late: "Mr. Shizhi only took two breaths, and then he breathed no more."[112] The driver was devastated. "'Master [*fuzi*], this is how you have gone?'" he reportedly sighed. "He embraced Mr. Shizhi's corpse, screamed, and tears ran, filling his cheeks."[113]

Another person the papers were interested in was Hu Shi's widow, Jiang Dongxiu (1890–1975). The marriage between Hu and Jiang had been arranged by his mother in the 1910s. Like many of his peers, Hu Shi was initially unhappy about the prospect of getting married to a relatively uneducated woman, who did not fit the ideal of a "new woman" of May Fourth. But unlike most of his peers, Hu did not divorce her.[114] Jiang Dongxiu, the Taiwan newspaper *United Daily News*

---

[110] Feng Aiqun, ed., "Dao yidai zheren Hu Shi" (Mourning the Philosopher of a Whole Era Hu Shi), in *Hu Shizhi xiansheng jinianji* (Commemorative Volume for Mr. Hu Shizhi) (Taibei: Xuesheng chubanshe, 1962), 133.

[111] Cheng Jingyu, ed., *Hu Shi boshi jinian jikan* (Collected Papers to Commemorate Dr. Hu Shi) (Hong Kong: Duli luntanshe, 1962), No page. For pictures of Fu Sinian's dead body, see Guoli Taiwan daxue jinian Fu guxiaozhang choubei weiyuanhui aiwanlu bianyin xiaozu, ed., "Fu guxiaozhang yixiang ji sangzang jidian deng zhaopian" (Photos of the Portrait of the Deceased Late President Fu, the Funeral and so Forth), in *Fu guxiaozhang aiwanlu* (Elegies on the Former President Fu) (Taibei: Taiwan daxue, 1951), Tuban.

[112] Liu Fanggang, "Xuezhe yu siji" (The Scholar and the Driver), in *Hu Shizhi xiansheng jinianji* (Commemorative Volume for Mr. Hu Shizhi), ed. Feng Aiqun (Taibei: Xuesheng chubanshe, 1962), 67.

[113] Ibid., 65.

[114] Grieder, *Hu Shih and the Chinese Renaissance*, 352–53.

(*Lianhebao*) wrote, had been in downtown Taibei when Hu Shi died. She was summoned to the Academia Sinica, which is in the outskirts of Taibei and where Hu had collapsed, but when she arrived, Hu had already passed away. Understandably, she almost suffered a nervous breakdown. Hu Shi had left the flat that day without saying a word to her, because he was busy with his work, she lamented, and now he was dead.[115] A picture was also circulating, which showed Madame Chiang (Song Meiling, 1898–2003) herself consoling Hu Shi's widow.[116] Such stories could only have been interesting for the public to read (and for newspapers to print), because Hu Shi was a celebrity on the island.

Large funerals were staged for both Fu Sinian and Hu Shi. The *National Evening Post* (*Minzu wanbao*) even suggested that Hu Shi should get a state funeral.[117] Later on, the newspaper articles on their deaths and other commemorative materials were reprinted in book collections, which were often compiled by Fu Sinian's and Hu Shi's friends, colleagues and students. One of them, the *Collection of Elegies on the Former President Fu*, was published in 1951 at Taiwan University.[118] Similar works were created for Hu Shi as well.[119]

Hu Shi's flat on the campus of the Academia Sinica – the one which Chiang Kai-shek had paid for in parts – was transformed into a Hu Shi Memorial Hall, which is still open today. A visitor to this Memorial Hall can see the flat fully furnished, including bed, sofas, garden furniture, desk and bathroom. Even Hu Shi's cane, his chopsticks and his tea service are preserved. In 1964, an "exhibition hall" was built and then enlarged to display some of Hu Shi's work, photos and the like, and the Hu Shi Memorial Hall complex also comprises the Hu Shi Memorial Gardens.[120] Fu Sinian too got a smallish Fu Sinian Memorial Garden with a Fu Sinian Mausoleum at its center, located on the campus of his university,

---

115 Li Yong, "Qishi'er sui Hu furen de shangxin" (The Grief of Seventy-Two-Year Old Mrs Hu), in *Hu Shi boshi jinian jikan* (Collected Papers to Commemorate Dr. Hu Shi), ed. Cheng Jingyu (Hong Kong: Duli luntanshe, 1962), 62–63.
116 Cheng, *Hu Shi boshi jinian jikan*, No page.
117 Feng Aiqun, ed., "Jianyi zhengfu guozang Hu Shi boshi" (We Recommend That the Government Give Dr Hu Shi a State Funeral), in *Hu Shizhi xiansheng jinianji* (Commemorative Volume for Mr. Hu Shizhi) (Taibei: Xuesheng chubanshe, 1962), 131. For Fu Sinian's funeral, see Guoli Taiwan daxue jinian Fu guxiaozhang choubei weiyuanhui aiwanlu bianyin xiaozu, "Fu guxiaozhang yixiang ji sangzang jidian deng zhaopian."
118 Guoli Taiwan daxue jinian Fu guxiaozhang choubei weiyuanhui aiwanlu bianyin xiaozu, ed., *Fu guxiaozhang aiwanlu* (Elegies on the Former President Fu) (Taibei: Taiwan daxue, 1951).
119 Feng Aiqun, ed., *Hu Shizhi xiansheng jinianji* (Commemorative Volume for Mr. Hu Shizhi) (Taibei: Xuesheng chubanshe, 1962); Cheng, *Hu Shi boshi jinian jikan*.
120 Pan Guangzhe, ed., *Rongren yu ziyou: Hu Shi sixiang jingxuan* (Tolerance and Freedom: An Anthology of Hu Shi's Thought) (Taibei: Nanfang jiayuan wenhua chuban, 2009), 4.

the National Taiwan University. It was built in 1951 and refurbished in 2004 with funding from the Ministry of Education.[121]

But all this star cult status could not gloss over the GMD's distaste for the New Culture Movement. This tension manifested itself in an elegiac couplet that Chiang Kai-shek wrote for Hu Shi. It called Hu Shi "The model of the old virtue in the New Culture; The paragon of the new thought in the old ethics."[122] Chiang, it seems, was unable to talk about Hu Shi's life without mentioning New Culture. But a May Fourth-era Hu Shi would have doubtlessly turned in his grave at the reference of "old virtue" and "old ethics."

Democracy-era Taiwan: A Blue and Green Taiwanese New Culture Movement

Martial law ended in 1987 and Taiwan democratized in the ensuing years, with the first democratic elections taking place in 1996. With this political turn, the New Culture Movement was reinvented as a buzzword in the form of the Taiwanese New Culture Movement to express differing visions for Taiwan's national identity.

The presidential debate of 2007

In July 2007, the GMD and DPP candidates for the upcoming presidential elections, Ma Ying-jeou (b. 1950) and Hsieh Chang-ting (b. 1946), debated Taiwanese history. Specifically, they quarreled over which party the activist of the Taiwanese New Culture Movement, Jiang Weishui, would have supported in 2007 and what his position would have been on the question of Taiwan's relationship with mainland China. Jiang Weishui, arguably, did not have a position on either issue. He had been active in the 1920s, when Taiwan was a Japanese colony and communist China did not yet exist. What Jiang had supported was Taiwanese independence from Japan. In order to advocate independence from Japan, Jiang Weishui had founded a Taiwan Cultural Association in 1921. Many of this Association's members also wrote for a newspaper called the *Taiwan People's News*.[123] (see chapter 3) Later on, he would be among the founders of the Taiwan People's Party.

Jiang Weishui was never exactly persona non grata in the martial-law era. But official interest in him was lukewarm in the 1950s and 1960s, because some

---

121 *Plaque at Fu Sinian Memorial Garden* (Guoli Taiwan daxue, n.d.), accessed August 20, 2015.
122 Jiang Jieshi, "Wanlian" (Elegiac Couplet), in *Hu Shi boshi jinian jikan* (Collected Papers to Commemorate Dr. Hu Shi), ed. Cheng Jingyu (Hong Kong: Duli luntanshe, 1962), 62–65.
123 Lamley, "Taiwan under Japanese Rule," 231–32.

of his family members were suspected of being communists. However, Jiang Weishui was discovered by the opposition in the 1970s.[124] In the 1990s, interest in Jiang grew into a veritable "Jiang Weishui fever."[125] Jiang's collected works were published in 1998, with a revised edition in 2005.[126] A Jiang Weishui Cultural Foundation was formally established in 2006, with strong involvement of Jiang's descendants and support by Ma Ying-jeou. In the same year, a highway was named after Jiang Weishui and a stamp showed his likeness.[127] This was part of a broader trend, in which other participants in the Taiwanese New Culture Movement were discovered and furnished with museums too.[128]

In 2007, then, the presidential candidates used Jiang Weishui and the Taiwanese New Culture Movement as buzzwords to argue for their own agendas and parties. GMD candidate (and future president) Ma Ying-jeou claimed that Jiang Weishui would have supported a rapprochement with the mainland. The basis for this claim was that, in 1924, Jiang had stated that "what the Taiwanese people understand is [this]: that they are of the Chinese nationality [*Zhonghua minzu*], that is, of the Han nationality [*Han minzu*], is a fact that cannot be denied by anybody."[129] The GMD under Ma Ying-jeou supported a rapprochement with mainland China so actively during his presidency (from 2008 to 2016) that this

---

[124] Thomas Fröhlich, "Identität und Widerstand: Jiang Weishuis Antikolonialismus und seine Nachwirkungen" (Identity and Resistance: Jiang Weishui's Anti-Colonialism and Its Legacy), in *Taiwans unvergänglicher Antikolonialismus: Jiang Weishui und der Widerstand gegen die japanische Kolonialherrschaft* (Taiwan's Eternal Anti-Colonialism: Jiang Weishui and the Resistance against Japanese Colonial Rule), ed. Thomas Fröhlich and Yishan Liu (Bielefeld: Transcript, 2011), 56–57.
[125] Zhang Fangyuan, "Yi ge Jiang Weishui, gezi-biaoshu: zhouxun lishi miwu zhong de Jiang Weishui zhenshi mianmao" (One Jiang Weishui, Many Narratives: A Search for the True Face of Jiang Weishui in the Dense Fog of History), *Haixia pinglun* (Cross-Strait Review), no. 249 (September 2011): 41.
[126] Jiang Weishui, *Jiang Weishui quanji* (Collected Works of Jiang Weishui), ed. Wang Xiaobo, vol. 2 (Taibei: Haixia xueshu chubanshe, 1998); Jiang Weishui, *Jiang Weishui quanji zengdingban* (Collected Works of Jiang Weishui, Revised and Expanded Edition), ed. Wang Xiaobo, vol. xia (Taibei: Haixia xueshu chubanshe, 2005).
[127] "Jijinhui dashiji ji Jiang Weishui xiangguan jinian huodong" (A Record of Great Events of the Foundation and Remembrance Activities for Jiang Weishui), *Jiang weishui wenhua jijinhui* (Chiang Wei-Shui's Cultural Foundation), accessed September 18, 2015, http://weishui.org/index-22.html; Shou Weng, "Da 'Jing Weishui shi shei?'" (Answering the Question: "Who Is Jiang Weishui?"), *Haixia pinglun* (Cross-Strait Review), no. 182 (February 2006): 60.
[128] Emily Graf, "Lu Xun Marginalized or Centered? Wen- and Wu- Readings of Lai He's Museum Space" (Popular Culture Group, Colloquium Workshop organized by Barbara Mittler, Heidelberg, May 26, 2017), 14, Heidelberg.
[129] Zhang, "Yi ge Jiang Weishui, gezi-biaoshu," 44.

would become one contributing factor for the harsh defeat his party suffered in the presidential elections of 2016.

Hsieh Chang-ting, running for the DPP, asserted that Jiang Weishui would have been opposed to the GMD. Hsieh argued that Jiang Weishui was against "a regime that had come from the outside" (*wailai zhengquan*), that is, a "foreign regime." Again, by a "foreign regime," Jiang Weishui would have meant imperialist Japan. But Hsieh Chang-ting took it to mean the GMD, which had "come from the outside," namely from the mainland, in the late 1940s.[130]

This usage of Jiang Weishui to debate Taiwanese identity was not new. The strategy had its fledgling origins in the 1970s, and in academic circles it was in full swing in the 1990s.[131] On the occasion of the presidential debate, the media now tapped into this repertoire of arguments about Jiang Weishui and combined them with issues that were especially inflammatory in 2007.

One such issue was the GMD's relationship to the 288 Incident, during which the GMD had killed a high number of Taiwanese in 1947. This had been set off by the arrest and beating of a woman who tried to illegally sell cigarettes on the evening of February 27, 1947, which started a series of violent protests all across Taiwan. Initially it looked as if these protests would result in the GMD paying greater attention to Taiwanese demands for self-rule. But soon afterwards, Chiang Kai-shek had thousands of Taiwanese massacred and executed, especially members of the Taiwanese elite, who were in a position to challenge GMD rule.[132]

In the 2000s, the GMD was just trying to get to grips with its role in the Incident, after DPP president Chen Shui-bian (b. 1950, in office from 2000 to 2008) had opened the files about the Incident, had held commemorations and made indemnity payments to the victims' descendants.[133] In 2007, the Green (that is, pro-DPP, pro-independence) press now pounced on the opportunity to draw

---

130 Ibid., 41; Wang Beilin and Wang Yuzhong, "Jiang Weishui jijinhui zuotan: wailai zhengquan lunzheng, Xie Ma jiaofeng" (Forum of the Jiang Weishui Cultural Foundation: Debate about Foreign Regimes, Hsieh and Ma Cross Swords), *Ziyou shibao* (Liberty Times Net), July 10, 2007, http://news.ltn.com.tw/news/politics/paper/140433.
131 Fröhlich, "Identität und Widerstand," 59–64.
132 Steven Phillips, "Between Assimilation and Independence: Taiwanese Political Aspirations under Nationalist Chinese Rule, 1945–1949," in *Taiwan: A New History*, ed. Murray A. Rubinstein (Armonk, N.Y: M.E. Sharpe, 2007), 292–96.
133 "Quzhiminhua, cai neng fazhan Taiwan de zhutixing: lun Ma Yingjiu de Taiwan lishi lunshu" (Only Decolonization Can Develop Taiwan's Subjectivity: Ma Ying-Jeou's Discourse on Taiwanese History), *Haixia pinglun* (Cross-Strait Review), no. 178 (October 2005): 1; Lutgard Lams and Xavier Li-wen Liao, "Tracing 'Taiwanization' Processes in Taiwanese Presidential Statements in Times," *Journal of Current Chinese Affairs* 40, no. 1 (2011): 74.

further attention to the GMD's inglorious role in the 288 Incident. The *Southern Express* (*Nanfang kuaibao*) and the *Liberty Times* (*Ziyou shibao*), for example, pointed out that Jiang Weishui would have certainly been executed in the 288 Incident, had he not already died in 1931.[134]

Speculating about Jiang Weishui's hypothetical fate under GMD rule was not the only strategy the Green press deployed. Another one was to declare the GMD's deployment of Jiang an act of misappropriation. The Green *Liberty Times* called the fact that a GMD candidate tried to associate himself with a Taiwanese historical figure – Jiang Weishui – and to thus carve out a *bentuhua* discourse for himself a "rape of this country [that is, of Taiwan]."[135] *Bentuhua* describes the formulation of an identity that is Taiwanese, instead of Chinese, a trend that had started in the 1970s and 1980s. This was a reversal from the national identity previously propagated by the GMD, which claimed that Taiwan, not the mainland, was the "real" and legitimate China. One strategy through which this Chinese identity was carved out was the suppression of Taiwanese dialects in favor of Mandarin[136] – a fact that will become important later in this section, in the discussion of a musical about Jiang Weishui.

The *bentuhua* discourse had long been a contested terrain between GMD and DPP. As soon as the DPP was forming, it took a leading role in the *bentuhua* discussions, combining Taiwanese nationalism with demands for democratization. But the GMD was not far behind. Already Lee Teng-hui (b. 1923, GMD, a native Taiwanese and president from 1988 to 2000) started appropriating the *bentuhua* discourse for the GMD.[137] In 2007, the Green public held it against Ma Ying-jeou that he had been born on the mainland, and Ma's wish to carve out a more solid position for himself in the *bentuhua* discourse was probably a contributing factor for his interest in the historical figure.[138]

---

134 Yan Jiatong, "Ma Yingjiu momingqimiao de yi bi" (The Baffling Pen of Ma Ying-Jeou), *Nanfang kuaibao* (Southern Express), July 17, 2007, Taibei, http://www.southnews.com.tw/polit/ma_in_9/00/00243.htm; "'Jin Henghui zhuanlan': Ma Yingjiu qiangbao Jiang Weishui! Weisui." ("Jin Henghui Column": Ma Ying-Jeou Rapes Jiang Weishui! Failed.), *Ziyou shibao* (Liberty Times Net), July 14, 2007, http://talk.ltn.com.tw/article/paper/141346.
135 "'Jin Henghui zhuanlan.'"
136 Xiaokun Song, *Between Civic and Ethnic: The Transformation of Taiwanese Nationalist Ideologies (1895–2000)* (Brussels: Vubpress, 2009), 135.
137 Ibid., 169, 180–81.
138 On Ma's creation of a Taiwanese identity for himself, see Jonathan Sullivan and Eliyahu V. Sapir, "Ma Ying-Jeou's Presidential Discourse," *Journal of Current Chinese Affairs* 41, no. 3 (2012): 39.

The *Liberty Times* now called this "rape." "In the martial-law era," an article explained, "the GMD could willfully rape democracy, violate the will of the people. Nowadays the son of the party-state Ma Ying-jeou still wants to rape a dead man [i. e. Jiang Weishui], rape reason."[139] Echoing Hsieh Chang-ting's accusation that the GMD was not really a Taiwanese party, because it had "come from the outside" (i. e. the mainland), the newspaper declared that the very attempt of Ma Ying-jeou to appropriate the *bentuhua* discourse in this way proved that the GMD was indeed "foreign": if there was no "foreign" regime in Taiwan, there would be no need to for a *bentuhua* discourse.[140] Jiang Weishui became a buzzword deployed in a competition about party politics and legitimacy.

A third strategy was to speculate which Taiwanese identity Jiang Weishui would have supported. Such speculations had already been deployed in the 1990s.[141] The trouble – and also the potential – was that Jiang Weishui had made contradictory statements on the matter. He had, as cited above, claimed that the Taiwanese were of the "Han nationality."[142] But he had also declared that they were "Taiwanese."[143] Of course for Jiang, who was concerned with ridding Taiwan of Japanese colonial rule, the two had been more or less the same. In the year 2007, when Japan was no longer a colonial power and the question was how to manoeuver the relationship with the mainland, they were diametrically opposite.

The press, academics and Jiang's descendants now drew out specific statements, which Jiang Weishui had made, and accused the opposite side of taking them out of context. Writing for the Blue (that is, pro-GMD, pro-rapprochement with the mainland) *Cross-Strait Review* (*Haixia pinglun*), the philosophy professor Wang Xiaobo (b. 1943) argued for the Chinese identity. He cited an article from 1992 by Jiang's daughter Jiang Biyu (no dates), in which she had argued against those who treated Jiang Weishui as a proponent of Taiwanese independence (from the mainland). The reason was, she said, that such people took Weishui's statement that the Taiwanese were "of the Taiwanese nation" (*Taiwan minzu*) out of its proper context. Put back into context, according to Jiang Biyu, it became

---

139 "'Jin Henghui zhuanlan.'"
140 Ibid.
141 On the debates in the 1990s, see Fröhlich, "Identität und Widerstand," 62–64.
142 Zhang, "Yi ge Jiang Weishui, gezi-biaoshu," 44.
143 Wang Xiaobo, "Qing wu panwu Taiwan kang-Ri shi he Jiang Weishui: Bo Lin Dushui he Chen Yishen" (Please Do Not Slander Taiwan's History of Resistance against Japan and Jiang Weishui: A Critique of Lin Dushui and Chen Yishen), *Haixia pinglun* (Cross-Strait Review), no. 200 (August 1, 2007): 39.

clear that Jiang Weishui had actually meant to say that Taiwan was Chinese.¹⁴⁴ Jiang Biyu, incidentally, and her husband were suspected to be communists in the 1950s, and her husband was executed for this reason.¹⁴⁵

The Green camp did exactly the same for Jiang Weishui's statement about the Taiwanese being of the "Chinese nation." This was drawn out of context, the *Liberty Times* for example explained. If Jiang's statements were put back into context, it would become clear that he favored Taiwanese independence.¹⁴⁶ In fact, the *Liberty Times* argued, Jiang Weishui had said after the Northern Expedition that now "the country is united." "The country," however, had then not included Taiwan, which implied that a "united country" only meant "mainland China." "Taiwanese independence" (lit. "the movement to normalize Taiwan's [identity] as a nation," *Taiwan guojia zhengchanghua yundong*) even "ran in a straight line" (*yimai-xiangchuan*) from Jiang Weishui's anti-Japanese activities, the article claimed.¹⁴⁷

High-school history textbooks
This contention around the Taiwanese New Culture Movement was not confined to politics and the press. It was, as Thomas Fröhlich points out, also vibrant in academia, in some quarters of which, for example, editions of Jiang Weishui's works were manipulated in a way that placed Jiang into the pro-Chinese identity camp. One of Jiang Weishui's texts from 1931 described Taiwan as having a certain "place of origin," but the name of the "place of origin" was censored by the Japanese. In an edition of Jiang's works of 1976, a Taiwanese editor, according to Fröhlich, simply filled the blank space with the words "Republic of China."¹⁴⁸

But the negotiation around the Taiwanese New Culture Movement also made its way into high-school education, where over the past ten years textbooks have been variously teaching the Taiwanese New Culture Movement as suggesting that Taiwan belonged to China or that it did not. The strategy for these arguments

---

144 Ibid. For Jiang Biyu's original article, see Jiang Biyu, Jiang Songhui, and Zhou Heyuan, "Wei Jiang Weishui yu Taiwan wenhua xiehui zhi 'Taiwan pinglun' de shengming" (Declaration to the *Taiwan Review* on Behalf of Jiang Weishui and the Taiwan Cultural Association), *Haixia pinglun* (Cross-Strait Review), no. 24 (December 1992): 94–96.
145 Fröhlich, "Identität und Widerstand," 57.
146 "Liqing Guomindang 'lianjie' Jiang Weishui de miulun" (Clarifying the Absurdity of the GMD's [Attempt] at Linking up with Jiang Weishui), *Ziyou shibao* (Liberty Times Net), July 11, 2007, http://talk.ltn.com.tw/article/paper/140799.
147 Ibid.
148 Fröhlich, "Identität und Widerstand," 66–67.

was different from the presidential debate: The books linked or delinked the Taiwanese New Culture Movement from the mainland Movement, by either claiming that the Movement on Taiwan was related to the one on the mainland or that it was not.

The Taiwanese New Culture Movement was taught to high-school children for the first time following government regulations of 2005. That it appeared in textbooks at all was part of a trend to teach the history of Taiwan not only as Chinese, but also as Taiwanese, history, which had started in the mid-1990s.[149] The 2005 regulation specified that history teaching should be "centered on Taiwan," and that in this context children should learn about the Taiwan Cultural Association (the one founded by Jiang Weishui).[150] A textbook based on these regulations therefore duly taught the Taiwanese New Culture Movement and kept mentions of its connection to the mainland to a minimum. The Taiwanese New Culture Movement was inspired by the "May Fourth *baihua* new literature movement" of the "late 1910s." But it differed from this movement in that it was also anti-colonial, the textbook explained.[151]

The next round of textbooks, based on a new set of regulations of 2011, eradicated any mention of the mainland Movement, thus delinking it as much as possible from its mainland cousin.[152] A textbook of this generation did not even call the event the "Taiwanese New Culture Movement," presumably since this made it sound like a derivative of its mainland counterpart. Instead, pupils learnt that the event had happened in light of "global" trends, "such as the tide of national self-determination in the political [sphere], liberalism, communism, etc., [which had] all spread to Taiwan."[153]

Taiwan, this story read, truly was no part of China. This account, of course, also hinted at the awkwardness of Taiwan's position vis-à-vis mainland China. In spite of all their attempts at detaching the Taiwanese New Culture Movement

---

149 Ya-Chen Su, "Ideological Representations of Taiwan's History: An Analysis of Elementary Social Studies Textbooks, 1978–1995," *Curriculum Inquiry* 37, no. 3 (11.2007): 212; Song, *Between Civic and Ethnic*, 203.
150 "Centerd on Taiwan": "Houqi zhongdeng jiaoyu gongtong hexin kecheng zhiyin" (Guide for common core curricula in for the higher mid-level education), 15, accessed September 17, 2015, http://edu.law.moe.gov.tw. The specification about the Taiwan Cultural Association: Ibid., 20. The same was also said in "Zonghe gaoji zhongxue zanxing kecheng gangyao" (Comprehensive outline of provisional curricula for senior high schools), 27, accessed September 17, 2015, http://edu.law.moe.gov.tw/LawContent.aspx?id=GL000357&KeyWord=%E8%AA%B2%E7%A8%8B%E7%B6%B1%E8%A6%81.
151 Wang Qi and Wang Jianwen, *Lishi* (History), vol. 1 (Hanlin chuban, 2006), 121.
152 On the 2011 regulations, see *Lishi* (History), vol. 1 (Nanyi shuju, 2012), i.
153 Ibid., 1:134.

from the mainland, the very fact that the Taiwanese New Culture Movement – by whichever name it was called – was declared a central stage in 20th-century Taiwanese history fashioned this history after mainland patterns. Students must have seen this pattern at least one year later, when they learned about the mainland Movement in a later volume of the textbook series.[154]

For the time being this 2011 cycle of textbooks was also the peak of Green interpretations of the Movement. The next round of textbooks, based on regulations of 2015, stood strongly under the auspices of Ma Ying-jeou, who had by then become infamous for his rapprochement with the mainland. These regulations decreed that history curricula should again emphasize Taiwan's connection to the mainland, leading to heavy protests in the summer of 2015. With respect to the Taiwanese New Culture Movement, they demanded an emphasis on "the influence of the [mainland's] May Fourth Movement and New Culture Movement."[155] It remains to be seen if and how the new DPP government under Cai Ying-wen (b. 1956, in office since 2016) will reinterpret the movement in textbooks. Over the past decade, however, it has been linked to, and delinked from, the mainland Movement to inculcate different visions for Taiwanese national identity.

A musical about the Taiwanese New Culture Movement

This debate is not confined to politics and a politically guided education, but extends to the realm of art too. In March 2016, a musical about Jiang Weishui was restaged in Taiwan. This was the time after the GMD had lost the presidential elections of January 2016, among other things thanks to Ma Ying-jeou's active rapprochement policies, but before the new president Cai Ying-wen had taken up her office in May.

The musical's title was *Weishui Spring Wind* (*Weishui chunfeng*) with the official English translation as *The Impossible Times*. It had first been performed in 2010 (in the presence of Ma Ying-jeou), and it had been commissioned by the Department for Cultural Affairs of the Taibei City Government.[156] This department has been quite active in propagating visions for Taiwanese national identity

---

154 *Lishi* (History), vol. 3 (Nanyi shuju, 2013), 46–51.
155 "Putong gaoji zhongxue yuwen ji shehui lingyu kecheng gangyao weitiao" (Fine tuning of the outline of the curriculum of the field of language and literature, as well as society for normal senior high schools), August 1, 2015, 5, http://www.k12ea.gov.tw/ap/news_view.aspx?sn=324aa1ef-22c2-40a5-9f1d-86b3fd5f1f6e.
156 On the 2010 performance, see "Linian yanchu jilu" (Record of Past Performances), *Weishui chunfeng – Yinyue shidai* (The Impossible Times – All Music Theatre), November 22, 2011, http://impossibletimes.allmusic.com.tw/archive.htm. Ma Ying-jeou's attendance: "Jijinhui dashiji

through the Taiwanese New Culture Movement. Under its auspices, a Taiwanese New Culture Movement Memorial Hall was founded in 2006, which emphasizes Taiwan's nature as a "pluralist" "immigrant society," according to the Memorial Hall's explanation of its own logo.[157] Taiwan as an "immigrant society" is another framework that seeks to come to grips with a history that has indeed been shaped by many waves of "immigration," the latest of which was the influx of GMD mainlanders after the Chinese Civil War.

The musical shows that it is apparently almost impossible to talk about the Taiwanese New Culture Movement in a public forum without recourse to party politics. Its creative director and play and lyrics writer Yang Zhongheng (b. 1963) expressed his wish to keep his musical out of party politics.[158] But the musical, the advertising machine around it and reviews in the press are full of allusions to what Yang Zhongheng himself calls typical Blue and Green interpretations of the Movement.[159] Even a piece of art – albeit a state-commissioned one – that seeks to be politically neutral features a combination of a variety of politically inspired categories.

Yang Zhongheng explained that calling Jiang Weishui "Taiwan's Sun Yat-sen" was a Blue interpretation. In line with this, the website of the troupe that performed the musical as well as a major ticket-selling organization refers to Jiang Weishui as "Taiwan's Sun Yat-sen." Within the musical, the character of Inagaki Tōbei (1892–1955), a New Culture-sympathetic Japanese, expresses the wish that Jiang Weishui start a "revolution" in the style of Sun Yat-sen.[160]

---

ji Jiang Weishui xiangguan jinian huodong." The 2016 restaging: "Yinyue shidai juchang 'Weishui chunfeng' 2016 yongheng zhuiyiban" (All Music Theater's *The Impossible Times*, 2016, Eternal Commemoration Version), *Liang tingyuan shoupiao* (National Theatre and Concert Hall Tickets), accessed March 7, 2016, https://www.artsticket.com.tw/CKSCC2005/Product/Product00/ProductsDeta.

157 Foundation of the museum: "Chengli zongzhi" (Purpose), *Taiwan xin wenhua yundong jinianguan* (Taiwan New Cultural Movement Memorial Hall), June 13, 2012, http://tncmmh.gov.taipei/ct.asp?xItem=2032903&CtNode=38914&mp=11900B. The logo: "Ben guan logo jieshao" (Introduction of Our Hall's Logo), *Taiwan xin wenhua yundong jinianguan* (Taiwan New Cultural Movement Memorial Hall), June 24, 2011, http://tncmmh.gov.taipei/ct.asp?xItem=2032904&CtNode=38915&mp=11900B.

158 Yang Zhongheng, "'Weishui chunfeng' – ruhe fuhuo Jiang Weishui" ("The Impossible Times" – How to Bring Jiang Weishui back to Life), *Weishui chunfeng – Yinyue shidai* (The Impossible Times – All Music Theatre), accessed March 8, 2016, http://impossibletimes.allmusic.com.tw/archive.htm; Zhu Anru, "'Weishui chunfeng' – rang lishi weiren 'you xue you rou'" ("The Impossible Times" – Giving a Great Man of History "Flesh and Bones"), *PAR biaoyan yishi zazhi* (PAR Acting and Arts Journal), no. 212 (August 2010): 80.

159 Yang, "'Weishui chunfeng'"; Zhu, "'Weishui chunfeng.'"

160 Ticket seller: "Yinyue shidai juchang 'Weishui chunfeng' 2016 yongheng zhuiyiban." The troupe's website: "Shouye" (Home), *Weishui chunfeng – Yinyue shidai* (The Impossible Times – All Music Theatre), November 22, 2011, http://impossibletimes.allmusic.com.tw/. The character

Taiwanese national identity, too, is negotiated in the musical, and here *The Impossible Times* has a rather Green thrust. First of all, the musical is performed in Taiwanese, which has been used as a symbol for *bentuhua*. For instance, when Ma Ying-jeou tried to carve out a Taiwanese identity for himself in the 2000s, in order to counter criticism that he was too fond of the mainland, he learnt Taiwanese languages.[161] Secondly, the musical's signature song incites, in the words of a critic who wrote for the Blue *Cross-Strait Review*, strong "feelings of 'love for Taiwan.'"[162] The musical, in other words, does not just use the (Taiwanese) New Culture Movement as a buzzword that makes mere intellectual claims, but as one that directly taps into emotions.

This signature song's title is "Taiwan, this is our name" (transliteration in Mandarin: *Taiwan, shi women de ming*), and it is performed at the very end of the first act, in a scene that portrays the foundation of the Taiwan Cultural Association.[163] After the character of Jiang Weishui has initiated the Association, the choir, portraying the Association members, starts dancing and singing the song. The lyrics outline what could be called Taiwan's identity crisis. The character of Chen Qichang (1904-?), another activist of the circle, starts, in a solo, with a description of Taiwan's colonization by the Dutch. The Dutch, he sings, found that Taiwan was "really uncivilized." Then the Ming Dynasty's turn towards isolationism, he continues, left Taiwan "an orphan, and nobody cared about [it]." The choir then asks four times: "What kind of people are we?"[164]

It then continues describing the identity dilemma: The Qing Dynasty "attacked Taiwan," and this formulation gives rise to the idea, as expressed in the song, that it might have "come from outside the pass" (*cong guanwai lai*). This taps into the rhetoric about *"wailai zhengquan,"* which I have outlined above. The same, the song continues, applied to the next foreign force that governed the

---

of Inagaki Tōbei in the musical: Yin Zhengyang, Hong Ruixiang, and Yinyue shidai juchang, *"Weishui chunfeng" linchuang jiangyi pian, Taiwan wenhua xiehui pian 9 fenzhong changban jingcai pianduan* (*The Impossible Times*, "Bedside Examination," "The Taiwanese Cultural Association," 9 Minutes of Choice Clips of the Long Version), *Weishui chunfeng* (The Impossible Times) (Taibei, 2010), Taibei, https://www.artsticket.com.tw/CKSCC2005/Product/Product00/ProductsDetailsPage.aspx?ProductId=hsobWfDDQ3RZoTusjZfyR. Yang Zhongheng's statement: Yang, "'Weishui chunfeng.'"

161 Sullivan and Sapir, "Ma Ying-Jeou's Presidential Discourse," 39.
162 Zhang, "Yi ge Jiang Weishui, gezi-biaoshu," 42.
163 Zhang Fangyuan claimed that this was the musical's signature song, Ibid.
164 Yin Zhengyang et al., *Taiwan, shi women de ming* ("Taiwan" Is Our Name), CD, *Weishui chunfeng* (The Impossible Times), Taiwan yinyueju san bu qu (Three Taiwanese Musicals) (Taibei: All Music Theatre, 2011), Taibei; Yin, Hong, and Yinyue shidai juchang, *"Weishui chunfeng" linchuang jiangyi pian* ...

island, namely the Japanese, who did not treat Taiwan well either. A new vision for Taiwan's status in the world is thus needed, declare thereupon the characters of Lin Xiantang and Jiang Weishui. In fact, the days in which Taiwan needs anyone to "care for" or "run" (*guan*) it are over. Instead, based on its new identity as "Taiwanese," the inhabitants of the island can now be truly independent: "'Taiwanese' is our name. Tomorrow waits for us to go and create a new future!"[165]

The message is stepped up after a brief interlude, during which Jiang Weishui and the assembled Association bravely declare to an intervening Japanese policeman that they would be happy to die a hero's death for their convictions. After chasing away the policeman, the whole Association, Taiwanese and Japanese members, choir and soloists alike, fall again into song, and now suggest that an awakening of Taiwan's national consciousness can bring about world peace.[166]

The song starts with the lyrics of the Hymn of the Taiwan Cultural Association, written by Jiang Weishui himself in 1921. The Hymn claims that the Taiwanese are "posed between the blood line of the Han race and the common people of Japan" (not part of either). As such they have not only received the "mission" from "Heaven" to reconcile Japan and China with each other and create peace in East Asia. They are also in a position to bring about world peace by uniting the "yellow and white" races.[167] The role that the emerging Taiwanese national consciousness plays in this is inserted through the artistic makeup of the song. While one part of the choir sings about bringing peace to the world (the lyrics of the Hymn), the other part repeats the chorus of the earlier song: "'Taiwanese' is our name."[168] Advertisements for the musical consequently drew out the "awakening [of] Taiwanese national and cultural awareness" in Jiang Weishui's life.[169] Critics, too, commented on this. Zhang Fangyuan (no dates), writing for the Blue *Cross-Strait Review*, conceded that the musical incited Taiwanese patriotism. But he regretted that there was no mention of Jiang Weishui's statement that the Taiwanese are of the "Chinese nationality."[170]

---

165 Yin et al., *Taiwan, shi women de ming*; Yin, Hong, and Yinyue shidai juchang, *"Weishui chunfeng" linchuang jiangyi pian* ... Zhang Fangyuan claimed that this was the musical's signature song, Zhang, "Yi ge Jiang Weishui, gezi-biaoshu," 42.
166 Yin, Hong, and Yinyue shidai juchang, *"Weishui chunfeng" linchuang jiangyi pian* ...
167 Jiang, *Jiang Weishui quanji zengdingban*, xia:736–37.
168 Yin Zhengyang et al., *Tian jiang da shiming: Taiwan wenhua xiehui huige* (A Great Mission Handed down from Heaven: The Hymn of the Taiwan Cultural Association), CD, *Weishui chunfeng* (The Impossible Times), Taiwan yinyueju san bu qu (Three Taiwanese Musicals) (Taibei: All Music Theatre, 2011), Taibei.
169 "Yinyue shidai juchang 'Weishui chunfeng' 2016 yongheng zhuiyiban" (All Music Theater's *The Impossible Times*, 2016, Eternal Commemoration Version), *Yourart*, accessed March 7, 2016, https://www.yourart.asia/news/show/47303.
170 Zhang, "Yi ge Jiang Weishui, gezi-biaoshu," 42.

A political dimension was unavoidably provided when the musical was commissioned by the Department for Cultural Affairs of the Taibei City Government. But in spite of the creator Yang Zhongheng's declared intentions to keep the musical out of party politics, the themes negotiated in the musical, in the advertisements and in the reviews around it show that the Taiwanese New Culture Movement can hardly be detached from its function as a buzzword for contemporary Taiwanese politics.

Conclusion

The New Culture Movement has had a very multifarious journey through the 20th and 21st centuries. In the process it was repeatedly written out of and back into history. But throughout the past hundred years, the New Culture Movement and May Fourth were used at important moments in history as buzzwords by individuals to boost their own fame, or by groups in a competition to promote their agendas. Very often these individuals were hostile to each other – for example, Hu Shi and Mao Zedong – and the agendas were mutually contradictory – such as the DPP and GMD interpretations of Jiang Weishui. Nevertheless, they all deployed the same buzzword.

In this way, the picture of the New Culture Movement that has arrived in our time is different from what it was in 1919, but it is, if anything, even more complex than at the time of its birth. The varying stories told about the New Culture Movement narrate mainland China's and Taiwan's political and social changes of the past hundred years. But beyond being merely an "indicator" of such change,[171] this usage of the New Culture Movement as a buzzword has also had an active quality: It has contributed to anchoring the New Culture Movement into the canons about 20th-century China and Taiwan.

The stories by Hu Shi and Mao Zedong were self-aggrandizing. But they also had the function of framing the making of Chinese culture within a teleological narrative. Mao Zedong placed the New Culture Movement and May Fourth into a linear, unavoidable and orderly narrative of historical materialism. Hu Shi took away the possibility of Chinese culture taking a different path, when he claimed that there was never any real opposition to the *baihua* project, and when he put the "Chinese renaissance" into a long line of renaissances, suggesting a global historical pattern. This was not only the European renaissance but also other Chinese renaissances, which he traced all the way back to the Tang Dynasty.[172]

---

171 Richter, "Begriffsgeschichte and the History of Ideas," 253.
172 On *baihua*: Hu, *The Chinese Renaissance*, 2010, 54. On the renaissances: Ibid., 44–46.

In a way, neat narratives are also created from the messiness of history, when mainland dissidents and contemporary Taiwanese politicians trace their agendas back to events that happened seventy or a hundred years ago, respectively. This establishes a linear line of development, not of the change in 1919, but towards events today.

How does this assertion of teleology fit with the usages of the New Culture Movement as a buzzword, especially by people like Mao and Hu, who claim a leadership role in the Movement? This question arises, since the epoch-making role of individuals suggests that the epoch could also have turned out differently. The answer is that it does not fit, and this contradiction is common for people who consider themselves leaders in big events. Richard Ned Lebow writes that many politicians and diplomats who were involved in the events that led to the end of the Cold War (which was not widely predicted) often displayed contradictory opinions in their interviews with Lebow and his collaborator Richard Herrman. One and the same person, for example, could say that the Cold War unavoidably had to end because of long-term developments and also that their own individual actions, connections and achievements were crucial in effecting these same developments. The latter claim of course denies the former.[173] These inherent contradictions in such accounts are also reflected in the old debate about "structure" versus "agency." If the individual action, as some claim, is shaped by long-term "social structures," how can individual action make a difference, and how can "structures" ever change?[174]

It is not the goal of this book to resolve this more than a century-old conundrum. What I am trying to say is that retrospective accounts of the New Culture Movement contain this conundrum. They have left us with a picture of China's cultural change through the New Culture Movement as a neat development, nevertheless propelled by visionary leaders, when it was, in fact, the "path-dependent,"[175] but by no means unavoidable, result of a competition between cultural agendas.

---

[173] Lebow, "Learning from Contingency," 450–51.
[174] Alex Callinicos, *Making History: Agency, Structure, and Change in Social Theory*, 2nd rev. ed (Leiden: Brill, 2004), vliii.
[175] North, *Institutions, Institutional Change and Economic Performance*, 99.

Conclusion

1919 was a year that changed China. It set its culture on a course, whose aftereffects still have an impact on mainland China and Taiwan until the present. More than that, it radically transformed China to the extent that contemporaries were left flabbergasted at the direction culture was taking. This astonishment indicates that this change happened fast, over the course of only a few months, the precise mechanisms of which I have traced in this book. It also indicates that this change could have worked out differently, with Chinese culture ending up on a different path.

I have argued that the cultural transformation of 1919 did not happen because any significantly new ideas or other elements were introduced or any unforeseeable events transpired. It occurred because "symbolic capital"[1] (prestige, and here also persuasiveness) were redistributed within a pool of competing agendas, which had existed for a while. This redistribution happened through the introduction of a particularly "hegemonic"[2] buzzword in the summer of 1919. This buzzword was the New Culture Movement. It came with a matrix of associations, in reference to which agendas now needed to be marketed. Programs now had to be identified with Hu Shi, Chen Duxiu, *baihua*, May Fourth and so forth.

This redistributed symbolic capital because this strategy worked better for some agendas (for example, the National Language) than for others (Literary Chinese, Christianity). To speak in the terms of Jeffrey N. Wasserstrom's model as elaborated on by Timothy Cheek, some agendas were better able to be "identif[ied]" with the "legitimating" associations surrounding the buzzword New Culture Movement than others, and therefore these agendas managed to move towards the "legitimate core" of the field, while the others ended up in the non-legitimate "periphery."[3]

This, I hope, makes two broader points about the cultural change of 1919. One is about how it worked; the other one is about its direction. On the first count, I argue that the transformation of 1919 was driven by marketing. This marketing happened within what Pierre Bourdieu frames as the "field"[4] – here the field of culture – as a space of competition for "capital" (cultural, symbolic, economic).[5] This model of cultural change through marketing shows the significance of observations in the study of Republican China of the past couple of decades, which

---

1 Thompson, "Editor's Introduction," 14.
2 Cheek, "The Names of Rectification," 6.
3 In modification of Ibid., 26. Originally "legitimating core."
4 Bourdieu, *Language and Symbolic Power*, 61.
5 Thompson, "Editor's Introduction," 14.

have emphasized the pragmatic orientation of intellectuals and have deemphasized intellectuals' idealist propensities – which had been the focus of much of the previous scholarship. Intellectuals' pragmatic orientation was more than merely another one of their features. It was a crucial force in determining hegemony within the field of culture.

My framing of cultural change also says something about why some ideas become more important than others: Ideas become influential, not necessarily because of their merit – because they are particularly "good" (however this would be defined) or fitting to the *Zeitgeist*. They become influential for much more cynical reasons, such as whether they can be communicated well with respect to certain rhetorical reference points. This, at least, is what happened in 1919.

The second major point I have hoped to make is about the direction of change. Retrospective narratives about any kind of change have a way of attributing teleology and linearity to change. Speaking about the social sciences, but in a way that is applicable more generally, Charles Kurzman says that "[t]hey take unexpected events and try to make them less unexpected after the fact."[6] My discussion of 1919 has reconfirmed that this is indeed sometimes a "retroactive prediction,"[7] or rather, a retroactive claim of linearity.

It has also explained why contemporaries tend to be confused about the change that happens. Scholars working on contingency in history often depart from observations similar to those put forward in this book: Contemporaries have a tendency to predict future developments wrongly or not at all. In the words of Richard Ned Lebow, such developments include "the sociopolitical revolution of the 1960s, the end of the Cold War, and the rise and political influence of fundamentalist religious groups."[8] In the case of the story about 1919 in China, the *Shanghai News* offered such a wrong prediction in April 1919, when it implied that Chinese culture would be shaped by those it classified as the "Old Faction."[9]

Scholars of contingency in history frequently offer the occurrence of unforeseeable events as an explanation for unpredictability. However, this is not what happened in 1919. As outlined in this book, nothing unforeseeable happened in that year. Western powers treated China badly and this led to protests. Warlord politicians were unpopular. Academics debated and were classified into "academic factions." Newspapers spread rumors and conspiracy theories. And

---

[6] Charles Kurzman, *The Unthinkable Revolution in Iran* (Cambridge, Massachusetts: Harvard University Press, 2004), 4.
[7] Ibid.
[8] Richard Ned Lebow, *Forbidden Fruit: Counterfactuals and International Relations* (Princeton: Princeton University Press, 2010), 12.
[9] Xin, "Riben dui wo xin sixiang shishi zhi tongqing," 6.

so forth. Both contemporaries' surprise and, even more crucially, in my view, the shift that Chinese culture experienced, were down to the combination of these structures. They were caused by what Sahlins calls the "structure of the conjuncture":[10] Change is created through the "intersection" of long-term structures, and since nobody can predict how they will combine, this change is often of the unforeseen variety.[11]

When I emphasize that this change is unforeseen, however, I do not merely want to make a statement about contingency and unpredictability. Instead, it shows how radical this transformation was, and, more importantly, that Chinese culture could easily have become something different. In spite of what the retrospective narratives claimed afterwards (see Hu Shi, "What surprised me most was the weakness and utter poverty of the opposition [towards *baihua* from its very beginning]"[12]), that Chinese culture turned out the way it did was not teleological. It was not linear. It had not been in the making for a long time. It happened, because a lot of structures and trends, which had indeed been around for a while, merged in uncontrolled ways in 1919, and in this way produced a transformation.

Roads not taken

To clarify this, I want to outline some of the roads Chinese culture could have taken, but which it did not.

Academic debates. In early 1919, the public could have continued to not care about the abstract debates at Beijing University. Debating and reforming language was a scholarly pursuit that had a centuries-old tradition in China. But this did not automatically mean that one of the suggestions put forward in the debates would be adopted by broader reaches of society. First of all, language was negotiated elsewhere too, such as by the state-sponsored National Language committees. Other ideas proposed in *New Youth* and *New Tide* were endorsed elsewhere as well, such as women's rights and popular education. Secondly, the debates at Beijing University had all the makings of ivory-tower sophistry soon to be forgotten. They were mostly conducted by students, and, as Fabio Lanza shows, students were in early 1919 not the central "political category" which they were after May Fourth.[13]

---

10 Sahlins, "Introduction," 192.
11 Erickson and Murphy, *Readings for a History of Anthropological Theory*, 626.
12 Hu, *The Chinese Renaissance*, 2010, 55.
13 Lanza, *Behind the Gate*, 16.

The debates were also extremely abstract and nuanced, and the opposing sides had hardly what could be called a concise agenda. Instead, they were each supporting a spectrum of ideas, from *baihua* to Esperanto, from newspaper-style Literary Chinese to archaic Literary Chinese. If Beijing University's debates had been forgotten, the New Culture Movement would not have emerged in this form and another set of reformist agendas might have been successful.

Factions. The classification of the debaters into "academic factions" by newspapers in the spring of 1919 could have continued to mean that the debates at Beijing University were anything but revolutionary. It was another long-term habit in China to classify debating academics into factions. So it is not surprising that newspapers did this, once Lin Shu had brought the debates to their attention. This newspaper decision intervenes in a longstanding academic debate about "academic factions," at one end of which are scholars who say that factions were constructed and at the other end of which are those who assume that they were quite real.[14] Contemporary opinion reflected these two poles, with some, like Liu Shipei, denying the existence of factions and others, like Huang Kan and Chen Duxiu, affirming it.

Constructed or not, the newspaper coverage made the "factions" *look* like real entities. In this way they became an unescapable category in the way newspaper readers viewed the debates. Still, the "factions" initially did not look like the game-changing categories which they would later turn out to be, when they formed the basis for associating May Fourth with the circle around Hu Shi and Chen Duxiu. When they first patterned the debates at Beijing University, they mostly implied that the discussions were nothing revolutionary and unprecedented. They were just one more instance in a long line of academic debates during which, the *Shanghai News* said somewhat apathetically, it could not do any harm if "scholars twisted their brains."[15] Again, Beijing University's debates were set to be forgotten.

Politics and academia. The widely assumed connection between politics and academia could have favored a different group or at least not had an impact on the "New Faction." This connection between politics and academia was doubtlessly another long-term structure.[16] Its history was firmly rooted in the civil service examination system of imperial times, and the belief that culture affected politics went all the way back to the Confucian Classics, among them the *Great*

---

14 Examples for sceptics: Elman, *Classicism, Politics, and Kinship*, 4; Hill, *Lin Shu, Inc.*, 156–57. Example for scholars assuming the reality of "academic factions": Li, "Liu Shipei yu Beijing daxue."
15 Jing, "Beijng daxue xin jiu zhi anchao," 6.
16 Lebow, *Forbidden Fruit*, 11.

Learning. The relationship between academia and politics was also a matter of heated debate in the 1910s, when scholars had to redefine their place in society after the end of the examination system in 1905. But the results of this assumption could have had very different effects.

First of all, since all reformist groups claimed to be intent on saving the nation, May Fourth could have been associated with any of them. Secondly, the rumors that politically polarized the "factions" at Beijing University could have been *not* spread. The fact that they appeared in many newspapers seems to suggest that they were created in many places at once, and that consequently there was some truth to them or even a necessity for them to arise. But they were printed in so many places, because newspapers printed the same articles by sharing journalists or copying from each other. Especially the rumors in the context of Cai Yuanpei's resignation appear to have been derived from very few sources. This set of rumors around Cai's resignation was crucial in connecting the "New Faction" and May Fourth, because it claimed that the government was holding the "New Faction" responsible for the protests and was threatening to burn down Beijing University. It could easily have happened that the few sources that started this rumor had not done so. Then May Fourth and the Hu Shi-Chen Duxiu circle would have remained unconnected.

Buzzwords. The expression "New Culture Movement" could have been not invented or it could have had a different matrix of reference points. That intellectuals were pragmatic and drew upon buzzwords to market their agendas was systemic, too. In the study of Chinese history, this pragmatism is a relatively recent discovery. In earlier decades, Republican scholars were seen as idealists. But books like Michael Gibbs Hill's *Lin Shu Inc.* have anchored intellectuals' pragmatism in our understanding of that social group.[17] This is not an observation peculiar to China historians, but is made on academia in the West too.[18] This book hopes to have enriched this trend by showing how endemic the deployment of buzzwords was, and how important an impact it could have on the creation of cultural change.

But just because it was common that intellectuals liked marketing does not mean that the expression "New Culture Movement" had to be invented. Just because it was clear that it had been invented, did not mean that it had to have this specific effect. Some Christians and some advocates of Literary Chinese did not think it would, when they used it for their purposes. The later history of the New Culture Movement confirms that the expression could have been used for

---

17 Hill, *Lin Shu, Inc.*
18 An example is Alex Csiszar, "Peer Review: Troubled from the Start," *Nature* 532 (April 21, 2016): 306–8.

many different agendas. Contemporaries in the 1920s would have certainly been surprised to see it used to argue both for and against a Taiwanese rapprochement with mainland China. It is virtually in the nature of buzzwords to be capable of embracing a broad range of meaning and have a correspondingly large array of potential effects. Even after the invention of the buzzword New Culture Movement, China's cultural future was not set in stone.

Possible roads

Even though cultural change could have taken different roads, it could not have just taken any road. For example, it could not have become an Islamic caliphate or a Neolithic society. The reason is that the options were constricted by the existing pool of agendas, available conceptualizations ("factions," and so forth) and international forces. To borrow Douglass C. North's words, cultural change was not "foreordained." However, it was "path-dependent."[19]

These "paths" were fed from both historical Chinese and international trends. I have already touched upon the available Chinese factors in the section above. In terms of international trends, there was the set of ideas which spread throughout the world piggyback on European imperialism. It had been reinvented in other parts of the world too, in similar but not the same ways as in China. In Japan, for example, it had been transformed into the culture of the Meiji period, which experienced political reform, the translation of Western works, calls for a "Japanese Enlightenment" expressed in journals, a belief in Social Darwinism and calls for women's rights.[20] The Meiji Restoration itself was again an influence on China.

In the Middle East, it became the Arab Nahda. Translated as "Arab enlightenment" or "Arab renaissance," this was a move towards Western-style modernization, centered around Syria, the Lebanon and Egypt in the late 19th and early 20th centuries. It included the translation of Western works, a reform of the written Arabic language, a fondness for science and Social Darwinism, the reinvention of the Arab scholar as an "activist thinker," demands for more rights for women and a reevaluation of Islam.[21] With imperialism, of course, also came the infrastructure:

---

[19] North, *Institutions, Institutional Change and Economic Performance*, 98–99.
[20] Christopher S. Goto-Jones, *Modern Japan: A Very Short Introduction*, Very Short Introductions (Oxford: Oxford University Press, 2009), 43–52.
[21] Yoav Di-Capua, "Nahda: The Arab Project of Enlightenment," in *The Cambridge Companion to Modern Arab Culture*, ed. Dwight F. Reynolds (Cambridge: Cambridge University Press, 2015), 59–67.

newspapers and the publishing industry, for example, both of which were important for the Nahda and the Meiji Restoration, and for the invention of the New Culture Movement too.[22]

Another such global factor was what Eres Manela calls the "Wilsonian moment." By this he means calls of dependent nations for independence from imperialism in the wake of World War I. The name derives from Manela's observation that these nations often made their case with reference to Woodrow Wilson's Fourteen Points. This Wilsonian moment spread across places like Ireland, Catalonia, Egypt, India, Korea and of course China.[23] Yet another factor was the spread of communism, crucially aided by the Russian October Revolution of 1917 and the efforts of the Comintern.[24]

These structures also limited the possible effects the buzzword New Culture Movement could have. Taiwanese independence from Japanese colonial rule, for example, could not be achieved by invoking the New Culture Movement. At the time, Japanese imperialism was still on the rise, and the country had no intention whatsoever to give up the island. Where these structures stood against the New Culture Movement, in other words, the buzzword could have no effect. Nor do I mean to say that after 1919 the course of Chinese culture was fixed. It was of course shaped by many different events that occurred afterwards, and the way they intersected with the path set out by the New Culture Movement will be for others to explore. Among these events was World War II, the Chinese Civil War, the Korean War, the Cultural Revolution, the opening reforms of the 1980s, the simultaneous democratization of Taiwan, the crackdown on the 1989 protests on Tian'anmen Square and so forth. But the New Culture Movement was a crucial turning point which shaped the setting for these future developments. It does not need much arguing for, for example, that most of the above events would have turned out differently or not happened at all without the popularization of communism in China.

This pool of structures available in 1919 also shows why my argument that the New Culture Movement did not invent something new, but decided between competing agendas, does not mean to repeat the story that China is "stagnant" and incapable of change. This story had been told in Europe since the Enlightenment and was reframed in Social Darwinist vocabulary in the 19th and early

---

22 Goto-Jones, *Modern Japan*, 49; Ilham Khuri-Makdisi, *The Eastern Mediterranean and the Making of Global Radicalism, 1860–1914* (Berkeley: University of California Press, 2010), 35–37.
23 On Ireland and Catalonia, see Manela, *The Wilsonian Moment*, 59. On Egypt, India, Korea and China, see Ibid., 56–135.
24 On the role of the October Revolution, see Meisner, *Li Ta-Chao and the Origins of Chinese Marxism*, 60–70. On the role of the Comintern, see Ibid., 114–21.

20th centuries.²⁵ In recent decades, it has been phased out with good reason. The agendas between which the New Culture Movement decided were all specific to the early 20th century. All of them had only been developed in the preceding few years or, at most, decades. The shift in culture created by the New Culture Movement was therefore time-dependent. It could not have happened in this way at another point in time.

1919 changed China, because a newly introduced buzzword – the New Culture Movement – reweighted persuasiveness within a pool of competing agendas. After a variety of long-term habits and foreseeable events had been combined, through the involvement of many but the orchestration of no one, into a new matrix of marketing reference points, Chinese culture was fundamentally transformed. This was a lively and at times ironic process involving academic infighting, rumors and conspiracy theories, newspaper stories and intellectuals (hell-)bent on selling agendas through a powerful buzzword.

---

25 Cohen, *Discovering History in China*, 59; Duara, *Rescuing History from the Nation*, 22.

Glossary of Terms

Pinyin	Characters	Translation
baihua	白話	Plain Language
Beijing daxue rikan	北京大學日刊	Beijing University Daily
Chenbao	晨報	Morning Post
Dagongbao	大公報	Impartial
Dongfang zazhi	東方雜誌	Eastern Miscellany
Funü zazhi	婦女雜誌	Ladies' Magazine
Gongyanbao	公言報	Public Voice
Guogu	國故	National Heritage
Guomin gongbao	國民公報	Citizen News
guoyu	國語	National Language
guwen	古文	ancient-style prose (Translation following Michael Gibbs Hill, *Lin Shu, Inc. : Translation and the Making of Modern Chinese Culture* [Oxford: Oxford University Press, 2013], 4.)
Jiangsu sheng jiaoyuhui	江蘇省教育會	Jiangsu Educational Association
jianrong bingbao	兼容並包	"broad-minded and encompassing tolerance of diverse points of view" (Translation following Vera Schwarcz, *The Chinese Enlightenment: Intellectuals and the Legacy of the May Fourth Movement of 1919* [Berkeley: University of California Press, 1986], 52.)
jiupai	舊派	Old Faction
jiuguo	救國	saving the nation
Meizhou pinglun	每週評論	Weekly Critic
Minguo ribao	民國日報	Republic Daily
Qingnian zazhi	青年雜誌	Youth Magazine
Renmin ribao	人民日報	People's Daily
Shangwu yinshuguan	商務印書館	Commercial Press
Shaonian Zhongguo	少年中國	Young China
Shenbao	申報	Shanghai News
Shengming	生命	Life
Shishi xinbao	時事新報	China Times
Taiwan minbao	臺灣民報	Taiwan People's News
Taiwan qingnian	臺灣青年	Taiwan Youth
Weishui chunfeng	渭水春風	*Weishui Spring Wind* (*The Impossible Times*)
wenyan	文言	Literary Chinese
xinpai	新派	New Faction
Xin qingnian	新青年	New Youth
xin wenhua yundong	新文化運動	New Culture Movement
Xinchao	新潮	New Tide
Xinghua	興華	Chinese Christian Advocate

Pinyin	Characters	Translation
Xinqgi pinglun	星期評論	*Weekly Review*
xuepai	學派	academic faction, faction of learning
Yadong tushuguan	亞東圖書館	East Asia Library
Yishibao	益世報	*Social Welfare Tiensin*
Zhengdaotuan	證道團	Apologetic Group
zhishi fenzi	知識分子	intellectuals

Bibliography

An?安. "Shandong wenti zhi Beijing xiaoxi" 山東問題之北京消息 (News from Beijing on the Shandong Question). *Shenbao* 申報 (Shanghai News), April 25, 1919, 6.
A Ying 阿英. "Aidao Li Kenong tongzhi" 哀悼李克農同志 (Mourning Comrade Li Kenong). *Renmin ribao* 人民日報 (People's Daily). February 14, 1962, 6. Beijing.
"Advertisement for *Construction*." *Shaonian zhongguo* 少年中國 (Young China) 1, no. 1 (November 20, 1919): 46.
"Advertisement for *Experiments*." *Shaonian zhongguo* 少年中國 (Young China) 1, no. 1 (November 20, 1919): 51.
"Advertisement for *Morning Post*." *Shaonian zhongguo* 少年中國 (Young China) 1, no. 1 (November 20, 1919): 49.
"Advertisement for *New Tide*." *Shenbao* 申報 (Shanghai News). October 23, 1919, 1. Shanghai.
"Advertisement for *New Tide*." *Shaonian zhongguo* 少年中國 (Young China) 1, no. 1 (November 20, 1919): 45.
"Advertisement for *New Tide*, vol. 1, no. 3." *Xinqun* 新群 (Social Reconstruction), no. 1 (November 1919).
"Advertisement for *New Youth*." *Shenbao* 申報 (Shanghai News). April 20, 1919, 1. Shanghai.
"Advertisement for *New Youth*." *Shenbao* 申報 (Shanghai News). August 3, 1919, 1. Shanghai.
"Advertisement for *New Youth*." *Shaonian zhongguo* 少年中國 (Young China) 1, no. 1 (November 20, 1919): 47.
"Advertisement for *Young World*." *Shaonian zhongguo* 少年中國 (Young China) 1, no. 1 (November 20, 1919): i.
"Advertisement for *Young World*." *Shaonian zhongguo* 少年中國 (Young China) 1, no. 6 (December 15, 1919): i.
"Advertisement for *Young World*." *Shaonian zhongguo* 少年中國 (Young China) 1, no. 7 (January 15, 1920): i.
Airlie, Shiona. *Scottish Mandarin: The Life and Times of Sir Reginald Johnston*. Hong Kong: Hong Kong University Press, 2012.
Anhui sheng jiaoyu ting bianshenshi 安徽省教育廳編審室, ed. *1961 nian gaozhong lishi fuxi tigang: Zhongguo shi bufen* 1961年高中歷史複習提綱：中國史部分 (Revising Senior High School History, 1961: Chinese History). Hefei: Anhui jiaoyu chubanshe, 1961.
"Annan duli yundong (xu di-san hao)" 安南獨立運動（續第三號） (Vietnam's Independence Movement (Continued from the Third Issue)). *Shishi huibao* 時事匯報 (Current Affairs), no. 6 (1914): 5–8.
"Anti-Foreign Spirit in China." *Times*. January 5, 1925, 9. The Times Digital Archive. London.
"Ao'guo yundong jiaru Zhongguo zhaizhu" 奧國運動加入中國債主 (Austria Lobbies to Join China's Creditors). *Xiehebao* 協和報 (Mutual Understanding) 2, no. 30 (1912): 25.
Aubié, Hermann. "Is Liu Xiaobo a Rooted Cosmopolitan? A Critical Examination of His Dissent from a Historical Perspective." In *Cosmopolitanism and the Legacies of Dissent*, edited by Tamara Caraus, 67–86. New York: Routledge, 2015.
Bai Ji 白吉庵. *Hu Shi zhuan* 胡適傳 (A Biography of Hu Shi). Changsha: Hunan jiaoyu chubanshe, 1987.
Bailey, Paul John. *Reform the People: Changing Attitudes towards Popular Education in Early Twentieth-Century China*. Edinburgh: Edinburgh University Press, 1990.
"Banner." *Piping* 批評 (Criticism). October 20, 1920, 1 edition, 1. Beijing; Shanghai.

Bao Yi 抱一. "Wo duiyu baihua wenti de yijian" 我對於白話文體的意見 (My Opinion on the Plain-Language Style of Writing). *Dagongbao* 大公報 (Impartial). July 12, 1919, 2. Changsha.

Barkun, Michael. *A Culture of Conspiracy: Apocalyptic Visions in Contemporary America*. Berkeley: University of California Press, 2003.

Barlow, Tani E. *Formations of Colonial Modernity in East Asia*. Durham: Duke University Press, 1997.

Barlow, Tani E. "Zhishifenzi [Chinese Intellectuals] and Power." *Dialectical Anthropology* 16, no. 3–4 (1991): 209–32.

Barmé, Geremie. *In the Red: On Contemporary Chinese Culture*. New York: Columbia University Press, 1999.

Bastid, Marianne, and Jian Zhang. *Educational Reform in Early Twentieth-Century China*. Translated by Paul John Bailey. Ann Arbor: Center for Chinese Studies, University of Michigan, 1988.

"Beijing daxue yaoyan zhi wugen" 北京大學謠言之無根 (The Untenable Nature of the Rumors about Beijing University). *Chenbao* 晨報 (Morning Post). March 10, 1919, 2. Beijing.

"Beijing daxue you qi jueda bolan: Cai xiaozhang cizhi chu Jing" 北京大學又起絕大波瀾：蔡校長辭職出京 (Another Big Wave Rises at Beijing University: Chancellor Cai Quits and Leaves Beijing). *Shenbao* 申報 (Shanghai News). May 12, 1919, 6. Shanghai.

"Beijing daxue zhi yaoyan" 北京大學之謠言 (The Rumors about Beijing University). *Guomin gongbao* 國民公報 (Citizen News). March 31, 1919, 2. Chengdu.

"Beijing nüxuesheng zhi waijiao yundong" 北京女學生之外交運動 (The Diplomatic Movement of Beijing's Female Students). *Funü zazhi* 婦女雜誌 (Ladies' Magazine), no. 7 (January 1, 1921): 11.

"Beijing xuejie da fengchao xuzhi" 北京學界大風潮續誌 (Record of the Great Student Protests in Beijing, Continued). *Gongyanbao* 公言報 (Public Voice). May 6, 1919, 907 edition, 2. Beijing.

"Ben bao de guanggao, faxing ji qita" 本報的廣告、發行及其他 (This Newspaper's Advertisement, Distribution and so on). *Shenbao* 申報 (Shanghai News). September 20, 1947, 22–23. Shanghai.

"Ben guan logo jieshao" 本館logo介紹 (Introduction of Our Hall's Logo). *Taiwan xin wenhua yundong jinianguan* 台灣新文化運動紀念館 (Taiwan New Cultural Movement Memorial Hall), June 24, 2011. http://tncmmh.gov.taipei/ct.asp?xItem=2032904&CtNode=38915&mp=11900B.

"Ben she jishi lu" 本社記事錄 (Records of This Society). *Guogu* 國故 (National Heritage), no. 1 (1919).

"Ben she qishi san" 本社啟事三 (Third Announcement of This Society). *Piping* 批評 (Criticism). October 20, 1920, 4. Beijing.

"Ben she qishi yi" 本社啓事一 (First Announcement of This Society). *Xin xuesheng* 新學生 (New Student) 1, no. 1 (December 1919).

"Ben yuekan jinyao qishi" 本月刊緊要啟事 (Important Notices from This Journal). *Shaonian zhongguo* 少年中國 (Young China) 1, no. 1 (November 20, 1919): 52.

"Ben zazhi bianji renyuan" 本雜誌編輯人員 (Editors of This Magazine). *Xinqun* 新群 (Social Reconstruction), no. 1 (November 1919).

Bender, Thomas. "The Cultures of Intellectual Life: The City and the Professions." In *Intellect and Public Life: Essays on the Social History of Academic Intellectuals in the United States*, 3–15. Baltimore: John Hopkins University Press, 1993.

Bergère, Marie-Claire. *Sun Yat-Sen*. Translated by Janet Lloyd. Stanford, California: Stanford University Press, 1998.

Bergère, Marie-Claire. *The Golden Age of the Chinese Bourgeoisie, 1911–1937*. Cambridge: Cambridge University Press, 1989.

Bernard, Henri. "Review of *The Chinese Renaissance* by Hu Shih." *Monumenta Serica* 1, no. 1 (1935): 214–15.

Bickers, Robert A. *Britain in China: Community, Culture and Colonialism 1900–1949*. Manchester: Manchester University Press, 1999.

Boorman, Howard L. "Fu Ssu-Nien." *Biographical Dictionary of Republican China*. New York: Columbia University Press, 1968. New York.

Boorman, Howard L. "Liu T'ing-Fang." *Biographical Dictionary of Republican China*. New York: Columbia University Press, 1968. New York.

Boorman, Howard L. "Lo Chia-Lun." *Biographical Dictionary of Republican China*. New York: Columbia University Press, 1968. New York.

Bourdieu, Pierre. *Language and Symbolic Power*. Edited by John B. Thompson. Translated by Gino Raymond and Matthew Adamson. Cambridge: Polity, 1991.

Bowles, David. "Finding the Way: The Nationalist Party Appropriation of Confucius and the Challenges of Revolutionary Traditionalism in China, 1919–1934." PhD. University of Oxford, 2013. University of Oxford.

"Boxer Indemnity." *Times*. May 3, 1926, 13. The Times Digital Archive. London.

"Boxer Indemnity Committee." *Times*. February 12, 1926, 11. The Times Digital Archive. London.

"Brief Reviews." *New York Times*. September 9, 1923, 25. New York Times (1923-Current File). New York.

Cai Dun 蔡惇. "Zhu Jingnong xiansheng yanjiang jilu" 朱經農先生演講紀錄 (A Record of Mr. Zhu Jingnong's Lecture). *Jiangsu shengli di-er nüzi shifan xuexiao xiaoyouhui huikan* 江蘇省立第二女子師範學校校友會彙刊 (Alumnae of the Second Women's Normal School of Jiangsu Province), no. 16 (November 1923): 6–13.

"Cai xiaozhang li Jing yu xuejie" 蔡校長離京與學界 (Chancellor Cai Leaves Beijing and Academia). *Shishi xinbao* 時事新報 (China Times). May 13, 1919, 1.2. Shanghai.

Cai Yuanpei 蔡元培. *Cai Yuanpei riji* 蔡元培日記 (Cai Yuanpei's Diary). Edited by Wang Shiru 王世儒. Vol. 1. Beijing: Beijing daxue chubanshe, 2010.

Cai Yuanpei 蔡元培. "Da Lin Qinnan shu" 答林琴南書 (Reply to Lin Qinnan). In *Wu si yundong zai Shanghai shiliao xuanji* 五四運動在上海史料選輯 (The May Fourth Movement in Shanghai: Selected Historical Materials), edited by Shanghai shehui xueyuan lishi yanjiusuo 上海社會學院歷史研究所, 95–100. Shanghai: Shanghai renmin chubanshe, 1980.

Cai Yuanpei 蔡元培. "Fu Zhang Liaozi han" 復張镠子函 (Reply to Zhang Liaozi). In *Cai Yuanpei xiansheng quanji* 蔡元培先生全集 (Collected Works of Mr. Cai Yuanpei), edited by Sun Changwei 孫常煒, 1093. Taibei: Taiwan shangwu yinshu guan, 1968.

Cai Yuanpei 蔡元培. "Qunian wu yue si ri yilai de huigu yu jinhou de xiwang" 去年五月四日以來的回顧與今後的希望 (A Review of [Events] since 4 May of Last Year and Hopes for the Future). In *Minguo shiqi mingren tan wu si: lishi jiyi yu lishi jieshi* 民國時期名人談五四：歷史記憶與歷史解釋（1919–1949）(Famous People of the Republican Period Talk about May Fourth: Historical Reminiscences and Historical Explanations), edited by Yang Hu 楊琥, 90–91. Fuzhou: Fujian jiaoyu chubanshe, 2011.

"Cai Yuanpei ciqu xiaozhang zhi zhenyin" 蔡元培辭去校長之真因 (The True Reasons for Cai Yuanpei's Resignation as Chancellor). *Chenbao* 晨報 (Morning Post). May 13, 1919, 2. Beijing.

"Cai Yuanpei cizhi zhi zhenyin" 蔡元培辭職之真因 (The True Reasons for Cai Yuanpei's Resignation). *Shishi xinbao* 時事新報 (China Times). May 15, 1919, 2.1. Shanghai.
"Cai Yuanpei qishi" 蔡元培啓事 (Cai Yuanpei's Note). *Guomin gongbao* 國民公報 (Citizen News). May 11, 1919, 1. Beijing.
"Cai Yuanpei zhi lai dian yu xuejie fengchao" 蔡元培之來電與學界風潮 (Telegram from Cai Yuanpei and the Student Protests). *Gongyanbao* 公言報 (Public Voice). May 21, 1919, 6. Beijing.
Cai Zhiguang 柴志光, and Xie Zewei 謝澤為. *Pudong mingren shujian baitong* 浦東名人書簡百通 (Collection of Letters by Famous People of Pudong). Shanghai: Shanghai yuandong chubanshe, 2010.
"Cai Zimin jue ci Beijing Daxue xiaozhang zhi zhenyin" 蔡子民決辭北京大學校長之真因 (The True Reasons for Cai Zimin's Decision to Resign as Chancellor of Beijing University). *Guomin gongbao* 國民公報 (Citizen News). May 13, 1919, 3. Beijing.
"Cai Zimin xiansheng yu qi furen jiehun yi nian jinian sheying" 蔡子民先生與其夫人結婚一年紀念攝影 (Photo Shooting on Occasion of the First Anniversary of the Wedding of Mr. Cai Zimin and His Wife). *Funü zazhi* 婦女雜誌 (Ladies' Magazine), no. 10 (October 1, 1924): 13.
"Cai Zimin zai Hang zhi tanhua" 蔡子民在杭之譚話 (Talks with Cai Zimin in Hangzhou). *Gongyanbao* 公言報 (Public Voice). June 17, 1919, 6. Beijing.
"Cai Zimin zhen huan shenjingbing ye" 蔡子民真患神經病耶 (Does Cai Zimin Really Suffer from Neurosis?). *Gongyanbao* 公言報 (Public Voice). June 26, 1919, 3. Beijing.
Callinicos, Alex. *Making History: Agency, Structure, and Change in Social Theory*. 2nd rev. ed. Leiden: Brill, 2004.
"Can China Find Its Gorbachev?" *Guardian*. April 24, 1989, 18. The Guardian (1959–2003). London.
Canmou benbu 參謀本部, and Lujunbu 陸軍部. "Beijing guowuyuan can, lubu ge dian" 北京國務院參、陸部歌電 (Telegram of the 5th [of September 1919] from the General Staff and the Army Ministry of the State Council in Beijing). In *Yan Xishan dang'an* 閻錫山檔案 (Yan Xishan Papers), edited by Qingfen Lin 林清芬, 5:84. Taibei: Guoshiguan, 2003.
Cao Boyan 曹伯言, and Ji Weilong 季維龍. *Hu Shi nianpu* 胡適年譜 (A Chronology of Hu Shi's Life). Anhui: Anhui jiaoyu chubanshe, 1989.
Carter, James Hugh. *Creating a Chinese Harbin: Nationalism in an International City, 1916–1932*. Ithaca, N.Y.: Cornell University Press, 2002.
Cha An 詧盦. *Xuejie fengchao ji* 學界風潮紀 (Chronicle of the Student Protests). Shanghai: Zhonghua shuju, 1919.
"'Chahua nü' xiaoshuo zhi xin dianying" "茶花女"小說之新電影 (The New Film about the Novel "The Lady of the Camellias"). *Shenbao* 申報 (Shanghai News). October 26, 1923, 18. Shanghai.
"Chajin 'fanghai zhi'an' de jihui, chuban zhi jingguo" 查禁《妨害治安》的集會、出版之經過 (The Process of Prohibiting Meetings and Publications That "harm the Public Order"). *Meizhou pinglun* 每週評論 (Weekly Critic). July 27, 1919, 1–2. Beijing.
Chang, Tuh Wei. "Letter to Emma Lester," December 15, 1931. Container 214. Lewis Nathaniel Chase Papers, Manuscript Division, Library of Congress, Washington, D.C.
"Chaoxian duli yundong" 朝鮮之獨立運動 (The Korean Independence Movement). *Shenbao* 申報 (Shanghai News). March 12, 1919, 6–7. Shanghai.
Chase, Lewis Nathaniel. "Letter to E.A. Chase," January 5, 1923. Container 171. Lewis Nathaniel Chase Papers, Manuscript Division, Library of Congress, Washington, D.C.

Chase, Lewis Nathaniel. "Letter to E.A. Chase," June 17, 1923. Container 171. Lewis Nathaniel Chase Papers, Manuscript Division, Library of Congress, Washington, D.C.
Chase, Lewis Nathaniel. "Letter to E.H. Cressy," March 26, 1925. Container 222. Lewis Nathaniel Chase Papers, Manuscript Division, Library of Congress, Washington, D.C.
Chase, Lewis Nathaniel. "Letter to Family," October 16, 1921. Container 171. Lewis Nathaniel Chase Papers, Manuscript Division, Library of Congress, Washington, D.C.
Chase, Lewis Nathaniel. "Letter to Family," December 16, 1921. Container 171. Lewis Nathaniel Chase Papers, Manuscript Division, Library of Congress, Washington, D.C.
Chase, Lewis Nathaniel. "Letter to Frank Chase," May 1, 1922. Container 173. Lewis Nathaniel Chase Papers, Manuscript Division, Library of Congress, Washington, D.C.
Chase, Lewis Nathaniel. "Letter to Frank Chase," June 4, 1925. Container 191. Lewis Nathaniel Chase Papers, Manuscript Division, Library of Congress, Washington, D.C.
Chase, Lewis Nathaniel. "Letter to Pearl Adell Chase," July 23, 1925. Container 205. Lewis Nathaniel Chase Papers, Manuscript Division, Library of Congress, Washington, D.C.
Chase, Lewis Nathaniel. "Letter to Shurman," June 2, 1924. Container 222. Lewis Nathaniel Chase Papers, Manuscript Division, Library of Congress, Washington, D.C.
Chase, Lewis Nathaniel. "My Ignorance of China." Lecture notes. El Centro, California, May 11, 1925. Container 217. Lewis Nathaniel Chase Papers, Manuscript Division, Library of Congress, Washington, D.C. El Centro, California.
Chase, Lewis Nathaniel. "Western Classics for Chinese Students: Appreciation of Ancient Greece by Chinese May Lead to Single World Civilization." Beijing, 1923. Container 220. Lewis Nathaniel Chase Papers, Manuscript Division, Library of Congress, Washington, D.C. Beijing.
Chase Lewis Nathaniel 柴義思. "Xifang wenxue jiezhu: wei Zhongguo xuesheng xuan de" 西方文學傑著: 為中國學生選的 (Classics of Western Literature: Chosen for Chinese Students). Translated by Shao Ming 紹明. *Yanda zhoukan* 燕大周刊 (Yen Ching Students' Weekly). October 11, 1923, 1. Container 220. Lewis Nathaniel Chase Papers, Manuscript Division, Library of Congress, Washington, D.C. Beijing.
Chatrchyan, S., V. Khachatryan, A.M. Sirunyan, A. Tumasyan, W. Adam, E. Aguilo, T. Bergauer, et al. "Observation of a New Boson at a Mass of 125 GeV with the CMS Experiment at the LHC." *Physics Letters B* 716, no. 1 (September 2012): 30–61.
"Chedi de furen jiefang yundong" 徹底的婦人解放運動 (A Thorough Movement for the Liberation of Women). *Taiwan minbao* 臺灣民報 (Taiwan People's News). April 15, 1923, 3–4. Tokyo.
Cheek, Timothy. *The Intellectual in Modern Chinese History*. Cambridge: Cambridge University Press, 2015.
Cheek, Timothy. "The Names of Rectification: Notes on the Conceptual Domains of CCP Ideology in the Yan'an Rectification Movement." *Indiana East Asian Working Paper Series on Language and Politics in Modern China*, no. 7 (January 1996): 1–42.
Chen Daqi 陳大齊. "Gonghe xinxi" 恭賀新禧 (Happy New Year). *Xin qingnian* 新青年 (New Youth) 6, no. 1 (January 15, 1919): 1–5.
Chen Duxiu 陳獨秀. "Gao xin wenhua yundong de zhu tongzhi" 告新文化運動的諸同志 (To All the Comrades of the New Culture Movement). In *Cai Yuanpei, Chen Duxiu, Hu Shi* 蔡元培、陳獨秀、胡適 (Cai Yuanpei, Chen Duxiu, Hu Shi), edited by Gong Haiyan 龔海燕, 14: 224–29. Shanghai: Shanghai wenyi chubanshe, 2010.
Chen Duxiu 陳獨秀. "Jinggao qingnian" 敬告青年 (Call to Youth). *Taiwan minbao* 臺灣民報 (Taiwan People's News). August 27, 1923, 3–5. Tokyo.

Chen Duxiu 陳獨秀. "Jinri zhi jiaoyu fangzhen" 今日之教育方針 (Contemporary Guiding Principles in Education). *Qingnian zazhi* 青年雜誌 (Youth Magazine) 1, no. 2 (October 15, 1915): 113–18.

Chen Duxiu 陳獨秀. "Tigao yu puji" 提高與普及 (Enhancement and Popularization). *Xin qingnian* 新青年 (New Youth) 8, no. 4 (1920): 5–6.

Chen Duxiu 陳獨秀. "Xin wenhua yundong shi shenme?" 新文化運動是什麼？(What Is the New Culture Movement?). *Xin qingnian* 新青年 (New Youth) 7, no. 5 (April 1920): 1–6.

Chen Duxiu 陳獨秀. "Xin wenhua yundong shi shenme?" 新文化運動是什麼？(What Is the New Culture Movement). In *Xin qingnian* 新青年 (New Youth), 8:697–702. Tokyo: Taian, 1963.

"Chen Duxiu bei bu" 陳獨秀被捕 (Chen Duxiu Arrested). *Shenbao* 申報 (Shanghai News). June 15, 1919, 7–8. Shanghai.

"Chen Duxiu bei bu" 陳獨秀被捕 (Chen Duxiu Arrested). *Shenbao* 申報 (Shanghai News), October 6, 1921, 14.

"Chen Duxiu guo Hu zhi tanpian" 陳獨秀過滬之談片 (Chen Duxiu's Speeches in Shanghai). *Shenbao* 申報 (Shanghai News), February 23, 1920, 14.

"Chen Duxiu xingjiang lai Hu" 陳獨秀行將來滬 (Chen Duxiu about to Come to Shanghai). *Shenbao* 申報 (Shanghai News), July 16, 1921, 14.

"Chen Duxiu zai E yanjiang zhi jingguo" 陳獨秀在鄂演講之經過 (Chen Duxiu's Speeches in Hubei). *Shenbao* 申報 (Shanghai News), February 15, 1920, 14.

"Chen Duxiu zai Jing bei bu xun" 陳獨秀在京被捕訊 (News on Chen Duxiu's Arrest in Beijing). *Shenbao* 申報 (Shanghai News), February 22, 1923, 14.

Chen Duxiu 陳獨秀. "Wenhua yundong yu shehui yundong" 文化運動與社會運動 (The Culture Movement and the Social Movement). In *Xin qingnian* 新青年 (New Youth), 9A:138–39. Tokyo: Taian, 1963.

Chen, L.Y. "Letter to Lewis Chase," 1923. Container 216. Lewis Nathaniel Chase Papers, Manuscript Division, Library of Congress, Washington, D.C.

Chen, Nai Yi. "China Now and England in the 19th Century." Student essay. Beijing, June 12, 1922. Container 216. Lewis Nathaniel Chase Papers, Manuscript Division, Library of Congress, Washington, D.C. Beijing.

Chen, Ping. *Modern Chinese: History and Sociolinguistics*. Cambridge: Cambridge University Press, 1999.

Chen Pingyuan 陳平原. "'Shaonian yiqi' yu 'jiaguo qinghuai' – Beida xuesheng de 'wu si' jiyi" 少年意氣'與'家國情懷——北大學生的"五四"記憶 ("Youthful Impulse" and "Patriotic Feelings" – Beida Students Remember May Fourth). Lecture presented at the Guangming jiangtan 光明講壇 (Guangming Forum), Beijing University, April 20, 2012. Beijing University.

Chen, Pingyuan. *Touches of History: An Entry into "May Fourth" China*. Translated by Michel Hockx. Leiden: Brill, 2011.

Chen Qi 陳奇. *Liu Shipei nianpu changbian* 劉師培年譜長編 (A Comprehensive Chronology of the Life of Liu Shipei). Guiyang: Guizhou renmin chubanshe, 2007.

Chen Qitian 陳啟天. "Shenme shi xin wenhua de jingshen" 什麼是新文化的精神 (What Is the Spirit of New Culture). *Shaonian zhongguo* 少年中國 (Young China) 2, no. 2 (August 15, 1920): 2–5.

Chen Shuping 陳樹萍. *Beixin shuju yu Zhongguo xiandai wenxue* 北新書局與中國現代文學 (New Northern Press and China's Contemporary Literature). Shanghai: Shanghai sanlin wenhua chuanbo youxian gongsi, 2008.

Chen Shuyu 陳漱渝. "Qingchun feiyang de suiyue" 青春飛揚的歲月 (The Time of the Rise of Youth). *Renmin ribao* 人民日報 (People's Daily). May 4, 2009, 16. Beijing.

Chen Sihe 陳思和. "Xu Shuzheng yu xin wenhua yundong" 徐樹錚與新文化運動 (Xu Shuzheng and the New Culture Movement). *Zhongguo xiandai wenxue yanjiu congkan* 中國現代文學叢刊 (Studies on Modern Chinese Literature), no. 3 (1996): 272–87.

Chen Tiesheng 陳鐵生, and Chen Gongzhe 陳公哲. *Xiaoshuo xinchao* 小說新潮 (Novel New Tide). Nanjing, 1921.

Chen, Zhongping. "The May Fourth Movement and Provincial Warlords: A Reexamination." *Modern China* 37, no. 2 (March 2011): 135–69.

Chen Zhuyun 陳竹筠, Xu Jilin 許紀霖, and Chen Qicheng 陳起誠. "Huang Yanpei" 黃炎培 (Huang Yanpei). Edited by Hu Hua 胡華. *Zhong-Gong dangshi renwu zhuan* 中共黨史人物傳 (Biographies of Figures in CCP History). Xi'an: Shaanxi renmin chubanshe, 1988. Xi'an.

Cheng Jingyu 程靖宇, ed. *Hu Shi boshi jinian jikan* 胡適博士紀念集刊 (Collected Papers to Commemorate Dr. Hu Shi). Hong Kong: Duli luntanshe, 1962.

Cheng Weixian 程維賢. "Zhuiyi Fu guxiaozhang zai sheng canyihui" 追憶傅故校長在省參議會 (Remembering the Late President Fu at the Consultative Meeting). In *Fu guxiaozhang aiwanlu* 傅故校長哀輓錄 (Elegies on the Former President Fu), edited by Guoli Taiwan daxue jinian Fu guxiaozhang choubei weiyuanhui aiwanlu bianyin xiaozu 國立臺灣大學紀念傅故校長籌備委員會哀輓錄編印小組, 18–19. Taibei: Taiwan daxue, 1951.

"Chengli zongzhi" 成立宗旨 (Purpose). *Taiwan xin wenhua yundong jinianguan* 台灣新文化運動紀念館 (Taiwan New Cultural Movement Memorial Hall), June 13, 2012. http://tncmmh.gov.taipei/ct.asp?xItem=2032903&CtNode=38914&mp=11900B.

"Chengzhong xiao zhi xin xun: xianzai xiaoyou Hu Shi zhi tongnian keyi" 澄衷校之新訊: 檢載校友胡適之童年課藝 (News from Chengzhong School: Discovery and Publication of Childhood Essays by Alumnus Hu Shi). *Shenbao* 申報 (Shanghai News). December 22, 1922, 17. Shanghai.

Chirgwin, A. M. "The Chinese Renaissance and Its Significance." *Contemporary Review* 125 (January 1, 1924): 62–71.

Chirgwin, A. M. *What China Wants*. London: Livingstone Press, 1928.

Chou, Eva Shan. "Learning to Read Lu Xun, 1918–1923: The Emergence of a Readership." *The China Quarterly* 172 (December 2002): 1042–64.

Chow, Tse-tsung. *The May Fourth Movement: Intellectual Revolution in Modern China*. Cambridge, Massachusetts: Harvard University Press, 1960.

"Chubanjie xiaoxi" 出版界消息 (News from the Publishing World). *Shenbao* 申報 (Shanghai News). March 31, 1925, 15. Shanghai.

Clifford, Nicholas Rowland. *Spoilt Children of Empire: Westerners in Shanghai and the Chinese Revolution of the 1920s*. Hanover: University Press of New England, 1991.

Cohen, Paul A. *Discovering History in China: American Historical Writing on the Recent Chinese Past*. New York: Columbia University Press, 1984.

Colbert, John W. "Journey on the Yangtze," n.d. Container 2. John W. Colbert Papers, Manuscript Division, Library of Congress, Washington, D.C.

"Contents." *Xinghua* 興華 (Chinese Christian Advocate) 17, no. 34 (September 8, 1920).

"Copyright Page." *Xinqun* 新群 (Social Reconstruction) 1, no. 1 (November 1919).

"Copyright Page." *Xin funü* 新婦女 (New Woman) 1, no. 2 (1920).

"Copyright page." *Shengming* 生命 (Life) 1, no. 1 (June 1, 1920).

Csiszar, Alex. "Peer Review: Troubled from the Start." *Nature* 532 (April 21, 2016): 306–8.

Dai Xian 呆僊. "Shangye xuesheng di-er ji bianyan" 商業學生第二集弁言 (Foreword to the Second Issue of *Commercial Student*). *Shangye xuesheng* 商業學生 (Commercial Student), no. 2 (December 1919): 1–3.

"Daxue xiaozhang zhi cizhi" 大學校長之辭職 (The Resignation of the Chancellor of the University). *Yishibao* 益世報 (Social Welfare Tiensin). May 10, 1919, 2. Tianjin.
DeFrancis, John. *Nationalism and Language Reform in China*. Princeton, N.J.: Princeton University Press, 1950.
Di-Capua, Yoav. "Nahda: The Arab Project of Enlightenment." In *The Cambridge Companion to Modern Arab Culture*, edited by Dwight F. Reynolds, 54–74. Cambridge: Cambridge University Press, 2015.
Dirlik, Arif. *The Origins of Chinese Communism*. New York: Oxford University Press, 1989.
Ditmanson, Peter. "The Early Ming National University and Xu Cunren." In *Long Live the Emperor! Uses of the Ming Founder across Six Centuries of East Asian History*, edited by Sarah Schneewind, 38–54. Minneapolis: Society of Ming Studies, 2008.
"Dizhi yundong yu tiyu yundong" 帝制運動與體育運動 (The Monarchy Movement and the Exercise Movement). *Jiaoyu zhoubao (Hangzhou)* 教育週報（杭州） (Education Weekly [Hangzhou]), no. 130 (1916): 28–29.
Doleželová-Velingerová, Milena, and Oldřich Král, eds. *The Appropriation of Cultural Capital: China's May Fourth Project*. Cambridge, Massachusetts: Harvard University Asia Center, 2001.
Dong Baoliang 董寶良, and Zhou Hongyu 周洪宇. *Zhongguo jin xiandai jiaoyu sichao yu liupai* 中國近現代教育思潮與流派 (Intellectual Tides and Schools in Education in China's Modern and Contemporary Period). Beijing: Renmin jiaoyu chubanshe, 1997.
Dorrill, William F. "Transfer of Legitimacy in the Chinese Communist Party: Origins of the Maoist Myth." *China Quarterly*, no. 36 (1968): 45–60.
Duan Huaiqing 段懷清. *Baibide yu Zhongguo wenhua* 白璧德與中國文化 (Babbitt and Chinese Culture). Beijing: Shoudu shifan daxue chubanshe, 2006.
Duan Qirui 段祺瑞. "Beijing Duan Qirui ban jing dian" 北京段祺瑞辦敬電 (Telegram of the 24th [of May 1919] by Duan Qirui in Beijing). In *Yan Xishan dang'an* 閻錫山檔案 (Yan Xishan Papers), edited by Lin Qingfen 林清芬, 5:48–50. Taibei: Guoshiguan, 2003.
Duara, Prasenjit. *Rescuing History from the Nation: Questioning Narratives of Modern China*. Chicago: University of Chicago Press, 1995.
"Duwei boshi lun Zhongguo xuesheng zhi aiguo yundong" 杜威博士論中國學生之愛國運動 (Doctor Dewey Discusses the Patriotic Movement of the Chinese Students). *Shenbao* 申報 (Shanghai News), October 18, 1919, 6.
Duyvendak, J.J.L. "Review of *The Chinese Renaissance* by Hu Shih." *Pacific Affairs* 8, no. 1 (March 1935): 102–3.
"Eguo xuesheng zhi shiwei yundong" 俄國學生之示威運動 (The Protest Movement of Russian Students). *Dongfang zazhi* 東方雜誌 (Eastern Miscellany) 8, no. 12 (1912): 13.
Elman, Benjamin A. *Classicism, Politics, and Kinship: The Ch'ang-Chou School of New Text Confucianism in Late Imperial China*. Berkeley: University of California Press, 1990.
Erickson, Paul A, and Liam D. Murphy, eds. *Readings for a History of Anthropological Theory*. Toronto: University of Toronto Press, 2010.
"Fakan 'Shengming yuekan' xuanyan" 發刊《生命月刊》宣言 (Manifesto for the Publication of *Life*). *Shengming* 生命 (Life) 1, no. 1 (June 1, 1920): 1–3.
"Fakanci" 發刊詞 (Manifesto). *Xin xuesheng* 新學生 (New Student) 1, no. 1 (December 1919): 1–3.
"Fakanci" 發刊詞 (Manifesto). *Piping* 批評 (Criticism). October 20, 1920, 1. Beijing; Shanghai.
Fang Yuan 芳圜. "Zhu Taiwan minbao fakan" 祝臺灣民報發刊 (Good Wishes for the Foundation of the *Taiwan People's News*). *Taiwan minbao* 臺灣民報 (Taiwan People's News). April 15, 1923, 24. Tokyo.

"Fayang 'wu si' geming jingshen – yi jiu yi jiu nian wu si yundong zhaopian jianji" 發揚"五四"革命精神——一九一九年五四運動照片剪輯 (Carrying on the Revolutionary Spirit of "May Fourth" – a Montage of Photos of the May Fourth Movement of 1919). *Renmin ribao* 人民日報 (People's Daily). May 3, 1979, 4. Beijing.

Feng Aiqun 馮愛群, ed. "Dao yidai zheren Hu Shi" 悼一代哲人胡適 (Mourning the Philosopher of a Whole Era Hu Shi). In *Hu Shizhi xiansheng jinianji* 胡適之先生紀念集 (Commemorative Volume for Mr. Hu Shizhi), 133–35. Taibei: Xuesheng chubanshe, 1962.

Feng Aiqun 馮愛群, ed. *Hu Shizhi xiansheng jinianji* 胡適之先生紀念集 (Commemorative Volume for Mr. Hu Shizhi). Taibei: Xuesheng chubanshe, 1962.

Feng Aiqun 馮愛群, ed. "Jianyi zhengfu guozang Hu Shi boshi" 建議政府國葬胡適博士 (We Recommend That the Government Give Dr Hu Shi a State Funeral). In *Hu Shizhi xiansheng jinianji* 胡適之先生紀念集 (Commemorative Volume for Mr. Hu Shizhi), 131. Taibei: Xuesheng chubanshe, 1962.

Feng Xiaocai 馮筱才. "Shanghai xiaceng minzhong dui 'wu si yundong' de fanying: yi 'Riren zhidu' fengchao wei zhongxin" 上海下層民衆對"五四運動"的反應：以"日人置毒"風潮爲中心 (The Reactions towards the May Fourth Movement of the Masses of Shanghai's Lower Classes: The Agitation about "the Poisoning [of Wells] by the Japanese"). *Dongfang lishi pinglun* 東方歷史評論 (Oriental History Review), no. 3 (2013): 84–101.

"Fengyu piaopiao zhi Jing xuejie" 風雨飄飄之京學界 (Academia in Beijing Shaking in Wind and Rain). *Shenbao* 申報 (Shanghai News). May 15, 1919, 7. Shanghai.

Fröhlich, Thomas. "Identität und Widerstand: Jiang Weishuis Antikolonialismus und seine Nachwirkungen" (Identity and Resistance: Jiang Weishui's Anti-Colonialism and Its Legacy). In *Taiwans unvergänglicher Antikolonialismus: Jiang Weishui und der Widerstand gegen die japanische Kolonialherrschaft* (Taiwan's Eternal Anti-Colonialism: Jiang Weishui and the Resistance against Japanese Colonial Rule), edited by Thomas Fröhlich and Yishan Liu, 43–92. Bielefeld: Transcript, 2011.

Fu Mengzhen 傅孟真. "Qing Liang Yusheng zhi shiji zhi yi sanshiliu juan" 清梁玉繩之史記志疑三十六卷 (The Doubtful Points in the *Records of the Historian* by the Qing Historian Liang Yusheng, Volume 36). In *Xinchao* 新潮 (New Tide), 1:145–47. Beijing, 2006.

Fu Sinian 傅斯年. "Duiyu Zhongguo jinri tan zhexue zhe zhi gannian" 對於中國今日談哲學者之感念 (Feelings on People Who Talk about Philosophy in China Today). In *Fu Sinian quanji* 傅斯年全集 (Collected Works of Fu Sinian), 4:1250–57. Taibei: Lianjing chuban shiye gongsi, 1980.

Fu Sinian 傅斯年. "Gu shu xin ping" 故書新評 (A Re-Evaluation of Old Books). In *Xinchao* 新潮 (New Tide), 1:145. Beijing, 2006.

Fu Sinian 傅斯年. "Hanyu gaiyong pinyin wenzi de chubu tan" 漢語改用拼音文字的初步談 (Abandoning Characters in Favour of Pinyin in Chinese: A Preliminary Discussion). In *Fu Sinian quanji* 傅斯年全集 (Collected Works of Fu Sinian), 4:1138–65. Taibei: Lianjing chuban shiye gongsi, 1980.

Fu Sinian 傅斯年. "Mao Zishui 'Guogu he kexue de jingshen' shiyu" 毛子水《國故和科學的精神》識語 (Editor's Note on Mao Zishui's "The *National Heritage* and the Scientific Spirit"). In *Fu Sinian quanji* 傅斯年全集 (Collected Works of Fu Sinian), 4:1258–59. Taibei: Lianjing chuban shiye gongsi, 1980.

Fu Sinian 傅斯年. "Rensheng wenti faduan" 人生問題發端 (The Beginnings of the Question of Life). In *Xinchao* 新潮 (New Tide), 1:9–23, 1966.

Fu Sinian 傅斯年. "Wen yan heyi caoyi" 文言合一草議 (The Integration of Written and Spoken Language). In *Fu Sinian quanji* 傅斯年全集 (Collected Works of Fu Sinian), 4:1065–74. Taibei: Lianjing chuban shiye gongsi, 1980.

Fu Sinian 傅斯年. "Wenxue gexin shenyi" 文學革新申義 (An Explanation of the Reform of Literature). In *Fu Sinian quanji* 傅斯年全集 (Collected Works of Fu Sinian), 4:1051–1064. Taibei: Lianjing chuban shiye gongsi, 1980.

Fu Sinian 傅斯年. "Xiju gailiang gemian guan" 戲劇改良各面觀 (A Comprehensive View of the Reform of Drama). In *Fu Sinian quanji* 傅斯年全集 (Collected Works of Fu Sinian), 4:1075–97. Taibei: Lianjing chuban shiye gongsi, 1980.

Fu Sinian 傅斯年. "Xinchao fakan zhiqushu" 《新潮》發刊旨趣書 (Aims behind the Publication of *New Tide*). In *Fu Sinian quanji* 傅斯年全集 (Collected Works of Fu Sinian), 4:1397–1401. Taibei: Lianjing chuban shiye gongsi, 1980.

Fu Sinian 傅斯年. "'Xinchao' zhi huigu yu qianzhan" 《新潮》之回顧與前瞻 (*New Tide*: Looking Back and Looking Ahead). *Xinchao* 新潮 (New Tide) 2, no. 1 (October 30, 1919): 199–205.

Fu Sinian 傅斯年. "'Xinchao' zhi huigu yu qianzhan" 《新潮》之回顧與前瞻 (*New Tide*: Looking Back and Looking Ahead). In *Wu si yundong huiyi lu* 五四運動回憶錄 (Records of Memories of the May Fourth Movement), edited by Zhongguo shehui kexue yuan jindaishi yanjiusuo 中國社會科學院近代史研究所, 171–76. Beijing: Zhongguo shehui kexue chubanshe, 1979.

Fu Sinian 傅斯年. "Zenyang zuo baihua wen" 怎樣做白話文 (How to Write Texts in the Plain Language). In *Fu Sinian quanji* 傅斯年全集 (Collected Works of Fu Sinian), 44:1119–35. Taibei: Lianjing chuban shiye gongsi, 1980.

Fu Sinian 傅斯年. "Zhongguo lishi fenqi zhi yanjiu" 中國歷史分期之研究 (Research on the Periodization of Chinese History). In *Fu Sinian quanji* 傅斯年全集 (Collected Works of Fu Sinian), 4:1224–33. Taibei: Lianjing chuban shiye gongsi, 1980.

Fu Sinian 傅斯年. "Zhongguo xueshu sixiangjie zhi jiben wumiu" 中國學術思想界之基本誤謬 (The Fundamental Faults in Chinese Scholarship and Thought). In *Fu Sinian quanji* 傅斯年全集 (Collected Works of Fu Sinian), 1213–1223. Taibei: Lianjing chuban shiye gongsi, 1980.

"Funü jiefang yundong de pubianhua" 婦女解放運動的普遍化 (Generalization of the Women's Emancipation Movement). *Funü zazhi* 婦女雜誌 (Ladies' Magazine) 7, no. 5 (May 5, 1921): 122.

Gao Pingshu 高平叔. *Cai Yuanpei nianpu changbian* 蔡元培年譜長編 (A Comprehensive Chronology of the Life of Cai Yuanpei). Vol. 2 (1917–1926). Beijing: Renmin jiaoyu chubanshe, 1996.

"Gao xiaoxuexiao fendeng yundonghui zhi yubei" 高小學校分等運動會之預備 (Preparations for the Graded Sports Festival of Higher Primary Schools). *Shenbao* 申報 (Shanghai News), December 6, 1919, 11.

"Gaodeng xiaoxue lianhe yundong zhi jijiang" 高等小學聯合運動之給獎 (Prizes Awarded at the Joint Sports [Festival] of the Upper Primary Schools). *Shenbao* 申報 (Shanghai News), July 16, 1919, 10.

"Gaoxing zhen jiang kai xiaoxue lianhe yundonghui" 高行鎮將開小學聯合運動會 (Gaoxing Will Hold a Joint Primary-School Sports Festival). *Shenbao* 申報 (Shanghai News), May 12, 1919, 11.

'Gaozhong lishi yongbiao' bianxiezu 《高中歷史用表》編寫組, ed. *Gaozhong lishi yongbiao* 高中歷史用表 (Tables for Senior High School History). Beijing: Zhongguo dui wai fanyi chuban gongsi, 2010.

Ge Jingyou 葛敬猷. "Beijing Ge canshi zhen dian" 北京葛參事真電 (Telegram of the 11th [of May 1919] from Councilor Ge in Beijing). In *Yan Xishan dang'an* 閻錫山檔案 (Yan Xishan Papers), edited by Lin Qingfen 林清芬, 5:24–25. Taibei: Guoshiguan, 2003.

Ge Wujue 戈悟覺. *Shiguang yousheng* 時光有聲 (Time Has a Voice). Beijing: Zhongguo qingnian chubanshe, 2011.

"Ge xiao xiaozhang zhi jianjue" 各校校長之堅決 (The Determination of the Principals of All Schools). *Dagongbao* 大公報 (Impartial). May 10, 1919, 3. Changsha.

Geertz, Clifford. *The Interpretation of Cultures: Selected Essays by Clifford Geertz*. New York: Basic Books, 1973.

Geng Yunzhi 耿雲志. *Hu Shi nianpu* 胡適年譜 (A Chronology of Hu Shi's Life). Chengdu: Sichuan renmin chubanshe, 1989.

Gillin, Donald G. "Education and Militarism in Modern China: Yen Hsi-Shan in Shansi Province, 1911–30." *The Journal of Modern History* 34, no. 2 (June 1962): 161–67.

Gillin, Donald G. "Portrait of a Warlord: Yen Hsi-Shan in Shansi Province, 1911–1930." *The Journal of Asian Studies* 19, no. 3 (May 1960): 289–306.

Gillin, Donald G. *Warlord: Yen Hsi-Shan in Shansi Province, 1911–1949*. Princeton: Princeton University Press, 1967.

Gittings, John. "Is China Heading towards Revolution? Recapturing 1919's Glory." *Guardian*. May 5, 1989, 14. The Guardian (1959–2003). London.

Gong Shuduo 龔書鐸. "Zhengque pingjia wu si xin wenhua yundong" 正確評價五四新文化運動 (Correctly Assessing the New Culture Movement of May Fourth). *Renmin ribao* 人民日報 (People's Daily). May 6, 1999, 9. Beijing.

Goto-Jones, Christopher S. *Modern Japan: A Very Short Introduction*. Very Short Introductions. Oxford: Oxford University Press, 2009.

Graf, Emily. "Lu Xun Marginalized or Centered? Wen- and Wu- Readings of Lai He's Museum Space." presented at the Popular Culture Group, Colloquium Workshop organized by Barbara Mittler, Heidelberg, May 26, 2017. Heidelberg.

Grieder, Jerome B. *Hu Shih and the Chinese Renaissance: Liberalism in the Chinese Revolution, 1917–1937*. Cambridge, Massachusetts: Harvard University Press, 1970.

Gu Xiuqing 谷秀青. *Qing mo Min chu Jiangsu sheng jiaoyuhui yanjiu* 清末民初江蘇省教育會研究 (A Study of the Jiangsu Education Association in the Late Qing and Early Republic). Guilin: Guangxi shifan daxue chubanshe, 2009.

"Guanggao jia mubiao" 廣告價目表 (Price List for Advertisements). *Jiefang yu gaizao* 解放與改造 (Emancipation and Reconstruction) 1, no. 1 + 2 (October 15, 1919).

"Guanggao jiamu" 廣告價目 (Price List for Advertisements). *Xinchao* 新潮 (New Tide) 1, no. 1 (January 1, 1919).

"Guanggao jiamu" 廣告價目 (Price List for Advertisements). *Guogu* 國故 (National Heritage), no. 1 (March 20, 1919).

"Guchui guoji zhuyi zhi jiguan" 鼓吹過激主義之機關 (Organs of Bolshevist Propaganda). *Yingyu zhoukan* 英語周刊 (English Weekly), no. 188 (1919): 1917.

"Gudai hanyu cidian" bianxiezu 《古代漢語詞典》編寫組. "Hui" 會 (Can, Meeting, Etc.). *Gudai hanyu cidian: suoyin ben* 古代漢語詞典：縮印本 (A Dictionary of Classical Chinese: Short Version). Beijing: Shangwu yinshuguan, 2007. Beijing.

Gui, Sheng 桂生. "Beijing tongxin" 北京通信 (Newsletter from Beijing). *Shenbao* 申報 (Shanghai News). April 12, 1919, 6. Shanghai.

Gulliver, Katrina. *Modern Women in China and Japan: Gender, Feminism and Global Modernity between the Wars*. London: Tauris, 2012.

Gunn, Edward M. *Rewriting Chinese: Style and Innovation in Twentieth-Century Chinese Prose*. Stanford, California: Stanford University Press, 1991.
Guo Fengqi 郭鳳歧, and He Huanzhen 何煥臻, eds. "Fu Zengxiang" 傅增湘 (Fu Zengxiang). *Zhiming renwu 100 wei* 知名人物100位 (100 Famous People). Tianjin: Tianjin guji chubanshe, 2009. Tianjin.
"Guogu yuekanshe zhi Gongyanbao han" 國故月刊社致公言報函 (A Letter from the National Heritage Society to the *Public Voice*). *Beijing daxue rikan* 北京大學日刊 (Beijing University Daily). March 24, 1919, 6. Beijing.
"Guoji zhuyi Bolshevism yu puji jiaoyu" 過激主義Bolshevism與普及教育 (Bolshevism and Promulgating Education). *Xin jiaoyu* 新教育 (New Education) 1, no. 3 (1919): 10.
"Guoji zhuyi qinru Siluofaniya" 過激主義侵入斯洛伐尼亞 (Bolshevism Invades Slovenia). *Dongfang zazhi* 東方雜誌 (Eastern Miscellany) 16, no. 8 (1919): 230.
"Guoji zhuyi zhi zhenxiang" 過激主義之真相 (The Truth about Bolshevism). *Yuehan sheng* 約翰聲 (The Voice of John) 30, no. 2 (1919): 13–16.
Guoli bianyiguan 國立編譯館. *Gaoji zhongxue lishi* 高級中學歷史 (History for Senior High Schools). 1st ed. Vol. 3. Guoli bianyiguan, 1972.
Guoli bianyiguan 國立編譯館. *Gaoji zhongxue lishi* 高級中學歷史 (History for Senior High Schools). Vol. 3. Guoli bianyiguan, 1985.
Guoli bianyiguan 國立編譯館. ed. *Gaoji zhongxue lishi* 高級中學歷史 (History for Senior High Schools). 9th ed. Vol. 3. Guoli bianyiguan, 1993.
Guoli bianyiguan 國立編譯館. *Gaoji zhongxue lishi jiaoshi shouce* 高級中學歷史教師手冊 (History for Senior High Schools – Teachers' Handbook). 2nd ed. Vol. 3. Guoli bianyiguan, 1978.
Guoli Taiwan daxue jinian Fu guxiaozhang choubei weiyuanhui aiwanlu bianyin xiaozu 國立臺灣大學紀念傅故校長籌備委員會哀輓錄編印小組, ed. *Fu guxiaozhang aiwanlu* 傅故校長哀輓錄 (Elegies on the Former President Fu). Taibei: Taiwan daxue, 1951.
Guoli Taiwan daxue jinian Fu guxiaozhang choubei weiyuanhui aiwanlu bianyin xiaozu 國立臺灣大學紀念傅故校長籌備委員會哀輓錄編印小組, ed. "Fu guxiaozhang yixiang ji sangzang jidian deng zhaopian" 傅故校長遺像及喪葬祭奠等照片 (Photos of the Portrait of the Deceased Late President Fu, the Funeral and so Forth). In *Fu guxiaozhang aiwanlu* 傅故校長哀輓錄 (Elegies on the Former President Fu), Tuban. Taibei: Taiwan daxue, 1951.
"Guomin dahui zhi yuwen" 國民大會之餘聞 (Miscellaneous News from the Citizens' Assembly). *Shenbao* 申報 (Shanghai News). May 9, 1919, 10. Shanghai.
"Guomin duiyu Shandong wenti zhi banfa" 國民對於山東問題之辦法 (Ways in Which the Citizens Deal with the Shandong Question). *Shenbao* 申報 (Shanghai News). May 6, 1919, 6. Shanghai.
"Guomin xuexiao lianhe yundonghui xiansheng" 國民學校聯合運動會先聲 (First Signs of the Joint Sports Festival of the Citizens' School). *Shenbao* 申報 (Shanghai News), October 14, 1919, 10.
Guowuyuan 國務院. "Beijing guowuyuan ma dian" 北京國務院麻電 (Telegram of the 6th [of May 1919] from the State Council in Beijing). In *Yan Xishan dang'an* 閻錫山檔案 (Yan Xishan Papers), edited by Lin Qingfen 林清芬, 5:9. Taibei: Guoshiguan, 2003.
Guowuyuan 國務院. "Beijing guowuyuan qing dian" 北京國務院青電 (Telegram of the 9th [of May 1919] from the State Council in Beijing). In *Yan Xishan dang'an* 閻錫山檔案 (Yan Xishan Papers), edited by Lin Qingfen 林清芬, 5:16–17. Taibei: Guoshiguan, 2003.

Guowuyuan 國務院. "Beijing guowuyuan zhi dian" 北京國務院支電 (Telegram of the 4th [of May 1919] from the State Council in Beijing). In *Yan Xishan dang'an* 閻錫山檔案 (Yan Xishan Papers), edited by Lin Qingfen 林清芬, 5:26–27. Taibei: Guoshiguan, 2003.

"Haishang xiaoshuojia manping (yi)" 海上小說家漫評（一） (Commentary of Foreign Novelists [1]). *Shenbao* 申報 (Shanghai News). January 16, 1921, 14. Shanghai.

Hamilton, Clarence H. "Review of *The Chinese Renaissance* by Hu Shih." *International Journal of Ethics* 46, no. 1 (October 1935): 121–23.

Hammerstrom, Erik J. "Buddhists Discuss Science in Modern China (1895–1949)." PhD, Indiana University, 2010.

"Hancheng duli yundong zhi fengqi" 漢城獨立運動之蜂起 (The Rise of the Independence Movement in Seoul). *Shenbao* 申報 (Shanghai News). April 6, 1919, 6. Shanghai.

"Hangzhou jiaoyuhui tiyu jiangxisuo yundonghui ge" 杭州教育會體育講習所運動會歌 (The Sports Festival Song of the Sports Institute of the Hangzhou Educational Association). *Hangzhou baihua bao* 杭州白話報 (Hangzhou Plain-Language News) 3, no. 16 (1900): 2.

"Hanmin duli yundong zhi waixun" 韓民獨立運動之外訊 (External News on the Korean Independence Movement). *Shenbao* 申報 (Shanghai News). April 10, 1919, 6. Shanghai.

Harrison, Henrietta. "Newspapers and Nationalism in Rural China 1890–1929." *Past & Present*, no. 166 (February 2000): 181–204.

Harrison, Henrietta. *The Man Awakened from Dreams: One Man's Life in a North China Village, 1857–1942*. Stanford, California: Stanford University Press, 2005.

Hashimoto Kaikan 橋本海關. "Deguo jiandui yundong" 德國艦隊運動 (The Movements of the German Armada). *Dong ye bao* 東業報 (Eastern Business), no. 5 (1898): 7.

Haydon, A. Eustace. "Foreword." In *The Chinese Renaissance: The Haskell Lectures 1933*, vii–viii. Whitefish, Montana: Kessinger Publishing, 2010.

Hickok Seelye, Laurens. "Review of *The Chinese Renaissance* by Hu Shih." *Church History* 4, no. 3 (June 1935): 153–54.

Hill, Michael Gibbs. *Lin Shu, Inc. : Translation and the Making of Modern Chinese Culture*. Oxford: Oxford University Press, 2013.

Hockx, Michel, ed. "Playing the Field: Aspects of Chinese Literary Life in the 1920s." In *The Literary Field of Twentieth-Century China*, 61–78. Richmond: Curzon, 1999.

Hockx, Michel, ed. *The Literary Field of Twentieth-Century China*. Richmond: Curzon, 1999.

"Houqi zhongdeng jiaoyu gongtong hexin kecheng zhiyin" 後期中等教育共同核心課程指引 (Guide for common core curricula in for the higher mid-level education). Accessed September 17, 2015. http://edu.law.moe.gov.tw.

"Hu Renyuan zhang daxue wenti: jiaoyuan xuesheng yizhi fandui" 胡仁源長大學問題：教員、學生一致反對 (Chancellor Hu Renyuan's Problem with the University: Professors and Students Unanimously Oppose Him). *Shenbao* 申報 (Shanghai News). June 10, 1919, 7. Shanghai.

Hu Shi 胡適. "Daxue kai nü de wenti" 大學開女的問題 (The Question of Opening Universities for Women). *Shaonian zhongguo* 少年中國 (Young China) 1, no. 4 (October 15, 1919): 1–3.

Hu Shi 胡適. *Fandong wenren Hu Shi dui "Shui hu" de kaozheng* 反動文人胡適對《水滸》的考證 (The Research on the *Water Margins* of the Reactionary Literatus Hu Shi). Edited by Renmin ribao tushu ziliaoshi 人民日報圖書資料室. Beijing: Renmin ribao chubanshe, 1975.

Hu Shi 胡適. *Hu Shi de riji* 胡適的日記 (Hu Shi's Diary). Edited by Zhongguo shehui kexueyuan jindaishi yanjiusuo Zhonghua minguoshi yanjiu 中國社會科學院近代史研究所中華民國史研究室. Vol. shang. Beijing: Zhonghua shuju, 1985.

Hu Shi 胡適. *Hu Shi jingdian wencun* 胡適經典文存 (Selected Classical Works by Hu Shi). Edited by Hong Zhigang 洪治綱. Shanghai: Shanghai daxue chubanshe, 2004.
Hu Shi 胡適. *Hu Shi liuxue riji* 胡適留學日記 (Hu Shi's Study-Abroad Diary). Vol. 1. Shangwu yinshuguan, 1947.
Hu Shi 胡適. *Hu Shi liuxue riji* 胡適留學日記 (Hu Shi's Study-Abroad Diary). Vol. 2. Shangwu yinshuguan, 1947.
Hu Shi 胡適. *Hu Shi liuxue riji* 胡適留學日記 (Hu Shi's Study-Abroad Diary). Vol. 3. Shangwu yinshuguan, 1947.
Hu Shi 胡適. *Hu Shi liuxue riji* 胡適留學日記 (Hu Shi's Study-Abroad Diary). Vol. 4. Shangwu yinshuguan, 1947.
Hu Shi 胡適. *Hu Shi liuxue riji* 胡適留學日記 (Hu Shi's Study-Abroad Diary). Taibei: Taiwan shangwu yinshuguan, 1959.
Hu Shi 胡適. *Hu Shi liuxue riji* 胡適留學日記 (Hu Shi's Study-Abroad Diary). Taibei: Taiwan shangwu, 1960.
Hu Shi 胡適. *Hu Shi liuxue riji* 胡適留學日記 (Hu Shi's Study-Abroad Diary). Taibei: Taiwan shangwu, 1961.
Hu Shi 胡適. *Hu Shi riji* 胡適日記 (Hu Shi's Diary). Wenhua yanjiushe, 1933.
Hu Shi 胡適. *Hu Shi riji* 胡適日記 (Hu Shi's Diary). Wenhua yanjiushe, 1934.
Hu Shi 胡適. *Hu Shi riji quanji* 胡適日記全集 (Hu Shi's Collected Diaries). Edited by Cao Boyan 曹伯言. Vol. 4. Taibei: Lianjing chuban shiye gongsi, 2004.
Hu Shi 胡適. *Hu Shi riji quanji* 胡適日記全集 (Hu Shi's Collected Diaries). Edited by Cao Boyan 曹伯言. Vol. 6. Taibei: Lianjing chuban shiye gongsi, 2004.
Hu Shi 胡適. *Hu Shi wencun* 胡適文存 (Selected Works of Hu Shi). Vol. 2. Shanghai: Yadong tushuguan, 1921.
Hu Shi 胡適. *Hu Shi wencun* 胡適文存 (Selected Works of Hu Shi). Vol. shang. Beijing: Zhongyang bianyi chubanshe, 1921.
Hu Shi 胡適. *Hu Shi wencun* 胡適文存 (Selected Works of Hu Shi). Vol. shang-xia. Beijing: Zhongyang bianyi chubanshe, 1921.
Hu Shi 胡適. *Hu Shi wencun* 胡適文存 (Selected Works of Hu Shi). 4th ed. Vol. shang. Shanghai: Yadong tushuguan, 1923.
Hu Shi 胡適. *Hu Shi wencun* 胡適文存 (Selected Works of Hu Shi). 4th ed. Vol. xia. Shanghai: Yadong tushuguan, 1923.
Hu Shi 胡適. *Hu Shi wencun* 胡適文存 (Selected Works of Hu Shi). Vol. 2. Shanghai: Yadong tushuguan, 1924.
Hu Shi 胡適. *Hu Shi wencun* 胡適文存 (Selected Works of Hu Shi). Vol. 3. Shanghai: Yadong tushuguan, 1924.
Hu Shi 胡適. *Hu Shi wencun* 胡適文存 (Selected Works of Hu Shi). 4th ed. Vol. 2.1. Shanghai: Yadong tushuguan, 1927.
Hu Shi 胡適. *Hu Shi wencun* 胡適文存 (Selected Works of Hu Shi). 4th ed. Vol. 2.2. Shanghai: Yadong tushuguan, 1927.
Hu Shi 胡適. *Hu Shi wencun* 胡適文存 (Selected Works of Hu Shi). 4th ed. Vol. 2.3. Shanghai: Yadong tushuguan, 1927.
Hu Shi 胡適. *Hu Shi wencun* 胡適文存 (Selected Works of Hu Shi). 4th ed. Vol. 2.4. Shanghai: Yadong tushuguan, 1927.
Hu Shi 胡適. *Hu Shi wencun* 胡適文存 (Selected Works of Hu Shi). 4th ed. Vol. 1. Shanghai: Yadong tushuguan, 1928.

Hu Shi 胡適. *Hu Shi wencun* 胡適文存 (Selected Works of Hu Shi). 4th ed. Vol. 2. Shanghai: Yadong tushuguan, 1928.
Hu Shi 胡適. *Hu Shi wencun* 胡適文存 (Selected Works of Hu Shi). 4th ed. Vol. 3. Shanghai: Yadong tushuguan, 1928.
Hu Shi 胡適. *Hu Shi wencun* 胡適文存 (Selected Works of Hu Shi). 4th ed. Vol. 4. Shanghai: Yadong tushuguan, 1928.
Hu Shi 胡適. *Hu Shi wencun* 胡適文存 (Selected Works of Hu Shi). Vol. shang. Beijing: Zhongyang bianyi chubanshe, 1929.
Hu Shi 胡適. *Hu Shi wencun* 胡適文存 (Selected Works of Hu Shi). Vol. xia. Beijing: Zhongyang bianyi chubanshe, 1929.
Hu Shi 胡適. *Hu Shi wencun* 胡適文存 (Selected Works of Hu Shi). 16th ed. Vol. 2. Shanghai: Yadong tushuguan, 1933.
Hu Shi 胡適. *Hu Shi wencun* 胡適文存 (Selected Works of Hu Shi). 16th ed. Vol. 3. Shanghai: Yadong tushuguan, 1933.
Hu Shi 胡適. *Hu Shi wencun* 胡適文存 (Selected Works of Hu Shi). 16th ed. Vol. 4. Shanghai: Yadong tushuguan, 1933.
Hu Shi 胡適. *Hu Shi wencun* 胡適文存 (Selected Works of Hu Shi). Taibei: Yuandong tushuguan, 1953.
Hu Shi 胡適. *Hu Shi yanlun ji* 胡適言論集 (Collection of Hu Shi's Speeches). Taibei: Huaguo chubanshe, 1953.
Hu Shi 胡適. *Hu Shi zishu* 胡適自述 (Hu Shi's Autobiography). Zhengzhou: Henan renmin chubanshe, 2004.
Hu Shi 胡適. "Introduction to 'Western Literature, Volume 1: Greece and Rome, by A. E. Zucker.'" In *Hu Shi quanji* 胡適全集 (Hu Shi's Collected Works), 35:287–97. Hefei: Anhui jiaoyu chubanshe, 2003.
Hu Shi 胡適. "Jianshe de wenxue geming lun" 建設的文學革命論 (Discussion of a Constructive Literary Revolution). *Xin qingnian* 新青年 (New Youth) 4, no. 4 (1918): 289–306.
Hu Shi 胡適. "Jieshao wo ziji de sixiang" 介紹我自己的思想 (Introducing My Own Thought). In *Hu Shi wenxuan* 胡適文選 (Selected Works of Hu Shi), 1–25. Shanghai: Yadong tushuguan, 1930.
Hu Shi 胡適. "Nüzi wenti (yi) Hu Shizhi xiansheng jiangyan" 女子問題(一)胡適之先生講演 (The Women's Question (1) a Speech by Mr Hu Shizhi). *Funü zazhi* 婦女雜誌 (Ladies' Magazine), no. 5 (May 1, 1921): 6–9.
Hu Shi 胡適. *Sishi zishu* 四十自述 (Autobiography at Forty). Shanghai: Yadong tushuguan, 1933.
Hu Shi 胡適. *Sishi zishu* 四十自述 (Autobiography at Forty). Shanghai: Yadong tushuguan, 1935.
Hu Shi 胡適. *Sishi zishu* 四十自述 (Autobiography at Forty). Shanghai: Yadong tushuguan, 1939.
Hu Shi 胡適. *Sishi zishu* 四十自述 (Autobiography at Forty). Shanghai: Yadong tushuguan, 1947.
Hu Shi 胡適. *Sishi zishu* 四十自述 (Autobiography at Forty). Shanghai: Yadong tushuguan, 1954.
Hu Shi 胡適. *Sishi zishu* 四十自述 (Autobiography at Forty). Taibei: Liu yi chubanshe, 1954.
Hu Shi 胡適. *Sishi zishu* 四十自述 (Autobiography at Forty). Taibei: Zhengzhong shuju, 1957.
Hu, Shi. *The Chinese Renaissance*. The Haskell Lectures, 1933. New York: Paragon Book Reprint Corp., 1963.
Hu, Shi. *The Chinese Renaissance*. The Haskell Lectures, 1933. Whitefish, Montana: Kessinger Publishing, 2010.

Hu, Shi. "The Development of the Logical Method in Ancient China." PhD, Columbia University, 1922.

Hu Shi 胡適. "Women duiyu Xiyang jindai wenming de taidu" 我們對於西洋近代文明的態度 (Our Attitude towards Modern Western Culture). *Xinghua* 興華 (Chinese Christian Advocate) 23, no. 30 (1926): 8–19.

Hu Shi 胡適. "Xin sichao de yiyi" 新思潮的意義 (The Meaning of the New Intellectual Tide). In *Xin qingnian* 新青年 (New Youth), 7A:9–16. Tokyo: Taian, 1963.

Hu Shi 胡適, and Jiang Menglin 蔣夢麟. "Women duiyu xuesheng de xiwang" 我們對於學生的希望 (Our Hopes for the Students). In *Minguo shiqi mingren tan wu si: lishi jiyi yu lishi jieshi* 民國時期名人談五四：歷史記憶與歷史解釋（1919–1949）(Famous People of the Republican Period Talk about May Fourth: Historical Reminiscences and Historical Explanations), edited by Yang Hu 楊琥, 93–97. Fuzhou: Fujian jiaoyu chubanshe, 2011.

"Hu Shi wencun" 胡適文存 (Selected Works of Hu Shi). *Taiwan minbao* 臺灣民報 (Taiwan People's News). April 15, 1923, 27. Tokyo.

"Hu Shi zuori di Hu" 胡適昨日抵滬 (Hu Shi Arrived in Shanghai Yesterday). *Shenbao* 申報 (Shanghai News). May 21, 1927, 11. Shanghai.

Hu, Shih. "Failure of Law in Nationalist China." In *The Search for Modern China: A Documentary Collection*, edited by Pei-kai Cheng, Michael Elliot Lestz, and Jonathan D. Spence, 1st ed., 271–75. New York: Norton, 1999.

Hu, Shih. *The Chinese Renaissance*. The Haskell Lectures, 1933. LaVergne, TN: Kessinger, 2009.

Hu, Shih. "The Renaissance in China." *Journal of the Royal Institute of International Affairs* 5, no. 6 (November 1926): 265–83.

Hu, Shih, T.T. Lew, Y.Y. Tsu, and Ching Yi Cheng. "China to-Day." In *China to-Day through Chinese Eyes*, 2nd ed. London: Student Christian Movement, 1922.

Hu, Shih, T.T. Lew, Y.Y. Tsu, and Ching Yi Cheng. *China to-Day through Chinese Eyes*. 2nd ed. London: Student Christian Movement, 1922.

Huang Banghe 黃邦和, and Pi Mingxiu 皮明庥, eds. "Zhang Zongxiang" 章宗祥 (Zhang Zongxiang). *Zhong-wai lishi renwu cidian* 中外歷史人物詞典 (Dictionary of Historical Figures in China and Abroad). Changsha: Hunan renmin chubanshe, 1987. Changsha.

Huang Songxian 黃頌顯. "1920 niandai Taiwan wenhua xiehui chengli beiying yinsu zhi fenxi" 1920年代臺灣文化協會成立背景因素之分析 (An Analysis of the Background and Factors Involved in the Foundation of the Taiwan Culture Association in the 1920s). *Mindao Riben yu jiaoyu* 明道日本語教育 (Mindao Japanese Education), no. 2 (July 2008): 237–74.

Huang Wenlin 黃文林, ed. *Gaozhong lishi* 高中歷史 (History for Senior High Schools). Beijing: Kexue jishu wenxian chubanshe, 1995.

Huang Yanpei 黃炎培. *Huang Yanpei riji* 黃炎培日記 (Huang Yanpei's Diary). Edited by Zhongguo shehui kexueyuan jindaishi yanjiusuo 中國社會科學院近代史研究所. Vol. 2. Beijing: Huawen chubanshe, 2008.

Huang Yanpei 黃炎培. "Huang Yanpei riji zhengli fanli" 黃炎培日記整理凡例 (Guide to the Structure of Huang Yanpei's Diary). In *Huang Yanpei riji* 黃炎培日記 (Huang Yanpei's Diary), edited by Zhongguo shehui kexueyuan jindaishi yanjiusuo 中國社會科學院近代史研究所, 2:1–2. Beijing: Huawen chubanshe, 2008.

Huang Yanpei 黃炎培. "Nanyang huaqiao jiaoyu shangque shu" 南洋華僑教育商榷書 (A Discussion of the Education of Chinese Nationals in the Southern Seas). *Zhongguo yu Nanyang* 中國與南洋 (China and the Southern Seas) 1, no. 1 (1918).

Huang Yanpei 黃炎培. "Zhiye jiaoyu shishi zhi xiwang" 職業教育實施之希望 (Hopes for Implementing Vocational Education). *Jiaoyu zazhi* 教育雜誌 (Education Magazine) 9, no. 1 (1917): 1–9.

Huang Yanpei 黃炎培, and Jiang Menglin 蔣夢麟. "Huang Yanpei, Jiang Menglin zhi Hu Shi" 黃炎培、蔣夢麟致胡適 (Letter from Huang Yanpei and Jiang Menglin to Hu Shi). In *Hu Shi laiwang shuxinxuan* 胡適來往書信選 (Hu Shi's Selected Correspondence), edited by Zhongguo shehui xueyuan jindaishi yanjiusuo Zhonghua minguoshi yanjiushi Fuhui 中國社會科學院近代史研究所中華民國史研究室, shang:35–36. Beijing: Zhongguo shehui kexue chubanshe, 2013.

"Huansong Yuandong yundonghui yusaiyuan" 歡送遠東運動會與賽員 (Seeing off the Participants in the Far Eastern Sports Festival). *Shenbao* 申報 (Shanghai News), May 4, 1919, 10.

"Huaqiao aiguo yundong zhi jinxun" 華僑愛國運動之近訊 (Recent News on the Patriotic Movement of Chinese Abroad). *Shenbao* 申報 (Shanghai News). July 7, 1919, 10. Shanghai.

Hunan sheng jiaoyuhui 湖南省教育會. "Hunan sheng jiaoyuhui, qing zhaoji quanguo jiaoyuhui lianhehui kai linshihui daidian" 湖南省教育會請召集全國教育會聯合會開臨時會代電 (Express Mail Letter from the Hunan Educational Association, Asking to Convene a Provisional Meeting of the National Union of the Educational Associations). Edited by Jiangsu sheng jiaoyuhui 江蘇省教育會. *Jiangsu sheng jiaoyuhui yuebao* 江蘇省教育會月報 (Jiangsu Educational Association Monthly Report), June 1919, 5–6.

Hung, Chang-tai. *Going to the People: Chinese Intellectuals and Folk Literature, 1918–1937*. Cambridge, Massachusetts: Council on East Asian Studies, Harvard University, 1985.

Hutchinson, Paul. *China's Real Revolution*. New York: Missionary Education Movement of the United States and Canada, 1924.

H.W.S. "Review of *The Chinese Renaissance* by Hu Shih." *Journal of Philosophy* 31, no. 13 (June 21, 1934): 363.

Isaacs, Arnold R. "Silencing the Best and the Brightest." *New York Times*. June 28, 1992, BR27. New York Times (1923-Current File). New York.

Jenco, Leigh. "Culture as History: Envisioning Change across and beyond 'Eastern' and 'Western' Civilizations in the May Fourth Era." *Twentieth-Century China* 38, no. 1 (January 2013): 34–51.

Jenco, Leigh. "The Problem of the Culturally Unprecedented: Cultural Difference as Historical Discontinuity after May Fourth," n.d.

Jian Ru 劍如. "Furen zanzheng yunong" 婦人參政運動 (The Movement for Women's Political Participation). *Taiwan minbao* 臺灣民報 (Taiwan People's News). April 15, 1923, 11. Tokyo.

Jian Ru 劍如. "Wenhua yundong" 文化運動 (The Culture Movement). *Taiwan minbao* 臺灣民報 (Taiwan People's News). August 1, 1923, 2–4. Tokyo.

Jiang Biyu 蔣碧玉, Jiang Songhui 蔣松輝, and Zhou Heyuan 周合源. "Wei Jiang Weishui yu Taiwan wenhua xiehui zhi 'Taiwan pinglun' de shengming" 為蔣渭水與台灣文化協會致《台灣評論》的聲明 (Declaration to the *Taiwan Review* on Behalf of Jiang Weishui and the Taiwan Cultural Association). *Haixia pinglun* 海峽評論 (Cross-Strait Review), no. 24 (December 1992): 94–96.

Jiang Jieshi 蔣介石. "Wanlian" 輓聯 (Elegiac Couplet). In *Hu Shi boshi jinian jikan* 胡適博士紀念集刊 (Collected Papers to Commemorate Dr. Hu Shi), edited by Cheng Jingyu 程靖宇, 62–65. Hong Kong: Duli luntanshe, 1962.

Jiang Qi 姜琦. "Xin wenhua yundong he jiaoyu" 新文化運動和教育 (The New Culture Movement and Education). *Jiefang yu gaizao* 解放與改造 (Emancipation and Reconstruction) 2, no. 5 (March 1, 1920): 88–95.

Jiang Weishui 蔣渭水. *Jiang Weishui quanji* 蔣渭水全集 (Collected Works of Jiang Weishui). Edited by Wang Xiaobo 王曉波. Vol. 2. Taibei: Haixia xueshu chubanshe, 1998.

Jiang Weishui 蔣渭水. *Jiang Weishui quanji zengdingban* 蔣渭水全集增訂版 (Collected Works of Jiang Weishui, Revised and Expanded Edition). Edited by Wang Xiaobo 王曉波. Vol. xia. Taibei: Haixia xueshu chubanshe, 2005.

"Jiang Zhe zhi jinian guochi yu zheng Qingdao" 江浙之紀念國恥與爭青島 (Jiangsu's and Zhejiang's Commemoration of the National Disgrace and Fight for Qingdao). *Shenbao* 申報 (Shanghai News). May 11, 1919, 7. Shanghai.

Jiangsu sheng jiaoyuhui 江蘇省教育會. "Cheng jiaoyu zongzhang zuzhi Zhonghua xin jiaoyushe wen" 呈教育總長組織中華新教育社文 (Petition to the Minister of Education Regarding the Foundation of the Chinese New-Education Society). *Jiangsu sheng jiaoyuhui yuebao* 江蘇省教育會月報 (Jiangsu Educational Association Monthly Report), January 1919, 2.

Jiangsu sheng jiaoyuhui 江蘇省教育會. "Cheng Qi shengzhang chenshu taolun xuechao hou jiuji fangfa wen" 呈齊省長陳述討論學潮後救濟方法文 (Petition to Provincial Governor Qi, Reporting about the Discussions on Rescue Methods after the Student Protests). *Jiangsu sheng jiaoyuhui yuebao* 江蘇省教育會月報 (Jiangsu Educational Association Monthly Report), September 1919, 6–7.

Jiangsu sheng jiaoyuhui 江蘇省教育會. "Fu yanshuo jingjinhui jianze" 附演說競進會簡則 (Attachment: Regulations for the Speech Competition). *Jiangsu sheng jiaoyuhui yuebao* 江蘇省教育會月報 (Jiangsu Educational Association Monthly Report), March 1918, 7–8.

Jiangsu sheng jiaoyuhui 江蘇省教育會. *Jiangsu sheng jiaoyu hui yuebao* 江蘇省教育會月報 (Jiangsu Educational Association Monthly Report), 1919.

Jiangsu sheng jiaoyuhui 江蘇省教育會. "Kaihui jilu" 開會紀錄 (Meeting Minutes). *Jiangsu sheng jiaoyuhui yuebao* 江蘇省教育會月報 (Jiangsu Educational Association Monthly Report), May 1919, 20–25.

Jiangsu sheng jiaoyuhui 江蘇省教育會. "Kaihui jilu" 開會紀錄 (Meeting Minutes). *Jiangsu sheng jiaoyuhui yuebao* 江蘇省教育會月報 (Jiangsu Educational Association Monthly Report), June 1919, 15–18.

Jiangsu sheng jiaoyuhui 江蘇省教育會. "Kaihui jilu" 開會紀錄 (Meeting Minutes). *Jiangsu sheng jiaoyuhui yuebao* 江蘇省教育會月報 (Jiangsu Educational Association Monthly Report), October 1919, 41–47.

Jiangsu sheng jiaoyuhui 江蘇省教育會. "Yanshuo jingjinhui bisai jishi" 演說競進會比賽紀事 (Record of the Contest of the Speech Competition). *Jiangsu sheng jiaoyuhui yuebao* 江蘇省教育會月報 (Jiangsu Educational Association Monthly Report), December 1918, 10–12.

Jiangsu sheng jiaoyuhui 江蘇省教育會. "Zhi da zongtong, guowuyuan, jiaoyubu chenming Shanghai ge xiao xuesheng yin jiaoyu zongzhang yiren deng wenti qun yi bake, qing fuxun yuqing dian" 致大總統、國務院、教育部陳明上海各校學生因教育總長易人等問題群議罷課，請俯順輿情電 (Telegram to the President, the Cabinet and the Ministry of Education, Explaining That the Students of All Schools in Shanghai Have Gone on Strike, due to Questions such as the Replacement of the Minister of Education, Etc., and Asking to Succumb to Public Sentiment). *Jiangsu sheng jiaoyuhui yuebao* 江蘇省教育會月報 (Jiangsu Educational Association Monthly Report), May 1919, 10.

Jiangsu sheng jiaoyuhui 江蘇省教育會. "Zhi da zongtong, guowuyuan qing duiyu Qingdao jiaoshe reng dian zhuanshi kangyi dian" 致大總統、國務院請對於青島交涉仍電專使抗議電 (Telegram to the President and the Cabinet, Asking to Intervene in the Qingdao [Question], and Send a Telegram to the Special Envoy [in Paris] Letting Him Resist). *Jiangsu sheng jiaoyuhui yuebao* 江蘇省教育會月報 (Jiangsu Educational Association Monthly Report), June 1919, 10–11.

Jiangsu sheng jiaoyuhui 江蘇省教育會. "Zhi ge zhongdeng xuexiao qing tongzhi xuesheng yu shujiaqi nei zuzhi jiangyantuan shu" 致各中等學校請通知學生於暑假期內組織講演團書 (Letter to All Middle Schools, Asking to Inform the Students to Form Lecture Corps during the Summer Holidays). *Jiangsu sheng jiaoyuhui yuebao* 江蘇省教育會月報 (Jiangsu Educational Association Monthly Report), May 1919, 13–14.

Jiangsu sheng jiaoyuhui 江蘇省教育會. "Zhi Mei zongtong, Mei guohui, Ying, Fa shouxiang, ji Ying, Fa guohui qing zhuchi gongdao dian" 致美總統、美國會、英、法首相、及英、法國會請主持公道電 (Telegram to the US President, the US Congress, the Prime Ministers of Britain and France, the Parliaments of Britain and France, Asking to Uphold Justice). *Jiangsu sheng jiaoyuhui yuebao* 江蘇省教育會月報 (Jiangsu Educational Association Monthly Report), June 1919, 1.

Jiangsu sheng jiaoyuhui 江蘇省教育會. "Zhi zhongdeng yishang ge xuexiao tongzhi dingqi juxing yanshuo jingjinhui shu" 致中等以上各學校通知定期舉行演說競進會書 (Letter to All [Educational Institutions] from Middle-School Level and Above, Informing Them That a Date Has Been Chosen to Conduct the Lecture Competition). *Jiangsu sheng jiaoyuhui yuebao* 江蘇省教育會月報 (Jiangsu Educational Association Monthly Report), October 1919, 18–21.

Jiangsu sheng jiaoyuhui 江蘇省教育會. "Zhi zhongdeng yishang xuexiao paiyuan daohui shu" 致中等以上學校派員到會書 (Letter to Schools of a Higher Level than Middle [Schools, Instructing Them] to Send People to the Conference). *Jiangsu sheng jiaoyuhui yuebao* 江蘇省教育會月報 (Jiangsu Educational Association Monthly Report), June 1919, 7–8.

"Jiangsu zhongdeng yishang xuexiao jiaoyu yanjiuhui zhi yijue'an" 江蘇中等以上學校教育研究會之議決案 (Resolution of the Educational Research Conference for Schools in Jiangsu of a Middle Level and above). *Shenbao* 申報 (Shanghai News). August 20, 1919, 10. Shanghai.

Jiaoyubu 教育部. "Tongsu jiaoyu jiangyan guize" 通俗教育講演規則 (Regulations on Lectures for Popular Education). In *Zhonghua minguo jiaoyu fagui xuanbian* 中華民國教育法規選編 (Anthology of Education Laws and Regulations of the Republic of China), edited by Song Enrong 宋恩榮 and Zhang Xian 章咸, 533. Nanjing: Jiangsu jiaoyu chubanshe, 2005.

"Jijinhui dashiji ji Jiang Weishui xiangguan jinian huodong" 基金會大事記及蔣渭水相關紀念活動 (A Record of Great Events of the Foundation and Remembrance Activities for Jiang Weishui). *Jiang weishui wenhua jijinhui* 蔣渭水文化基金會 (Chiang Wei-Shui's Cultural Foundation). Accessed September 18, 2015. http://weishui.org/index-22.html.

Jilin sheng jiaoyu xueyuan 吉林省教育學院, ed. *Gaozhong lishi fuxi ziliao* 高中歷史複習資料 (Revision Material for History at Senior High Schools). Changchun: Jilin renmin chubanshe, 1979.

"Jimo Xu sheng" 寂寞徐生 (Lonely Scholar Xu). *Shenbao* 申報 (Shanghai News). February 20, 1921, 14. Shanghai.

"'Jin Henghui zhuanlan': Ma Yingjiu qiangbao Jiang Weishui! Weisui." 《金恆煒專欄》馬英九強暴蔣渭水！未遂。 ("Jin Henghui Column": Ma Ying-Jeou Rapes Jiang Weishui! Failed.). *Ziyou shibao* 自由時報 (Liberty Times Net), July 14, 2007. http://talk.ltn.com.tw/article/paper/141346.

Jing Guan 靜觀. "Beijing daxue xin jiu zhi anchao" 北京大學新舊之暗潮 (The Latent Trends of Old and New at Beijing University). *Shenbao* 申報 (Shanghai News). March 6, 1919, 6. Shanghai.

Jing Guan 靜觀. "Dumen xuejie xiaoxi" 都門學界消息 (News from Academia in the Capital). *Shenbao* 申報 (Shanghai News). November 5, 1919, 6. Shanghai.

Jing Guan 靜觀. "Gao xin wenhua yundong de tongzhi" 告新文化運動的同志 (To the Comrades of the New Culture Movement). *Xin funü* 新婦女 (New Woman) 1, no. 2 (1920): 31–33.

"Jing xuejie jin xun" 京學界近訊 (Recent News from Academia in Beijing). *Shenbao* 申報 (Shanghai News). August 11, 1919, 6–7. Shanghai.

"Jing xuejie you fasheng da wenti: Beijing daxue xiaozhang chuzou" 京學界又發生大問題：北京大學校長出走 (Big Problem Happens Again in Beijing's Academia: The Chancellor of Beijing University Walks out). *Dagongbao* 大公報 (Impartial). May 15, 1919, 3. Changsha.

"Jing xuejie zhi zuijin xiaoxi" 京學界之最近消息 (Most Recent News from Academia in Beijing). *Shenbao* 申報 (Shanghai News). May 18, 1919, 7. Shanghai.

"Jing xuejie zhi zuijin xingdong" 京學界之最近行動 (Latest Events in Beijing's Academia). *Shenbao* 申報 (Shanghai News). May 27, 1919, 7. Shanghai.

"Jinghua duanjian" 京華短簡 (Short Letters from the Capital). *Shenbao* 申報 (Shanghai News). March 31, 1919, 7. Shanghai.

"Jinghua duanjian" 京華短簡 (Short Letters from the Capital). *Shenbao* 申報 (Shanghai News). April 5, 1919, 7. Shanghai.

"Jinian Makesi danchen, zhanlanhui zuori zai shoudu kaimu" 紀念馬克思誕辰，展覽會昨日在首都開幕 (Remembering the Birth of Marx, Opening of the Exhibition Yesterday in the Capital). *Renmin ribao* 人民日報 (People's Daily). May 6, 1958, 4. Beijing.

Jun Shi 君實. "Guoji zhuyi yu minzhuzhuyi zhi duikang" 過激主義與民主主義之對抗 (The Antagonism of Extremism and Democracy). *Dongfang zazhi* 東方雜誌 (Eastern Miscellany) 16, no. 8 (1919): 105–10.

"Juxing yundonghui" 舉行運動會 (Conducting a Sports Festival). *Dalubao* 大陸報 (Mainland News), no. 5 (1904): 72–73.

Kang Baiqing 康白情. "Lun Zhongguo zhi minzu qizhi" 論中國之民族氣質 (On the Disposition of the Chinese Nation). In *Xichao* 新潮 (New Tide), 1:211–58, 1966.

Kaske, Elisabeth. *The Politics of Language in Chinese Education, 1895–1919*. Leiden: Brill, 2008.

Khuri-Makdisi, Ilham. *The Eastern Mediterranean and the Making of Global Radicalism, 1860–1914*. Berkeley: University of California Press, 2010.

Koo Z. C., and Chang S. L. "This 'Chest Protector' Newly Invented in America ...." *Yingyu zhoubao* 英語週刊 (English Language Weekly), no. 154 (1918): 1172.

Koselleck, Reinhart. "Begriffsgeschichte and Social History." Translated by Keith Tribe. *Economy and Society* 11, no. 4 (November 1982): 409–27.

Koselleck, Reinhart. *Futures Past: On the Semantics of Historical Time*. Cambridge, Massachusetts: MIT Press, 1985.

Koselleck, Reinhart. *Keywords: A Vocabulary of Culture and Society*. London: Croom Helm, 1976.

Kuang Seng 匡僧. "Daxue jiaoyuan wuyang" 大學教員無恙 (University Professors Safe). *Shishi xinbao* 時事新報 (China Times). March 7, 1919, 3.3. Shanghai.

Kurzman, Charles. *The Unthinkable Revolution in Iran*. Cambridge, Massachusetts: Harvard University Press, 2004.

Lamley, Steven. "Taiwan under Japanese Rule, 1895–1945: The Vicissitudes of Colonialism." In *Taiwan: A New History*, edited by Murray A. Rubinstein, 201–60. Armonk, N.Y: M.E. Sharpe, 2007.

Lams, Lutgard, and Xavier Li-wen Liao. "Tracing 'Taiwanization' Processes in Taiwanese Presidential Statements in Times." *Journal of Current Chinese Affairs* 40, no. 1 (2011): 63–98.

Lanza, Fabio. *Behind the Gate: Inventing Students in Beijing*. New York: Columbia University Press, 2010.

Lanza, Fabio. "Of Chronology, Failure, and Fidelity: When Did the May Fourth Movement End?" *Twentieth-Century China* 38, no. 1 (January 2013): 53–70.

"Laodongjie zhi jiaxin yundong" 勞働界之加薪運動 (The Pay-Rise Movement of the Workers' World). *Shenbao* 申報 (Shanghai News), October 17, 1919, 11.

Lary, Diana. "Warlord Studies." *Modern China* 6, no. 4 (October 1980): 439–70.

Lebow, Richard Ned. *Forbidden Fruit: Counterfactuals and International Relations*. Princeton: Princeton University Press, 2010.

Lebow, Richard Ned. "Learning from Contingency: The Case of World War I." *International Journal* 63, no. 2 (2008): 447–59.

Lee, Leo Ou-fan. "Incomplete Modernity: Rethinking the May Fourth Intellectual Project." In *The Appropriation of Cultural Capital: China's May Fourth Project*, edited by Milena Doleželová-Velingerová and Oldřich Král, 31–65. Cambridge, Massachusetts: Harvard University Asia Center, 2001.

Lee, Leo Ou-fan., ed. *Lu Xun and His Legacy*. Berkeley: University of California Press, 1985.

Lee, Leo Ou-fan, and Merle Goldman. *An Intellectual History of Modern China*. Cambridge: Cambridge University Press, 2002.

Lee, Nelson K. "How Is a Political Public Space Made? – The Birth of Tiananmen Square and the May Fourth Movement." *Political Geography* 28, no. 1 (January 2009): 32–43.

Leese, Daniel. "'Revolution': Conceptualizing Political and Social Change in the Late Qing Dynasty." *Oriens Extremus*, no. 51 (2012): 25–61.

Legge, James. *The Chinese Classics*. Vol. 1. Hong Kong: Hong Kong University Press, 1960.

Legge, James. *The Chinese Classics*. 2nd ed. Vol. 4: The She King. Taibei: SMC Publishing Inc, 1991.

Lew, T. T. "China's Renaissance." In *China to-Day through Chinese Eyes*, 2nd ed. London: Student Christian Movement, 1922.

Li, Cheng. "My Reflections and Querries [Sic] on the Question of the Creation of the Chinese Imaginative Literature of Interest to Non Chinese." Examination paper, 22.1.24. Container 221. Lewis Nathaniel Chase Papers, Manuscript Division, Library of Congress, Washington, D.C.

Li, Chun 李純. "Nanjing Li dujun geng dian" 南京李督軍庚電 (Telegram of the 8th [of June 1919] from Military Governor Li in Nanjing). In *Yan Xishan dang'an* 閻錫山檔案 (Yan Xishan Papers), edited by Qingfen Lin 林清芬, 5:58–59. Taibei: Guoshiguan, 2003.

Li Da 李達. *Hu Shi fandong sixiang pipan* 胡適反動思想批判 (A Criticism of Hu Shi's Reactionary Thought). Wuhan: Hubei renmin chubanshe, 1955.

Li Dazhao 李大釗. "Funü jiefang yu Democracy" 婦女解放與 Democracy (The Liberation of Women and Democracy). *Shaonian zhongguo* 少年中國 (Young China) 1, no. 4 (October 15, 1919): 27–32.

Li Dazhao 李大釗. "'Shaonian zhongguo' de 'shaonian yundong'" 《少年中國》的《少年運動》 (Young China's "Movement of the Young"). *Shaonian zhongguo* 少年中國 (Young China) 1, no. 3 (September 15, 1919): 1–3.

Li Fan 李帆. "Liu Shipei yu Beijing daxue" 劉師培與北京大學 (Liu Shipei and Beijing University). *Beijing daxue xuebao (Zhexue shehui kexueban)* 北京大學學報（哲學社會科學版）

(Journal of Peking University [Humanities and Social Sciences Edition]) 38, no. 6 (2001): 108–18.

Li, Huaiyin. "Between Tradition and Revolution: Fan Wenlan and the Origins of Marxist Historiography of Modern China." *Modern China* 36, no. 3 (May 2010): 269–301.

Li Jinxi 黎錦熙, ed. "Duyin tongyihui Zhili daibiao Wang Pu deng cheng jiaoyubu qing banxing zhuyin zimu wen" 讀音統一會直隸代表王璞等呈教育部請頒行注音字母文 (Petition to the Ministry of Education from Wang Pu, Etc., Representative of the Commission for the Unification of Pronunciation, Requesting the Promotion of Bopomofo). In *Guoyuxue jiangyi* 國語學講義 (Lecture Notes on the Study of the National Language). Shanghai: Shangwu yinshuguan, 1919.

Li Jinxi 黎錦熙, ed. *Guoyu yundong shigang* 國語運動史綱 (A Survey of the National-Language Movement). Beijing: Shangwu yinshuguan, 2011.

Li Jinxi 黎錦熙, ed. *Guoyuxue jiangyi* 國語學講義 (Lecture Notes on the Study of the National Language). Shanghai: Shangwu yinshuguan, 1919.

Li Longgeng 李隆庚, ed. *Zhongguo lishi* 中國歷史 (Chinese History). Vol. 3. Beijing: Renmin jiaoyu chubanshe, 1987.

Li Qingfang 李慶芳. "Beijing Li Fenpu qing dian" 北京李芬圃青電 (Telegram of the 9th [of May 1919] from Li Fenpu in Beijing). In *Yan Xishan dang'an* 閻錫山檔案 (Yan Xishan Papers), edited by Lin Qingfen 林清芬, 5:12–14. Taibei: Guoshiguan, 2003.

Li Quan 李泉. *Fu Sinian xueshu sixiang pingzhuan* 傅斯年學術思想評傳 (A Critical Biography of the Scholarship and Thought of Fu Sinian). Beijing: Beijing tushuguan chubanshe, 1999.

Li Ruihuan 李瑞環. "Jianchi zhengmian xuanchuan wei zhu de fangzhen: zai xinwen gongzuo yantaoban shang de jianghua (1989 nian 11 yue 25 ri)" 堅持正面宣傳為主的方針：在新聞工作研討班上的講話（1989年11月25日） (The Policy of Emphasizing the Continuation of Direct Propaganda: A Talk at the News Work Study and Discussion Class [25 November 1989]). *Renmin ribao* 人民日報 (People's Daily). March 3, 1990, 1. Beijing.

Li Xiaofeng 李小峰. "Xinchaoshe de shimo" 新潮社的始末 (Beginning and End of the New Tide Society). In *Wu si yundong huiyilu xu* 五四運動回憶錄續 (Records of Memories of the May Fourth Movement, Part Two), edited by Zhongguo shehui kexueyuan jindaishi yanjiusuo 中國社會科學院近代史研究所, 200–242. Beijing: Zhongguo shehui kexue chubanshe, 1979.

Li Xin 李新. "Xu" 序 (Preface). In *Hu Shi zhuan* 胡適傳 (A Biography of Hu Shi), by Bai Ji 白吉庵, 1–4. Changsha: Hunan jiaoyu chubanshe, 1987.

Li Yong 李勇. "Qishi'er sui Hu furen de shangxin" 七十二歲胡夫人的傷心 (The Grief of Seventy-Two-Year Old Mrs Hu). In *Hu Shi boshi jinian jikan* 胡適博士紀念集刊 (Collected Papers to Commemorate Dr. Hu Shi), edited by Cheng Jingyu 程靖宇, 62–64. Hong Kong: Duli luntanshe, 1962.

Li Yuanxiu 李元秀, and Wu Di 武迪, eds. *Shijie quanshi* 世界全史 (World History). Vol. 41. Beijing: Junshi yiwen chubanshe, 2006.

Lian Qing 廉情. "Taiwan yihui shezhi qingyuan weiyuan shang Jing" 台灣議會設置請願委員上京 (The Representatives of the Taiwan Parliament Petition [Movement] Go to Tokyo). *Taiwan minbao* 臺灣民報 (Taiwan People's News). June 21, 1924, 2. Tokyo.

Liang Shu 梁淑安. "Zhang Yuanji" 張元濟 (Zhang Yuanji). *Zhongguo wenxuejia da cidian* 中國文學家大辭典 (Great Dictionary of Chinese Writers). Beijing: Zhonghua shuju, 1997. Beijing.

Liang Yiqun 梁義群. "Duan Qirui" 段祺瑞 (Duan Qirui). Edited by Qu Lindong 瞿林東. *Zhongguo zhongxue jiaoxue baike quanshu* 中國中學教學百科全書 (Chinese Middle-School Teaching Encyclopedia). Shenyang: Shenyang chubanshe, 1991. Shenyang.

"Lianhe yundong" 聯合運動 (Joint Sports). *Sichuan guanbao* 四川官報 (Sichuan Official News), no. 29 (1905): 36.

Lin Cizhou 林慈舟. "Gaizheng Taiwan difang zhidu gailun (shang)" 改正臺灣地方制度概論（上）(Outline of the Reform of Taiwan's Local System [One]). *Taiwan qingnian* 臺灣青年 (Taiwan Youth) 1, no. 4 (1920): 1–2.

Lin, Diana. *Peking University: Chinese Scholarship and Intellectuals, 1898–1937*. Albany: State University of New York, 2005.

Lin Shu 林紓. "Da daxuetang xiaozhang Cai Heqing taishi shu" 答大學堂校長蔡鶴卿太史書 (Reply to the Chancellor of the University, Hanlin Scholar Cai Heqing). In *Lin Shu wenxuan* 林紓文選 (Selected Works of Lin Shu), edited by Xu Guiting 許桂亭, 106–12. Tianjin: Baihua wenyi chubanshe, 2006.

Lin Shu 林紓. "Jing sheng" 荊生 (Scholar Jing). In *Canchun* 殘春 (Last Days of Spring), edited by Zhang Ren 張韌, 212–13. Changchun: Jilin shying chubanshe, 1996.

Lin, Shu. "Nightmare." In *Modern Chinese Literary Thought: Writings on Literature, 1893–1945*, edited by Kirk A. Denton, translated by Timothy Wong, 146–50. Stanford, 1996.

Lin Shu 林紓. "Yaomeng" 妖夢 (Nightmare). In *Canchun* 殘春 (Last Days of Spring), edited by Zhang Ren 張韌, 214–16. Changchun: Jilin shying chubanshe, 1996.

Lin, Yü-sheng. *The Crisis of Chinese Consciousness: Radical Antitraditionalism in the May Fourth Era*. Madison: University of Wisconsin Press, 1979.

Lin, Yutang. *A History of the Press and Public Opinion in China*. Chicago: University of Chicago Press, 1936.

"Linian yanchu jilu" 歷年演出記錄 (Record of Past Performances). *Weishui chunfeng – Yinyue shidai* 渭水春風——音樂時代 (The Impossible Times – All Music Theatre), November 22, 2011. http://impossibletimes.allmusic.com.tw/archive.htm.

"Liqing Guomindang 'lianjie' Jiang Weishui de miulun" 釐清國民黨「連結」蔣渭水的謬論 (Clarifying the Absurdity of the GMD's [Attempt] at Linking up with Jiang Weishui). *Ziyou shibao* 自由時報 (Liberty Times Net), July 11, 2007. http://talk.ltn.com.tw/article/paper/140799.

Lishi 歷史 (History). Vol. 1. Nanyi shuju, 2012.

Lishi 歷史 (History). Vol. 3. Nanyi shuju, 2013.

Liu Boming 劉伯明. "Xuesheng yingyou de taidu ji jingshen" 學生應有的態度及精神 (The Attitude and Spirit Students Should Have). *Xuesheng* 學生 (Students' Magazine) 7, no. 9 (September 5, 1920): 1–3.

Liu Fanggang 劉芳剛. "Xuezhe yu siji" 學者與司機 (The Scholar and the Driver). In *Hu Shizhi xiansheng jinianji* 胡適之先生紀念集 (Commemorative Volume for Mr. Hu Shizhi), edited by Feng Aiqun 馮愛群, 65–67. Taibei: Xuesheng chubanshe, 1962.

Liu Jianming 劉建明, ed. "Dagong bao" 大公報 (Impartial). *Xuanchuan yulunxue da cidian* 宣傳輿論學大辭典 (Great Dictionary of the Study of Propaganda and Public Opinion). Beijing: Jingji ribao chubanshe, 1993. Beijing.

Liu Jingquan 劉景泉. *Beijing minguo zhengfu, yihui, zhengzhi yanjiu* 北京民國政府、議會、政治研究 (Research on Government, Parliament and the Politics of the Beijing Republic). Tianjin: Tianjin jiaoyu chubanshe, 2006.

Liu Kedi 劉克敵. *Hua luo chun reng zai: Wu Mi yu "Xueheng"* 花落春仍在：吳宓與《學衡》(The Flowers Have Wilted but Spring Is Still There: Wu Mi and the *Critical Review*). Beijing: Zhongguo wenlian chubanshe, 2001.

Liu, Lydia. *Translingual Practice: Literature, National Culture, and Translated Modernity – China, 1900–1937*. Stanford: Stanford University Press, 1995.

Liu, Lydia He, Dorothy Ko, and Rebecca E. Karl, eds. *The Birth of Chinese Feminism: Essential Texts in Transnational Theory*. New York: Columbia University Press, 2013.

Liu, Qian. "Creative Translation and Creativity via Translation: The Transformation of Emotional Expression in Early Modern Chinese Fiction (1900–1925)." PhD, University of Oxford, 2013.

Liu Shipei 劉師培. "Liu Shipei zhi Gongyanbao han" 劉師培致公言報函 (Letter by Liu Shipei to the *Public Voice*). *Beijing daxue rikan* 北京大學日刊 (Beijing University Daily). March 24, 1919, 6. Beijing.

Liu, Taotao. "Conversation with the author," June 25, 2014.

Liu, Taotao. "E-mail message to the author," June 22, 2014.

Liu, Te Yuan. "The Educational Value of Chinese Character Writing." Student essay, n.d. Container 219. Lewis Nathaniel Chase Papers, Manuscript Division, Library of Congress, Washington, D.C.

Liu Tingfang 劉廷芳. "Xin wenhua yundong zhong jidujiao xuanjiaoshi de zeren (xu)" 新文化運動中基督教宣教師的責任 （續) (The Duty of Christian Missionaries in the New Culture Movement [Continued]). *Xinghua* 興華 (Chinese Christian Advocate) 18, no. 24 (June 22, 1921): 1–19.

Liu Weijian 劉偉見. "Shidai huhuan da bianji" 時代呼喚大編輯 (Great Edition of an Epoch's Call). *Renmin ribao* 人民日報 (People's Daily). January 4, 2009, 8. Beijing.

"Liu Xiaobo" 劉曉波 (Liu Xiaobo). *Lingba xianzhang* 零八憲章 (Charter 08). Accessed November 11, 2015. http://www.2008xianzhang.info/000-xiaobo--liebiao.php.

Livingston Schuyler, Robert. "Contingency in History." *Political Science Quarterly* 74, no. 3 (September 1959): 321–33.

Luo Jialun 羅家倫. "Jinri Zhongguo de zazhijie" 今日中國的雜誌界 (The Chinese World of Magazines Today). In *Xinchao* 新潮 (New Tide), 2:73–82. Minguo zhenxi qikan 民國珍稀期刊 (Valuable Republican Journals). Beijing: Quanguo tushuguan wenxian suowei fuzhi zhongxin, 2006.

Luo Jialun 羅家倫. "'Wu si yundong' de jingshen" "五四運動"的精神 (The Spirit of the "May Fourth Movement"). In *Minguo shiqi mingren tan wu si: lishi jiyi yu lishi jieshi* 民國時期名人談五四：歷史記憶與歷史解釋（1919–1949） (Famous People of the Republican Period Talk about May Fourth: Historical Reminiscences and Historical Explanations), edited by Yang Hu 楊琥, 78–79. Fuzhou: Fujian jiaoyu chubanshe, 2011.

Luo Zhitian 羅志田. "Xin wenhua yundong shiqi guanyu zhengli guogu de sixiang lunzheng" 新文化運動時期關於整理國故的思想論爭 (Intellectual Debates about "Tidying up China's National Heritage" in the Period of the New Culture Movement). In *Guojia yu xueshu: Qingji minchu guanyu "guoxue" de sixiang lunzheng* 國家與學術：清季民初關於"國學"的思想論爭 (Country and Scholarship: Intellectual Debates on "National Learning" at the End of the Qing and in the Early Republic). Beijing: Shenghui dushu xinzhi sanlian shudian, 2003.

MacKinnon, Stephen R. "Toward a History of the Chinese Press in the Republican Period." *Modern China* 23, no. 1 (January 1997): 3–32.

MacNair, Harley Farnsworth. "Review of *The Chinese Renaissance* by Hu Shih." *American Journal of Sociology* 41, no. 3 (November 1935): 389.

Malong Maiyuke 馬龍麥雨柯. "Nüzi fayu shidai zhi yundong" 女子發育時代之運動 (Exercises for Women during Puberty). Translated by Diao Jun 調均. *Funü zazhi* 婦女雜誌 (Ladies' Magazine), no. 1 (January 5, 1915): 16.

Manela, Erez. *The Wilsonian Moment: Self-Determination and the International Origins of Anti-colonial Nationalism*. Oxford: Oxford University Press, 2007.

"Mangtong xuexiao dingqi youyi yundong" 盲童學校定期游藝運動 (The Blind Children's School Has Scheduled a Recreation Movement). *Shenbao* 申報 (Shanghai News), December 11, 1919, 10.

Manuscript Division. "Biographical and Organizational Note: Lewis Nathaniel Chase." *A Finding Aid to the Collection in the Library of Congress*, 2012. http://findingaids.loc.gov.

Mao, Zedong. "On New Democracy (January 15, 1940)." In *Mao's Road to Power: Revolutionary Writings 1912–1949*, edited by Stuart Schram and Nancy J. Hodes, 7:330–69. Armonk, N.Y.: M.E. Sharpe, 2005.

Mao, Zedong. "The May Fourth Movement (May 1939)." In *Mao's Road to Power: Revolutionary Writings 1912–1949*, edited by Stuart Schram and Nancy J. Hodes, 7:66–68. Armonk, N.Y.: M.E. Sharpe, 2005.

Mao Zedong 毛澤東. "Xin minzhu zhuyi lun" 新民主主義論 (On New Democracy). In *Mao Zedong ji* 毛澤東集 (Collected Writings of Mao Zedong), edited by Takeuchi Minoru 竹内実, 147–206. New York: Tianwai chubanshe, 1998.

Mao Zishui 毛子水. "'Bo Xinchao "Guogu he kexue de jingshen" pian' dingwu" 《駁新潮〈國故和科學的精神〉篇》訂誤 (Corrections of "Against the Article 'the *National Heritage* and the Scientific Spirit' in the *New Tide*"). *Xinchao* 新潮 (New Tide) 2, no. 1 (October 30, 1919): 37–57.

Mao Zishui 毛子水. "Guogu he kexue de jingshen" 國故和科學的精神 (The *National Heritage* and the Scientific Spirit). *Xinchao* 新潮 (New Tide) 5, no. 1 (January 5, 1919).

Mao Zishui 毛子水. "Guogu he kexue de jingshen" 國故和科學的精神 (The *National Heritage* and the Scientific Spirit). In *Xinchao* 新潮 (New Tide), 2:191–204. Beijing: Quanguo tushuguan wenxian suowei fuzhi zhongxin, 2006.

McCarthy, Peggy. "A Support for Students Who Grieve for China." *New York Times*. July 2, 1989, CN1, CN7. New York Times (1923-Current File). New York.

"Mei bao zhi Hanren yundong duli shuo" 美報之韓人運動獨立說 (American Newspapers on Koreans' Lobbying for Independence). *Shenbao* 申報 (Shanghai News). March 13, 1919, 6. Shanghai.

Mei Feuerwerker, Yi-tsi. *Ideology, Power, Text: Self-Representation and the Peasant "Other" in Modern Chinese Literature*. Stanford: Stanford University Press, 1998.

Mei Feuerwerker, Yi-tsi. "Reconsidering Xueheng: Neo-Conservatism in Republican China." In *Literary Societies Of Republican China*, edited by Michel Hockx and Kirk A. Denton, 137–70. Plymoth: Lexington Books, 2008.

"Meiguo nü xiaoshuojia Shituhuo furen xiaoying" 美國女小說家施土活夫人小影 (A Photo of the Female American Writer Mrs. Stowe). *Shenbao* 申報 (Shanghai News). April 10, 1921, 14. Shanghai.

"Meiren you lai yundong zhengfu" 美人又來運動政府 (The Americans Again Lobby the Government). *Di-yi Jin huabao* 第一晉話報 (The First Shanxi Dialect Newspaper), no. 3 (1905): 39.

Meisner, Maurice J. *Li Ta-Chao and the Origins of Chinese Marxism*. Cambridge, Massachusetts: Harvard University Press, 1967.

Meng Xianli 孟憲勵. "Guotu zhanchu zhengui wu si wenxian" 國圖展出珍貴五四文獻 (The National Library Exhibits Precious May Fourth Documents). *Renmin ribao* 人民日報 (People's Daily). May 5, 1999, 5. Beijing.

Miao Jinyuan 繆金源. "Miao Jinyuan zhi Hu Shi" 繆金源致胡適 (Miao Jinyuan to Hu Shi). In *Hu Shi laiwang shuxinxuan* 胡適來往書信選 (Hu Shi's Selected Correspondence), 117–19. Beijing: Zhonghua shuju, 1979.

Miao Jinyuan 繆金源. "Suowei 'xin wenhua yundong' de chachao yu pochan" 所謂"新文化運動"的查抄與破產 (Confiscation and Bankruptcy of the So-Called "New Culture Movement"). *Piping* 批評 (Criticism). October 20, 1920, 3–4. Shanghai.

"Mimi zhi yundong" 秘密之運動 (Secret Movements). *Dalu (Shanghai 1902)* 大陸（上海 1902）(Mainland [Shanghai 1902]) 2, no. 8 (1904): 11–12.

"Mingri huanghua zhi dizhi yundong ji" 明日黃花之帝制運動記 (A Record of the Obsolete Monarchy Movement). *Xuesheng* 學生 (Student) 3, no. 9 (1916): 1–4.

Mitter, Rana. *A Bitter Revolution: China's Struggle with the Modern World*. Oxford: Oxford University Press, 2004.

Mitter, Rana, and Micah S. Muscolino. "Further Subject: China since 1900 (History Faculty of the University of Oxford : Reading List)." Oxford, 2015. Oxford.

Mittler, Barbara. *A Newspaper for China?: Power, Identity, and Change in Shanghai's News Media, 1872–1912*. Cambridge, Massachusetts: Harvard University Asia Center, 2004.

Moser, E. "Das heutige China" (China Today). *Schweizerische pädagogische Zeitschrift* (Swiss Pedagogical Journal) 33, no. 8 (1923): 229–37.

"Muci" 目次 (Table of Contents). *Xin xuesheng* 新學生 (New Student) 1, no. 1 (December 1919).

"Multiple Display Advertisements." *Times*. January 1, 1924, 18. The Times Digital Archive. London.

"Mulu" 目錄 (Table of Contents). *Guogu* 國故 (National Heritage), no. 3 (1919).

"My Reflections and Queries on the Subject of Revealing or Interpreting China and the Chinese to Non-China, by Means of Imaginative Literature." Examination paper, January 22, 1924. Container 221. Lewis Nathaniel Chase Papers, Manuscript Division, Library of Congress, Washington, D.C.

"Nanfang zhi guoqingri (Guangdong nan-nü xuesheng da yundonghui)" 南方之國慶日（廣東男女學生大運動會）(The National Holiday in the South [Great Sports Festival of Male and Female Students from Guangdong]). *Zhenxiang huabao* 真相畫報 (Truth Pictorial) 1, no. 10 (1912): 14.

Nathan, Andrew J. "A Constitutional Republic: The Peking Government, 1916–28." In *The Cambridge History of China*, 1st ed., 12:256–83. Cambridge: Cambridge Histories Online, 1983. http://universitypublishingonline.org/cambridge/histories/.

Nathan, Andrew J. *Peking Politics, 1918–1923: Factionalism and the Failure of Constitutionalism*. Berkeley, Calif.: University of California Press, 1976.

Neiwubu 內務部. "Beijing neiwubu hao dian" 北京內務部皓電 (Telegram of the 19th [of September 1919] from the Ministry for Internal Affairs in Beijing). In *Yan Xishan dang'an* 閻錫山檔案 (Yan Xishan Papers), edited by Qingfen Lin 林清芬, 5:86. Taibei: Guoshiguan, 2003.

Neiwubu 內務部, Lujunbu 陸軍部, and Jiaotongbu 交通部. "Beijing neiwubu, lujunbu, jiaotongbu dong dian" 北京內務部、陸軍部、交通部冬電 (Telegram of the 2nd [of December 1919] from the Ministry for Internal Affairs, the Army Ministry and the Ministry of Communications in Beijing). In *Yan Xishan dang'an* 閻錫山檔案 (Yan Xishan Papers), edited by Qingfen Lin 林清芬, 5:88–89. Taibei: Guoshiguan, 2003.

Niu, Minghua. "Letter to Emma Lester," May 9, 1933. Container 209. Lewis Nathaniel Chase Papers, Manuscript Division, Library of Congress, Washington, D.C.

Niu, Minghua. "Letter to Emma Lester," December 10, 1933. Container 209. Lewis Nathaniel Chase Papers, Manuscript Division, Library of Congress, Washington, D.C.
Niu, Minghua. "Letter to Emma Lester," February 28, 1934. Container 209. Lewis Nathaniel Chase Papers, Manuscript Division, Library of Congress, Washington, D.C.
Niu, Minghua. "Letter to Emma Lester," June 2, 1934. Container 209. Lewis Nathaniel Chase Papers, Manuscript Division, Library of Congress, Washington, D.C.
Niu, Minghua. "Letter to Emma Lester," July 23, 1937. Container 209. Lewis Nathaniel Chase Papers, Manuscript Division, Library of Congress, Washington, D.C.
North, Douglass C. *Institutions, Institutional Change and Economic Performance*. Cambridge: Cambridge University Press, 1996.
Ouyang Junxi 歐陽軍喜. "Guomindang yu xin wenhua yundong: yi 'Xingqi pinglun,' 'Jianshe' wei zhongxin" 國民黨與新文化運動：以《星期評論》、《建設》為中心 (The Nationalist Party and the New Culture Movement: With a Focus on *Weekly Review* and *Construction*). *Nanjing daxue xuebao* 南京大學學報 (Journal of Nanjing University), no. 1 (2009): 72–84.
P., J. "Review of *The Chinese Renaissance* by Hu Shih." *International Affairs* 14, no. 2 (1935): 288.
Pan Guangzhe 潘光哲, ed. *Rongren yu ziyou: Hu Shi sixiang jingxuan* 容忍與自由：胡適思想精選 (Tolerance and Freedom: An Anthology of Hu Shi's Thought). Taibei: Nanfang jiayuan wenhua chuban, 2009.
Pang Ju 龐菊愛. *Kua wenhua guanggao yu shimin wenhua de bianqian: 1910–1930 nian Shenbao kua-wenhua guanggao yanjiu* 跨文化廣告與市民文化的變遷：1910–1930年《申報》跨文化廣告研究 (Developments in Cross-Cultural Advertisement and Urbanites' Culture: Research on Cross-Cultural Advertisement in the *Shanghai News*, 1910–1930). Shanghai: Shanghai jiaotong daxue chubanshe, 2010.
Pantsov, Alexander. *The Bolsheviks and the Chinese Revolution, 1919–1927*. Richmond: Curzon, 2000.
Pei Xiaowei 裴效維. "Huang Kan" 黃侃 (Huang Kan). Edited by Ma Liangchun 馬良春 and Li Futian 李福田. *Zhongguo wenxue da cidian* 中國文學大辭典 (Great Dictionary of Chinese Literature). Tianjin: Tianjin renmin chubanshe, 1991. Tianjin.
Peng Ming 彭明. "Jianping 'Wu si shiqi qikan jieshao'" 簡評"五四時期期刊介紹" (A Review of *Periodicals of the May Fourth Era*). *Renmin ribao* 人民日報 (People's Daily). March 7, 1959, 7. Beijing.
Peng Peng 彭鵬. *Yanjiuxi yu wu si shiqi xin wenhua yundong: yi 1920 nian qianhou wei zhongxin* 研究系與五四時期新文化運動：以1920年前後為中心 (The Research Clique and the New Culture Movement in the May Fourth Period: With a Focus on the Time around the Year 1920). Guangzhou: Zhongshan daxue chubanshe, 2003.
Phillips, Steven. "Between Assimilation and Independence: Taiwanese Political Aspirations under Nationalist Chinese Rule, 1945–1949." In *Taiwan: A New History*, edited by Murray A. Rubinstein, 275–319. Armonk, N.Y: M.E. Sharpe, 2007.
Phillips, Steven E. *Between Assimilation and Independence: The Taiwanese Encounter Nationalist China, 1945–1950*. Stanford, California: Stanford University Press, 2003.
Pils, Eva, Jean-Philippe Béja, and Hualing Fu. "Introduction." In *Liu Xiaobo, Charter 08, and the Challenges of Political Reform in China*, edited by Jean-Philippe Béja and Hualing Fu, 1–12. Hong Kong: Hong Kong University Press, 2012.
Plaque at Fu Sinian Memorial Garden. Guoli Taiwan daxue 國立台灣大學, n.d. Accessed August 20, 2015.

"ProQuest Historical Newspapers: The Guardian and The Observer." Database, n.d. http://search.proquest.com/hnpguardianobserver.

"Pudong ge xiao zhi lianhe yundonghui" 浦東各校之聯合運動會 (The Joint Sports Festival of All Pudong Schools). *Shenbao* 申報 (Shanghai News), May 25, 1919, 12.

"Putong gaoji zhongxue yuwen ji shehui lingyu kecheng gangyao weitiao" 普通高級中學語文及社會領域課程綱要微調 (Fine tuning of the outline of the curriculum of the field of language and literature, as well as society for normal senior high schools), August 1, 2015. http://www.k12ea.gov.tw/ap/news_view.aspx?sn=324aa1ef-22c2-40a5-9f1d-86b3fd5f1f6e.

Pye, Lucian W. "Review of *A Bitter Revolution*." *Foreign Affairs*, November–December 2004.

Qi Yaolin 齊耀琳. "Qi shengzhang pi" 齊省長批 (Approval by Provincial Governor Qi). Edited by Jiangsu sheng jiaoyuhui 江蘇省教育會. *Jiangsu sheng jiaoyuhui yuebao* 江蘇省教育會月報 (Jiangsu Educational Association Monthly Report), September 1919, 9.

"Qian Dian zhi aiguo yundong" 黔滇之愛國運動 (Guizhou's and Yunnan's Patriotic Movements). *Shenbao* 申報 (Shanghai News). July 14, 1919, 6–7. Shanghai.

Qian Jian 淺見. "Jiake Gegen zhuyan xinming jiang kaiyan" 賈克哥根主演新明將開演 (Lead Actor Jackie Coogan Will Newly Star in a Movie). *Shenbao* 申報 (Shanghai News). September 5, 1924, 19. Shanghai.

"Qing kan Beijing xuejie sixiang chao bianqian zhi jinzhuang" 請看北京學界思想潮變迁之近狀 (Let's Have a Look at the Recent Changes in Intellectual Trends in Beijing's Academia). *Gongyanbao* 公言報 (Public Voice). March 18, 1919, 3, 6. Beijing.

"Qingdao ying jiaohuan Zhongguo zhi wailun" 青島應交還中國之外論 (External Opinions on [Why] Qingdao Should Be Returned to China). *Shenbao* 申報 (Shanghai News). May 8, 1919, 7. Shanghai.

"Qingnianhui zhongxue yudonghui yuji" 青年會中學運動會預紀 (Announcement of a Sports Festival of the Youth Association Middle School). *Shenbao* 申報 (Shanghai News), May 14, 1919, 11.

Qiu Changwei 邱昌渭. "Lun xin wenhua yundong (da Wu Mi jun)" 論新文化運動（答吳宓君） (A Discussion of the New Culture Movement [a Reply to Mr. Wu Mi]). *Liu Mei xuesheng jibao* 留美學生季報 (Chinese Students' Quarterly) 8, no. 4 (1921): 1–13.

Qiu Shihuang 邱沛篁, Wu Xinxun 吳信訓, and Xiang Chunwu 向純武, eds. "Jiefang yu gaizao" 解放與改造 (Emancipation and Reconstruction). *Xinwen chuanbo baike quanshu* 新聞傳播百科全書 (Encyclopedia of News and Broadcasting). Chengdu: Sichuan renmin chubanshe, 1998. Chengdu.

Qiu Shihuang 邱沛篁, Wu Xinxun 吳信訓, and Xiang Chunwu 向純武, eds. "Piping" 批評 (Criticism). *Xinwen chuanbo baike quanshu* 新聞傳播百科全書 (Encyclopedia of News and Broadcasting). Chengdu: Sichuan renmin chubanshe 向純武, 1998. Chengdu.

Qiu Shihuang 邱沛篁, Wu Xinxun 吳信訓, and Xiang Chunwu 向純武, eds. "Shenbao" 申報 (Shanghai News). *Xinwen chuanbo baike quanshu* 新聞傳播百科全書 (Encyclopedia of News and Broadcasting). Chengdu: Sichuan renmin chubanshe, 1998. Chengdu.

Qiu Shihuang 邱沛篁, Wu Xinxun 吳信訓, and Xiang Chunwu 向純武, eds. "Shishi xinbao" 時事新報 (China Times). *Xinwen chuanbo baike quanshu* 新聞傳播百科全書 (Encyclopedia of News and Broadcasting). Chengdu: Sichuan renmin chubanshe, 1998. Chengdu.

Qiu Shihuang 邱沛篁, Wu Xinxun 吳信訓, and Xiang Chunwu 向純武, eds. "Xueheng" 學衡 (Critical Review). *Xinwen chuanbo baike quanshu* 新聞傳播百科全書 (Encyclopedia of News and Broadcasting). Chengdu: Sichuan renmin chubanshe, 1998. Chengdu.

Quan Zhe 泉哲. "Taiwan zizhizhi ping" 臺灣自治制評 (An Assessment of Taiwan's System of Self-Government). *Taiwan qingnian* 臺灣青年 (Taiwan Youth) 1, no. 3 (February 12, 1920): 34–39.

Quanguo baokan suoyin 全國報刊索引 (National Index of Chinese Newspapers and Periodicals [Database]). Accessed January 8, 2013. http://www.cnbksy.com.

Quanguo baokan suoyin, qikan daohang 全國報刊索引，期刊導航 (National Index of Chinese Newspapers and Periodicals, Guide). Accessed August 1, 2013. http://www.cnbksy.com/shlib_tsdc/originNavSearch.do.

Quanguo jiaoyuhui lianhehui 全國教育會聯合會. "Qing ding guoyu biaozhun bing tuixing zhuyin zimu yiqi yuyan tongyi" 請定國語標準並推行注音字母以期語言統一 (Request for Determination of a Standard for the National Language and the Promotion of Bopomofo, so as to Unify the Language). In *Lijie jiaoyu huiyi yijue'an huibian* 歷屆教育會議議決案彙編 (Collection of the Resolutions of All Historical Meetings of the Educational Associations), edited by Tai Shuangqiu 邰爽秋, 12–13. Beijing: Quanguo tushuguan wenxian suowei zhongxin, 2010.

Quanguo jiaoyuhui lianhehui 全國教育會聯合會. "Tongyi guoyu fangfa'an" 統一國語方法案 (Motion for the Unification of the National Language). In *Lijie jiaoyu huiyi yijue'an huibian* 歷屆教育會議議決案彙編 (Collection of the Resolutions of All Historical Meetings of the Educational Associations), edited by Tai Shuangqiu 邰爽秋, 2–3. Beijing: Quanguo tushuguan wenxian suowei zhongxin, 2010.

"Quzhiminhua, cai neng fazhan Taiwan de zhutixing: lun Ma Yingjiu de Taiwan lishi lunshu" 去殖民化，才能展現出台灣的主體性：論馬英九的台灣歷史論述 (Only Decolonization Can Develop Taiwan's Subjectivity: Ma Ying-Jeou's Discourse on Taiwanese History). *Haixia pinglun* 海峽評論 (Cross-Strait Review), no. 178 (October 2005): 1–4.

Rahav, Shakhar. *The Rise of Political Intellectuals in Modern China: May Fourth Societies and the Roots of Mass-Party Politics*. New York: Oxford University Press, 2015.

"Read the *Shanghai Gazette*." *Moti* 墨梯 (McTyeirean), no. 3 (June 1919).

Ren Fangqiu 任訪秋. "Xu" 序 (Preface). In *Hu Shi zhuan* 胡適傳 (A Biography of Hu Shi), by Shen Weiwei 沈衛威, 1–8. Kaifeng: Henan daxue chubanshe, 1988.

"Review of *What China Wants* by A. M. Chirgwin." *North China Herald*. July 21, 1928, 130. Shanghai.

"Riben furen tongqinghui de zixha fangzhi yundong" 日本婦人同情會的自殺防止運動 (Suicide Prevention Movement of the Japanese Women's Sympathy Organization). *Funü zazhi* 婦女雜誌 (Ladies' Magazine) 7, no. 2 (February 5, 1921): 18.

Richter, Melvin. "Begriffsgeschichte and the History of Ideas." *Journal of the History of Ideas* 48, no. 2 (June 1987): 247–63.

Rosenbaum, Arthur Lewis. *New Perspectives on Yenching University, 1916–1952*. Leiden: Brill, 2012.

Rubinstein, Murray A., ed. *Taiwan: A New History*. Armonk, N.Y.: M.E. Sharpe, 2007.

Sahlins, Marshall. "Introduction [Islands of History] [1985]." In *Readings for a History of Anthropological Theory*, edited by Paul A Erickson and Liam D. Murphy, 188–95. Toronto: University of Toronto Press, 2010.

"Sailuonijia shimin zhi shiwei yundong" 塞羅尼加市民之示威運動 (The Demonstration Movement of Thessaloniki's Citizens). *Dongfang zazhi* 東方雜誌 (Eastern Miscellany) 12, no. 4 (1915): 11.

Sang, Bing. "The Divergence and Convergence of China's Written and Spoken Languages: Reassessing the Vernacular Language during the May Fourth Period." *Twentieth-Century China* 28, no. 1 (January 2013): 71–93.

Schneider, Axel. *Wahrheit und Geschichte: zwei chinesische Historiker auf der Suche nach einer modernen Identität für China* (Truth and History: Two Chinese Historians in Search of a Modern Identity for China). Wiesbaden: Harrassowitz, 1997.

Schwarcz, Vera. "A Curse on the Great Wall: The Problem of Enlightenment in Modern China." *Theory and Society* 13, no. 3 (May 1984): 455–70.

Schwarcz, Vera. "China: The Hard Road to Now." *New York Times*. May 13, 1990, BR1, BR32. New York Times (1923-Current File). New York.

Schwarcz, Vera. *The Chinese Enlightenment: Intellectuals and the Legacy of the May Fourth Movement of 1919*. Berkeley: University of California Press, 1986.

Schwarcz, Vera. *Time for Telling the Truth Is Running Out: Conversations with Zhang Shenfu*. New Haven: Yale University Press, 1992.

Schwartz, Benjamin Isadore. *In Search of Wealth and Power: Yen Fu and the West*. Cambridge: Belknap Press of Harvard University Press, 1964.

Se Lu 瑟廬. "Zuijin shi nian nei funü jie de huigu" 最近十年內婦女界的回顧 (Review of the World of Women of the Last Ten Years). *Funü zazhi* 婦女雜誌 (Ladies' Magazine), no. 1 (January 1, 1924): 16–22.

Semanov, Vladimir Ivanovich, and Charles J. Alber. *Lu Hsün and His Predecessors*. White Plains: M. E. Sharpe, 1980.

Seth, Michael J. *A History of Korea: From Antiquity to the Present*. Lanham, Md.: Rowman & Littlefield, 2010.

"Shandong wenti shibai hou zhi dong xun" 山東問題失敗後之東訊 (News from the East after the Failure in the Shandong Question). *Shishi xinbao* 時事新報 (China Times). May 13, 1919, 2.1. Shanghai.

"Shandong wenti yi jiejue" 山東問題已解決 (Shandong Question Solved). *Yishibao* 益世報 (Social Welfare Tiensin). May 10, 1919, 2. Tianjin.

"Shandong wenti Zhong-Ri huanwen zhi pilu" 山東問題中日換文之披露 (Disclosure of Sino-Japanese Diplomatic Correspondence on the Shandong Question). *Shenbao* 申報 (Shanghai News). February 22, 1919, 6. Shanghai.

Shangguan furong 上官芙蓉. "Fu Sinian shishi qianhou jixiang" 傅斯年逝世前後紀詳 (Detailed Record of the Time around Fu Sinian's Death). In *Fu guxiaozhang aiwanlu* 傅故校長哀輓錄 (Elegies on the Former President Fu), edited by Guoli Taiwan daxue jinian Fu guxiaozhang choubei weiyuanhui aiwanlu bianyin xiaozu 國立臺灣大學紀念傅校長籌備委員會哀輓錄編印小組, 19. Taibei: Taiwan daxue, 1951.

Shanghai shehui xueyuan lishi yanjiusuo 上海社會學院歷史研究所, ed. *Wu si yundong zai Shanghai shiliao xuanji* 五四運動在上海史料選輯 (The May Fourth Movement in Shanghai: Selected Historical Materials). Shanghai: Shanghai renmin chubanshe, 1980.

"Shanxi Gelaohui zhi yundong" 陝西哥老會之運動 (The Movements of the Elder Brother Society in Shaanxi). *Lu jiang bao* 鷺江報 (Lu River News), no. 87 (1904).

"Shanxi geming dang zhi yundong" 陝西革命黨之運動 (The Movements of the Shaanxi Revolutionary Party). *Lu jiang bao* 鷺江報 (Lu River News), no. 70 (1904).

"'Shaonian zhongguo' yuekan de xuanyan" 《少年中國》月刊的宣言 (Young China's Manifesto). *Shaonian zhongguo* 少年中國 (Young China) 1, no. 3 (September 15, 1919): i.

"'Shaonian zhongguo' yuekan de xuanyan" 《少年中國》月刊的宣言 (Young China's Manifesto). *Shaonian zhongguo* 少年中國 (Young China) 1, no. 4 (October 15, 1919): i.

Shapiro, Ian, and Sonu Bedi. "Introduction." In *Political Contingency: Studying the Unexpected, the Accidental, and the Unforeseen*, edited by Ian Shapiro and Sonu Bedi, 1–18. New York: New York University Press, 2007.

Shen Weiwei 沈衛威. *Hu Shi zhuan* 胡適傳 (A Biography of Hu Shi). Kaifeng: Henan daxue chubanshe, 1988.

Shen Weiwei 沈衛威. *"Xueheng pai" biannian wenshi* 《學衡派》編年文事 (Compiling the Literary Matters of the "Critical Review Faction"). Vol. 1. Nanjing: Nanjing daxue chubanshe, 2015.

Shen Yinmo 沈尹默. "Wo he Chen Duxiu" 我和陳獨秀 (I and Chen Duxiu). In *Chen Duxiu yanjiu cankao ziliao* 陳獨秀研究參考資料 (Study and Reference Material on Chen Duxiu), edited by Anqing shi lishi xuehui 安慶市歷史學會, 1:89–91. Anyang: Anyang shi chubanshe, 1981.

Shenbao 1872–1949 申報1872–1949 (Shanghai News 1872–1949 [Database]). Accessed January 12, 2016. http://shunpao.egreenapple.com.

"Shengli di-yi shangxiao yundonghui ji" 省立第一商校運動會紀 (Record of the Sports Festival of the First Provincial Business School). *Shenbao* 申報 (Shanghai News), October 10, 1919, 10.

Sheridan, James E. "The Warlord Era: Politics and Militarism under the Peking Government, 1916–28." In *The Cambridge History of China*, 1st ed., 12:284–321. Cambridge: Cambridge Histories Online, 1983. http://universitypublishingonline.org/cambridge/histories/.

Shi Zhong 史眾. "Wu si shiqi pi Kong douzheng de lishi jingyan – jinian wu si yundong wushiwu zhounian" 五四時期批孔鬥爭的歷史經驗——紀念五四運動五十五週年 (The Historical Experience of the Struggle to Criticize Confucius during the May Fourth Period – Commemorating the 55th Anniversary of the May Fourth Movement). *Renmin ribao* 人民日報 (People's Daily). May 5, 1974, 2. Beijing.

Shih, Shu-mei. *The Lure of the Modern: Writing Modernism in Semicolonial China, 1917–1937*. Berkeley: University of California Press, 2001.

"Shijie tang shi yu Riben canxun" 世界糖市與日本蠶汛 (The Global Sugar Market and the Destruction of Japanese Silkworms). *Shenbao* 申報 (Shanghai News). April 29, 1919, 6. Shanghai.

Shou Chang 守常. "Xin jiu sichao zhi jizhan" 新舊思潮之激戰 (The Fierce Battle between New and Old Intellectual Trends). *Chenbao* 晨報 (Morning Post). March 4, 1919, 7. Beijing.

Shou Chang 守常. "Xin jiu sichao zhi jizhan" 新舊思潮之激戰 (The Fierce Battle between New and Old Intellectual Trends). *Chenbao* 晨報 (Morning Post). March 5, 1919, 7. Beijing.

Shou Chang 守常. "Xin jiu sichao zhi jizhan" 新舊思潮之激戰 (The Fierce Battle between New and Old Intellectual Trends). *Meizhou pinglun* 每週評論 (Weekly Critic). March 9, 1919, 3. Beijing.

Shou Chang 守常. "Xin jiu sichao zhi jizhan" 新舊思潮之激戰 (The Fierce Battle between New and Old Intellectual Trends). *Shishi xinbao* 時事新報 (China Times). March 10, 1919, 3.3. Shanghai.

Shou Chang 守常. "Xin jiu sichao zhi jizhan" 新舊思潮之激戰 (The Fierce Battle between New and Old Intellectual Trends). *Shishi xinbao* 時事新報 (China Times). March 17, 1919, 3.3. Shanghai.

Shou Weng 壽翁. "Da 'Jing Weishui shi shei?'" 答《蔣渭水是誰？》 (Answering the Question: "Who Is Jiang Weishui?"). *Haixia pinglun* 海峽評論 (Cross-Strait Review), no. 182 (February 2006): 60.

"Shouye" 首頁 (Home). *Weishui chunfeng – Yinyue shidai* 渭水春風——音樂時代 (The Impossible Times – All Music Theatre), November 22, 2011. http://impossibletimes.allmusic.com.tw/.

Shuang Yu 霜羽. "Daxue xiaozhang wenti zhi guoqu, xianzai, weilai" 大學校長問題之過去現在未來 (Past, Present and Future of the Problems with the University's Chancellor). *Shenbao* 申報 (Shanghai News). May 13, 1919, 6. Shanghai.

"Shuo yundong" 說運動 (Talking about "Movement"). *Shaoxing baihuabao* 紹興白話報 (Shaoxing Plain-Language News), no. 82 (190?): 1–2.

Sichuan jiaoyu xinchao 四川教育新潮 (Sichuan Educational New Tide). Sichuan, 1920.

Sili Fujian Xiehe daxue xueshenghui xuanchuanbu 私立福建協和大學學生會宣傳部. *Xieda xinchao* 協大新潮 (Xiehe University New Tide). Fuzhou, 1927.

Smith, S.A. *A Road Is Made: Communism in Shanghai, 1920–1927*. Richmond: Curzon, 2000.

Smith, S.A. *Like Cattle and Horses: Nationalism and Labor in Shanghai, 1895–1927*. Durham: Duke University Press, 2002.

Song Qiang 宋強, Zhang Zangzang 張藏藏, and Qiao Bian 橋邊. *Zhongguo keyi shuo bu: lengzhan hou shidai de zhengzhi yu qinggan jueze* 中國可以說不：冷戰後時代的政治與情感抉擇 (China Can Say No: Political and Emotional Choices in the Post-Cold War Era). Beijing: Zhonghua gongshang lianhe chubanshe, 1996.

Song Xiaojun 宋曉軍. *Zhongguo bu gaoxing: da shidai, da mubiao ji women de neiyou-waihuan* 中國不高興：大時代，大目標及我們的內憂外患 (Unhappy China: The Great Time, Grand Vision and Our Challenges). Nanjing: Jiangsu renmin chubanshe, 2009.

Song, Xiaokun. *Between Civic and Ethnic: The Transformation of Taiwanese Nationalist Ideologies (1895–2000)*. Brussels: Vubpress, 2009.

Spence, Jonathan. *The Search for Modern China*. 2nd ed. New York: Norton, 1999.

Strand, David. "'A High Place Is No Better than a Low Place': The City in the Making of Modern China." In *Becoming Chinese: Passages to Modernity and beyond*, edited by Wen-hsin Yeh, 98–127. University of California Press, 2000.

Strand, David. *An Unfinished Republic: Leading by Word and Deed in Modern China*. Berkeley: University of California Press, 2011.

Su, K'e Ju. "The Educational Value of Chinese Character Writing." Student essay, n.d. Container 219. Lewis Nathaniel Chase Papers, Manuscript Division, Library of Congress, Washington, D.C.

Su, Ya-Chen. "Ideological Representations of Taiwan's History: An Analysis of Elementary Social Studies Textbooks, 1978–1995." *Curriculum Inquiry* 37, no. 3 (11.2007): 205–37.

Sullivan, Jonathan, and Eliyahu V. Sapir. "Ma Ying-Jeou's Presidential Discourse." *Journal of Current Chinese Affairs* 41, no. 3 (2012): 33–68.

"Sunduan kai yundonghui" 孫端開運動會 (Sunduan Starts a Sports Festival). *Shaoxing baihuabao* 紹興白話報 (Shaoxing Plain-Language News), no. 92 (1900): 2.

Sze Be Tsung. "Letter to Emma Lester," September 18, 1929. Container 218. Lewis Nathaniel Chase Papers, Manuscript Division, Library of Congress, Washington, D.C.

Taiwan qingnian zazhishe 臺灣青年雜誌社. *Taiwan qingnian* 臺灣青年 (Taiwan Youth). Tokyo, 1920.

Tan Mingqian 譚鳴謙. "Laodong wenti zhi jiejue" 勞動問題之解決 (The Solution of the Workers' Question). *Xinchao* 新潮 (New Tide) 1, no. 4 (April 1, 1919): 603–10.

Tang Xiu 唐雋. "Du Chen Duxiu de 'Xin wenhua yundong shi shenme?'" 讀陳獨秀的"新文化運動是什麼？" (Reading Chen Duxiu's "What Is the New Culture Movement?"). *Meishu* 美術 (Art [Shanghai]) 2, no. 2 (1920): 105–8.

Tao Yinghui 陶英惠. *Dianxing zai suxi: zuihuai Zhongyang yanjiuyuan liu wei yigu yuanzhang* 典型在夙昔：追懷中央研究院六位已故院長 (A Model of Past Times: Commemorating the Late Sixth President of the Academia Sinica). Taibei: Xiuwei zixun keji gufen youxian gongsi, 2007.

Tawney, R.H. "Review of *The Chinese Renaissance* by Hu Shih." *Philosophy* 11, no. 44 (October 1936): 484–85.

T.C.W. "Review of 'China's Renaissance' by Timothy Tingfang Lew." *American Journal of Sociology* 29, no. 5 (3.1924): 636.
T.C.W. "Review of 'The Chinese Renaissance and Its Significance' by Chirgwin." *American Journal of Sociology* 30, no. 1 (July 1924): 111.
"The Chinese Renaissance: Lecture in Trinity College." *Irish Times*, November 17, 1926, 7. The Irish Times (1921-Current File).
"The *Shanghai Gazette*." *Moti* 墨梯 (McTyeirean), no. 2 (June 1918).
"'The Tragedy of China': Dr. Hu Shih on Failure of the Revolution." *Manchester Guardian*. October 11, 1926, 6. The Manchester Guardian (1901–1959). Manchester.
Thompson, John B. "Editor's Introduction." In *Language and Symbolic Power*, by Pierre Boudieu, 1–31. edited by John B. Thompson, translated by Gino Raymond and Matthew Adamson. Cambridge: Polity, 1991.
Tian Hao 天豪. "Beijing zhi daxue xiaoxi" 北京之大學消息 (News from Beijing's Universities). *Shenbao* 申報 (Shanghai News). July 3, 1924, 11. Shanghai.
Tianjin lishi bowuguan 天津歷史博物館, and Nankai daxue lishixi "Wu si yundong zai Tianjin" bianxiezu 南開大學歷史系《五四運動在天津》編寫組, eds. *Wu si yundong zai Tianjin: lishi ziliao xuanji* 五四運動在天津: 歷史資料選輯 (The May Fourth Movement in Tianjin: Selected Historical Materials). Tianjin: Tianjin renmin chubanshe, 1979.
"Tianwen yi zhi er ke: lun diqiu yundong" 天文易知二課：論地球運動 (Easy Knowledge about the Heavenly Bodies, Lesson Two: Discussing the Movement of the Earth). *Xiaohai yuebao* 小孩月報 (Child Monthly), no. 14 (1876): 3.
Tilly, Charles. *The Contentious French*. Cambridge, Massachusetts: Harvard University Press, 1986.
"Times Digital Archive (1785–1985)." Database, n.d. http://www.thetimes.co.uk/tto/archive.
Ting Hao 廷浩. "'Gu'er ku yu' zhi pinglun" "孤兒苦遇"之評論 (Evaluation of *Oliver Twist*). *Shenbao* 申報 (Shanghai News). September 10, 1924, 15. Shanghai.
Ting, Vung Yuin. "Letter to Emma Lester," January 11, 1937. Container 209. Lewis Nathaniel Chase Papers, Manuscript Division, Library of Congress, Washington, D.C.
Vargas, Philippe de. *Some Elements in the Chinese Renaissance*. Shanghai, 1922.
Vargas, Philippe de. "Some Elements in the Chinese Renaissance (Manuscript)." Beijing, February 15, 1922. Container 221. Lewis Nathaniel Chase Papers, Manuscript Division, Library of Congress, Washington, D.C. Beijing.
Ven, Hans J. van de. *From Friend to Comrade*. Berkeley: University of California Press, 1991.
Vittinghoff, Natascha. *Die Anfänge des Journalismus in China (1860–1911)* (The Beginnings of Journalism in China [1860–1911]). Wiesbaden: Harrassowitz, 2002.
Wagner, Rudolf G. "The Canonization of May Fourth." In *The Appropriation of Cultural Capital: China's May Fourth Project*, edited by Milena Doleželová-Velingerová and Oldřich Král, 66–120. Cambridge, Massachusetts: Harvard University Asia Center, 2001.
"Waibao lun nan-bei jianghe yaodian" 外報論南北講和要點 (Foreign Newspapers Discuss Crucial Points about the Peace Talks between South and North). *Shenbao* 申報 (Shanghai News). December 17, 1918, 6. Shanghai.
"Waijiao jinji yu heju polie (liu)" 外交緊急與和局破裂（六）(The Urgency of Diplomacy and the Destruction of Peace [Six]). *Yishibao* 益世報 (Social Welfare Tiensin). May 21, 1919, 2. Tianjin.
"Waijiao jinji yu heju polie (si)" 外交緊急與和局破裂（四）(The Urgency of Diplomacy and the Destruction of Peace [Four]). *Yishibao* 益世報 (Social Welfare Tiensin). May 19, 1919, 2. Tianjin.

"Waijiaobu gongbiao ge xiang miyue" 外交部公表各項密約 (The Foreign Ministry Publishes All Secret Agreements). *Dongfang zazhi* 東方雜誌 (Eastern Miscellany) 16, no. 5 (May 1919): 178–90.

"Waijiaobu gongbiao ge xiang miyue (xu)" 外交部公表各項密約（續） (The Foreign Ministry Publishes All Secret Agreements [Continued]). *Dongfang zazhi* 東方雜誌 (Eastern Miscellany) 16, no. 6 (June 1919): 166–79.

Waijiaobu 外交部, Neiwubu 內務部, and Jiaotongbu 交通部. "Beijing guowuyuan waijiao deng bu jing dian" 北京國務院外交等部敬電 (Telegram of the 24th [of April 1920] from the Foreign Ministry, Etc., of the State Council in Beijing). In *Yan Xishan dang'an* 閻錫山檔案 (Yan Xishan Papers), edited by Qingfen Lin 林清芬, 5:102–4. Taibei: Guoshiguan, 2003.

Wang Beilin 王貝林, and Wang Yuzhong 王寓中. "Jiang Weishui jijinhui zuotan: wailai zhengquan lunzheng, Xie Ma jiaofeng" 蔣渭水基金會座談:外來政權論戰，謝馬交鋒 (Forum of the Jiang Weishui Cultural Foundation: Debate about Foreign Regimes, Hsieh and Ma Cross Swords). *Ziyou shibao* 自由時報 (Liberty Times Net), July 10, 2007. http://news.ltn.com.tw/news/politics/paper/140433.

Wang, David Der-wei. "Chinese Literature from 1841 to 1937." In *The Cambridge History of Chinese Literature*, edited by Kang-i Sun Chang, Cambridge Histories Online., 2:413–564. Cambridge: Cambridge University Press, 2010. http://universitypublishingonline.org/cambridge/histories/.

Wang Guangqi 王光祈. "'Shaonian Zhongguo' zhi chuangzao" 《少年中國》之創造 (The Creation of *Young China*). *Shaonian zhongguo* 少年中國 (Young China) 1, no. 2 (August 15, 1919): 1–6.

Wang Guangyuan 王光遠. *Chen Duxiu nianpu 1879–1942* 陳獨秀年譜 1879–1942 (A Chronology of the Life of Chen Duxiu, 1879–1942). Chongqing: Chongqing chubanshe, 1987.

Wang Jingfang 王敬芳. "Fakanci" 發刊辭 (Manifesto). *Xin qun* 新群 (Social Reconstruction), no. 1 (November 1919): 1–7.

Wang Jingwei 汪精衛. "Wang huizhang jiuzhi ri yanshuoci" 汪會長就職日演說辭 (Speech given by President Wang upon Taking Office). *Guangdong sheng jiaoyuhui zazhi* 廣東省教育會雜誌 (Journal of the Guangdong Educational Association) 1, no. 1 (July 1921): 2–6.

Wang Minchuan 王敏川. "Nüzi jiaoyu" 女子教育 (Women's Education). *Taiwan qingnian* 臺灣青年 (Taiwan Youth) 1, no. 3 (September 12, 1920): 41–43.

Wang Qi 王琪, and Wang Jianwen 王健文. *Lishi* 歷史 (History). Vol. 1. Hanlin chuban, 2006.

Wang Runian 王儒年. *Yuwang de xiangxiang: 1920–1930 niandai Shenbao guanggao de wenhuashi yanjiu* 欲望的想像：1920–1930年代《申報》廣告的文化史研究 (The Imagination of Desire : A Cultural History of Advertisement in the *Shanghai News* in the 1920s and 1930s). Shanghai: Shanghai renmin chubanshe, 2007.

Wang Shanzhi 王善治. "Liu Boming boshi shishi" 劉伯明博士逝世 (Dr. Liu Boming Dead). *Xinghua* 興華 (Chinese Christian Advocate) 20, no. 47 (December 5, 1923): 23.

Wang Su 王遬. "Du 'Xin funü' de ganxiang" 讀《新婦女》的感想 (Feelings on Reading *New Woman*). *Funü zazhi* 婦女雜誌 (Ladies' Magazine) 6, no. 5 (April 30, 1920): 33–34.

Wang Wenqi 王文祺. "My Reflections and Queries on the Question of the Creation of the Chinese Imaginative Literature of Interest to Non Chinese." Examination paper, January 22, 1924. Container 221. Lewis Nathaniel Chase Papers, Manuscript Division, Library of Congress, Washington, D.C.

Wang Xiaobo 王曉波. "Qing wu panwu Taiwan kang-Ri shi he Jiang Weishui: Bo Lin Dushui he Chen Yishen" 請勿攀誣台灣抗日史和蔣渭水：駁林濁水和陳儀深 (Please Do Not Slander

Taiwan's History of Resistance against Japan and Jiang Weishui: A Critique of Lin Dushui and Chen Yishen). *Haixia pinglun* 海峽評論 (Cross-Strait Review), no. 200 (August 1, 2007): 38–40.

Wang Xiaodan 王曉丹. "'Funü zazhi' dui jindai dushi nüxing shenghuo de suzao he yingxiang" 《婦女雜誌》對近代都市女性生活的塑造和影響 (The Formation Of, and Influence On, the Life of Modern Urban Women by the *Ladies' Magazine*). *Xueshu tansuo* 學術探索 (Academic Exploration), no. 8 (August 2011): 99–129.

Wang Yinxue 王吟雪. "Shishi xinbao: cong wu si yundong yilai Shanghai gua xin wenhua yundong zhaopai de baozhi ..." 時事新報：從五四運動以來上海掛新文化運動招牌的報紙...... (The *China Times*: Newspapers That Hang up the Signboard of the New Culture Movement in Shanghai since the May Fourth Movement ...). *Xin fojiao* 新佛教 (New Buddhism) 1, no. 6 (1920): 9–10.

Wang Yuanfang 汪原放. *Huiyi Yadong tushuguan* 回憶亞東圖書館 (Remembering East Asia Library). Shanghai: Xuelin chubanshe, 1983.

Wang Yuanfang 汪原放. *Yadong tushuguan yu Chen Duxiu* 亞東圖書館與陳獨秀 (East Asia Library and Chen Duxiu). Shanghai: Xuelin chubanshe, 2006.

Ward, Colin. *Anarchism: A Very Short Introduction*. Oxford: Oxford University Press, 2004.

Wasserstrom, Jeffrey N. *Student Protests in Twentieth-Century China: The View from Shanghai*. Stanford, California: Stanford University Press, 1991.

"Weiwei gongsi xindao dapi xiaoshuo" 微微公司新到大批小說 (A Great Amount of Novels Newly Arrive at Weiwei Company). *Shenbao* 申報 (Shanghai News). February 3, 1923, 17. Shanghai.

Wenyou hui. "Invitation to Hu Shi's Lecture," November 17, 1922. Container 220. Lewis Nathaniel Chase Papers, Manuscript Division, Library of Congress, Washington, D.C.

Wenyou hui. "Invitation to Hu Shi's Lecture," February 20, 1924. Container 187. Lewis Nathaniel Chase Papers, Manuscript Division, Library of Congress, Washington, D.C.

Weston, Timothy B. "The Formation and Positioning of the New Culture Community, 1913–1917." *Modern China* 24, no. 3 (July 1998): 255–84.

Weston, Timothy B. *The Power of Position: Beijing University, Intellectuals, and Chinese Political Culture, 1898–1929*. Berkeley, Calif.: University of California Press, 2004.

Williams, Raymond. *Keywords: A Vocabulary of Culture and Society*. Revised edition. New York: Oxford University Press, 1976.

Wood, G. Zay. *The Shantung Question: A Study in Diplomacy and World Politics*. New York: Fleming H. Revell, 1922.

Wu Lichang 吳立昌, ed. *Wenxue de xiaojie yu fan xiaojie: Zhongguo xiandai wenxue paibie lunzheng shilun* 文學的消解與反消解：中國現代文學派別論爭史論 (Dispelling Literature and the Opposition to Dispelling It: A History of the Factions and Debates in Modern Chinese Literature). Shanghai: Fudan daxue chubanshe, 2004.

Wu Mi 吳宓. "Lun xin wenhua yundong (jielu *Liu Mei xuesheng jibao*)" 論新文化運動（節錄留美學生季報） (A Discussion of the New Culture Movement [An Excerpt from the *Chinese Students' Quarterly*]). *Xueheng* 學衡 (Critical Review), no. 4 (1922): 36–58.

Wu Mi 吳宓. "Zai lun xin wenhua yundong (da Qiu Changwei jun)" 再論新文化運動(答邱昌渭君) (Another Discussion of the New Culture Movement [A Reply to Mr. Qiu Changwei]). *Liu Mei xuesheng jibao* 留美學生季報 (Chinese Students' Quarterly) 8, no. 4 (1921): 13–38.

Wu Ti 伍俶. "Yi Mengzhen" 憶孟真 (Remembering Mengzhen). In *E'e zhi shi: mingren bixia de Fu Sinian, Fu Sinian bixia de mingren* 諤諤之士：命人筆下的傅斯年傅斯年筆下的名人 (Outspoken Gentlemen: Fu Sinian in the Words of Famous People, Famous People in the Words of Fu Sinian), edited by Wang Furen 王富仁 and Shi Xingze 石興澤, 82–86. Shanghai: Dongfang chuban zhongxin, 1999.

Wu Wang 毋忘. "Xin jiu sixiang zhi chongtu" 新舊思想之衝突 (The Clash between Old and New Thought). *Guomin gongbao* 國民公報 (Citizen News). March 9, 1919, 1. Beijing.

"Wu wang 'liu si'" 勿忘"六四" (Do Not Forget June Fourth). *Lingba xianzhang* 零八憲章 (Charter 08). Accessed November 11, 2015. http://www.2008xianzhang.info/June-Fourth/000198964.html.

Wu Xiang 吳翔. "Lun Xu Shuzheng yu Wanxi junfa de xingshuai" 論徐樹錚與皖系軍閥的興衰 (The Rise and Fall of Xu Shuzheng and the Anhui Warlord Clique). Master's, Huazhong shifan daxue 華中師範大學, 2009.

"Wu yue qi ri zhi guomin dahui" 五月七日之國民大會 (The National Assembly of 7 May). *Shenbao* 申報 (Shanghai News). May 8, 1919, 10. Shanghai.

"Xi bao ji feichu zaohun zhi yundong" 西報紀廢除早婚之運動 (Western Newspapers Chronicle the Movement to Abolish Early Marriages). *Shenbao* 申報 (Shanghai News), December 5, 1919, 6.

Xi Jinping 習近平. "Qingnian yao zijue jianxing shehui zhuyi hexin jiazhiguan – zai Beijing daxue shi-sheng zuojianghui shang de jianghua" 青年要自覺踐行社會主義核心價值觀——在北京大學師生座談會上的講話 (The Young People Must Consciously Fulfill the Core Value System of Socialism – Talk at the Beijing University Teacher and Student Forum). *Zhonghua renmin gongheguo jiaoyubu* 中華人民共和國教育部 (Ministry of Education of the People's Republic of China), May 4, 2014. http://www.moe.gov.cn/publicfiles/business/htmlfiles/moe/moe_176/201405/167911.html.

Xi Ping 希平. "Duiyu 'Liu Boming jun yanjiang xin wenhua yundong zhi yiyi ji biyao' de piping" 對於"劉伯明君演講新文化運動之意義及必要"的批評 (A Criticism of "Liu Boming's Talk on the Meaning and Necessity of the New Culture Movement"). *Juewu* 覺悟 (Enlightenment). July 1, 1920, 4. Shanghai.

Xi, Zhen. "Is a Knowledge of Ancient Greek and Roman Literature such as Indicated by Dr Zucker's Book of Interest to You Either Personally or as Chinese?" Student essay. Beijing, 1923. Container 220. Lewis Nathaniel Chase Papers, Manuscript Division, Library of Congress, Washington, D.C. Beijing.

Xian Jin 先進. "Xin wenhua yundong de wuqi" 新文化運動的武器 (The Weapons of the New Culture Movement). *Xingqi pinglun* 星期評論 (Weekly Review). August 31, 1919, 13 edition, 4. Shanghai.

"Xiang jiang pinglun ..." 湘江評論…… (Xiang River Review ...). *Meizhou pinglun* 每週評論 (Weekly Critic). August 24, 1919, 4. Beijing.

Xiang Jingyu 向警予. "Nüzi jiefang yu gaizao de shangque" 女子解放與改造的商榷 (A Discussion of the Liberation and Reform of Women). *Shaonian zhongguo* 少年中國 (Young China) 2, no. 2 (August 15, 1920): 29–37.

"Xian'gao xiaoxuexiao jiang kai yundonghui" 賢高小學校將開運動會 (Xian'gao Primary School Will Hold a Sports Festival). *Shenbao* 申報 (Shanghai News), October 17, 1919, 10.

"Xianzhang zhengwen" 憲章正文 (Text of the Charter). *Lingba xianzhang* 零八憲章 (Charter 08). Accessed November 11, 2015. http://www.2008xianzhang.info/chinese.htm.

"Xiaoshuo xianping" 小說閒評 (Casual Evaluation of Novels). *Shenbao* 申報 (Shanghai News). February 20, 1921, 14. Shanghai.

"Xijujia huanyan Hu Shizhi: Hu yun hui Jing hou zuo changshi juben" 戲劇家歡宴胡適之：胡允回京後作嘗試劇本 (Actors Give a Banquet in Hu Shizhi's Honor: Hu Consents to Write a Trial Script after His Return to Beijing). *Shenbao* 申報 (Shanghai News). November 20, 1923, 13. Shanghai.

"Xin Funü xuanyan" 新婦女宣言 (Manifesto of *New Woman*). *Xin funü* 新婦女 (New Woman) 1, no. 1 (reprint) (October 10, 1920): 1.

"Xin jiu sichao chongtu zhi di-yi sheng" 新舊思潮衝突之第一聲 (First Voice on the Clash between New and Old Intellectual Trends). *Guomin gongbao* 國民公報 (Citizen News). March 30, 1919, 1. Beijing.

Xin qingnian 新青年 (New Youth). Vol. 6. 14 vols. Tokyo: Taian, 1963.

Xin Wei 心危. "Riben dui wo xin sixiang shishi zhi tongqing" 日本對我新思想失勢之同情 (Japan's Sympathy for Our New Intellectual Tide Losing Power). *Shenbao* 申報 (Shanghai News), April 25, 1919, 6.

"Xin wenhua congshu" 新文化叢書 (New Culture Collections). *Shaonian zhongguo* 少年中國 (Young China) 4, no. 6 (August 1923).

"Xin wenhua yundong zhi jieshi" 新文化運動之解釋 (Explanation of the New Culture Movement). *Xinghua* 興華 (Chinese Christian Advocate) 16, no. 44 (November 12, 1919): 28–29.

"Xin wenhua zhi shuguang" 新文化之曙光 (The Dawn of New Culture). *Beida shenghuo* 北大生活 (Life at Beida), December 1921.

Xinchao 新潮 (New Tide). Vol. 3. Minguo zhenxi qikan 民國珍稀期刊 (Valuable Republican Journals). Beijing: Quanguo tushuguan wenxian suowei fuzhi zhongxin, 2006.

"Xinchaoshe jishi" 新潮社紀事 (Records of the New Tide Society). In *Xinchao* 新潮 (New Tide), 3:200–204. Beijing, 2006.

"Xingzheng gexin de hao ji" 行政革新的好機 (A Good Opportunity for Administrative Reform). *Taiwan minbao* 臺灣民報 (Taiwan People's News). November 11, 1923, 1. Tokyo.

Xiu Chao 秀潮. "Zhongguo xin wenxue yundong de guoqu, xianzai he jianglai" 中國新文學運動的過去現在和將來 (Past, Present and Future of the Chinese New Literature Movement). *Taiwan minbao* 臺灣民報 (Taiwan People's News). July 13, 1923, 3. Tokyo.

Xu Baoqian 徐寶謙. "Beijing jidujiao xuexiao shiye lianhehui gaizu shimo" 北京基督教學校事業聯合會改組始末 (The Full Story of the Reorganization of the Beijing Christian Union for School Affairs). *Shengming* 生命 (Life) 1, no. 1 (June 1, 1920): 1–12.

Xu Baoqian 徐寶謙. "Jidujiao xin sichao" 基督教新思潮 (The New Intellectual Tide of Christianity). *Shengming* 生命 (Life) 1, no. 1 (June 1, 1920): 1–7.

Xu Guoyu 徐國俞. "My Reflections and Queries on the Question of the Creation of the Chinese Imaginative Literature of Interest to Non Chinese." Examination paper, January 22, 1924. Container 221. Lewis Nathaniel Chase Papers, Manuscript Division, Library of Congress, Washington, D.C.

Xu Jilin 許紀霖. *Jindai Zhongguo zhishi fenzi de gongong jiaowang* 近代中國知識分子的公共交往 (Interactions between Modern Chinese Intellectuals). Shanghai: Shanghai renmin chubanshe, 2007.

Xu Weiming 徐為民, ed. "Bao Yi" 抱一 (Bao Yi). *Zhongguo jin xiandai renwu bieming cidian* 中國近現代人物別名詞典 (Dictionary of the Pseudonyms of Chinese Figures in the Modern and Contemporary Period). Shenyang: Shenyang chubanshe, 1993. Shenyang.

Xu, Xiaoqun. *Chinese Professionals and the Republican State: The Rise of Professional Associations in Shanghai, 1912–1937*. Cambridge: Cambridge University Press, 2001.

Xue Xiangsui 薛祥綏. "Du gushu fa ju yu" 讀古書法舉隅 (How to Read Old Books). *Guogu* 國故 (National Heritage), no. 1 (1919): 1B–2B.

"Xuejie fengchao you qi" 學生界風潮又起 (Student Protests Flare up Again). *Gongyanbao* 公言報 (Public Voice). May 10, 1919, 2. Beijing.

"Xuejie fengchao zhong ge fangmian zhi taidu" 學界風潮中各方面之態度 (The Attitude of All Parties in the Student Protests). *Shenbao* 申報 (Shanghai News). May 8, 1919, 6. Shanghai.

"Xuesheng aiguo yundong chengji zhi wailun" 學生愛國運動成績之外論 (External Discussions of the Achievements of the Students' Patriotic Movement). *Shenbao* 申報 (Shanghai News). July 1, 1919, 6. Shanghai.

"Xuesheng shiwei yundong zhi waiping" 學生示威運動之外評 (External Comments on the Students' Protest Movement). *Shenbao* 申報 (Shanghai News), May 10, 1919, 7.

"Xuzhou" 徐州 (Xuzhou). *Shenbao* 申報 (Shanghai News). June 1, 1920, 7. Shanghai.

Yan Jiatong 嚴家同. "Ma Yingjiu momingqimiao de yi bi" 馬英九莫名其妙的一筆 (The Baffling Pen of Ma Ying-Jeou). *Nanfang kuaibao* 南方快報 (Southern Express). July 17, 2007. Taibei. http://www.southnews.com.tw/polit/ma_in_9/00/00243.htm.

Yan Xishan 閻錫山. "Dujun yu zixing shi dui ge ji junguan jiangci" 督軍於自省時對各級軍官講詞 (Speech before the Officers of All Ranks by the Military Governor While Self-Reflecting), August 3, 1919. Ge fang minguo 8 nian wanglai dianwen lucun (shi yi), Taibei Guoshiguan Yan Xishan shiliao 各方民國8年往來電文祿存（十一）, 台北國史館閻錫山史料 (Telegram correspondences of 1919 [11], Yan Xishan papers, Academia Historica, Taibei).

Yan Xishan 閻錫山. "Fu Beijing Zhao canmouzhang xian dian" 復北京趙參謀長咸電 (Telegram of the 15th [of May 1919], in Reply to Chief of Staff Zhao in Beijing). In *Yan Xishan dang'an* 閻錫山檔案 (Yan Xishan Papers), edited by Lin Qingfen 林清芬, 5:29–30. Taibei: Guoshiguan, 2003.

Yan Xishan 閻錫山. "Shanxi dujun jian shengzhang wei quanguo jiaoyu lianhehui di-wu ci kaihui zhici" 山西督軍兼省長為全國教育聯合會第五次開會致辭 (Speech by the Shanxi Military Governor and Provincial Governor on the Fifth Conference of the National Union of Educational Associations), October 10, 1919. Ge fang minguo 8 nian wanglai dianwen lucun (shi yi), Taibei Guoshiguan Yan Xishan shiliao 各方民國8年往來電文祿存（十一）, 台北國史館閻錫山史料 (Telegram correspondences of 1919 [11], Yan Xishan papers, Academia Historica, Taibei).

Yan Xishan 閻錫山. "Shanxi sheng zhengfu zhi Shilou zhishi han" 山西省政府致石樓知事函 (Letter by the Shanxi Provincial Government to the County Magistrate of Shilou). Taiyuan, 1919. Ge fang minguo 8 nian wanglai dianwen lucun (er), Taibei Guoshiguan Yan Xishan shiliao 各方民國8年往來電文祿存（二）, 台北國史館閻錫山史料 (Telegram correspondences of 1919 [2], Yan Xishan papers, Academia Historica, Taibei). Taiyuan.

Yang Zhensheng 楊振聲. "Huiyi wu si" 回憶五四 (Remembering May Fourth). In *Wu si yundong huiyilu xu* 五四運動回憶錄續 (Records of Memories of the May Fourth Movement, Continued), edited by Zhongguo shehui kexueyuan jindaishi yanjiusuo 中國社會科學院近代史研究所, 52–57. Beijing: Zhongguo shehui kexue chubanshe, 1959.

Yang Zhongheng 楊忠衡. "'Weishui chunfeng' – ruhe fuhuo Jiang Weishui" 《渭水春風》——如何復活蔣渭水 ("The Impossible Times" – How to Bring Jiang Weishui back to Life). *Weishui chunfeng – Yinyue shidai* 渭水春風——音樂時代 (The Impossible Times – All Music Theatre). Accessed March 8, 2016. http://impossibletimes.allmusic.com.tw/archive.htm.

"Yangzhou" 揚州 (Yangzhou). *Shenbao* 申報 (Shanghai News). May 22, 1920, 8. Shanghai.

"Yanshuo jingjinhui di-er ci kaihuiji" 演說競進會第二次開會紀 (Record of the Second Lecture Competition). *Shenbao* 申報 (Shanghai News). December 25, 1919, 10. Shanghai.

"Yanshuo jingjinhui dingqi zai Ning kaihui" 演說競進會定期在寧開會 (The Lecture Competition Is Schedule to Be Held in Nanjing). *Shenbao* 申報 (Shanghai News), October 31, 1919.

"Yanshuo jingjinhui yanti zhi jieshi" 演說競進會演題之解釋 (Explanation of the Topic of the Lecture Competition). *Shenbao* 申報 (Shanghai News), November 2, 1919, 10.

Ye Juan 葉雋. *Deyu wenxue yanjiu yu xiandai Zhongguo* 德語文學研究與現代中國 (Research on German Literature and Contemporary China). Beijing: Beijing daxue chubanshe, 2008.

Ye Shixiang 葉世祥, and Zhang Dongmei 張東梅. "Xiandaixing shiye zhong de 'guocui pai' he 'Xueheng pai'" 現代性視野中的'國粹派'和'學衡派 (The "National Essence Group" and the "Critical Review Group" from a Modern Perspective). *Wenzhou daxue xuebao* 溫州大學學報 (Journal of Wenzhou University) 21, no. 4 (2008): 1–4.

Ye Yun 野雲. "Ji Beijing daxue shiye shi (xu)" 紀北京大學始業式 (續) (Remembering Beijing University's Opening Ceremony for the New Academic Year [Continued]). *Shenbao* 申報 (Shanghai News), September 15, 1920.

Ye Yun 野雲. "Jing xuejie yaoren zhi diaoxie" 京學界要人之凋謝 (The Passing-Away of Important Figures in Beijing Academia). *Shenbao* 申報 (Shanghai News), November 27, 1919, 7.

Yeh, Wen-hsin. *Provincial Passages: Culture, Space, and the Origins of Chinese Communism*. Berkeley: University of California Press, 1996.

Yeh, Wen-hsin. *Shanghai Splendor: Economic Sentiments and the Making of Modern China, 1843–1949*. Berkeley, Calif.: University of California Press, 2007.

Yeh, Wen-hsin. *The Alienated Academy: Culture and Politics in Republican China, 1919–1937*. Cambridge, Massachusetts: Council on East Asian Studies, Harvard University, 1990.

Yi Sheng 遺生. "Zuijin zhi xueshu xinchao" 最近之學術新潮 (Recent New Trends in Scholarship). In *Wu si yundong zai Shanghai shiliao xuanji* 五四運動在上海史料選輯 (The May Fourth Movement in Shanghai: Selected Historical Materials), edited by Shanghai shehui xueyuan lishi yanjiusuo 上海社會學院歷史研究所, 106–7. Shanghai: Shanghai renmin chubanshe, 1980.

Yi Wan 億萬. "Yi zhou Beijing de gongmin da huodong" 一週北京的公民大活動 (One Week of Great Activities by the Citizens of Beijing). *Meizhou pinglun* 每週評論 (Weekly Critic). May 11, 1919, 1–3. Beijing.

"Yi xiaoshuo yi xi tan" 譯小說一席談 (A Talk about the Translation of Novels). *Shenbao* 申報 (Shanghai News). April 3, 1921, 14. Shanghai.

Yi Zuoxian 易作賢. *Hu Shi zhuan* 胡適傳 (A Biography of Hu Shi). Wuhan: Hubei renmin chubanshe, 1987.

Yin Zhengyang 殷正洋, Cheng Boren 稱伯仁, Yinyue shidai juchang 音樂時代劇場, and Ye Wenhao 葉文豪. *Taiwan, shi women de ming* 台灣，是我們的名 ("Taiwan" Is Our Name). CD. *Weishui chunfeng* 渭水春風 (The Impossible Times). Taiwan yinyueju san bu qu 台灣音樂劇三部曲 (Three Taiwanese Musicals). Taibei: All Music Theatre, 2011. Taibei.

Yin Zhengyang 殷正洋, Hong Ruixiang 洪瑞襄, and Yinyue shidai juchang 音樂時代劇場. "Weishui chunfeng" linchuang jiangyi pian, Taiwan wenhua xiehui pian 9 fenzhong changban jingcai pianduan 《渭水春風》臨床講義篇、台灣文化協會篇9分鐘長版精彩片段 (*The Impossible Times*, "Bedside Examination," "The Taiwanese Cultural Association," 9 Minutes of Choice Clips of the Long Version). *Weishui chunfeng* 渭水春風 (The Impossible Times). Taibei, 2010. Taibei. https://www.artsticket.com.tw/CKSCC2005/Product/Product00/ProductsDetailsPage.aspx?ProductId=hsobWfDDQ3RZoTusjZfyR.

Yin Zhengyang 殷正洋, Hong Ruixiang 洪瑞襄, Yinyue shidai juchang 音樂時代劇場, and Ye Wenhao 葉文豪. *Tian jiang da shiming: Taiwan wenhua xiehui huige* 天降大使命：台灣文化協會會歌 (A Great Mission Handed down from Heaven: The Hymn of the Taiwan Cultural Association). CD. *Weishui chunfeng* 渭水春風 (The Impossible Times). Taiwan yinyueju san bu qu 台灣音樂劇三部曲 (Three Taiwanese Musicals). Taibei: All Music Theatre, 2011. Taibei.

"Yingguo yundong xila jiaru zhanzheng" 英國運動希臘加入戰爭 (Britain Lobbies Greece to Join the War). *Dongfang zazhi* 東方雜誌 (Eastern Miscellany) 12, no. 12 (1915): 9.

"Yingguo zhuming xiaoshuo shecheng yingju" 英國著名小說攝成影戲 (A Famous English Novel Is Adapted for the Screen). *Shenbao* 申報 (Shanghai News). December 16, 1922, 18. Shanghai.

"Yingyin shuoming" 影印說明 (Explanations to the Photo-Offset). In *Yishibao* 益世報 (Social Welfare Tiensin), 20:i. Tianjin: Nankai daxue chubanshe, 2004.

"Yinyue shidai juchang 'Weishui chunfeng' 2016 yongheng zhuiyiban" 音樂時代劇場《渭水春風》2016永恆追憶版 (All Music Theater's *The Impossible Times*, 2016, Eternal Commemoration Version). *Liang tingyuan shoupiao* 兩廳院售票 (National Theatre and Concert Hall Tickets). Accessed March 7, 2016. https://www.artsticket.com.tw/CKSCC2005/Product/Product00/ProductsDeta.

"Yinyue shidai juchang 'Weishui chunfeng' 2016 yongheng zhuiyiban" 音樂時代劇場《渭水春風》2016永恆追憶版 (All Music Theater's *The Impossible Times*, 2016, Eternal Commemoration Version). *Yourart*. Accessed March 7, 2016. https://www.yourart.asia/news/show/47303.

Yu Chunmei 喻春梅. *Dadao wei gong: Changsha "Dagong bao" (1915–1927) yu Hunan shehui sichao* 大道為公：長沙《大公報》（1915–1927）與湖南社會思潮 (The Grand Course Pursues a Public Spirit: *Impartial* in Changsha (1915–1927) and Intellectual Tides Hunanese Society). Changsha: Hunan renmin chubanshe, 2011.

Yu Jiaju 余家菊. "Shenme shi geming de zuihao fangfa?" 什麼是革命的最好方法？ (What Is the Best Method for Revolution?). *Shaonian zhongguo* 少年中國 (Young China) 2, no. 1 (July 15, 1920): 35–40.

Yu Shizhen 俞士鎮. "Gu jin xueshu goutong siyi" 古今學術鉤通私議 (Connecting Old and New Scholarship). *Guogu* 國故 (National Heritage), no. 1 (1919): 1B–3A.

Yu Tiandong 余天棟. "Xin wenhua yundong zhi zhongzhong wenti ji tuixing fa" 新文化運動之種種問題及推行法 (The Various Questions of the New Culture Movement and Ways to Promote It). *Xuesheng* 學生 (Students' Magazine) 7, no. 3 (1920): 1–5.

Yu Ying 育英. "Wu si yundong de zhen jingshen" 五四運動的真精神 (The True Spirit of the May Fourth Movement). *Gong jin* 共進 (Advancing Together), no. 61 (1924): 1–2.

Yü, Ying-shih. "Neither Renaissance nor Enlightenment: A Historian's Reflection on the May Fourth Movement." In *The Appropriation of Cultural Capital: China's May Fourth Project*, edited by Milena Doleželová-Velingerová and Oldřich Král, 299–326. Cambridge, Massachusetts: Harvard University Asia Center, 2001.

Yuan Hui 袁暉. *Hanyu biaodian fuhao liubianshi* 漢語標點符號流變史 (A History of the Development of Chinese Punctuation Marks). Wuhan: Hubei jiaoyu chubanshe, 2002.

Yuan Hui 袁暉. "Jiushi biaodian fuhao" 舊式標點符號 (Old-Style Punctuation Marks). *Biaodian fuhao cidian* 標點符號詞典 (A Dictionary of Punctuation Marks). Shanghai: Shanghai chubanshe, 2000. Shanghai.

"Yuandong yundong yusai yuan jinri chufa" 遠東運動與賽員今日出發 (The Participants in the Far Eastern Sports [Festival] Depart Today). *Shenbao* 申報 (Shanghai News), May 4, 1919, 10.

"Yuandong yundonghui ji Beibu yundonghui gaiqi" 遠東運動會及北部運動會改期 (Changes in the Dates of the Far Eastern Sports Festival and the Northern Sports Festival). *Beijing gaodeng shifan xuexiao zhoubao* 北京高等師範學校週報 (Beijing Higher Normal School Weekly), no. 49 (1918): 11.

"Yue xuesheng shifang hou zhi da yundong" 粵學生釋放後之大運動 (The Great Movement after the Release of the Cantonese Students). *Shenbao* 申報 (Shanghai News), October 3, 1919, 7.

Yun Chao 蘊巢. "Lun Daxue xin jiu zhi zheng" 論大學新舊之爭 (Discussing the Quarrel between New and Old at the University). *Yishibao* 益世報 (Social Welfare Tiensin). April 7, 1919, 2. Tianjin.

"Yundonghui jishi" 運動會記事 (Record of the Sports Festival). *Jiangsu shengli di-er shifan xuexiao xiaoyouhui zazhi* 江蘇勝利第二師範學校校友會雜誌 (Alumni of the Second Jiangsu Provincial Normal School), no. 5 (1912): 39–42.

Zarrow, Peter. *Anarchism and Chinese Political Culture*. New York: Columbia University Press, 1990.

"Zhan dian" 戰電 (War Telegrams). *Shenbao* 申報 (Shanghai News). November 8, 1918, 2. Shanghai.

Zhang Fangyuan 張方遠. "Yi ge Jiang Weishui, gezi-biaoshu: zhouxun lishi miwu zhong de Jiang Weishui zhenshi mianmao" 一個蔣渭水，各自表述：追尋歷史迷霧中的蔣渭水真實面貌 (One Jiang Weishui, Many Narratives: A Search for the True Face of Jiang Weishui in the Dense Fog of History). *Haixia pinglun* 海峽評論 (Cross-Strait Review), no. 249 (September 2011): 41–47.

Zhang Jianming 張建明, and Qi Dazhi 齊大之. *Hua shuo Jing shang* 話說京商 (Talking about Business in Beijing). Beijing: Zhonghua gongshang lianhe chubanshe, 2006.

Zhang Juncai 張俊才. *Lin Shu pingzhuan* 林紓評傳 (A Critical Biography of Lin Shu). Beijing: Zhonghua shuju, 2007.

Zhang Liaozi 張謬子. "Zhang Liaozi yuan han" 張謬子原函 (Original Letter from Zhang Liaozi). In *Cai Yuanpei xiansheng quanji* 蔡元培先生全集 (Collected Works of Mr. Cai Yuanpei), edited by Sun Changwei 孫常煒, 1093–94. Taibei: Taiwan shangwu yinshuguan, 1968.

Zhang Liushi 張六師. "Beijing xuesheng you you wu si yundong shi de jingshen" 北京學生猶有五四運動時的精神 (Beijing's Students Still Have the Spirit from the Time of the May Fourth Movement). *Juewu* 覺悟 (Enlightenment). 1924, 4–6. Shanghai.

Zhang Xuan 張煊. "Bo Xinchao guogu he kexue de jingshen pian" 駁新潮國故和科學的精神篇 (Against the Article "The *National Heritage* and the Scientific Spirit" in the *New Tide*). *Guogu* 國故 (National Heritage), no. 3 (May 20, 1919): 1B–4A.

Zhang Xuan 張煊. "Mozi jing shuo xin jie: xu" 墨子經說新解：續 (New Explanations of the *Mozi*, Continued). *Guogu* 國故 (National Heritage), no. 3 (1919): 1B–3A.

Zhang Xuan 張煊. "Wen yan heyi pingyi" 文言合一平議 (The Integration of Written and Spoken Language). *Guogu* 國故 (National Heritage), no. 1 (1919): 1–5.

Zhang Xuan 張煊. "Zhongguo wenxue gailiang lun" 中國文學改良論 (The Reform of Chinese Literature). *Guogu* 國故 (National Heritage), no. 4 (1919): 1B–4A.

Zhao, Daiwen 趙戴文. "Beijing Zhao canmouzhang han dian" 北京趙參謀長寒電 (Telegram of the 14th [of May 1919] from Chief of Staff Zhao in Beijing). In *Yan Xishan dang'an* 閻錫山檔案 (Yan Xishan Papers), edited by Qingfen Lin 林清芬, 5:31–32. Taibei: Guoshiguan, 2003.

Zheng Shiqu 鄭師渠. "Wu si hou guanyu 'xin wenhua yundong' de taolun" 五四后關于"新文化運動"的討論 (Discussions about the "New Culture Movement" after May Fourth). Conference paper presented at the "Wu si de lishi yu lishi de wu si" xueshu taolunhui "五四的歷史與歷史中的五四"學術討論會 ("The History of May Fourth and the

May Fourth of History." An Academic Symposium), Beijing, June 6, 2009. Beijing. http://www.wanfangdata.com.

Zhi Yan 隻眼. "Guanyu Beijing daxue de yaoyan" 關於北京大學的謠言 (The Rumors about Beijing University). In *Wu si yundong zai Shanghai shiliao xuanji* 五四運動在上海史料選輯 (The May Fourth Movement in Shanghai: Selected Historical Materials), edited by Shanghai shehui xueyuan lishi yanjiusuo 上海社會學院歷史研究所, 103–4. Shanghai: Shanghai renmin chubanshe, 1980.

Zhong Hengxu 種恒續. "The triumph of the students." *Shangye xuesheng* 商業學生 (Commercial Student), no. 2 (December 1919): 22–29.

Zhongguo shehui kexueyuan jindaishi yanjiusuo "jindaishi ziliao" bianyishi 中國社會科學院近代史研究所《近代史資料》編譯室, ed. *Wu si aiguo yundong* 五四愛國運動 (The Patriotic Movement of May Fourth). Vol. 1. Beijing: Zhishi chanquan chubanshe, 2013.

"Zhongguo xin wenhua yundong de xianqu, wenyi jie zhuoyue lingdaoren Yang Hansheng tongzhi shishi" 中國新文化運動的先驅、文藝界卓越領導人陽翰笙同志逝世 (The Pioneer of China's New Culture Movement and Outstanding Leader in the Field of Art and Literature, Comrade Yang Hansheng, Has Passed Away). *Renmin ribao* 人民日報 (People's Daily). June 11, 1993, 4. Beijing.

"Zhonghua zhiye jiaoyushe xuanyanshu" 中華職業教育社宣言書 (Manifesto of the Chinese Society for Vocational Education). *Dongfang zazhi* 東方雜誌 (Eastern Miscellany) 14, no. 7 (1917): 163–69.

"Zhong-Ri gongtong tiaoyue zhi jinxun" 中日共同條約之近訊 (Latest News on the Sino-Japanese Mutual Treaty). *Shenbao* 申報 (Shanghai News), June 3, 1918, 3.

"Zhong-Ri miyue hanri fabiao shuo" 中日密約寒日發表說 (Publication of Sino-Japanese Secret Agreements on the 14th). *Shenbao* 申報 (Shanghai News), March 13, 1920, 3.

Zhongxue biaozhun jiaokeshu lishike bianji weiyuanhui 中學標準教科書歷史科編輯委員會, ed. *Gaozhong lishi* 高中歷史 (Chinese History for Senior High Schools). 6th ed. Vol. 2. Taibei: Taiwan xinsheng yinshuachang, 1968.

Zhongxue biaozhun jiaokeshu lishike bianji weiyuanhui 中學標準教科書歷史科編輯委員會, ed. *Gaozhong Zhongguo wenhuashi* 高中中國文化史 (The History of Chinese Culture for Senior High Schools). Vol. xia. Taibei: Taiwan xinsheng yinshuachang, 1967.

Zhou Changxian 周長憲. "Fuyuan xuezhang dajian" 伏園學長大鑒 (To Principal Fuyuan). In *Qingnian bi dushu* 青年必讀書 (Young People Must Study), edited by Wang Shijia 王世家, 88–89. Kaifeng: Henan daxue chubanshe, 2006.

Zhou Changxian 周長憲. "Piping de jingshen he xin wenhua yundong" 批評的精神和新文化運動 (The Critical Spirit and the New Culture Movement). *Piping* 批評 (Criticism). 1920, 2. Shanghai.

Zhou, Gang. *Placing the Modern Chinese Vernacular in Transnational Literature*. New York: Palgrave Macmillan, 2011.

Zhou Lingsun 周玲蓀. "Xin wenhua yundong he meiyu" 新文化運動和美育 (The New Culture Movement and Aesthetic Education). *Meiyu* 美育 (Arts Education), no. 3 (June 1920): 1–16.

Zhou, Zuoren 周作人. "Christmas Card to Lewis Chase," 192? Container 220. Lewis Nathaniel Chase Papers, Manuscript Division, Library of Congress, Washington, D.C.

Zhu Anru 朱安如. "'Weishui chunfeng' – rang lishi weiren 'you xue you rou'" 《渭水春風》——讓歷史偉人「有血有肉」 ("The Impossible Times" – Giving a Great Man of History "Flesh and Bones"). *PAR biaoyan yishi zazhi* PAR 表演藝術雜誌 (PAR Acting and Arts Journal), no. 212 (August 2010): 80.

Zhu Daihen 朱黛痕. "Ni yu tongxiang mou jun taolun xin wenhua yundong shixing fangfa shu" 擬與同鄉某君討論新文化運動施行方法書 (Pretending to Discuss Ways to Implement the New Culture Movement with Someone from My Native Village). *Jiangsu shengli di-er nüzi shifan xuexiao xiaoyouhui huikan* 江蘇省立第二女子師範學校友會彙刊 (Alumnae of the Second Women's Normal School of Jiangsu Province), no. 9 (November 1919): 36–38.

Zhu Shuangyi 朱雙一. "'Taiwan minbao' dui wu si xin wenxue zuopin de jieshao ji qi yingxiang he zuoyong" 《台灣民報》對五四新文學作品的介紹及其影響和作用 (The Introduction, Influence and Function of May Fourth Works of New Literature by the *Taiwan People's News*). *Taiwan yanjiu jikan* 台灣研究集刊 (Taiwan Research Quarterly), no. 4 (2008): 84–93.

"Zhuandian" 專電 (Special Telegram). *Shenbao* 申報 (Shanghai News). May 6, 1919, 3. Shanghai.

"Zonghe gaoji zhongxue zanxing kecheng gangyao" 綜合高級中學暫行課程綱要 (Comprehensive outline of provisional curricula for senior high schools). Accessed September 17, 2015. http://edu.law.moe.gov.tw/LawContent.aspx?id=GL000357&KeyWord=%E8%AA%B2%E7%A8%8B%E7%B6%B1%E8%A6%81.

Zucker, A.E. *Western Literature: Specimens of Literature with Introductions Embodying the Chief Traditions of Europeans and Americans*. Vol. 2: The Bible and the Middle Ages. Shanghai: Commercial Press, 1922.

Zucker, A.E. *Western Literature: Specimens of Literature with Introductions Embodying the Chief Traditions of Europeans and Americans*. Vol. 1. Shanghai: Commercial Press, 1927.

Zung, Tsing Tuh. "Contemporary Drama of China." Student essay, July 29, 1924. Container 220. Lewis Nathaniel Chase Papers, Manuscript Division, Library of Congress, Washington, D.C.

Zuo Xuexun 左學訓. "Wen Beijing daxue jiaoyuan bei zhu xiaoxi jinggao ge fangmian" 聞北京大學教員被逐消息警告各方面 (Comprehensive Information about the News That Beijing University's Professors Are Being Pursued). *Shishi xinbao* 時事新報 (China Times). March 11, 1919, 3.3. Shanghai.

Index

anarchism 3, 6, 9, 25, 52, 87, 91
Anfu Club 19, 20, 24, 73, 77, 78, 82, 83, 86, 87
Anhui Clique 19
Apologetic Group 104, 105, 157

baihua 3, 6, 10, 11, 13, 15, 27–29, 31, 37, 38, 42, 45, 47–52, 57, 58, 61, 62, 70, 72, 73, 83, 85, 87, 89, 91–93, 96, 112, 118, 122–124, 128, 130, 132, 134, 135, 137, 141, 142, 154, 162, 165, 176, 178, 188, 193, 195, 197, 198
– *baihua* movement 27, 160, 165
Beijing Normal University 141, 142, 172
Beijing University 1, 9–12, 17, 21, 23, 24, 27, 31, 33, 39, 46–52, 54, 57, 58, 60, 61, 63, 64, 68, 70–72, 75–83, 85–89, 92–96, 103, 108, 121, 122, 126, 132, 135, 144–146, 151, 152, 165, 169, 172–174, 178, 199
Beijing University Daily 24, 32, 38, 109
Beijing University Monthly 148
bentuhua 186, 191

Cai Ying-wen 189
Cai Yuanpei 17, 22, 25, 35, 48–50, 54, 62, 63, 68, 72, 77, 79, 86, 88, 105, 107, 111, 118, 122, 133, 145, 146, 174, 199
– fame after May Fourth 63
– *jianrong bingbao* 37, 38
– resignation 84
– restructuring of Beijing University 34
Cha An 84, 85
Chase, Lewis Nathaniel 144, 149, 155, 157
Chen Duxiu 1–3, 6, 9–12, 24, 25, 27, 28, 30, 34, 35, 37, 45–48, 50, 57, 58, 61–63, 65, 70, 72, 75–77, 82, 83, 92–94, 96–98, 103, 105, 107, 120–123, 125–127, 133, 141–143, 146, 149, 195, 198, 199
– dismissal from Beijing University 48, 50, 75, 77, 82, 84, 165
– fame after May Fourth 62, 63
– foundation of *New Youth* 31
– on *baihua* 45, 124, 165
Chiang Kai-shek 18, 133, 171, 175–178, 181, 182, 184

China Times 24, 29, 76–81, 134
Chinese Christian Advocate 32, 92, 112, 145, 158
Citizen News (Beijing) 31, 79, 81, 125
Citizen News (Chengdu) 29, 49, 79
Commercial Press 46, 103, 117, 146
communism 6, 13, 27, 59, 60, 85, 86, 91, 92, 94, 102, 112, 125, 129, 135, 156, 174, 175, 182, 183, 187, 188, 201
Construction 116, 133, 148, 158
Critical Review 139, 140
Criticism 121, 132, 137, 144, 145, 170

de Vargas, Philippe 11, 70, 83, 84, 150
Dewey, John 101, 102, 136, 138
Duan Qirui 18–20, 66, 67, 73, 83, 84

East Asia Library 25, 31, 64, 65, 75, 116, 146, 148, 149, 177, 178
Emancipation and Reconstruction 133, 134, 147

Fu Sinian 2, 9, 17, 31, 39, 49, 57, 58, 64, 70, 94, 124, 126, 130, 132, 142, 149, 155, 169
– death 180, 182
– debates at Beijing University 45
– foundation of *New Tide* 30
Fu Zengxiang 21, 68, 77, 84, 88, 107, 117

Giles, Herbert Allen 163
Giles, Lionel 163
Guo Moruo 134, 170
guwen 32, 36, 203

He-yin Zhen 52, 117
Hsieh Chang-ting 182, 184, 186
Hu Shi 1–3, 6, 9–13, 21, 24, 27, 28, 30, 34, 37, 38, 43, 44, 46–48, 50, 56–58, 61, 62, 70, 72, 76, 77, 82, 83, 92–95, 101, 103, 105, 107, 115, 116, 118, 120, 122, 123, 125–127, 132, 133, 137, 138, 141–146, 150–156, 158, 160–163, 170, 171, 177–179, 193, 195, 198, 199
– death 182
– debate on "problems and isms" 125

– fame after May Fourth 63
– Haskell Lectures 166
– on *baihua* 45, 124, 165
– trip to Canada and the United States 166
– trip to Europe 163
Huang Kan 29, 33, 37, 38, 47, 139, 198
Huang Yanpei 1, 10, 11, 22, 52, 54, 59–61, 89, 111, 133, 145, 146
Hutchinson, Paul 159

Impossible Times (Weishui chunfeng) 189, 191

Jiang Qi 116, 134
Jiang Weishui 119, 188, 189, 192, 193
Jiang Zemin 174
Jiangsu Educational Association 5, 9–11, 22, 52–54, 56, 74, 85, 92, 93, 106–108, 110–112, 122, 123, 126, 133, 135, 146
Johnston, Reginald F. 163

Kropotkin, Peter 25, 116

Ladies' Magazine 62, 63, 117, 118, 158
Lester, Emma 135, 136
Li Dazhao 9, 30, 35, 76, 78, 115, 125, 133, 169
Li Jinxi 58, 122
Li Yuanhong 19
Liang Qichao 20, 117, 134, 146
Life 104, 105
Lin Shu 33, 36, 46–49, 64, 72, 76, 77, 81, 83, 122, 140, 165, 198, 199
Lin Xiantang 119, 121, 191
Literary Chinese 1, 3, 6, 7, 9–11, 13, 27–30, 32, 37, 38, 40–42, 47–52, 54, 57, 62, 72, 92, 103, 117, 128, 135–138, 144, 195, 198, 199
Liu Boming 3, 6, 91, 92, 104, 106, 128, 136, 137, 139
Liu Shipei 23, 29, 33, 34, 37, 38, 47, 52, 64, 117, 139, 146, 198
Liu Tingfang 104, 105, 158, 160, 161
Liu Xiaobo 175
Lu Xun 13, 33, 55, 56, 120, 130, 151, 169, 170, 173, 178
Luo Jialun 2, 9, 30, 58, 70, 71, 74, 148, 169, 179

Ma Ying-jeou 182, 183, 185, 186, 189, 191
Mao Dun 134
Mao Zedong 13, 30, 148, 155, 156, 167–169, 171, 193
Marx, Karl 115
Mei Guangdi 139
Miao Jinyuan 95, 121, 125, 126, 132, 144
Morning Post 24, 29, 49, 71, 72, 76–79, 81, 82, 116, 133, 134

National Heritage 24, 30, 32, 37–40, 44–47, 64, 65, 95, 117, 137–139, 148
– foundation 30
National Language 2, 3, 6, 10, 13, 27, 53, 56, 58, 60, 73, 91, 92, 106, 111, 122–124, 128, 135, 136, 142, 165, 195, 197
– introduction into primary schools 27, 62, 87, 129, 142, 165
New Faction (*xinpai*) 1, 7, 12, 29, 30, 33–36, 46, 47, 49, 50, 58, 61, 65, 69–73, 75–77, 81–88, 96, 124, 128, 135, 139, 141, 146, 198, 199
New Tide 10, 24, 30, 32, 37–40, 42–46, 62, 64, 65, 70, 77, 95, 96, 116, 123, 124, 138, 142, 145, 148, 149, 151, 158, 162, 197
New Woman 118, 122, 131, 148, 149
New Youth 1, 10, 24, 30–32, 34, 37, 62, 65, 70, 93, 95, 96, 105, 116, 119, 126, 138, 145, 148, 169

Old Faction (*jiupai*) 1, 2, 7, 10, 12, 33–35, 37, 41, 47, 49, 61, 64, 72, 75, 76, 82–84, 87, 91, 139, 141, 196

People's Daily 169, 171, 172
popular education 3, 9, 10, 13, 15, 27, 28, 51, 53, 56, 60, 91, 106, 108, 112, 122, 123, 197
Public Voice 23, 24, 29, 33, 38, 48, 49, 77, 78, 87, 88

Qian Xuantong 9, 33, 37, 48, 76, 96
Qiu Changwei 137

Republic Daily 24, 91, 121, 132
Research Clique 19, 20, 24, 59, 76, 78, 85, 86, 116, 133, 134

Revolutionary Alliance 33, 145
Russell, Bertrand 138

Scholar's Lantern 133, 134
Shanghai News 10, 17, 23–25, 27–29, 32, 33, 46, 49, 50, 52, 58, 61, 63–67, 71, 74–79, 81, 82, 84, 92, 98, 99, 102, 110, 112, 139, 140, 143, 146, 147, 196, 198
Shi Liangcai 146
Social Reconstruction 131, 132, 145, 148, 149
Sun Yat-sen 19, 20, 133, 139, 175, 176, 179, 190

Taiwan 13, 17, 95, 119–121, 156, 157, 173, 175–178, 180–182, 188, 192, 193, 195, 201, 203
– debates about national identity 182, 193
– independence from Japanese rule 3, 6, 91, 119–121, 128, 182, 186, 187, 201
Taiwan People's News 119, 120, 182
Taiwan Youth 95, 119, 120
Tiger 25, 138, 148

vocational education 9, 54, 106, 111, 112
– Chinese Society for Vocational Education 54, 111, 145, 146

Waley, Arthur 163
Wang Mengzou 31, 34, 62, 146
Wang Yuanfang 25, 31, 62, 75, 133, 148
Weekly Critic (Meizhou pinglun) 10, 24, 76, 92, 125, 148, 169
Weekly Review (Xingqi pinglun) 92, 133, 175
Wilhelm, Richard 163

Wilson, Woodrow 14, 66, 158, 201
women's rights 3, 6, 9, 10, 13, 27, 28, 51, 60, 91, 92, 108, 119, 120, 129, 197, 200
Wu Mi 137, 138
Wu Rulun 32, 53

Xi Jinping 172
Xiang River Review 148, 168, 169
Xu Shuzheng 19, 83, 84, 86
Xue Xiangsui 29, 44, 140

Yan Fu 32, 146
Yan Xishan 9–11, 18, 51, 52, 56, 85, 87, 89, 117, 123
Yang Hansheng 171
Yen Ching Students' Weekly 153
Young China 117, 118
Yu Pingbo 178
Yu Shizhen 29, 39, 44, 139
Yuan Shikai 18, 20, 25, 53, 66
Yun Daiying 113

Zhang Henshui 130
Zhang Jian 146
Zhang Shenfu 15
Zhang Shizhao 138
Zhang Taiyan 32, 33
– Taiyan Disciples 33
Zhang Xuan 29, 39–41, 138, 139
Zhang Xun 18
Zhili Clique 19
Zhou Enlai 170
Zhou Zuoren 103, 142, 151, 178
Zucker, A. E. 154

www.ingramcontent.com/pod-product-compliance
Lightning Source LLC
Chambersburg PA
CBHW030618230426

43661CB00053B/2041